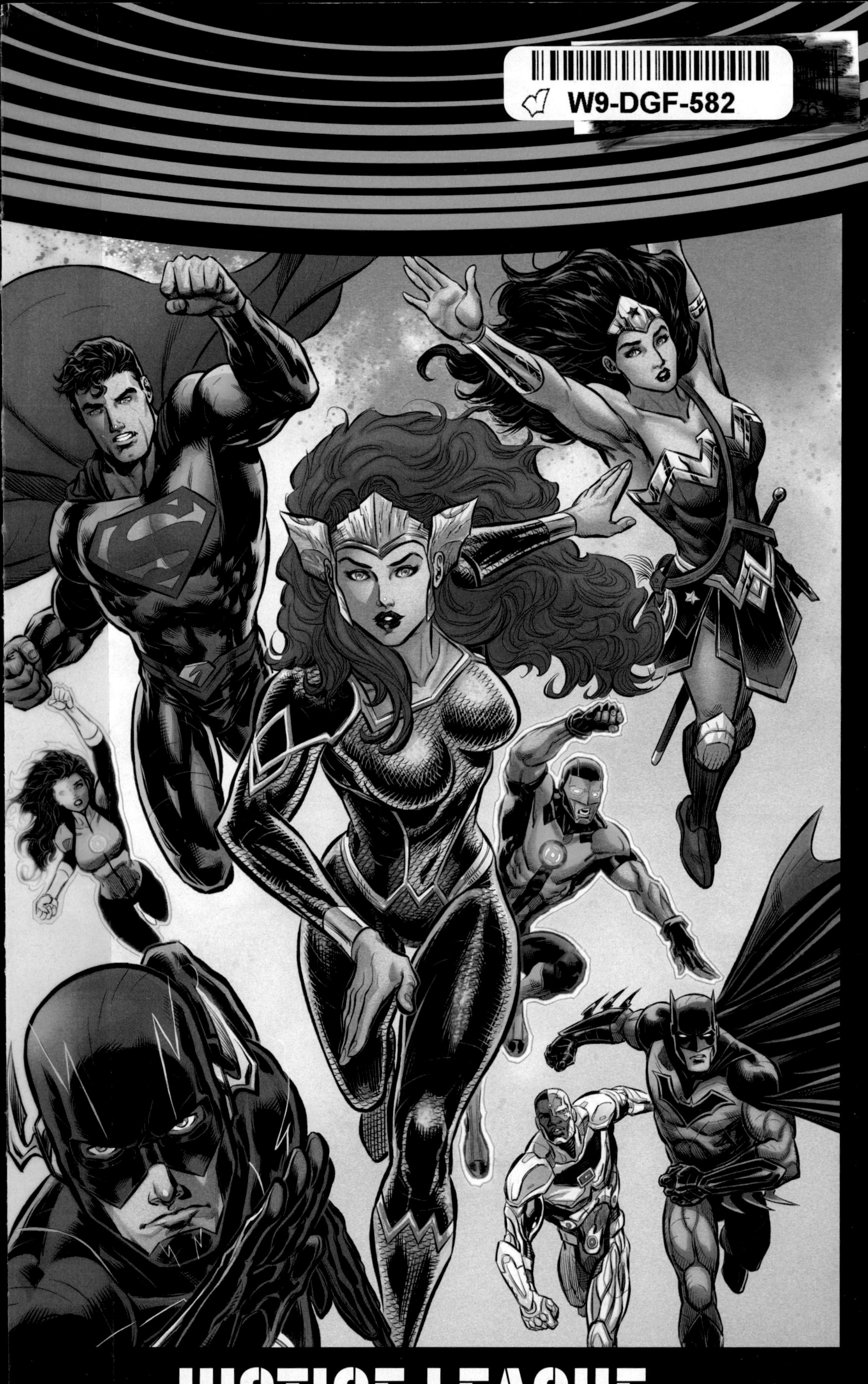

JUSTICE LEAGUE
VOL.4 ENDLESS

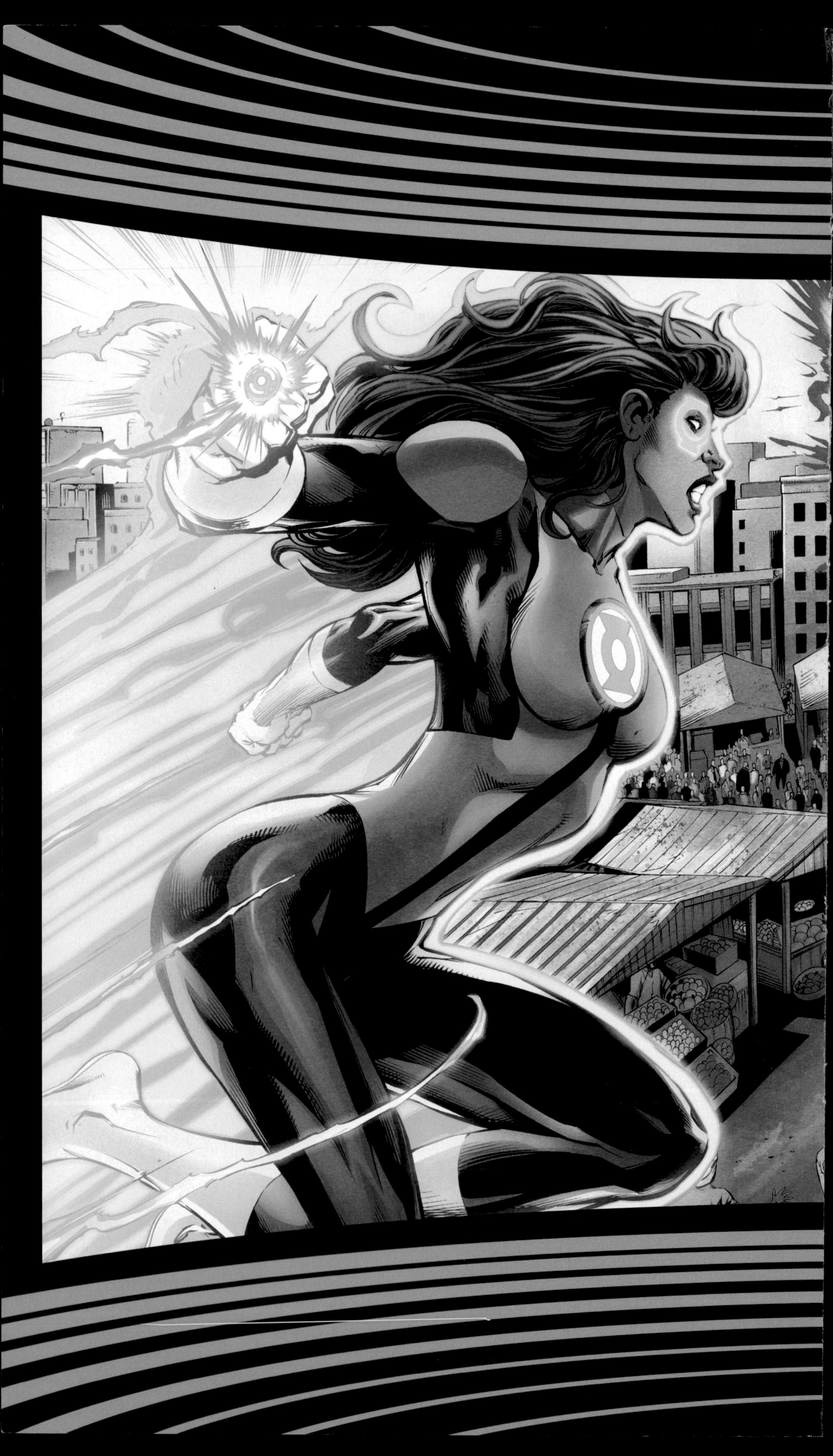

JUSTICE LEAGUE
VOL.4 ENDLESS

BRYAN HITCH * **SHEA FONTANA**
TOM DeFALCO * **DAN ABNETT**
writers

BRYAN HITCH * **TOM DERENICK** * **PHILIPPE BRIONES**
IAN CHURCHILL * **DANIEL HENRIQUES** * **ANDY OWENS**
SCOTT HANNA * **TREVOR SCOTT** * **ANDREW CURRIE**
PAUL NEARY * **TONY KORDOS** * **BATT**
artists

ALEX SINCLAIR * **GABE ELTAEB** * **JEROMY COX**
PETE PANTAZIS * **ADRIANO LUCAS** * **HI-FI**
colorists

RICHARD STARKINGS & COMICRAFT
DAVE SHARPE * **JOSH REED**
letterers

BRYAN HITCH & ALEX SINCLAIR
collection cover artists

SUPERMAN created by **JERRY SIEGEL** and **JOE SHUSTER**
By special arrangement with the Jerry Siegel family

BRIAN CUNNINGHAM Editor - Original Series ＊ **AMEDEO TURTURRO** Associate Editor - Original Series
JEB WOODARD Group Editor - Collected Editions ＊ **ROBIN WILDMAN** Editor - Collected Edition
STEVE COOK Design Director - Books ＊ **SHANNON STEWART** Publication Design

BOB HARRAS Senior VP - Editor-in-Chief, DC Comics
PAT McCALLUM Executive Editor, DC Comics

DIANE NELSON President ＊ **DAN DiDIO** Publisher ＊ **JIM LEE** Publisher ＊ **GEOFF JOHNS** President & Chief Creative Officer
AMIT DESAI Executive VP - Business & Marketing Strategy, Direct to Consumer & Global Franchise Management
SAM ADES Senior VP & General Manager, Digital Services ＊ **BOBBIE CHASE** VP & Executive Editor, Young Reader & Talent Development
MARK CHIARELLO Senior VP - Art, Design & Collected Editions ＊ **JOHN CUNNINGHAM** Senior VP - Sales & Trade Marketing
ANNE DePIES Senior VP - Business Strategy, Finance & Administration ＊ **DON FALLETTI** VP - Manufacturing Operations
LAWRENCE GANEM VP - Editorial Administration & Talent Relations ＊ **ALISON GILL** Senior VP - Manufacturing & Operations
HANK KANALZ Senior VP - Editorial Strategy & Administration ＊ **JAY KOGAN** VP - Legal Affairs
THOMAS LOFTUS VP - Business Affairs ＊ **JACK MAHAN** VP - Business Affairs
NICK J. NAPOLITANO VP - Manufacturing Administration ＊ **EDDIE SCANNELL** VP - Consumer Marketing
COURTNEY SIMMONS Senior VP - Publicity & Communications ＊ **JIM (SKI) SOKOLOWSKI** VP - Comic Book Specialty Sales & Trade Marketing
NANCY SPEARS VP - Mass, Book, Digital Sales & Trade Marketing ＊ **MICHELE R. WELLS** VP - Content Strategy

JUSTICE LEAGUE VOL. 4: ENDLESS

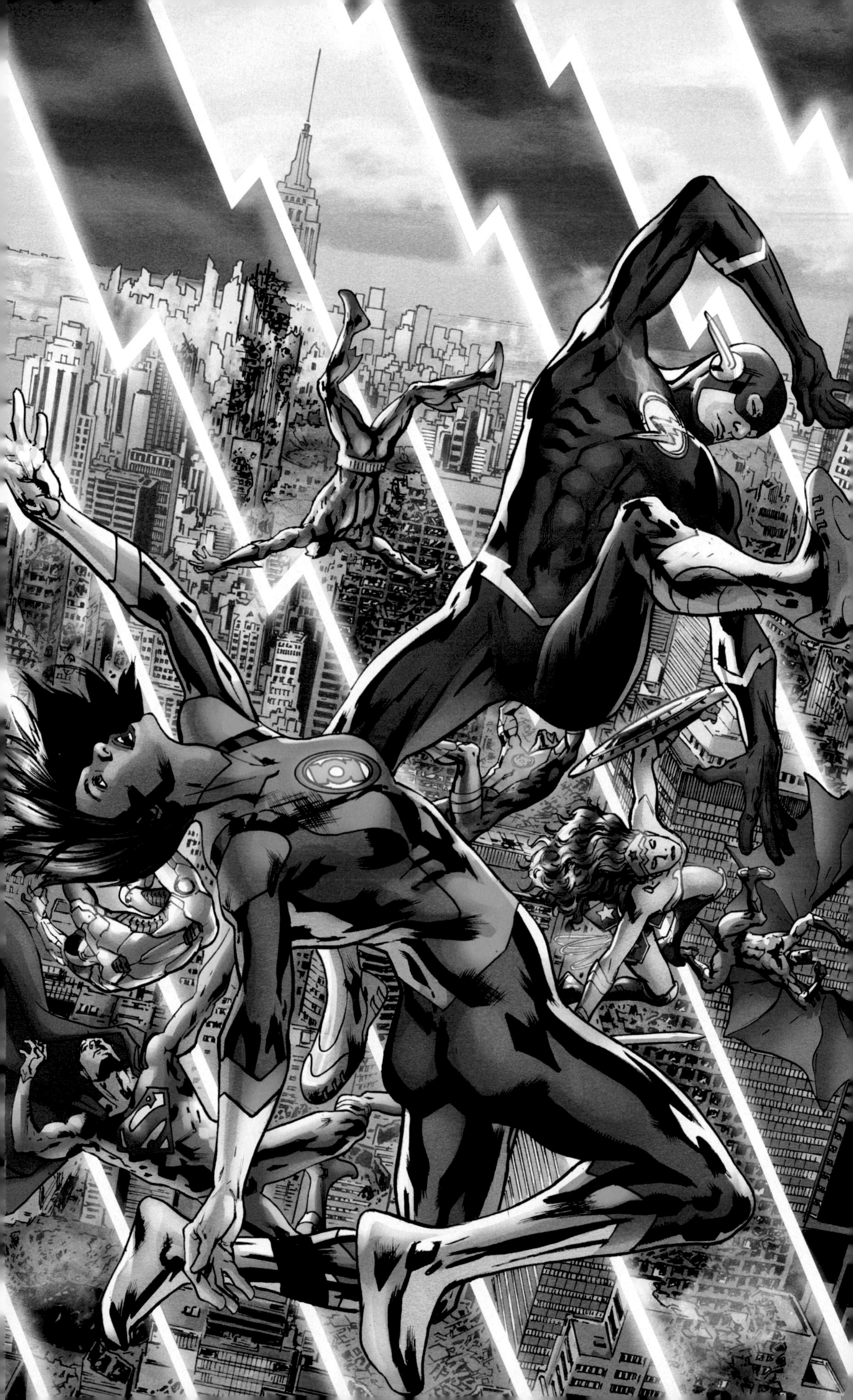

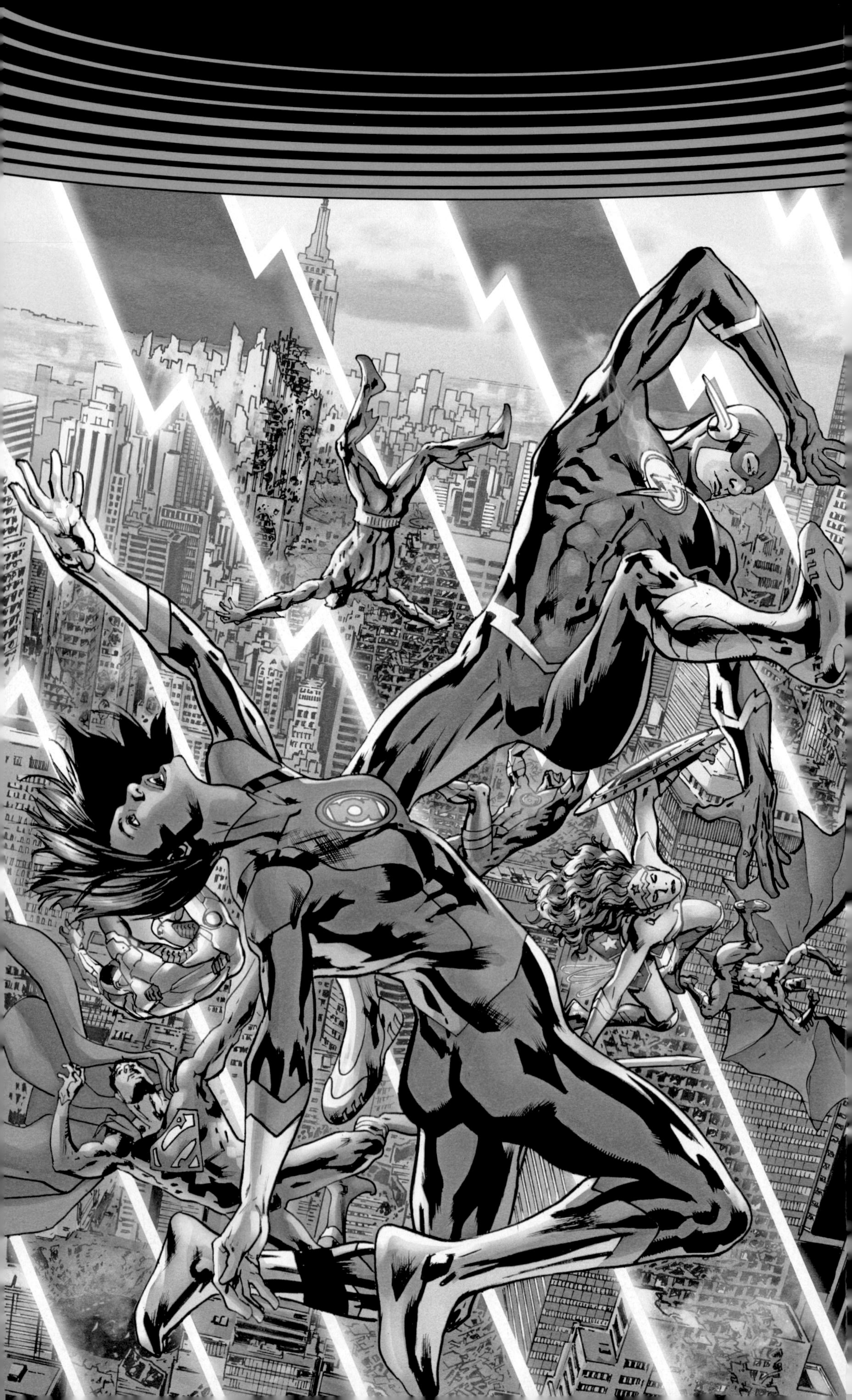

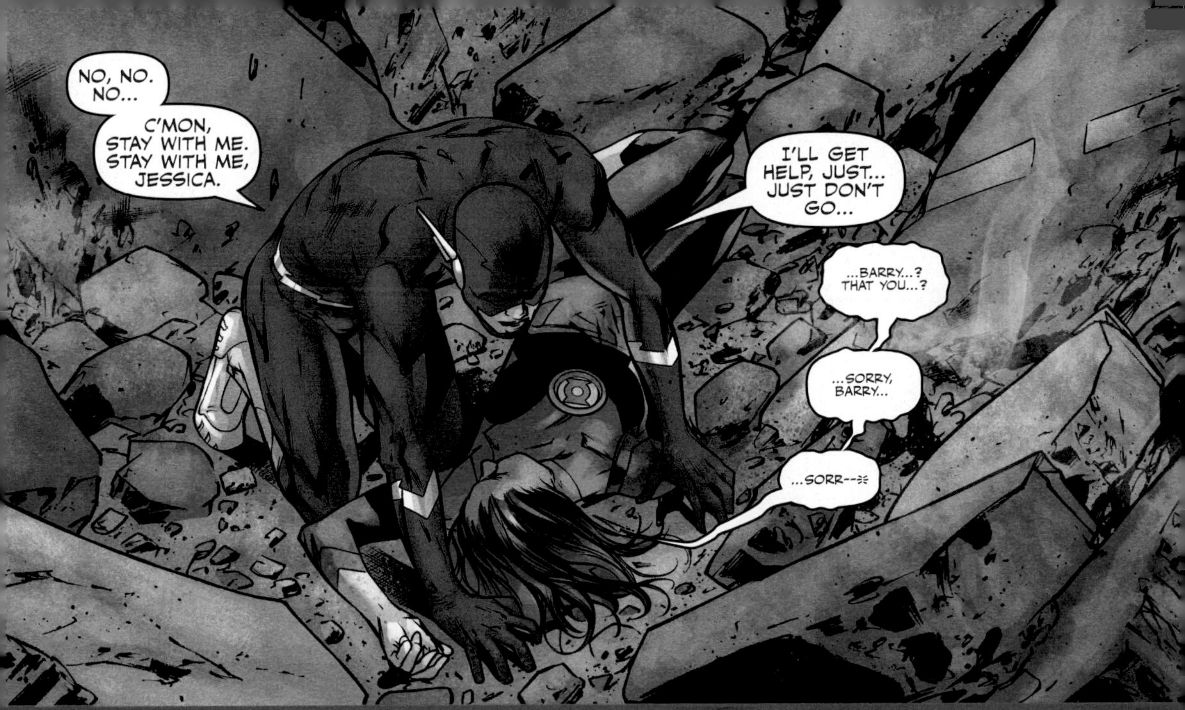
NO, NO. NO...
C'MON, STAY WITH ME. STAY WITH ME, JESSICA.
I'LL GET HELP, JUST... JUST DON'T GO...
...BARRY...? THAT YOU...?
...SORRY, BARRY...
...SORR--

ENDLESS

PART ONE

BRYAN HITCH Writer & Artist

DANIEL HENRIQUES, ANDREW CURRIE & PAUL NEARY Inkers

ALEX SINCLAIR, JEROMY COX & PETE PANTAZIS Colorists

RICHARD STARKINGS & COMICRAFT Lettering

BRYAN HITCH & ALEX SINCLAIR Cover

NICK BRADSHAW & ALEX SINCLAIR Variant Cover

AMEDEO TURTURRO Assistant Editor

BRIAN CUNNINGHAM Editor

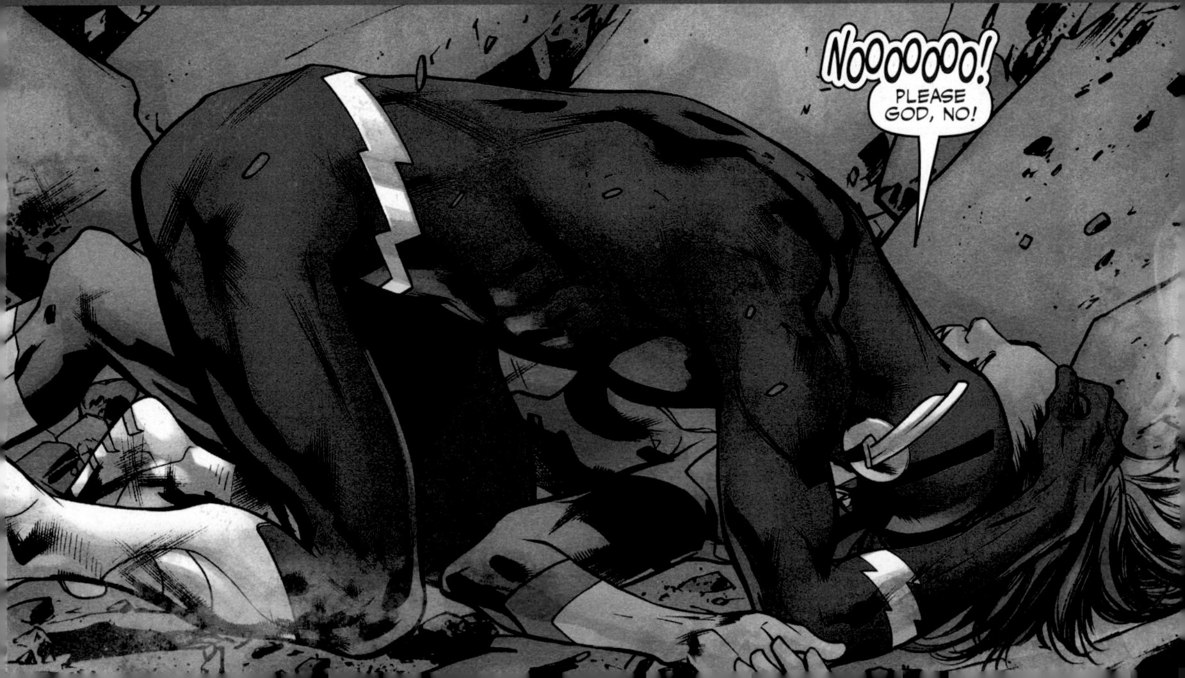
NOOOOOOO!
PLEASE GOD, NO!

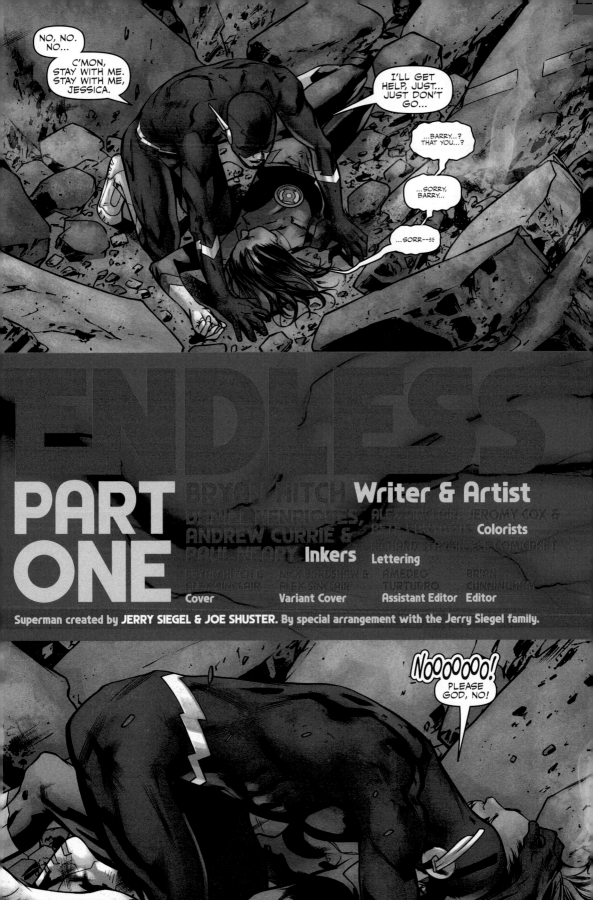

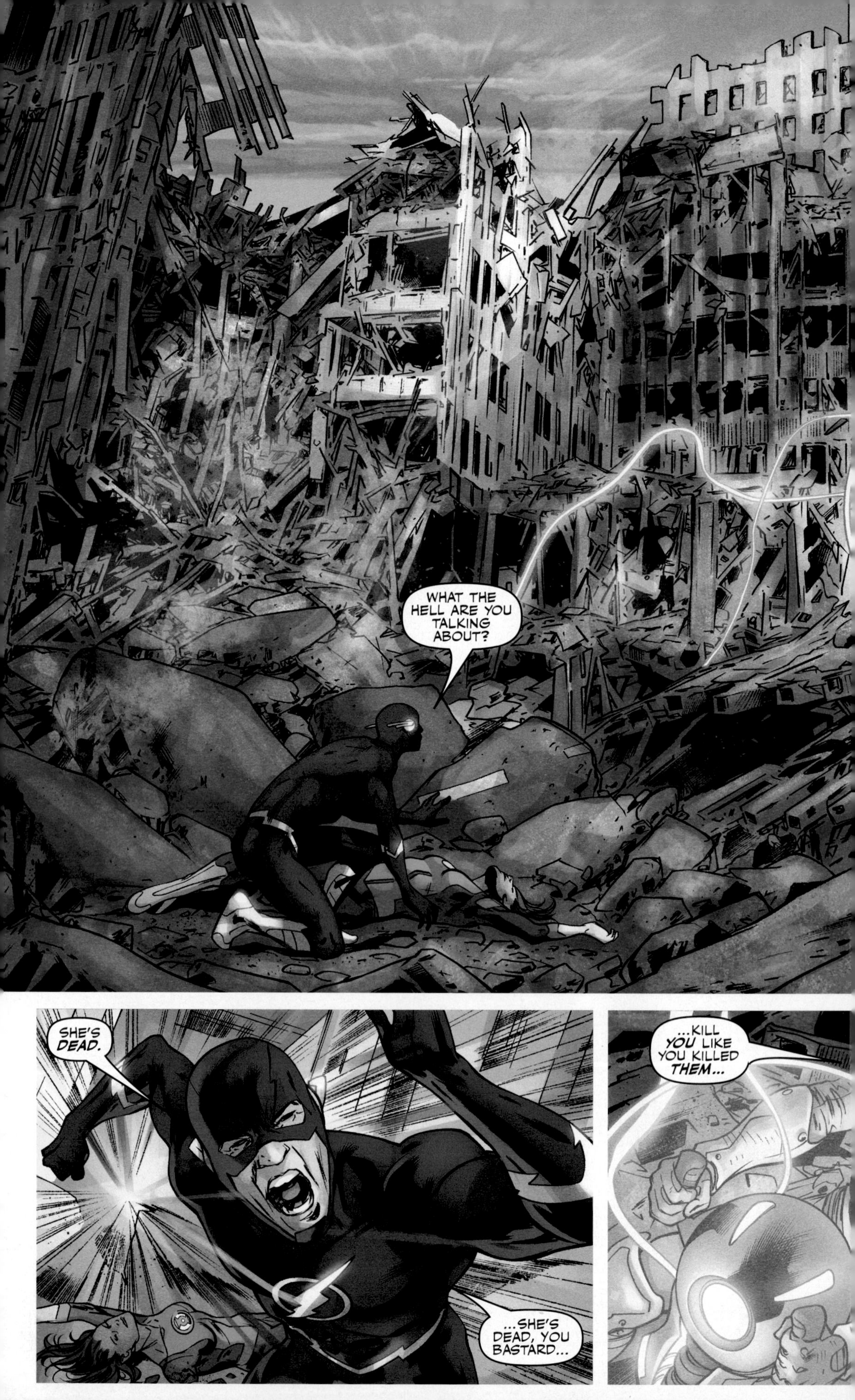
WHAT THE HELL ARE YOU TALKING ABOUT?
SHE'S *DEAD.*
...SHE'S DEAD, YOU BASTARD...
...KILL *YOU* LIKE YOU KILLED *THEM*...

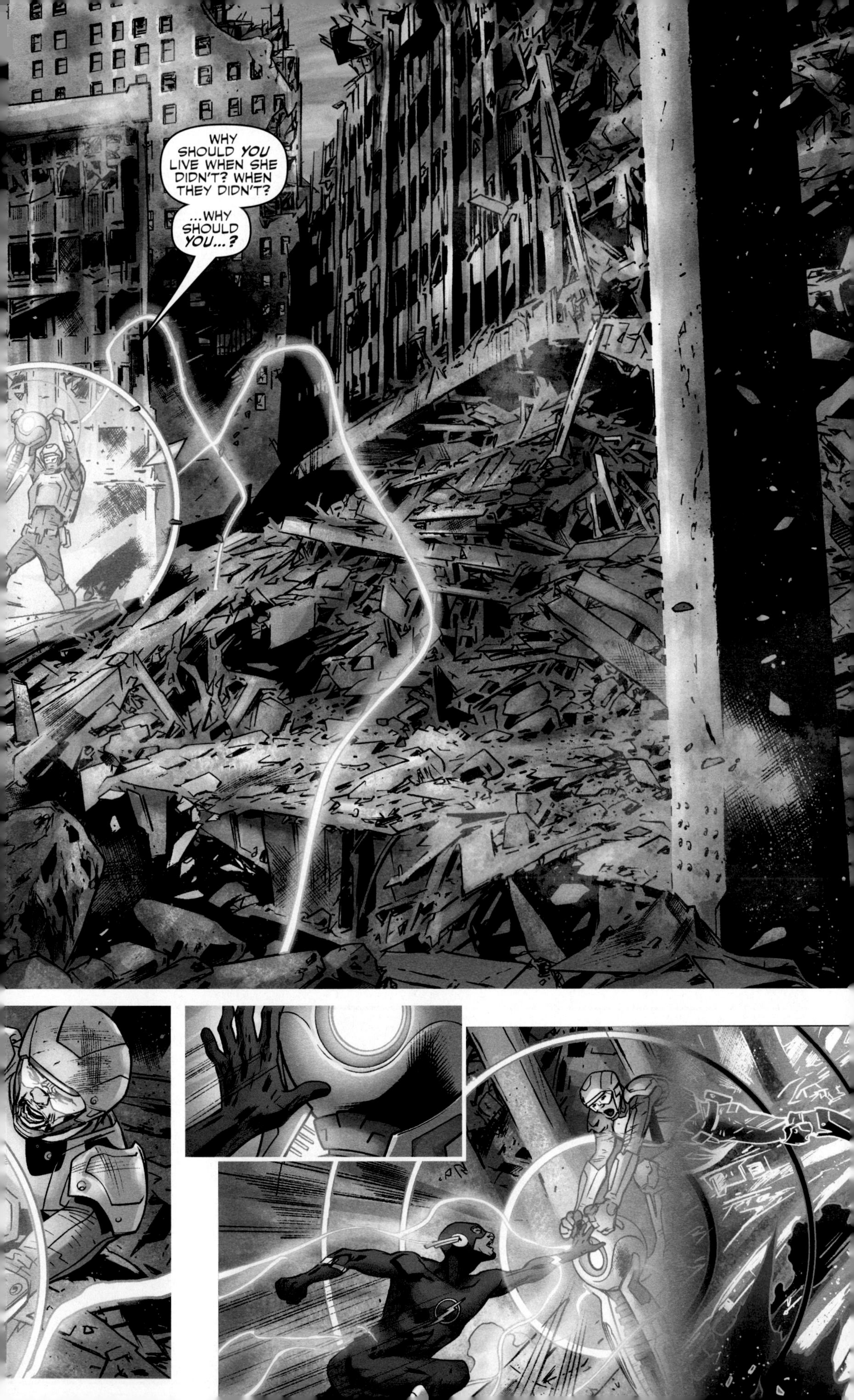
WHY SHOULD YOU LIVE WHEN SHE DIDN'T? WHEN THEY DIDN'T?
...WHY SHOULD YOU...?

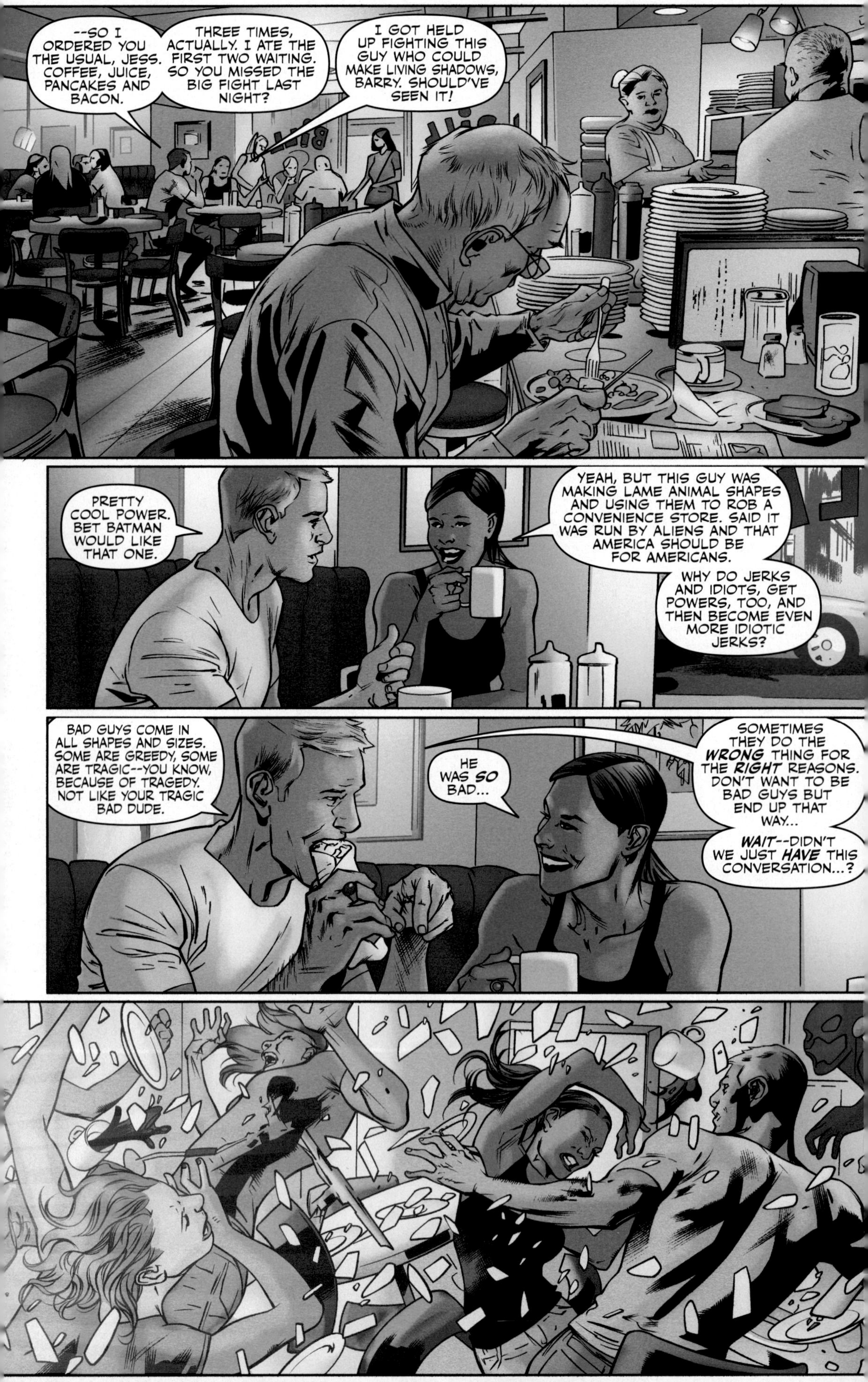
--SO I ORDERED YOU THE USUAL, JESS. COFFEE, JUICE, PANCAKES AND BACON.
THREE TIMES, ACTUALLY. I ATE THE FIRST TWO WAITING. SO YOU MISSED THE BIG FIGHT LAST NIGHT?
I GOT HELD UP FIGHTING THIS GUY WHO COULD MAKE LIVING SHADOWS, BARRY. SHOULD'VE SEEN IT!
PRETTY COOL POWER. BET BATMAN WOULD LIKE THAT ONE.
YEAH, BUT THIS GUY WAS MAKING LAME ANIMAL SHAPES AND USING THEM TO ROB A CONVENIENCE STORE. SAID IT WAS RUN BY ALIENS AND THAT AMERICA SHOULD BE FOR AMERICANS.
WHY DO JERKS AND IDIOTS, GET POWERS, TOO, AND THEN BECOME EVEN MORE IDIOTIC JERKS?
BAD GUYS COME IN ALL SHAPES AND SIZES. SOME ARE GREEDY, SOME ARE TRAGIC--YOU KNOW, BECAUSE OF TRAGEDY. NOT LIKE YOUR TRAGIC BAD DUDE.
HE WAS SO BAD...
SOMETIMES THEY DO THE WRONG THING FOR THE RIGHT REASONS. DON'T WANT TO BE BAD GUYS BUT END UP THAT WAY...
WAIT--DIDN'T WE JUST HAVE THIS CONVERSATION...?

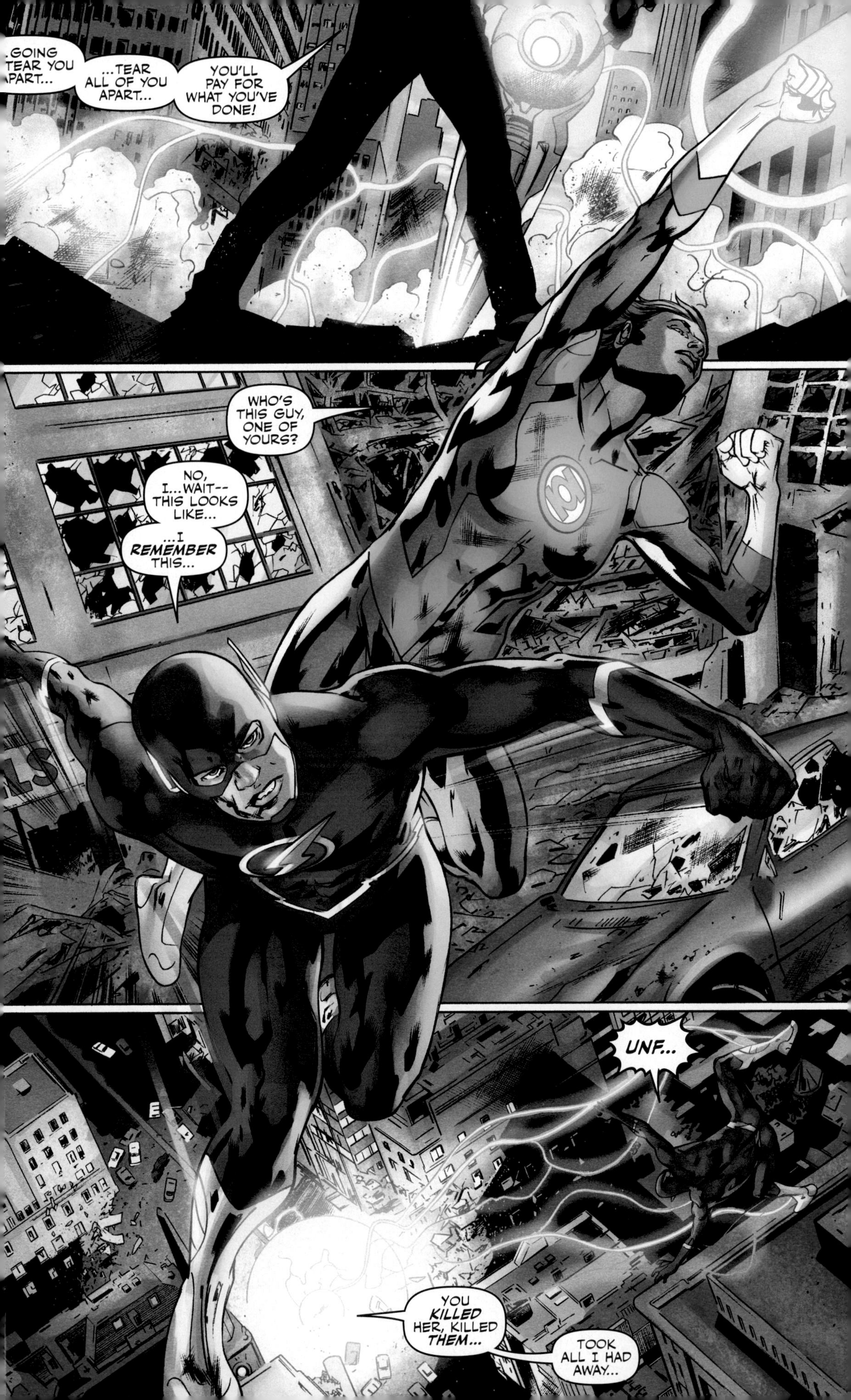

...GOING TO TEAR YOU APART...
...TEAR ALL OF YOU APART...
YOU'LL PAY FOR WHAT YOU'VE DONE!
WHO'S THIS GUY, ONE OF YOURS?
NO, I...WAIT-- THIS LOOKS LIKE...
...I REMEMBER THIS...
UNF...
YOU KILLED HER, KILLED THEM...
TOOK ALL I HAD AWAY...

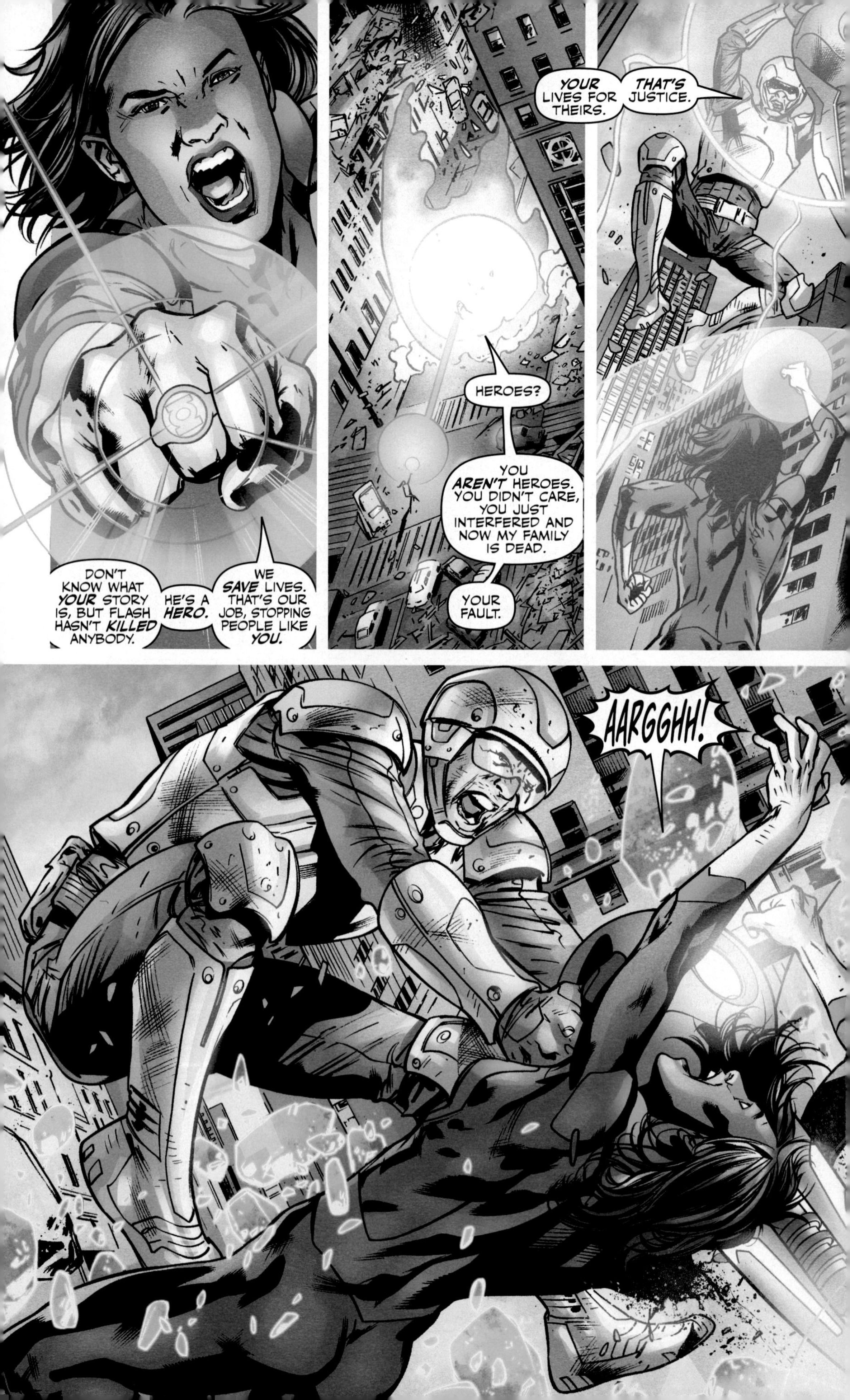
DON'T KNOW WHAT YOUR STORY IS, BUT FLASH HASN'T KILLED ANYBODY.
HE'S A HERO.
WE SAVE LIVES. THAT'S OUR JOB, STOPPING PEOPLE LIKE YOU.
HEROES?
YOU AREN'T HEROES. YOU DIDN'T CARE, YOU JUST INTERFERED AND NOW MY FAMILY IS DEAD.
YOUR FAULT.
YOUR LIVES FOR THEIRS.
THAT'S JUSTICE.
AARGGHH!

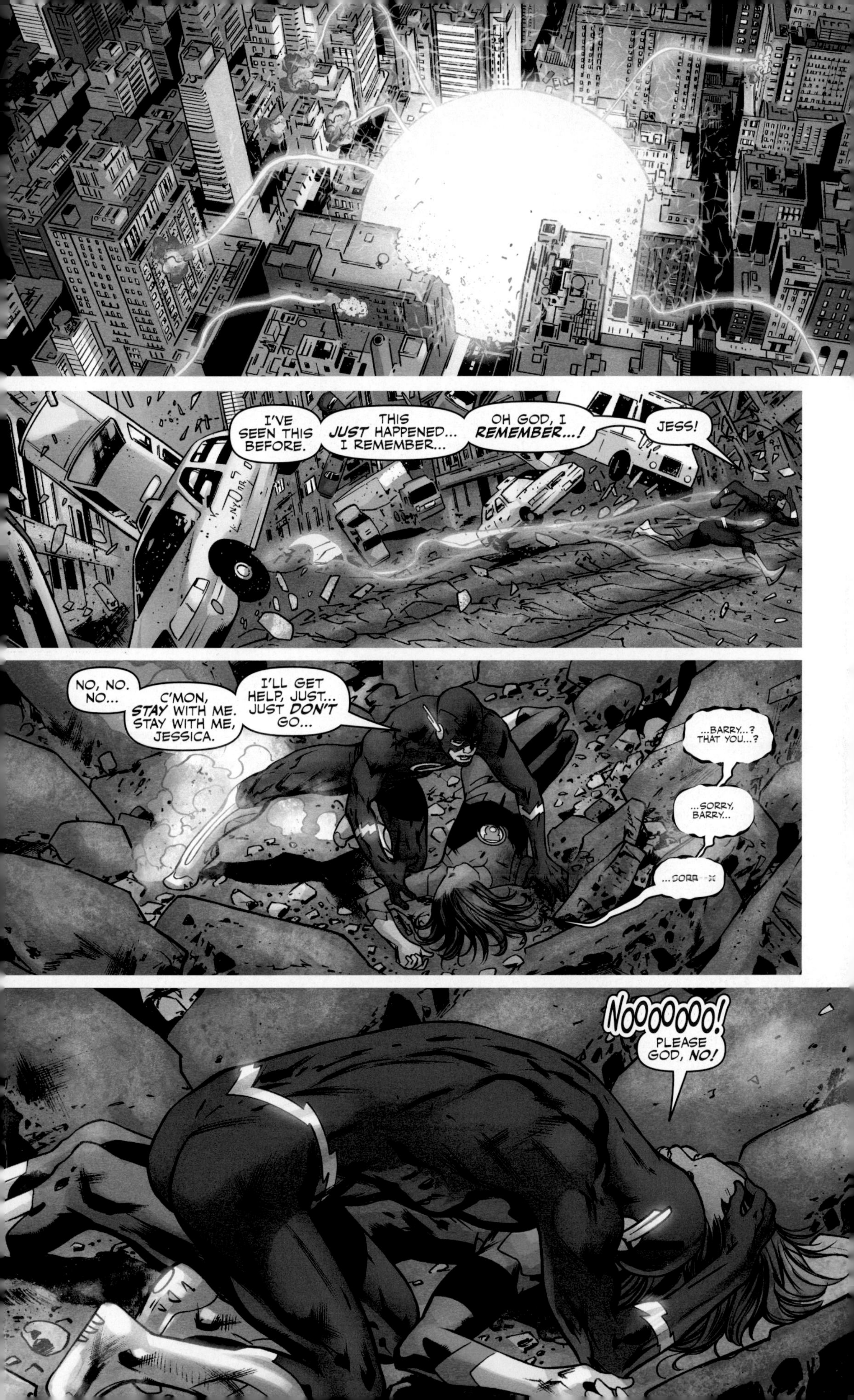
I'VE SEEN THIS BEFORE.
THIS JUST HAPPENED... I REMEMBER...
OH GOD, I REMEMBER...!
JESS!
NO, NO. NO...
C'MON, STAY WITH ME. STAY WITH ME, JESSICA.
I'LL GET HELP, JUST... JUST DON'T GO...
...BARRY...? THAT YOU...?
...SORRY, BARRY...
...SORR--
NOOOOOOO! PLEASE GOD, NO!

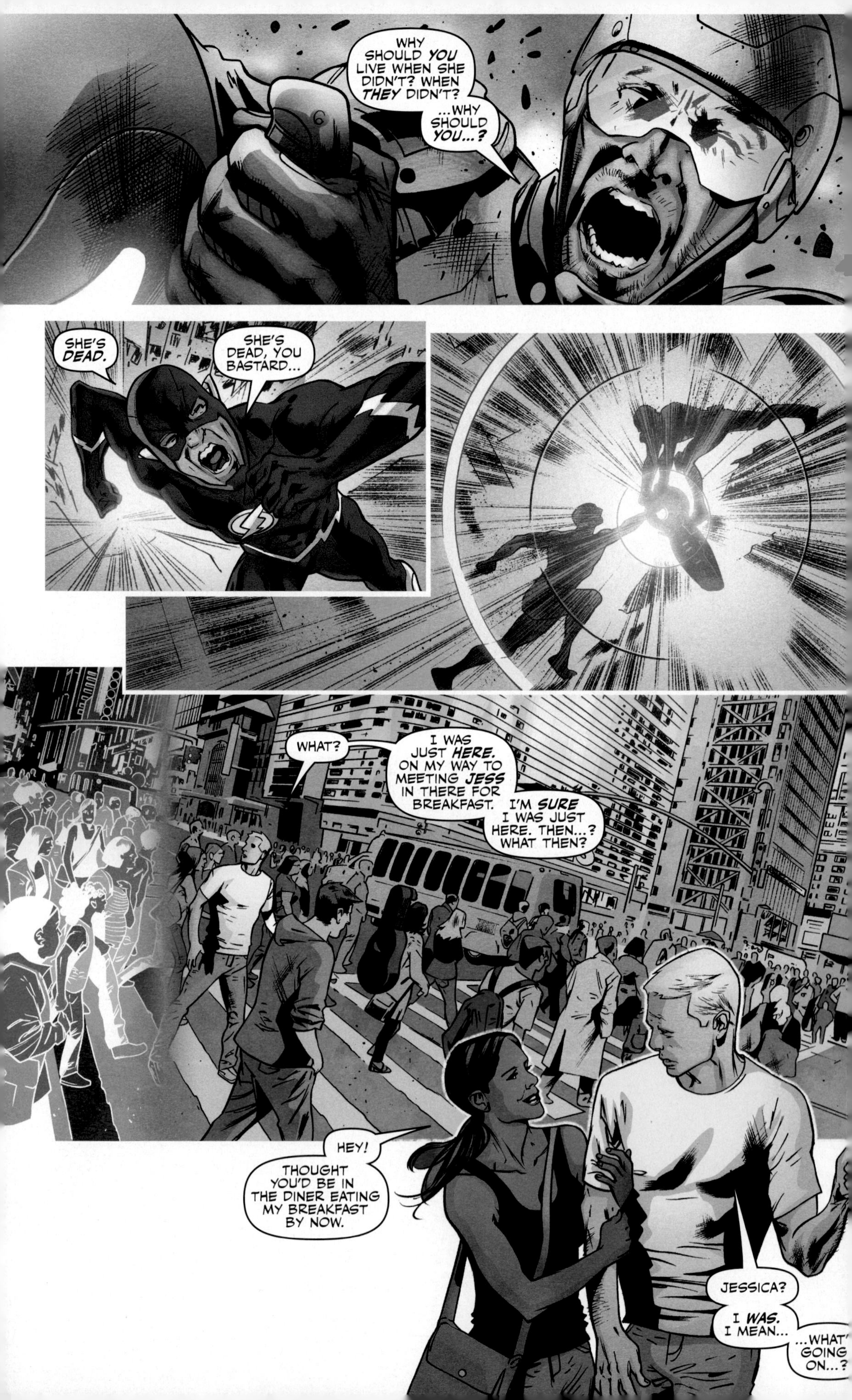
WHY SHOULD *YOU* LIVE WHEN SHE DIDN'T? WHEN *THEY* DIDN'T?
...WHY SHOULD *YOU...?*
SHE'S *DEAD.*
SHE'S DEAD, YOU BASTARD...
WHAT?
I WAS JUST *HERE.* ON MY WAY TO MEETING *JESS* IN THERE FOR BREAKFAST.
I'M *SURE* I WAS JUST HERE. THEN...? WHAT THEN?
HEY!
THOUGHT YOU'D BE IN THE DINER EATING MY BREAKFAST BY NOW.
JESSICA?
I *WAS.* I MEAN...
...WHAT' GOING ON...?

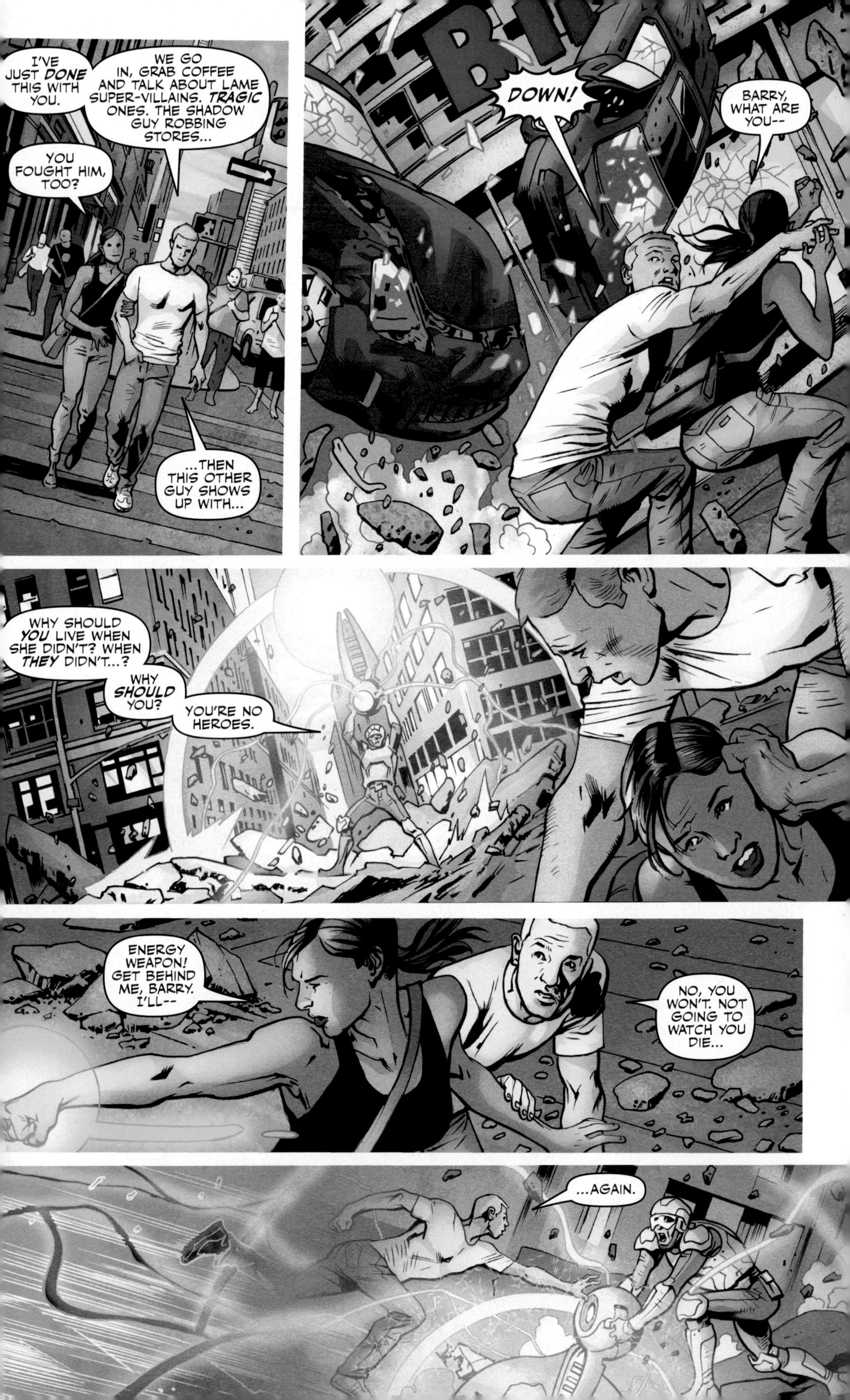
I'VE JUST DONE THIS WITH YOU.
WE GO IN, GRAB COFFEE AND TALK ABOUT LAME SUPER-VILLAINS. TRAGIC ONES. THE SHADOW GUY ROBBING STORES...
YOU FOUGHT HIM, TOO?
...THEN THIS OTHER GUY SHOWS UP WITH...
DOWN!
BARRY, WHAT ARE YOU--
WHY SHOULD YOU LIVE WHEN SHE DIDN'T? WHEN THEY DIDN'T...?
WHY SHOULD YOU?
YOU'RE NO HEROES.
ENERGY WEAPON! GET BEHIND ME, BARRY. I'LL--
NO, YOU WON'T. NOT GOING TO WATCH YOU DIE...
...AGAIN.

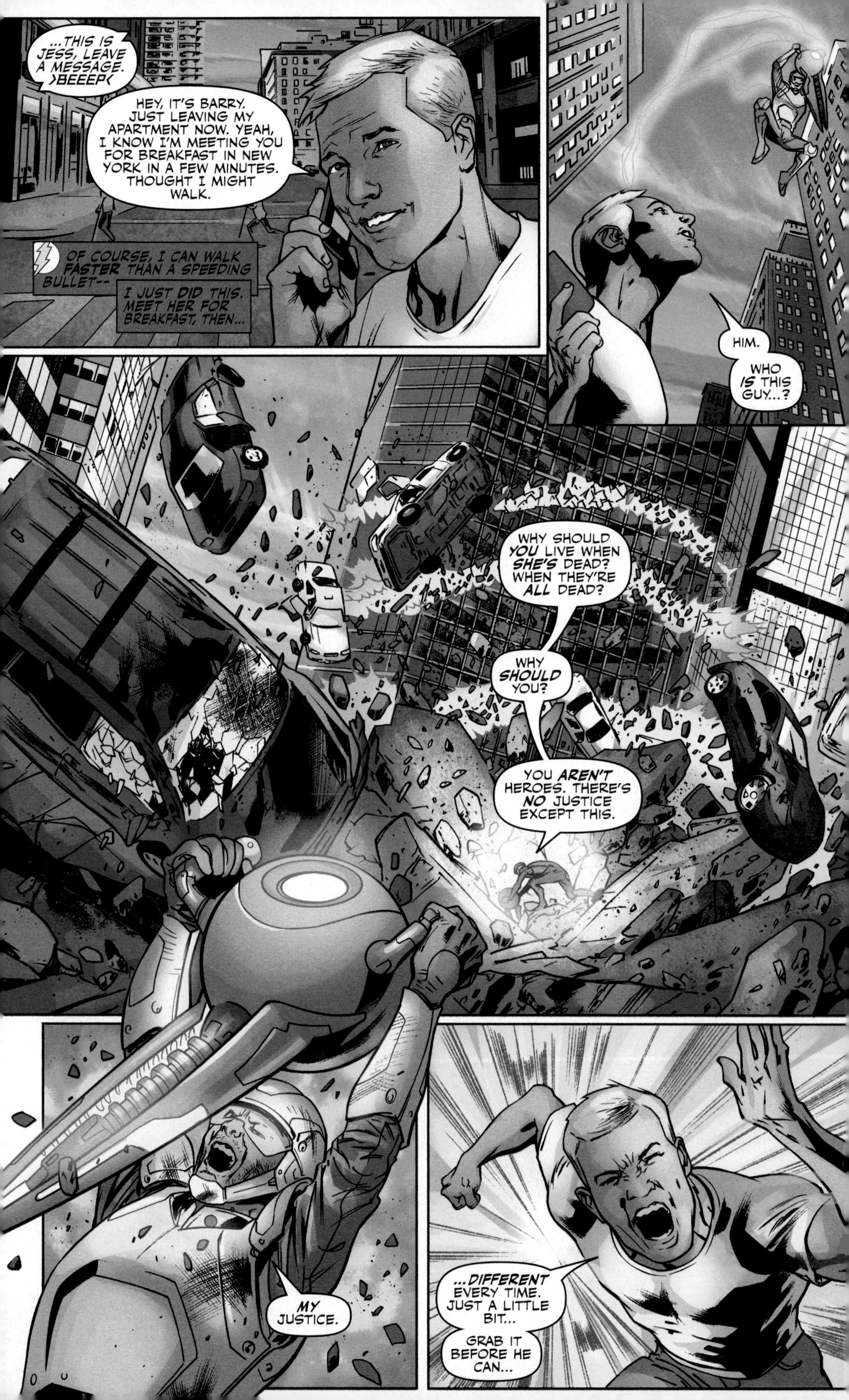

...THIS IS JESS, LEAVE A MESSAGE. >BEEEP<
HEY, IT'S BARRY. JUST LEAVING MY APARTMENT NOW. YEAH, I KNOW I'M MEETING YOU FOR BREAKFAST IN NEW YORK IN A FEW MINUTES. THOUGHT I MIGHT WALK.
OF COURSE, I CAN WALK FASTER THAN A SPEEDING BULLET--
I JUST DID THIS. MEET HER FOR BREAKFAST, THEN...
HIM.
WHO IS THIS GUY...?
WHY SHOULD YOU LIVE WHEN SHE'S DEAD? WHEN THEY'RE ALL DEAD?
WHY SHOULD YOU?
YOU AREN'T HEROES. THERE'S NO JUSTICE EXCEPT THIS.
MY JUSTICE.
...DIFFERENT EVERY TIME. JUST A LITTLE BIT...
GRAB IT BEFORE HE CAN...

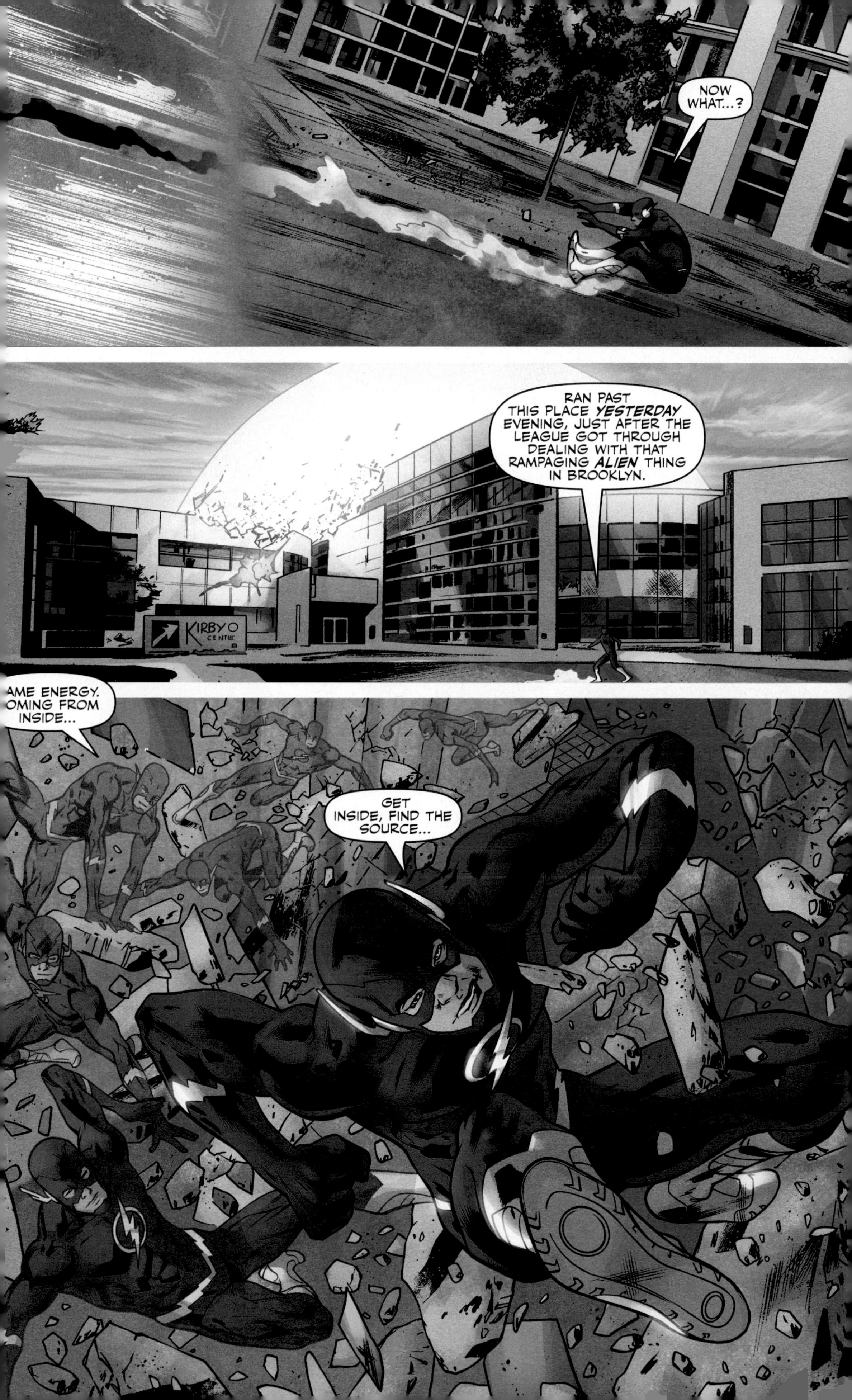
NOW WHAT...?
RAN PAST THIS PLACE *YESTERDAY* EVENING, JUST AFTER THE LEAGUE GOT THROUGH DEALING WITH THAT RAMPAGING *ALIEN* THING IN BROOKLYN.
KIRBY
CENTRE
AME ENERGY. OMING FROM INSIDE...
GET INSIDE, FIND THE SOURCE...

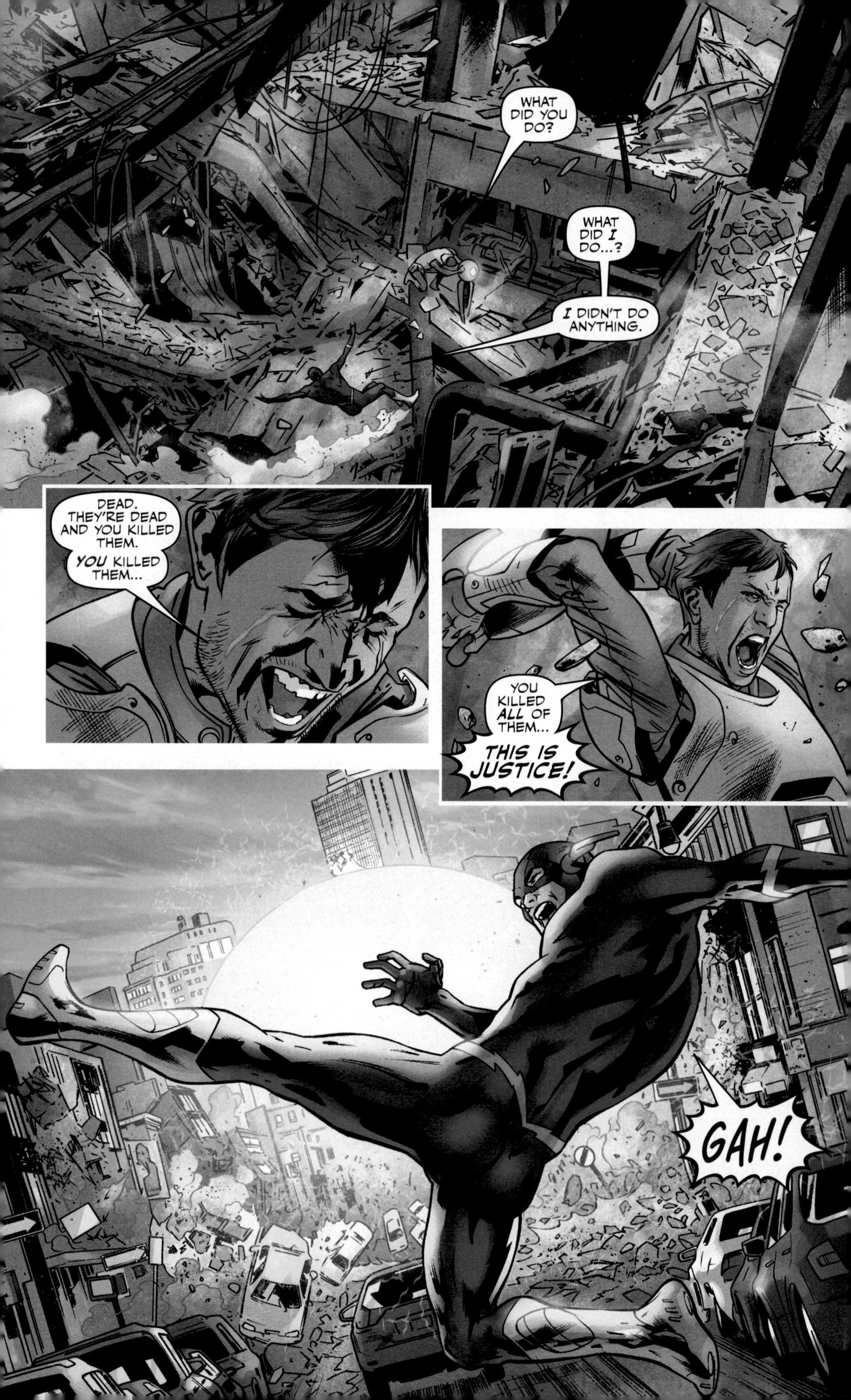
WHAT DID YOU DO?
WHAT DID *I* DO...?
I DIDN'T DO ANYTHING.
DEAD. THEY'RE DEAD AND YOU KILLED THEM. *YOU* KILLED THEM...
YOU KILLED *ALL* OF THEM...
THIS IS JUSTICE!
GAH!

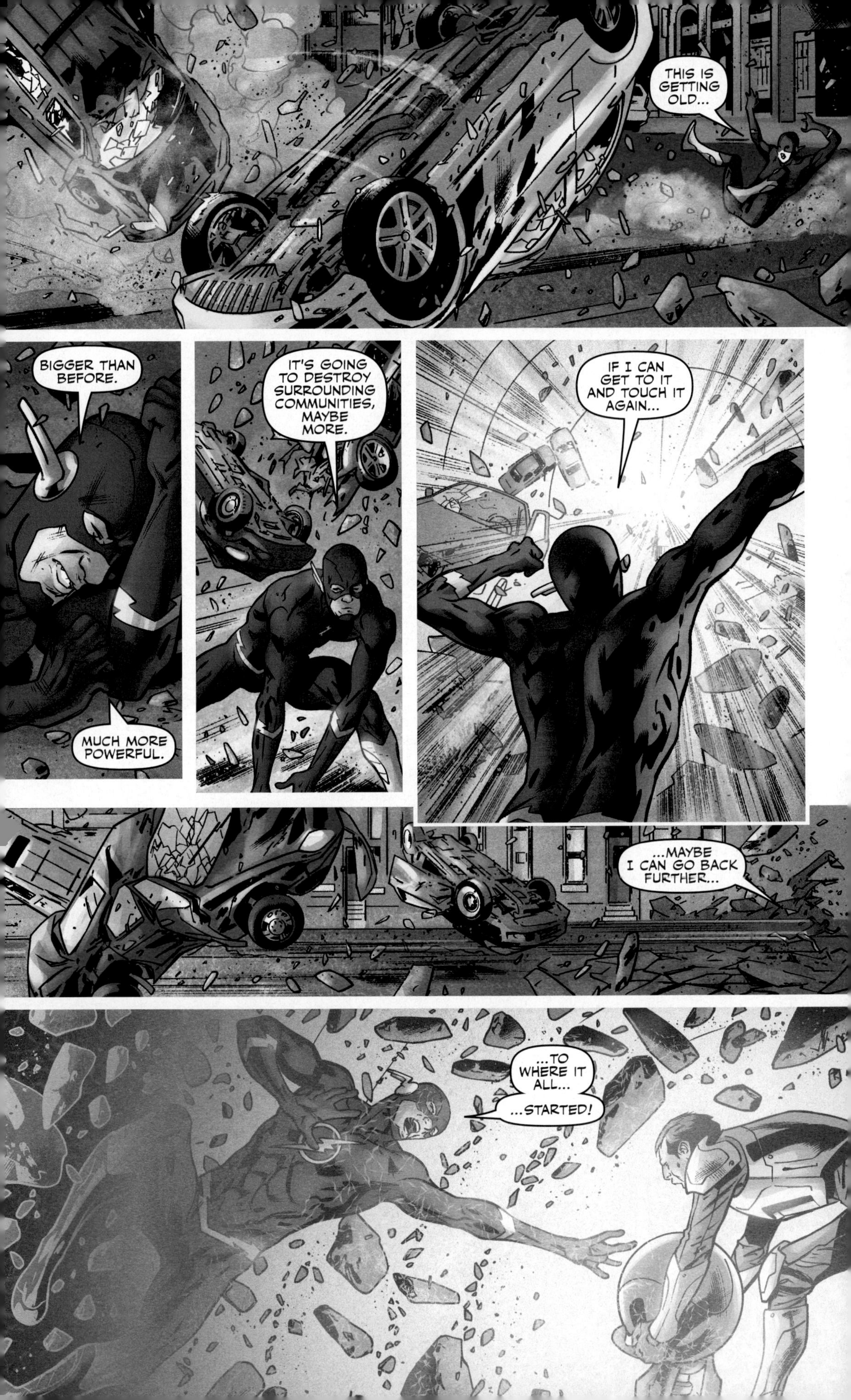
THIS IS GETTING OLD...
BIGGER THAN BEFORE.
MUCH MORE POWERFUL.
IT'S GOING TO DESTROY SURROUNDING COMMUNITIES, MAYBE MORE.
IF I CAN GET TO IT AND TOUCH IT AGAIN...
...MAYBE I CAN GO BACK FURTHER...
...TO WHERE IT ALL...
...STARTED!

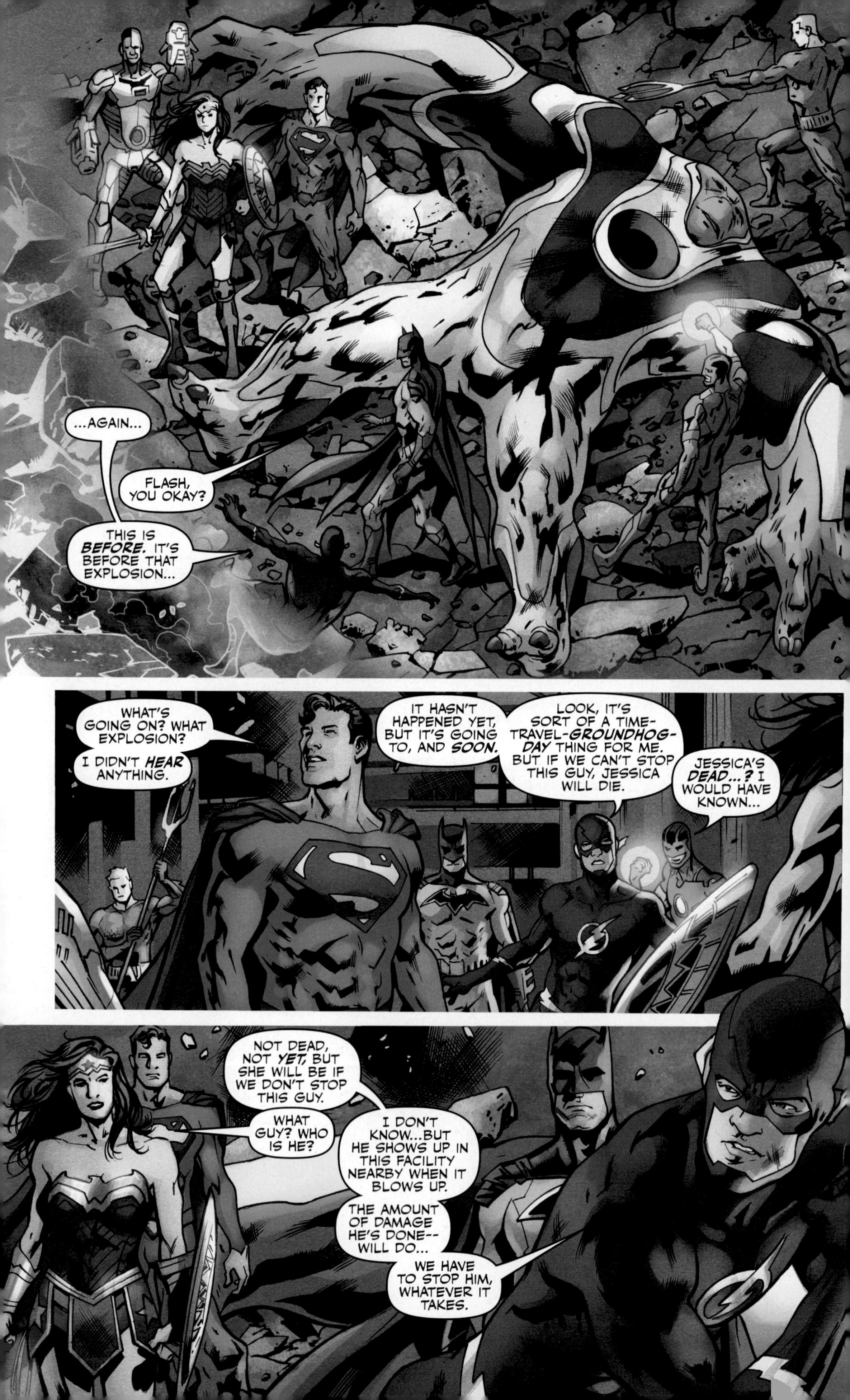
...AGAIN...
FLASH, YOU OKAY?
THIS IS BEFORE. IT'S BEFORE THAT EXPLOSION...
WHAT'S GOING ON? WHAT EXPLOSION?
I DIDN'T HEAR ANYTHING.
IT HASN'T HAPPENED YET, BUT IT'S GOING TO, AND SOON.
LOOK, IT'S SORT OF A TIME-TRAVEL-GROUNDHOG-DAY THING FOR ME. BUT IF WE CAN'T STOP THIS GUY, JESSICA WILL DIE.
JESSICA'S DEAD...? I WOULD HAVE KNOWN...
NOT DEAD, NOT YET, BUT SHE WILL BE IF WE DON'T STOP THIS GUY.
WHAT GUY? WHO IS HE?
I DON'T KNOW...BUT HE SHOWS UP IN THIS FACILITY NEARBY WHEN IT BLOWS UP.
THE AMOUNT OF DAMAGE HE'S DONE-- WILL DO...
WE HAVE TO STOP HIM, WHATEVER IT TAKES.

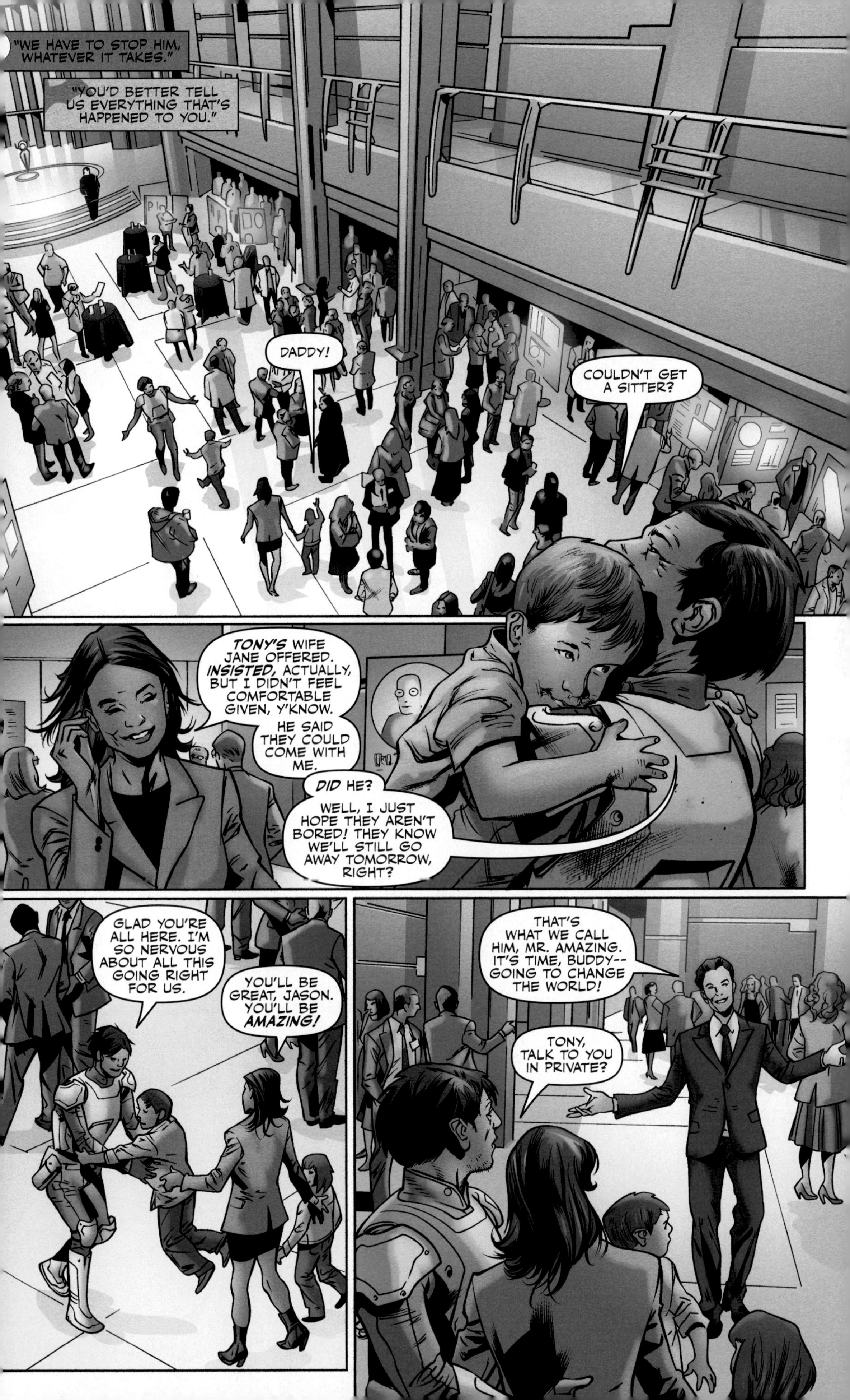
"WE HAVE TO STOP HIM, WHATEVER IT TAKES."
"YOU'D BETTER TELL US EVERYTHING THAT'S HAPPENED TO YOU."
DADDY!
COULDN'T GET A SITTER?
TONY'S WIFE JANE OFFERED. INSISTED, ACTUALLY, BUT I DIDN'T FEEL COMFORTABLE GIVEN, Y'KNOW.
HE SAID THEY COULD COME WITH ME.
DID HE?
WELL, I JUST HOPE THEY AREN'T BORED! THEY KNOW WE'LL STILL GO AWAY TOMORROW, RIGHT?
GLAD YOU'RE ALL HERE. I'M SO NERVOUS ABOUT ALL THIS GOING RIGHT FOR US.
YOU'LL BE GREAT, JASON. YOU'LL BE AMAZING!
THAT'S WHAT WE CALL HIM, MR. AMAZING. IT'S TIME, BUDDY-- GOING TO CHANGE THE WORLD!
TONY, TALK TO YOU IN PRIVATE?

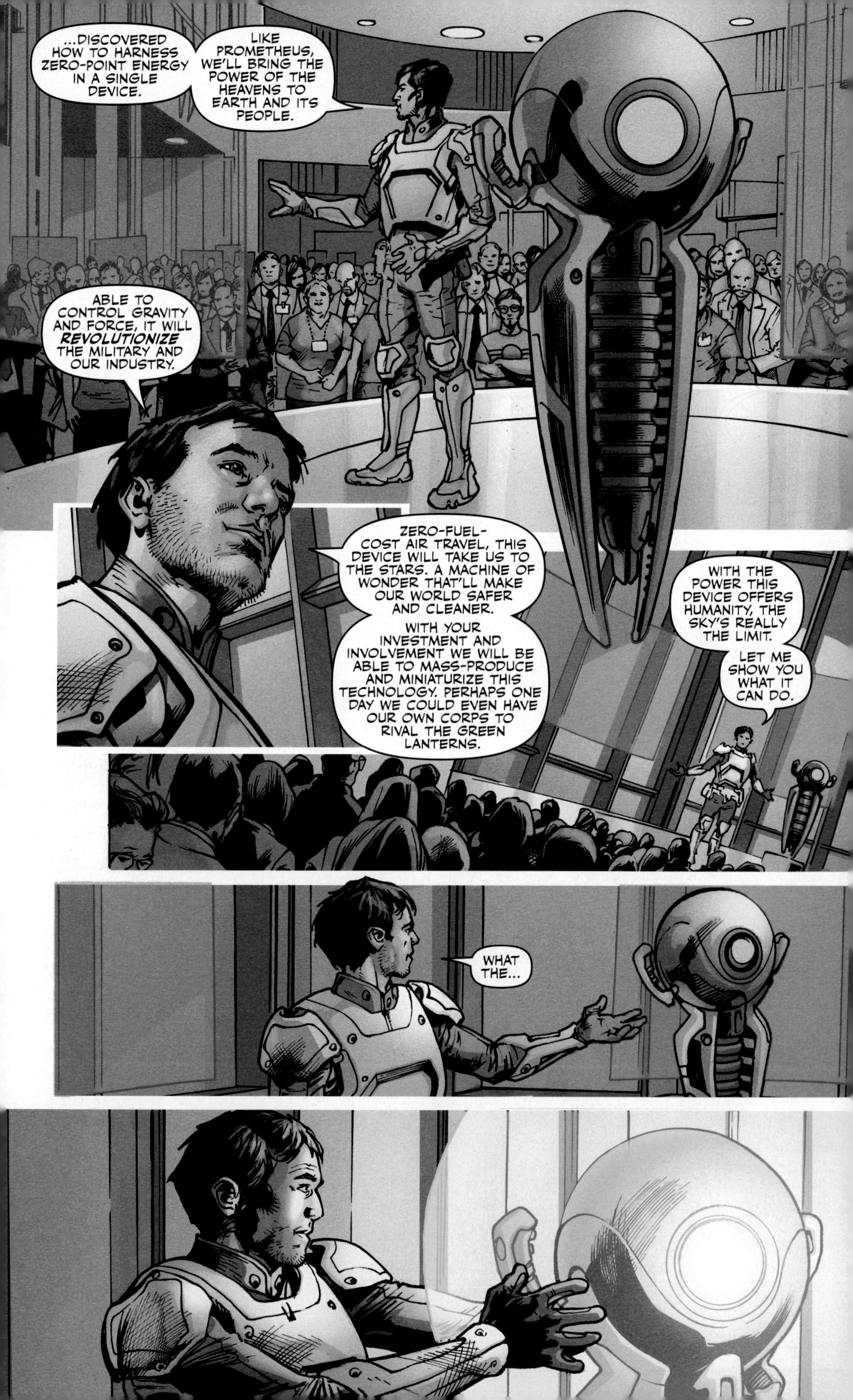
...DISCOVERED HOW TO HARNESS ZERO-POINT ENERGY IN A SINGLE DEVICE.
LIKE PROMETHEUS, WE'LL BRING THE POWER OF THE HEAVENS TO EARTH AND ITS PEOPLE.
ABLE TO CONTROL GRAVITY AND FORCE, IT WILL *REVOLUTIONIZE* THE MILITARY AND OUR INDUSTRY.
ZERO-FUEL-COST AIR TRAVEL, THIS DEVICE WILL TAKE US TO THE STARS. A MACHINE OF WONDER THAT'LL MAKE OUR WORLD SAFER AND CLEANER.
WITH YOUR INVESTMENT AND INVOLVEMENT WE WILL BE ABLE TO MASS-PRODUCE AND MINIATURIZE THIS TECHNOLOGY. PERHAPS ONE DAY WE COULD EVEN HAVE OUR OWN CORPS TO RIVAL THE GREEN LANTERNS.
WITH THE POWER THIS DEVICE OFFERS HUMANITY, THE SKY'S REALLY THE LIMIT.
LET ME SHOW YOU WHAT IT CAN DO.
WHAT THE...

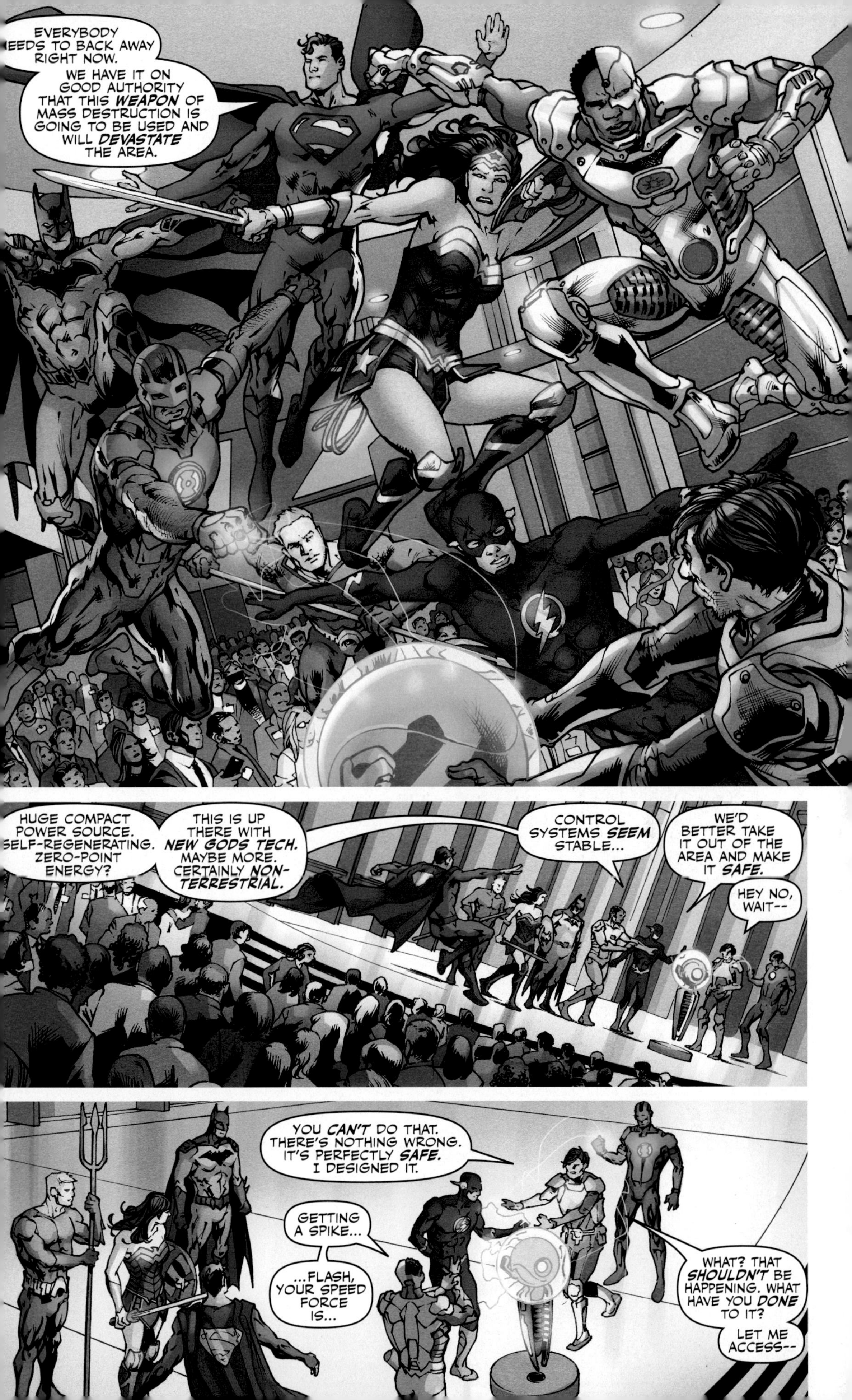
EVERYBODY NEEDS TO BACK AWAY RIGHT NOW.
WE HAVE IT ON GOOD AUTHORITY THAT THIS WEAPON OF MASS DESTRUCTION IS GOING TO BE USED AND WILL DEVASTATE THE AREA.
HUGE COMPACT POWER SOURCE. SELF-REGENERATING. ZERO-POINT ENERGY?
THIS IS UP THERE WITH NEW GODS TECH. MAYBE MORE. CERTAINLY NON-TERRESTRIAL.
CONTROL SYSTEMS SEEM STABLE...
WE'D BETTER TAKE IT OUT OF THE AREA AND MAKE IT SAFE.
HEY NO, WAIT--
YOU CAN'T DO THAT. THERE'S NOTHING WRONG. IT'S PERFECTLY SAFE. I DESIGNED IT.
GETTING A SPIKE...
...FLASH, YOUR SPEED FORCE IS...
WHAT? THAT SHOULDN'T BE HAPPENING. WHAT HAVE YOU DONE TO IT?
LET ME ACCESS--

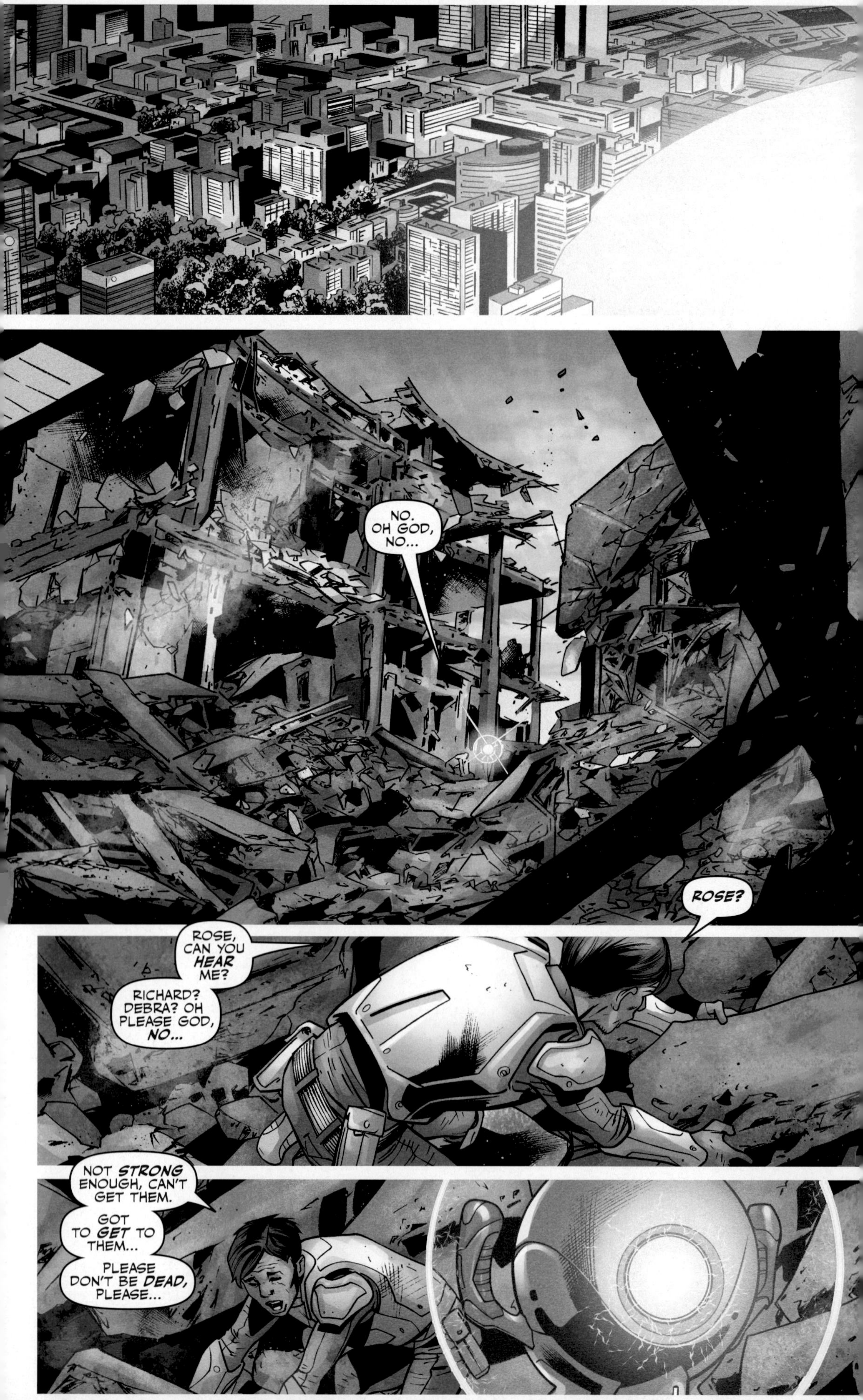

NO. OH GOD, NO...
ROSE?
ROSE, CAN YOU HEAR ME?
RICHARD? DEBRA? OH PLEASE GOD, NO...
NOT STRONG ENOUGH, CAN'T GET THEM.
GOT TO GET TO THEM...
PLEASE DON'T BE DEAD, PLEASE...

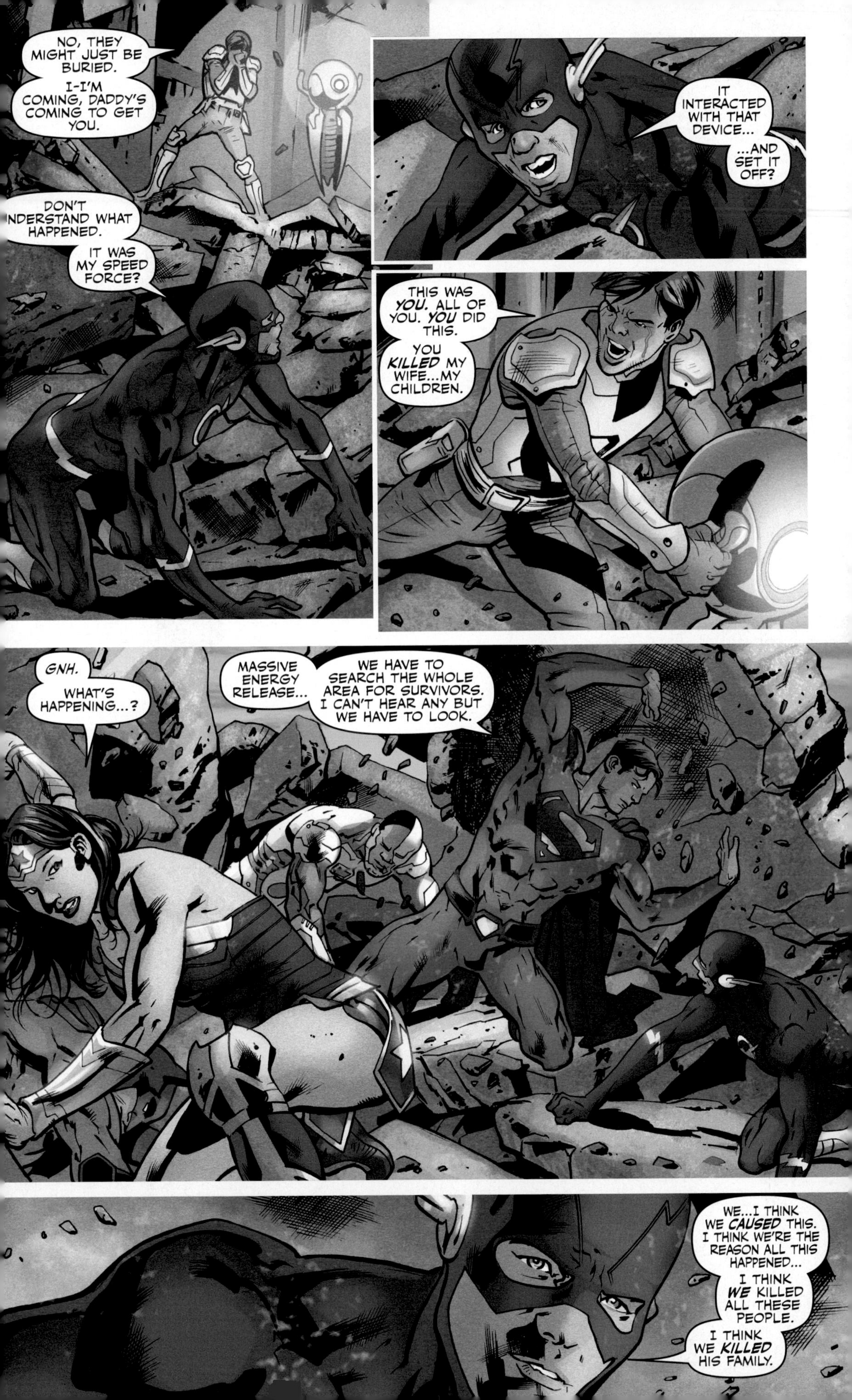

NO, THEY MIGHT JUST BE BURIED.
I-I'M COMING, DADDY'S COMING TO GET YOU.
IT INTERACTED WITH THAT DEVICE...
...AND SET IT OFF?
DON'T NDERSTAND WHAT HAPPENED.
IT WAS MY SPEED FORCE?
THIS WAS *YOU.* ALL OF YOU. *YOU* DID THIS.
YOU *KILLED* MY WIFE...MY CHILDREN.
GNH.
WHAT'S HAPPENING...?
MASSIVE ENERGY RELEASE...
WE HAVE TO SEARCH THE WHOLE AREA FOR SURVIVORS. I CAN'T HEAR ANY BUT WE HAVE TO LOOK.
WE...I THINK WE *CAUSED* THIS. I THINK WE'RE THE REASON ALL THIS HAPPENED...
I THINK *WE* KILLED ALL THESE PEOPLE.
I THINK WE *KILLED* HIS FAMILY.

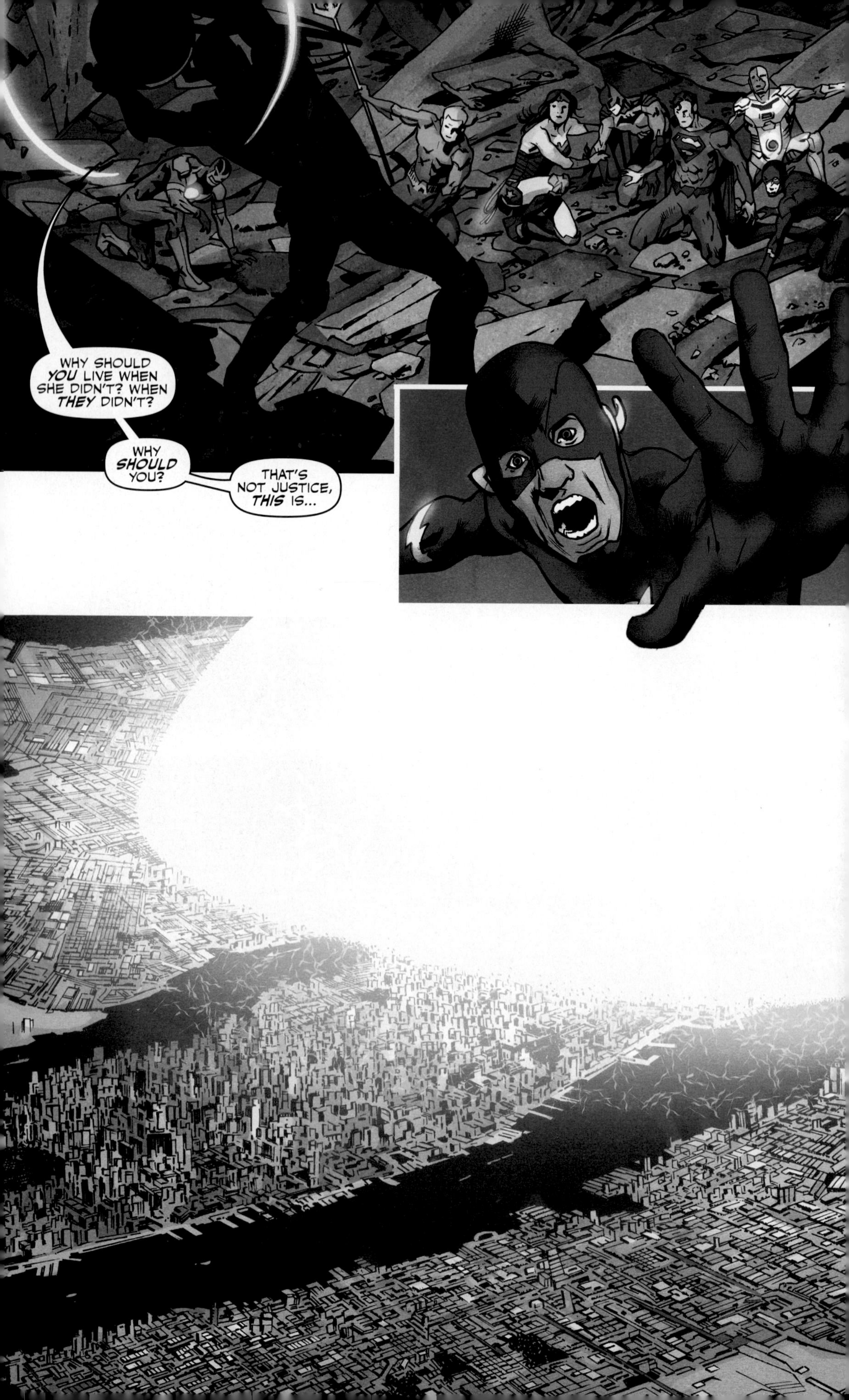
WHY SHOULD YOU LIVE WHEN SHE DIDN'T? WHEN THEY DIDN'T?
WHY SHOULD YOU?
THAT'S NOT JUSTICE, THIS IS...

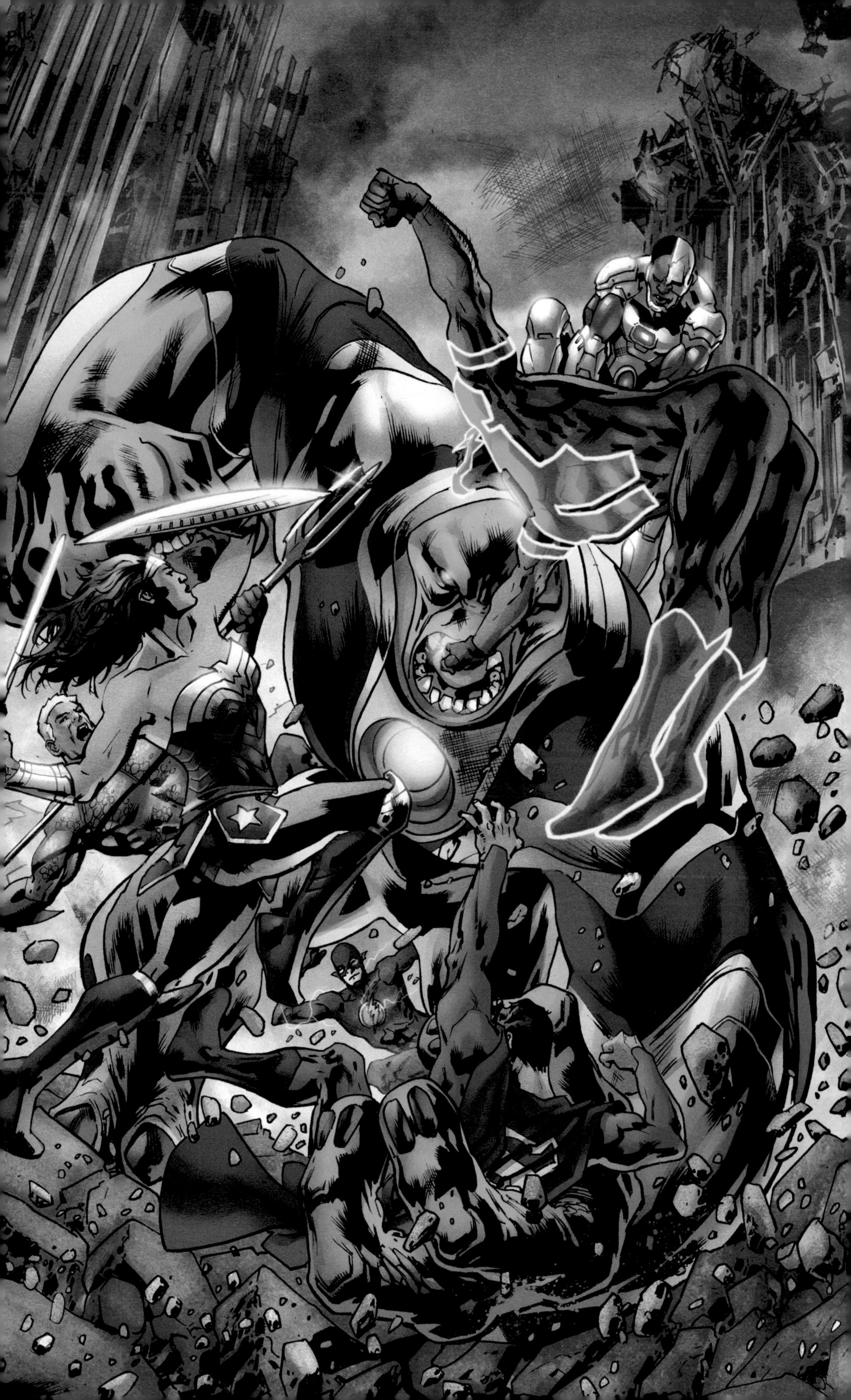

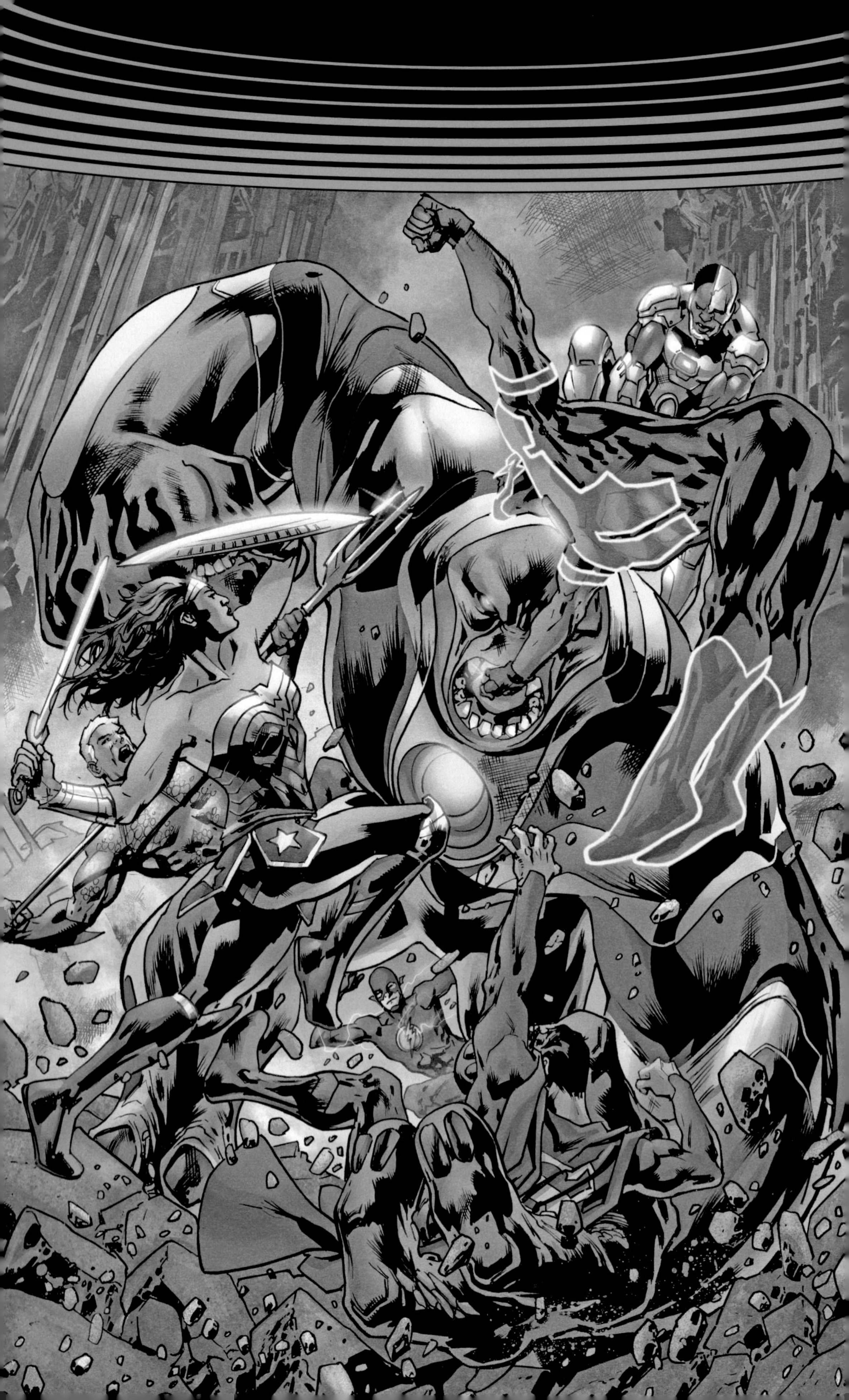

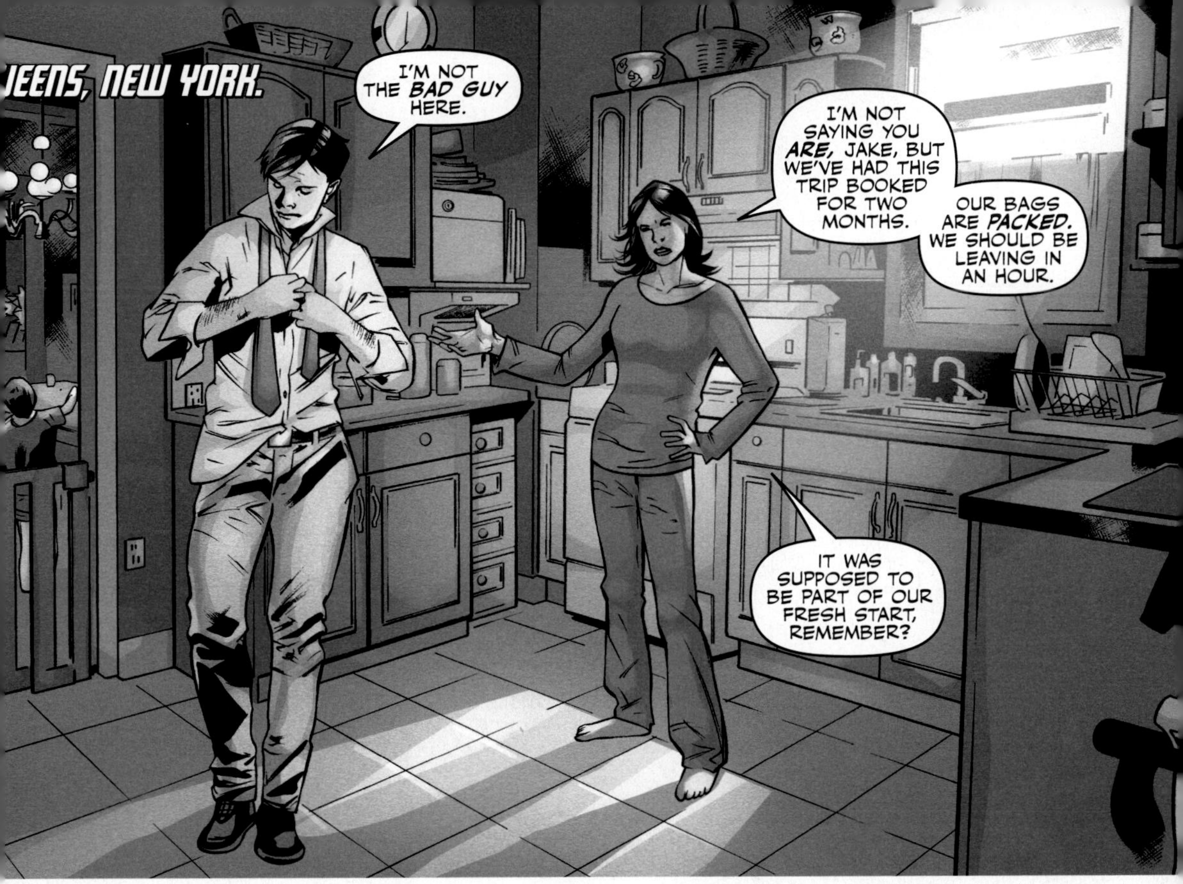
EENS, NEW YORK.
I'M NOT THE BAD GUY HERE.
I'M NOT SAYING YOU ARE, JAKE, BUT WE'VE HAD THIS TRIP BOOKED FOR TWO MONTHS.
OUR BAGS ARE PACKED. WE SHOULD BE LEAVING IN AN HOUR.
IT WAS SUPPOSED TO BE PART OF OUR FRESH START, REMEMBER?

ENDLESS

PART TWO

BRYAN HITCH Writer & Artist
DANIEL HENRIQUES & SCOTT HANNA Inkers
ALEX SINCLAIR Colorist
RICHARD STARKINGS & COMICRAFT Lettering
BRYAN HITCH & ALEX SINCLAIR Cover
NICK BRADSHAW & ALEX SINCLAIR Variant Cover
AMEDEO TURTURRO Assistant Editor
BRIAN CUNNINGHAM Editor

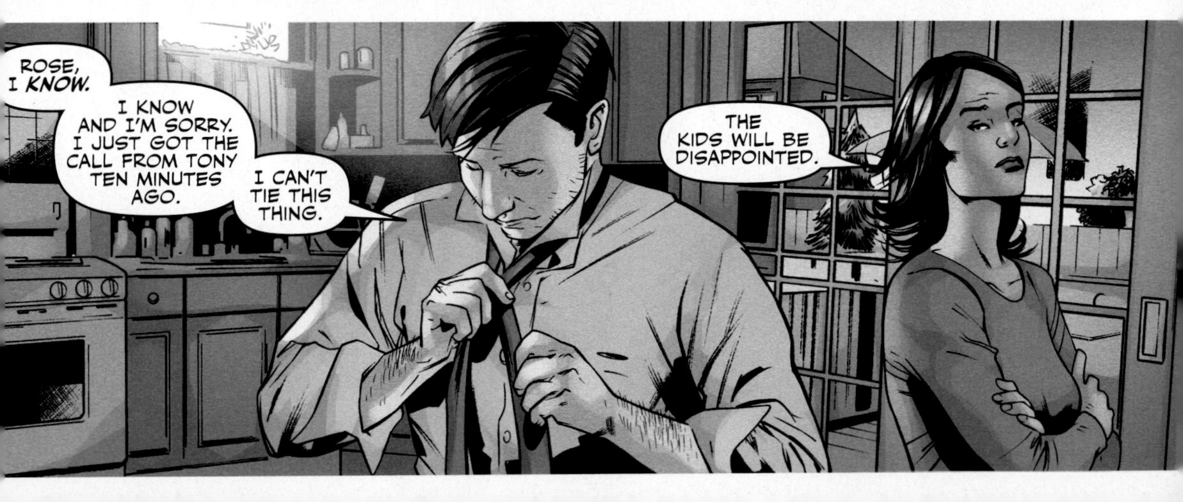
ROSE, I KNOW.
I KNOW AND I'M SORRY. I JUST GOT THE CALL FROM TONY TEN MINUTES AGO.
I CAN'T TIE THIS THING.
THE KIDS WILL BE DISAPPOINTED.

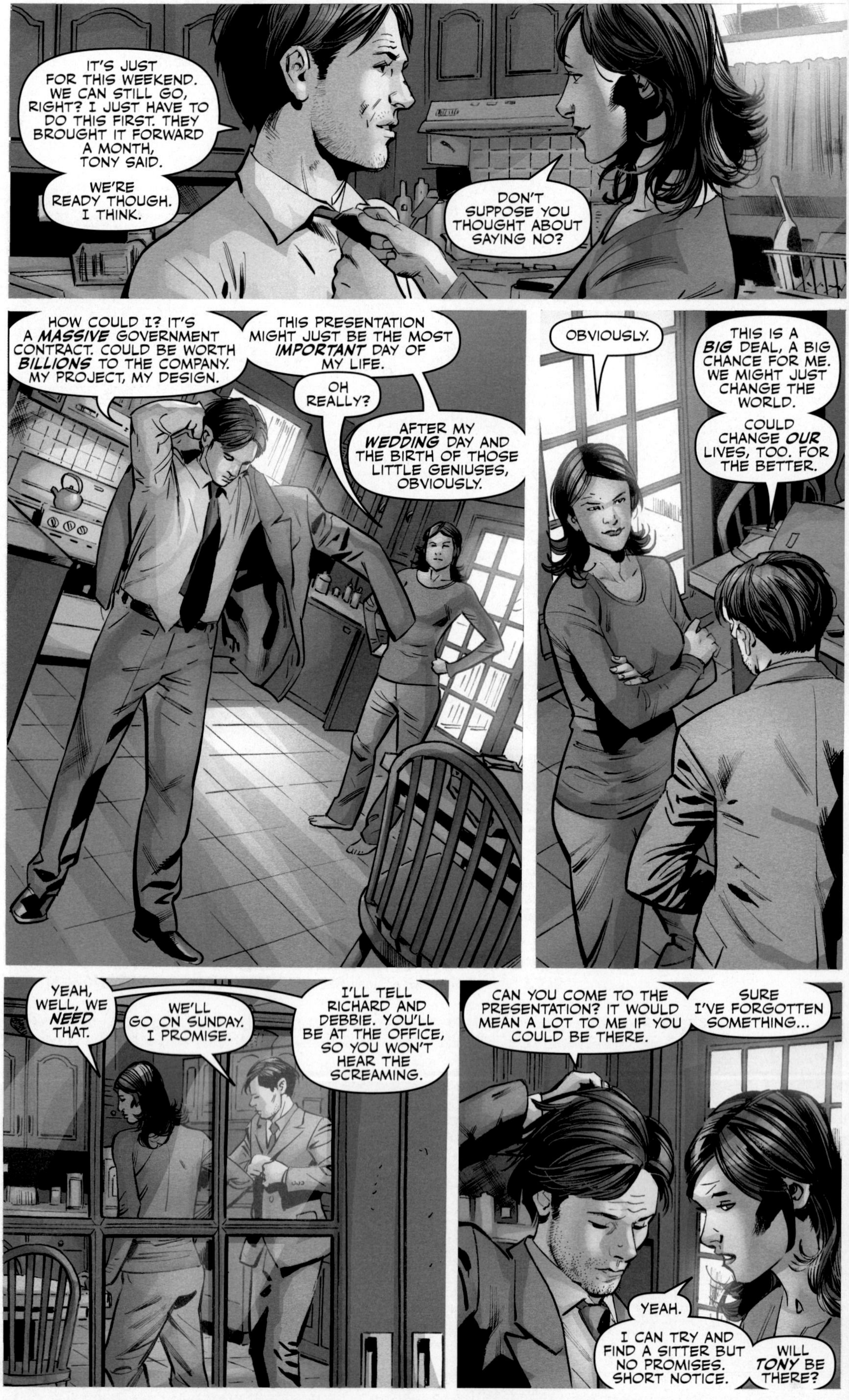
IT'S JUST FOR THIS WEEKEND. WE CAN STILL GO, RIGHT? I JUST HAVE TO DO THIS FIRST. THEY BROUGHT IT FORWARD A MONTH, TONY SAID.
WE'RE READY THOUGH. I THINK.
DON'T SUPPOSE YOU THOUGHT ABOUT SAYING NO?
HOW COULD I? IT'S A *MASSIVE* GOVERNMENT CONTRACT. COULD BE WORTH *BILLIONS* TO THE COMPANY. MY PROJECT, MY DESIGN.
THIS PRESENTATION MIGHT JUST BE THE MOST *IMPORTANT* DAY OF MY LIFE.
OH REALLY?
AFTER MY *WEDDING* DAY AND THE BIRTH OF THOSE LITTLE GENIUSES, OBVIOUSLY.
OBVIOUSLY.
THIS IS A *BIG* DEAL, A BIG CHANCE FOR ME. WE MIGHT JUST CHANGE THE WORLD.
COULD CHANGE *OUR* LIVES, TOO. FOR THE BETTER.
YEAH, WELL, WE *NEED* THAT.
WE'LL GO ON SUNDAY. I PROMISE.
I'LL TELL RICHARD AND DEBBIE. YOU'LL BE AT THE OFFICE, SO YOU WON'T HEAR THE SCREAMING.
CAN YOU COME TO THE PRESENTATION? IT WOULD MEAN A LOT TO ME IF YOU COULD BE THERE.
SURE I'VE FORGOTTEN SOMETHING...
YEAH.
I CAN TRY AND FIND A SITTER BUT NO PROMISES. SHORT NOTICE.
WILL *TONY* BE THERE?

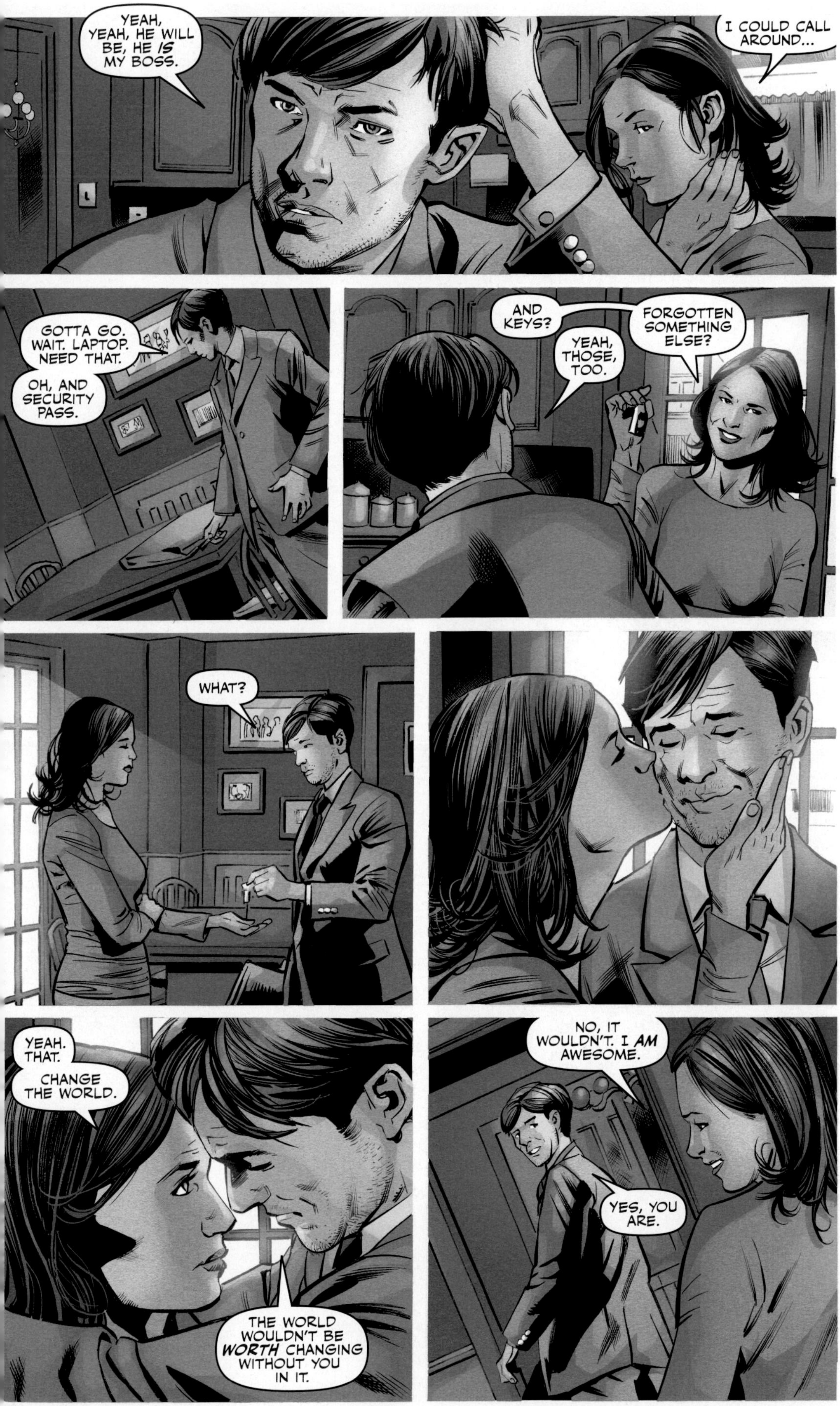
YEAH, YEAH, HE WILL BE, HE *IS* MY BOSS.
I COULD CALL AROUND...
GOTTA GO. WAIT. LAPTOP. NEED THAT.
OH, AND SECURITY PASS.
FORGOTTEN SOMETHING ELSE?
AND KEYS?
YEAH, THOSE, TOO.
WHAT?
YEAH. THAT.
CHANGE THE WORLD.
THE WORLD WOULDN'T BE *WORTH* CHANGING WITHOUT YOU IN IT.
NO, IT WOULDN'T. I *AM* AWESOME.
YES, YOU ARE.

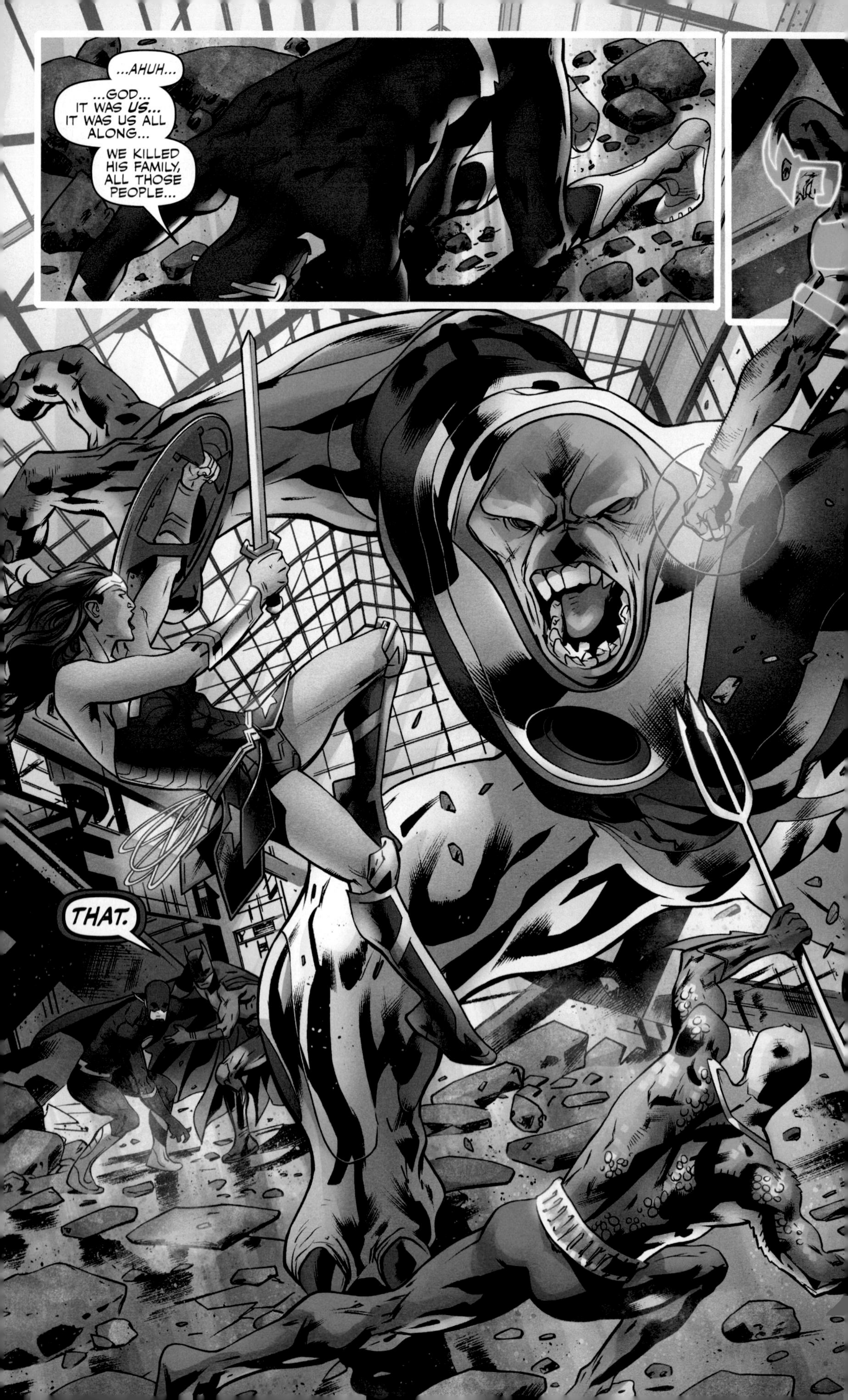
...AHUH...
...GOD... IT WAS US... IT WAS US ALL ALONG...
WE KILLED HIS FAMILY, ALL THOSE PEOPLE...
THAT.

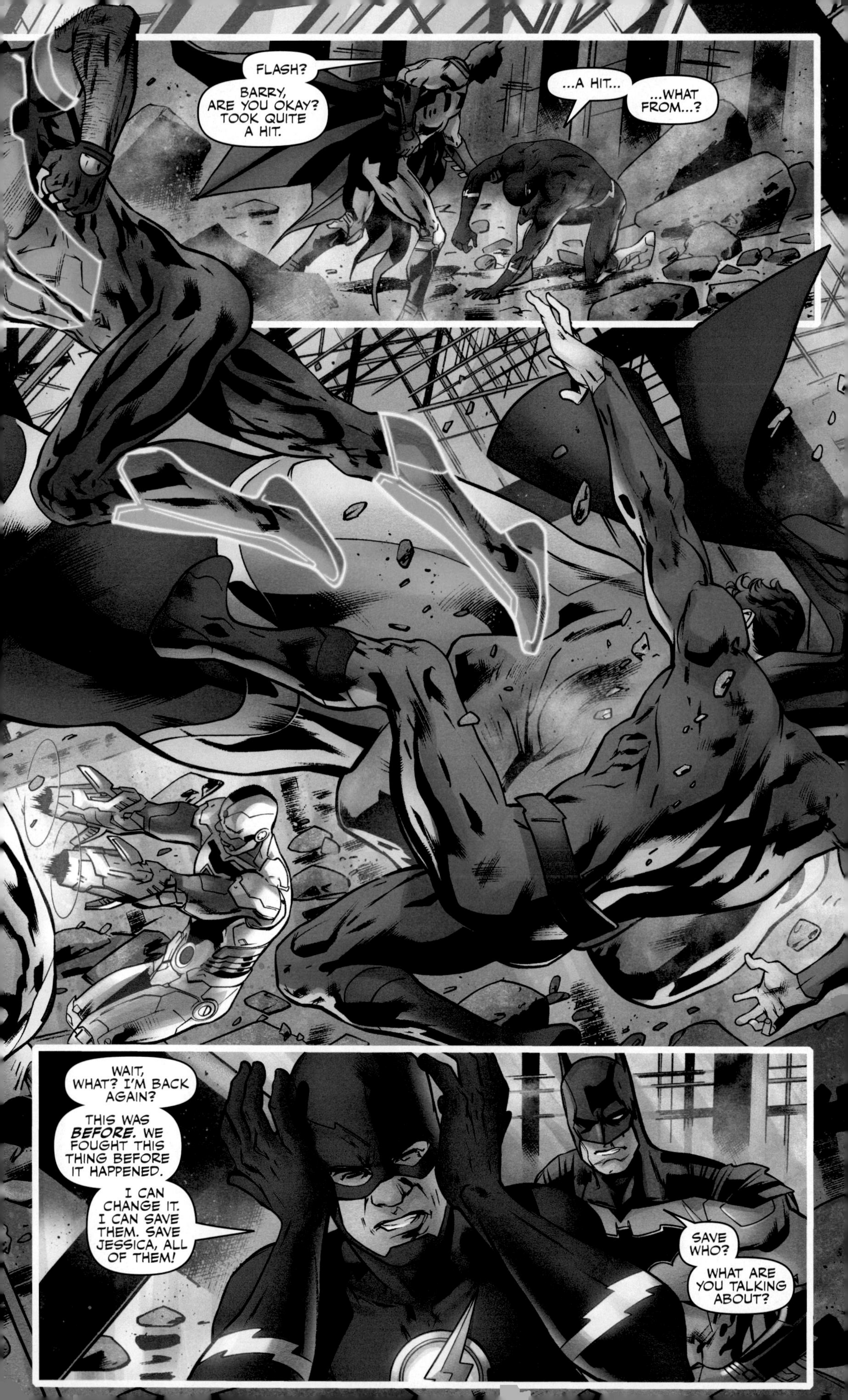
FLASH?
BARRY, ARE YOU OKAY? TOOK QUITE A HIT.
...A HIT...
...WHAT FROM...?
WAIT, WHAT? I'M BACK AGAIN?
THIS WAS *BEFORE.* WE FOUGHT THIS THING BEFORE IT HAPPENED.
I CAN CHANGE IT. I CAN SAVE THEM. SAVE JESSICA, ALL OF THEM!
SAVE WHO?
WHAT ARE YOU TALKING ABOUT?

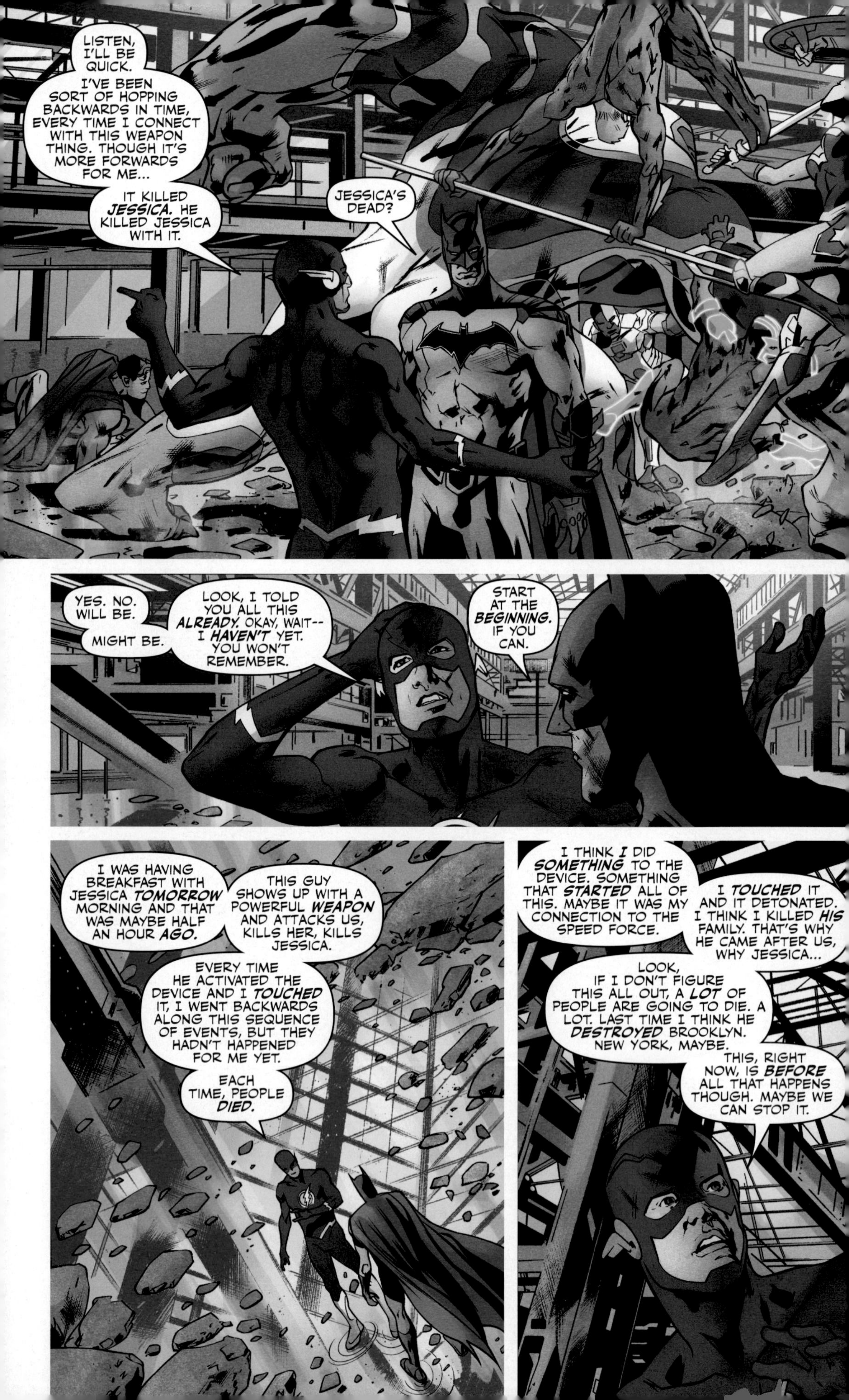

LISTEN, I'LL BE QUICK.
I'VE BEEN SORT OF HOPPING BACKWARDS IN TIME, EVERY TIME I CONNECT WITH THIS WEAPON THING. THOUGH IT'S MORE FORWARDS FOR ME...
IT KILLED JESSICA. HE KILLED JESSICA WITH IT.
JESSICA'S DEAD?
YES. NO. WILL BE.
MIGHT BE.
LOOK, I TOLD YOU ALL THIS ALREADY. OKAY, WAIT-- I HAVEN'T YET. YOU WON'T REMEMBER.
START AT THE BEGINNING. IF YOU CAN.
I WAS HAVING BREAKFAST WITH JESSICA TOMORROW MORNING AND THAT WAS MAYBE HALF AN HOUR AGO.
THIS GUY SHOWS UP WITH A POWERFUL WEAPON AND ATTACKS US, KILLS HER, KILLS JESSICA.
EVERY TIME HE ACTIVATED THE DEVICE AND I TOUCHED IT, I WENT BACKWARDS ALONG THIS SEQUENCE OF EVENTS, BUT THEY HADN'T HAPPENED FOR ME YET.
EACH TIME, PEOPLE DIED.
I THINK I DID SOMETHING TO THE DEVICE. SOMETHING THAT STARTED ALL OF THIS. MAYBE IT WAS MY CONNECTION TO THE SPEED FORCE.
I TOUCHED IT AND IT DETONATED. I THINK I KILLED HIS FAMILY. THAT'S WHY HE CAME AFTER US, WHY JESSICA...
LOOK, IF I DON'T FIGURE THIS ALL OUT, A LOT OF PEOPLE ARE GOING TO DIE. A LOT. LAST TIME I THINK HE DESTROYED BROOKLYN. NEW YORK, MAYBE.
THIS, RIGHT NOW, IS BEFORE ALL THAT HAPPENS THOUGH. MAYBE WE CAN STOP IT.

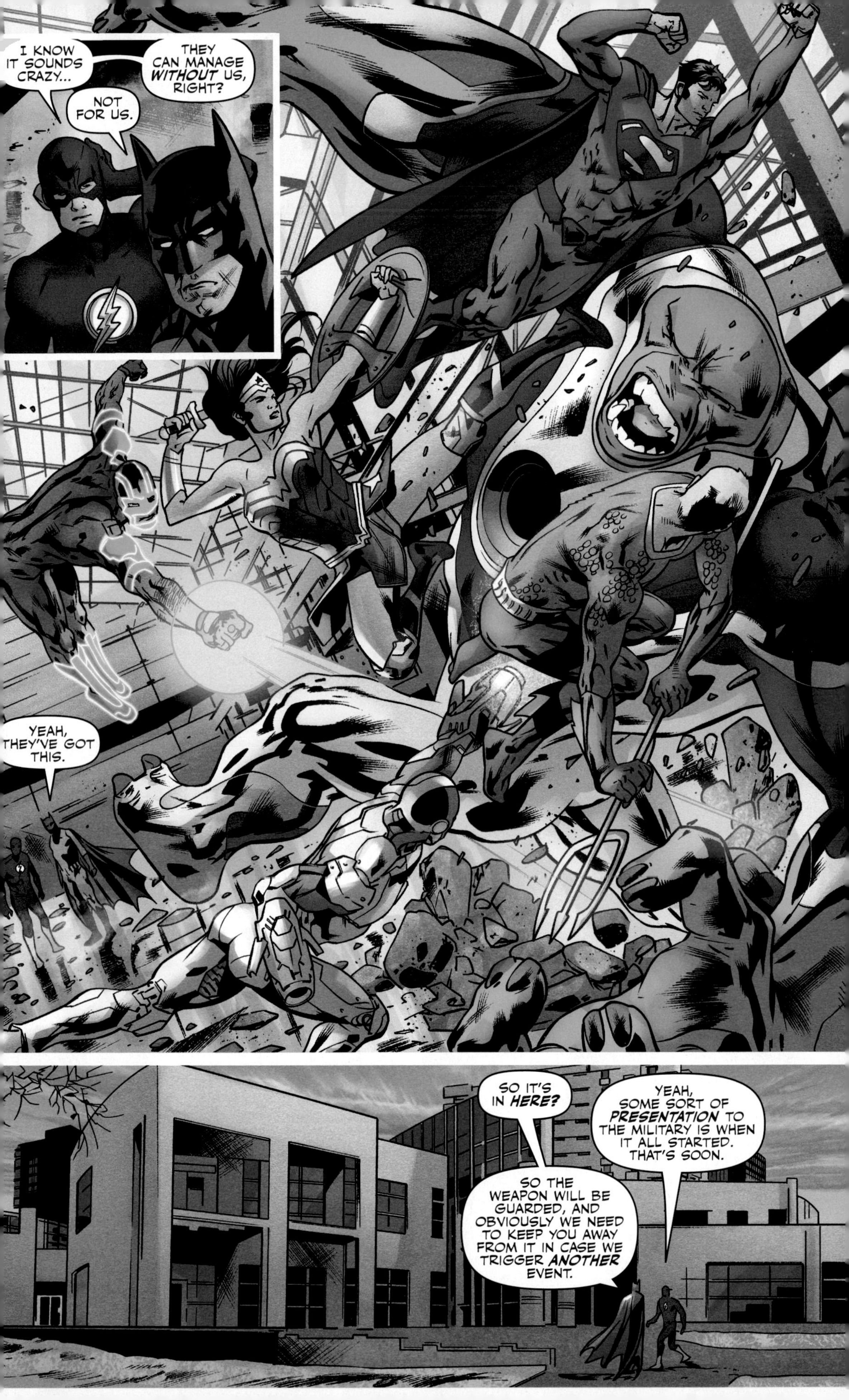
I KNOW IT SOUNDS CRAZY...
THEY CAN MANAGE *WITHOUT* US, RIGHT?
NOT FOR US.
YEAH, THEY'VE GOT THIS.
SO IT'S IN *HERE?*
YEAH, SOME SORT OF *PRESENTATION* TO THE MILITARY IS WHEN IT ALL STARTED. THAT'S SOON.
SO THE WEAPON WILL BE GUARDED, AND OBVIOUSLY WE NEED TO KEEP YOU AWAY FROM IT IN CASE WE TRIGGER *ANOTHER* EVENT.

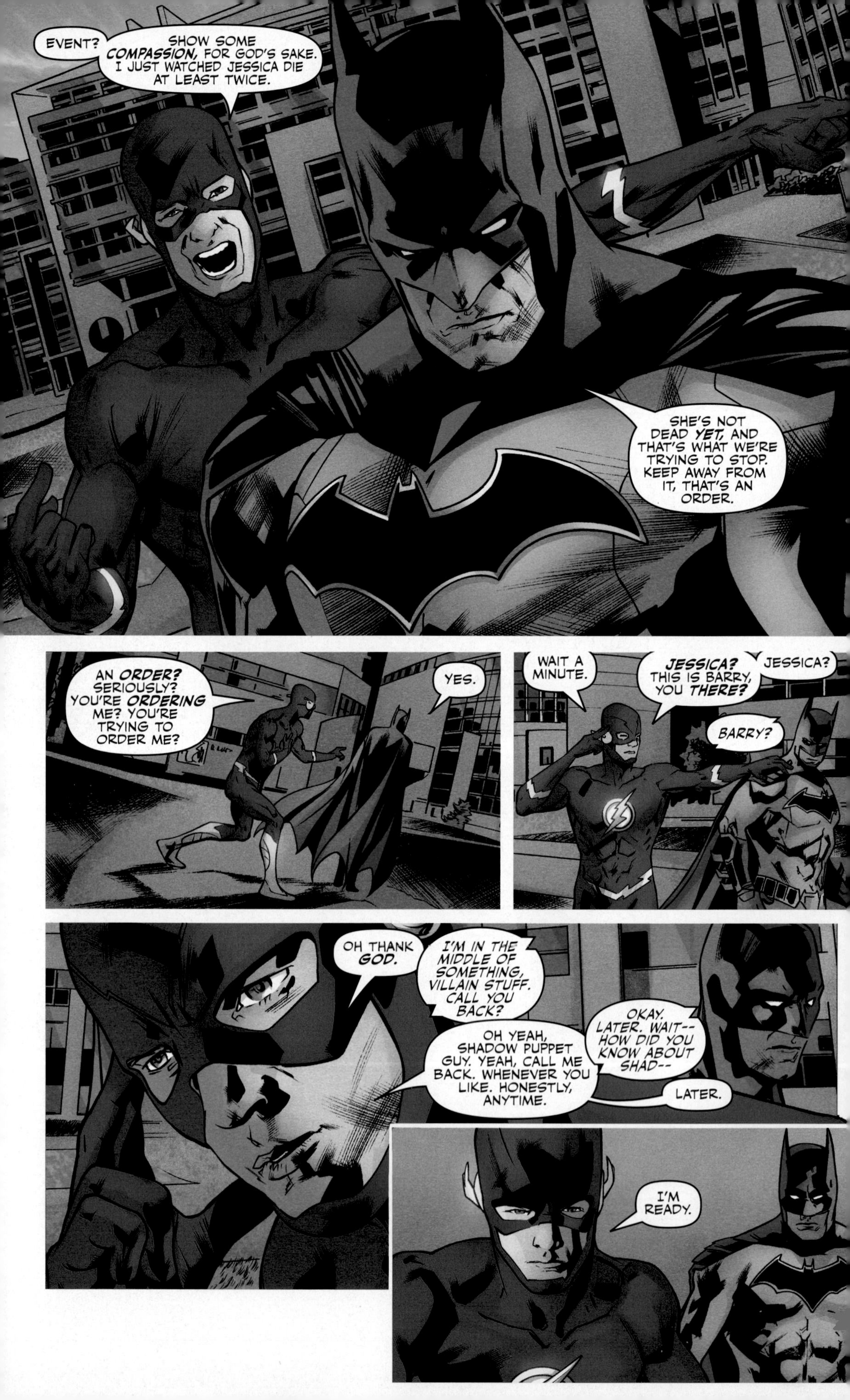
EVENT?
SHOW SOME COMPASSION, FOR GOD'S SAKE. I JUST WATCHED JESSICA DIE AT LEAST TWICE.
SHE'S NOT DEAD YET, AND THAT'S WHAT WE'RE TRYING TO STOP. KEEP AWAY FROM IT, THAT'S AN ORDER.
AN ORDER? SERIOUSLY? YOU'RE ORDERING ME? YOU'RE TRYING TO ORDER ME?
YES.
WAIT A MINUTE.
JESSICA? THIS IS BARRY, YOU THERE?
JESSICA?
BARRY?
OH THANK GOD.
I'M IN THE MIDDLE OF SOMETHING, VILLAIN STUFF. CALL YOU BACK?
OH YEAH, SHADOW PUPPET GUY. YEAH, CALL ME BACK. WHENEVER YOU LIKE. HONESTLY, ANYTIME.
OKAY. LATER. WAIT-- HOW DID YOU KNOW ABOUT SHAD--
LATER.
I'M READY.

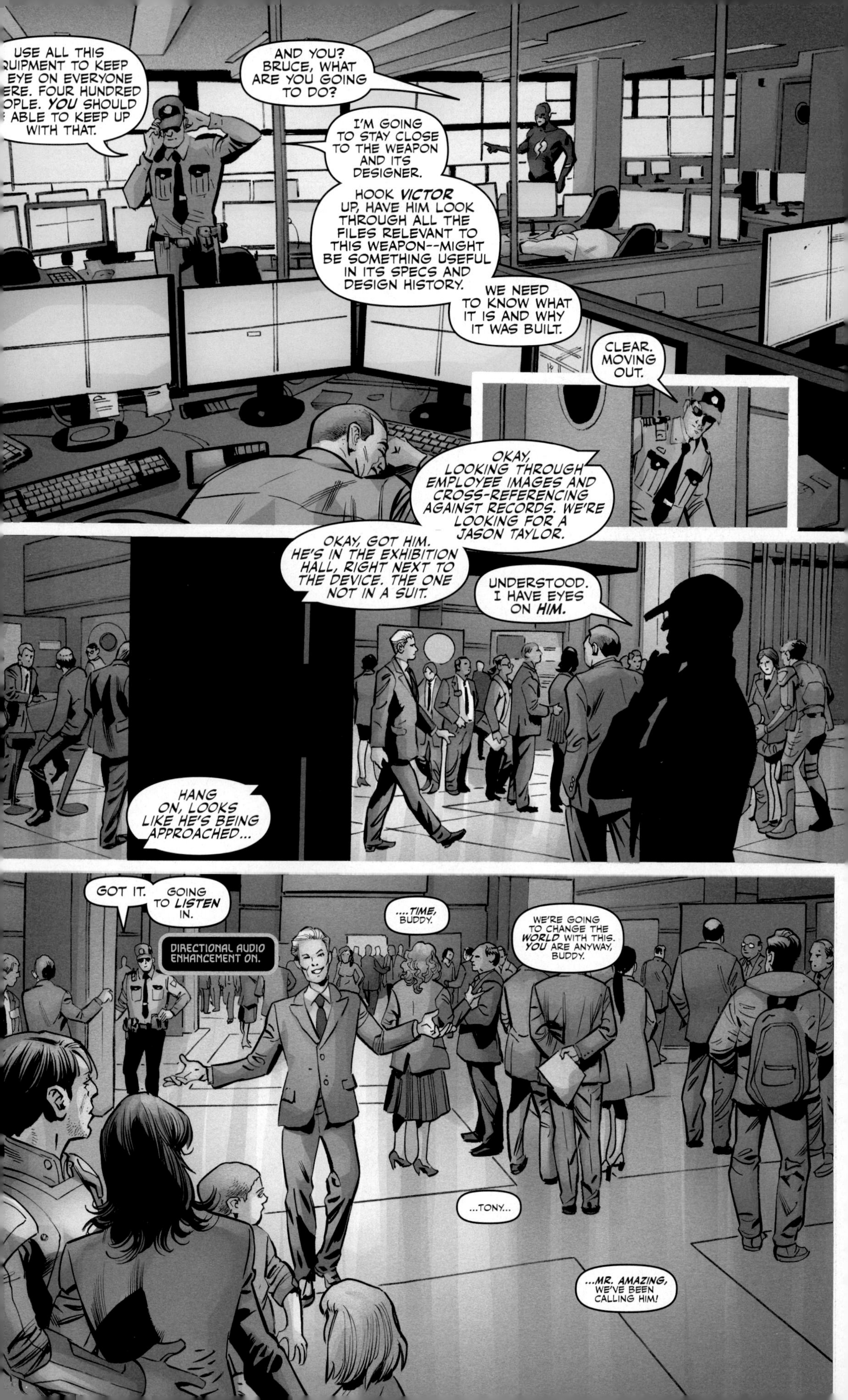
USE ALL THIS QUIPMENT TO KEEP EYE ON EVERYONE ERE. FOUR HUNDRED OPLE. *YOU* SHOULD ABLE TO KEEP UP WITH THAT.
AND YOU? BRUCE, WHAT ARE YOU GOING TO DO?
I'M GOING TO STAY CLOSE TO THE WEAPON AND ITS DESIGNER.
HOOK *VICTOR* UP, HAVE HIM LOOK THROUGH ALL THE FILES RELEVANT TO THIS WEAPON--MIGHT BE SOMETHING USEFUL IN ITS SPECS AND DESIGN HISTORY.
WE NEED TO KNOW WHAT IT IS AND WHY IT WAS BUILT.
CLEAR. MOVING OUT.
OKAY, LOOKING THROUGH EMPLOYEE IMAGES AND CROSS-REFERENCING AGAINST RECORDS. WE'RE LOOKING FOR A JASON TAYLOR.
OKAY, GOT HIM. HE'S IN THE EXHIBITION HALL, RIGHT NEXT TO THE DEVICE. THE ONE NOT IN A SUIT.
UNDERSTOOD. I HAVE EYES ON *HIM.*
HANG ON, LOOKS LIKE HE'S BEING APPROACHED...
GOT IT.
GOING TO *LISTEN* IN.
DIRECTIONAL AUDIO ENHANCEMENT ON.
....*TIME,* BUDDY.
WE'RE GOING TO CHANGE THE *WORLD* WITH THIS. *YOU* ARE ANYWAY, BUDDY.
...TONY...
...*MR. AMAZING,* WE'VE BEEN CALLING HIM!

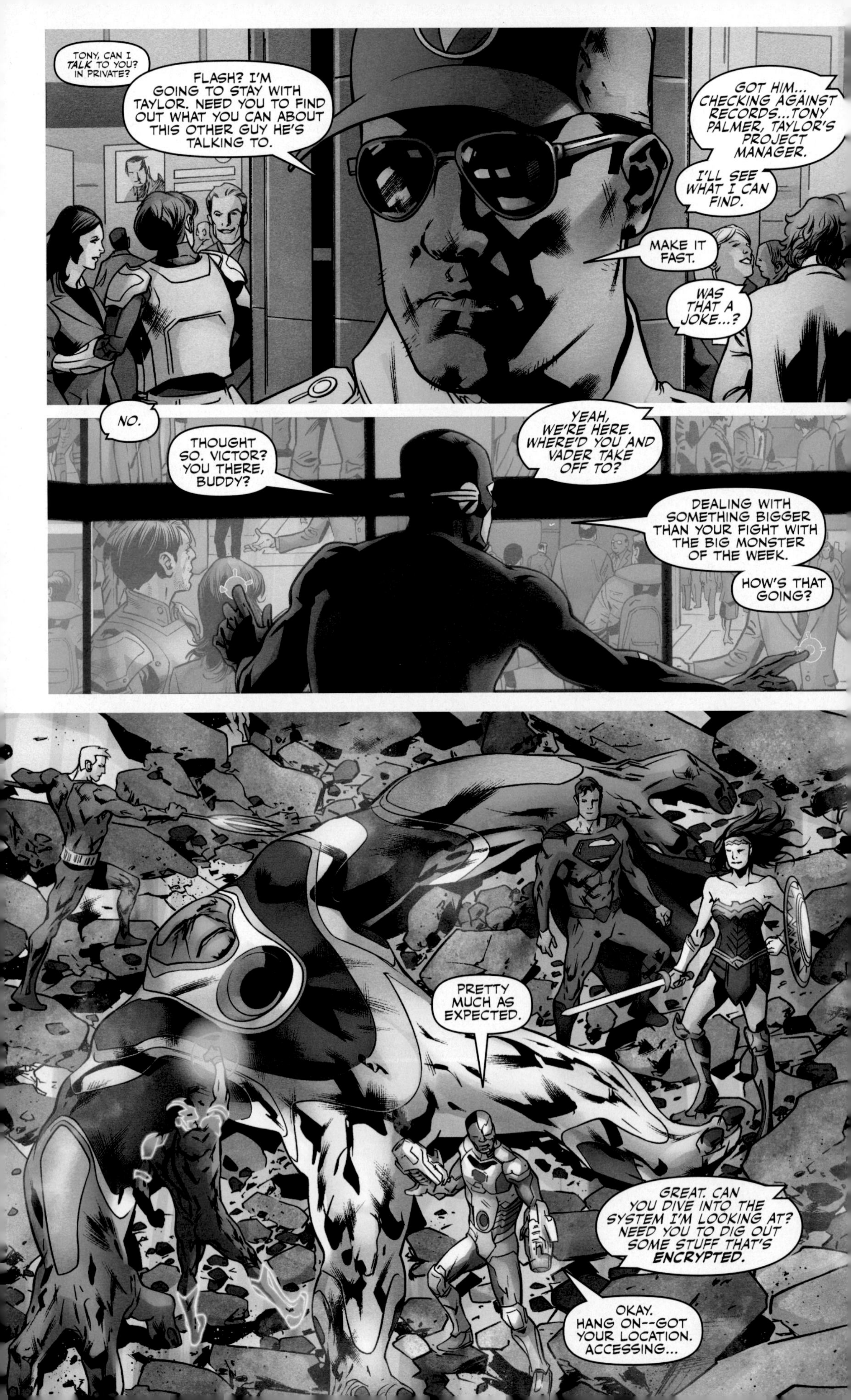
TONY, CAN I TALK TO YOU? IN PRIVATE?
FLASH? I'M GOING TO STAY WITH TAYLOR. NEED YOU TO FIND OUT WHAT YOU CAN ABOUT THIS OTHER GUY HE'S TALKING TO.
GOT HIM... CHECKING AGAINST RECORDS...TONY PALMER, TAYLOR'S PROJECT MANAGER.
I'LL SEE WHAT I CAN FIND.
MAKE IT FAST.
WAS THAT A JOKE...?
NO.
THOUGHT SO. VICTOR? YOU THERE, BUDDY?
YEAH, WE'RE HERE. WHERE'D YOU AND VADER TAKE OFF TO?
DEALING WITH SOMETHING BIGGER THAN YOUR FIGHT WITH THE BIG MONSTER OF THE WEEK.
HOW'S THAT GOING?
PRETTY MUCH AS EXPECTED.
GREAT. CAN YOU DIVE INTO THE SYSTEM I'M LOOKING AT? NEED YOU TO DIG OUT SOME STUFF THAT'S ENCRYPTED.
OKAY. HANG ON--GOT YOUR LOCATION. ACCESSING...

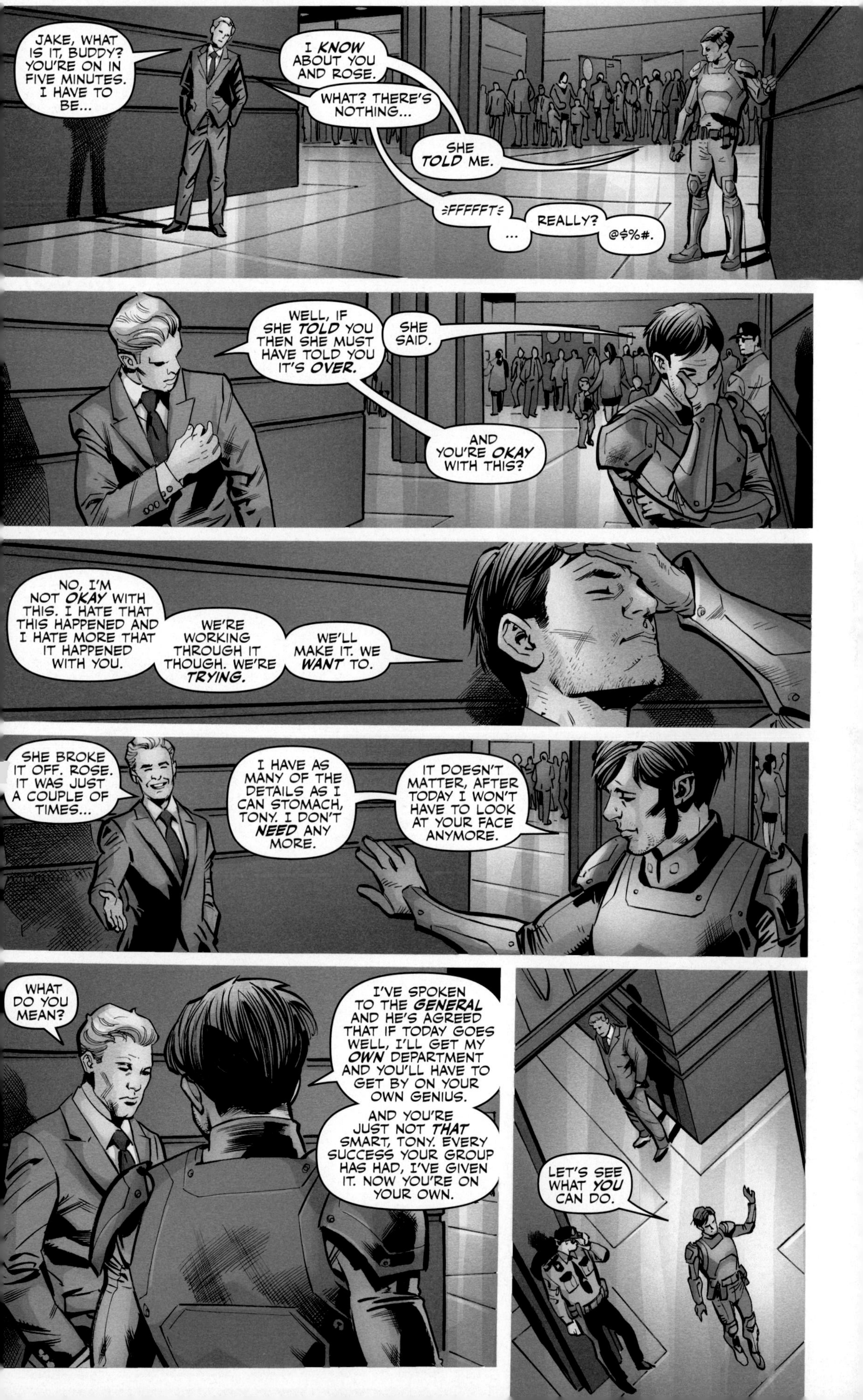
JAKE, WHAT IS IT, BUDDY? YOU'RE ON IN FIVE MINUTES. I HAVE TO BE...
I KNOW ABOUT YOU AND ROSE.
WHAT? THERE'S NOTHING...
SHE TOLD ME.
FFFFFT
...
REALLY?
@$%#.
WELL, IF SHE TOLD YOU THEN SHE MUST HAVE TOLD YOU IT'S OVER.
SHE SAID.
AND YOU'RE OKAY WITH THIS?
NO, I'M NOT OKAY WITH THIS. I HATE THAT THIS HAPPENED AND I HATE MORE THAT IT HAPPENED WITH YOU.
WE'RE WORKING THROUGH IT THOUGH. WE'RE TRYING.
WE'LL MAKE IT. WE WANT TO.
SHE BROKE IT OFF. ROSE. IT WAS JUST A COUPLE OF TIMES...
I HAVE AS MANY OF THE DETAILS AS I CAN STOMACH, TONY. I DON'T NEED ANY MORE.
IT DOESN'T MATTER, AFTER TODAY I WON'T HAVE TO LOOK AT YOUR FACE ANYMORE.
WHAT DO YOU MEAN?
I'VE SPOKEN TO THE GENERAL AND HE'S AGREED THAT IF TODAY GOES WELL, I'LL GET MY OWN DEPARTMENT AND YOU'LL HAVE TO GET BY ON YOUR OWN GENIUS.
AND YOU'RE JUST NOT THAT SMART, TONY. EVERY SUCCESS YOUR GROUP HAS HAD, I'VE GIVEN IT. NOW YOU'RE ON YOUR OWN.
LET'S SEE WHAT YOU CAN DO.

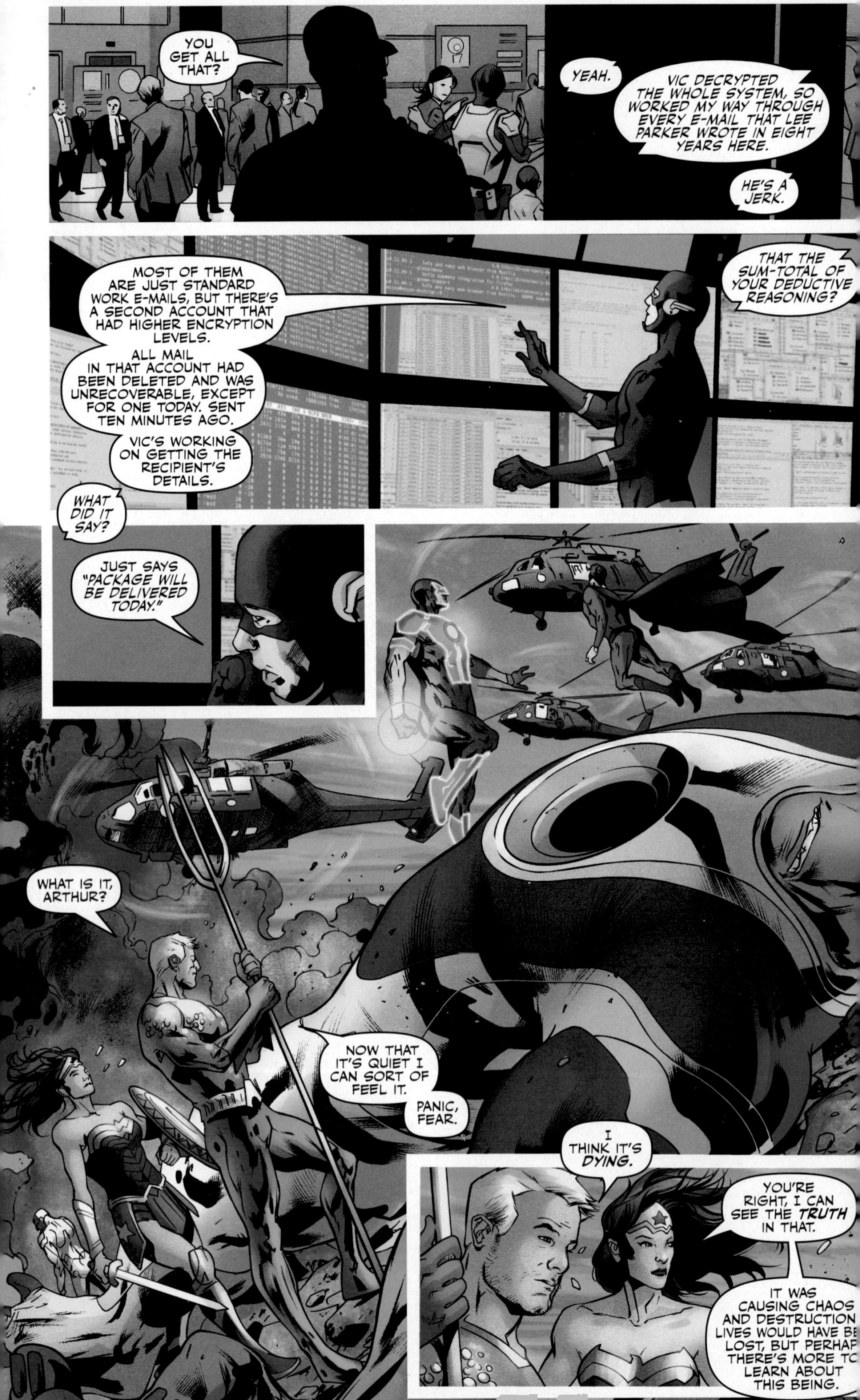
YOU GET ALL THAT?
YEAH.
VIC DECRYPTED THE WHOLE SYSTEM, SO WORKED MY WAY THROUGH EVERY E-MAIL THAT LEE PARKER WROTE IN EIGHT YEARS HERE.
HE'S A JERK.
MOST OF THEM ARE JUST STANDARD WORK E-MAILS, BUT THERE'S A SECOND ACCOUNT THAT HAD HIGHER ENCRYPTION LEVELS.
ALL MAIL IN THAT ACCOUNT HAD BEEN DELETED AND WAS UNRECOVERABLE, EXCEPT FOR ONE TODAY. SENT TEN MINUTES AGO.
VIC'S WORKING ON GETTING THE RECIPIENT'S DETAILS.
THAT THE SUM-TOTAL OF YOUR DEDUCTIVE REASONING?
WHAT DID IT SAY?
JUST SAYS "PACKAGE WILL BE DELIVERED TODAY."
WHAT IS IT, ARTHUR?
NOW THAT IT'S QUIET I CAN SORT OF FEEL IT.
PANIC, FEAR.
I THINK IT'S *DYING.*
YOU'RE RIGHT, I CAN SEE THE *TRUTH* IN THAT.
IT WAS CAUSING CHAOS AND DESTRUCTION LIVES WOULD HAVE BE LOST, BUT PERHAP THERE'S MORE TO LEARN ABOUT THIS BEING.

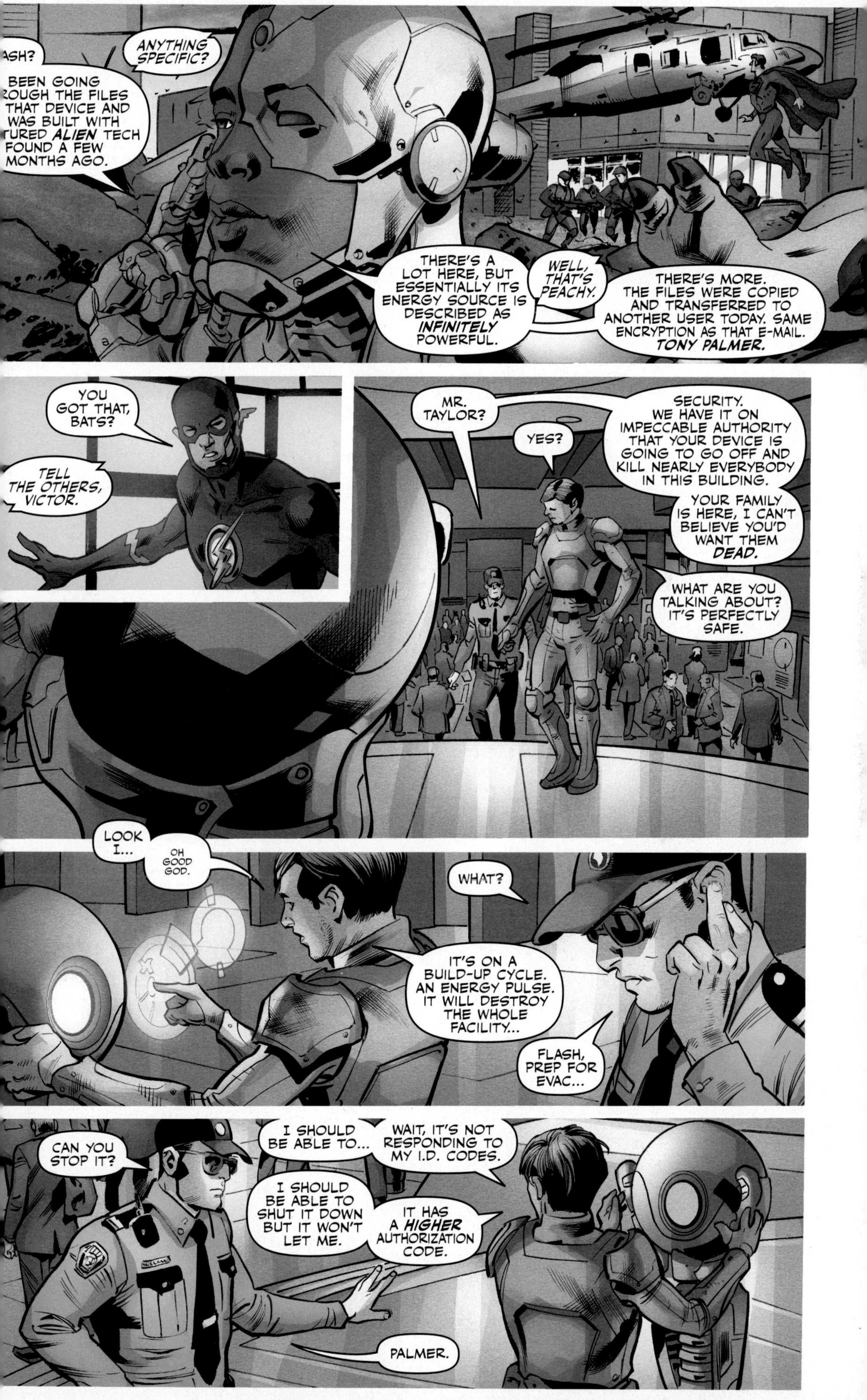

ASH?
BEEN GOING
ROUGH THE FILES
THAT DEVICE AND
WAS BUILT WITH
TURED ALIEN TECH
FOUND A FEW
MONTHS AGO.
ANYTHING SPECIFIC?
THERE'S A LOT HERE, BUT ESSENTIALLY ITS ENERGY SOURCE IS DESCRIBED AS INFINITELY POWERFUL.
WELL, THAT'S PEACHY.
THERE'S MORE. THE FILES WERE COPIED AND TRANSFERRED TO ANOTHER USER TODAY. SAME ENCRYPTION AS THAT E-MAIL. TONY PALMER.
YOU GOT THAT, BATS?
TELL THE OTHERS, VICTOR.
MR. TAYLOR?
YES?
SECURITY. WE HAVE IT ON IMPECCABLE AUTHORITY THAT YOUR DEVICE IS GOING TO GO OFF AND KILL NEARLY EVERYBODY IN THIS BUILDING.
YOUR FAMILY IS HERE, I CAN'T BELIEVE YOU'D WANT THEM DEAD.
WHAT ARE YOU TALKING ABOUT? IT'S PERFECTLY SAFE.
LOOK I...
OH GOOD GOD.
WHAT?
IT'S ON A BUILD-UP CYCLE. AN ENERGY PULSE. IT WILL DESTROY THE WHOLE FACILITY...
FLASH, PREP FOR EVAC...
CAN YOU STOP IT?
I SHOULD BE ABLE TO...
WAIT, IT'S NOT RESPONDING TO MY I.D. CODES.
I SHOULD BE ABLE TO SHUT IT DOWN BUT IT WON'T LET ME.
IT HAS A HIGHER AUTHORIZATION CODE.
PALMER.

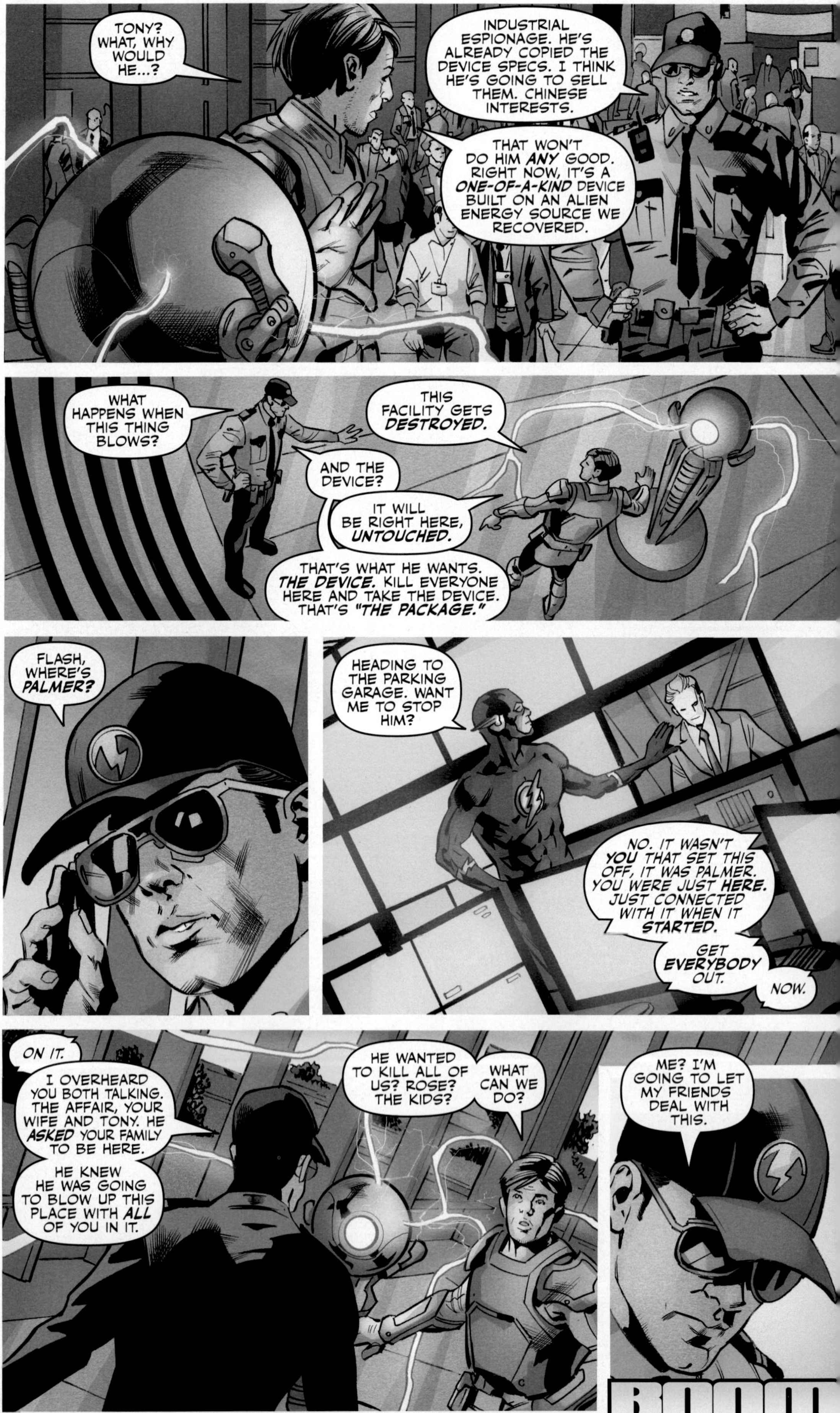
TONY? WHAT, WHY WOULD HE...?
INDUSTRIAL ESPIONAGE. HE'S ALREADY COPIED THE DEVICE SPECS. I THINK HE'S GOING TO SELL THEM. CHINESE INTERESTS.
THAT WON'T DO HIM ANY GOOD. RIGHT NOW, IT'S A ONE-OF-A-KIND DEVICE BUILT ON AN ALIEN ENERGY SOURCE WE RECOVERED.
WHAT HAPPENS WHEN THIS THING BLOWS?
THIS FACILITY GETS DESTROYED.
AND THE DEVICE?
IT WILL BE RIGHT HERE, UNTOUCHED.
THAT'S WHAT HE WANTS. THE DEVICE. KILL EVERYONE HERE AND TAKE THE DEVICE. THAT'S "THE PACKAGE."
FLASH, WHERE'S PALMER?
HEADING TO THE PARKING GARAGE. WANT ME TO STOP HIM?
NO. IT WASN'T YOU THAT SET THIS OFF, IT WAS PALMER. YOU WERE JUST HERE. JUST CONNECTED WITH IT WHEN IT STARTED.
GET EVERYBODY OUT.
NOW.
ON IT.
I OVERHEARD YOU BOTH TALKING. THE AFFAIR, YOUR WIFE AND TONY. HE ASKED YOUR FAMILY TO BE HERE.
HE KNEW HE WAS GOING TO BLOW UP THIS PLACE WITH ALL OF YOU IN IT.
HE WANTED TO KILL ALL OF US? ROSE? THE KIDS?
WHAT CAN WE DO?
ME? I'M GOING TO LET MY FRIENDS DEAL WITH THIS.
BOOM

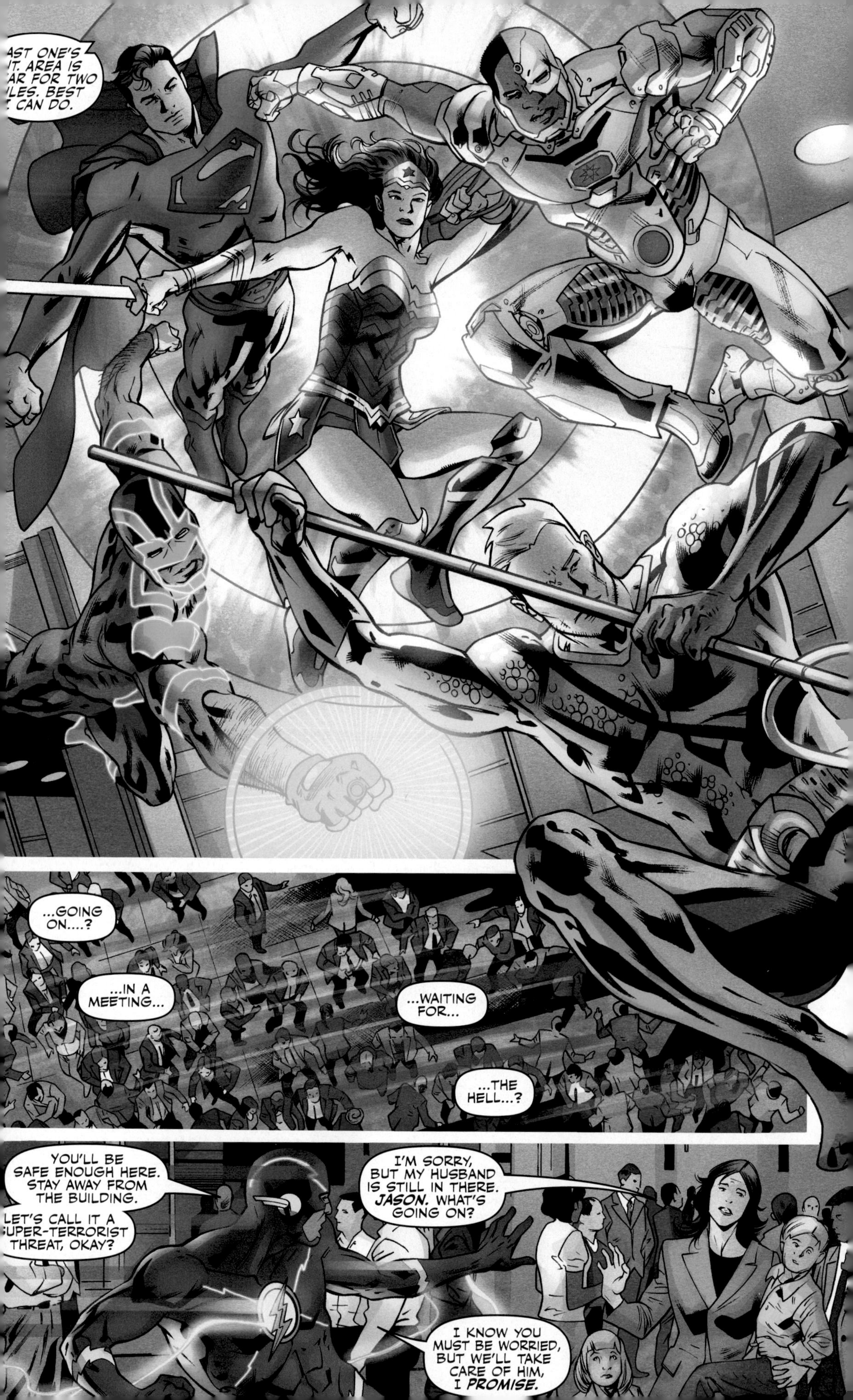
AST ONE'S
T. AREA IS
AR FOR TWO
LES. BEST
CAN DO.
...GOING ON....?
...IN A MEETING...
...WAITING FOR...
...THE HELL...?
YOU'LL BE SAFE ENOUGH HERE. STAY AWAY FROM THE BUILDING.
LET'S CALL IT A SUPER-TERRORIST THREAT, OKAY?
I'M SORRY, BUT MY HUSBAND IS STILL IN THERE. JASON. WHAT'S GOING ON?
I KNOW YOU MUST BE WORRIED, BUT WE'LL TAKE CARE OF HIM, I PROMISE.

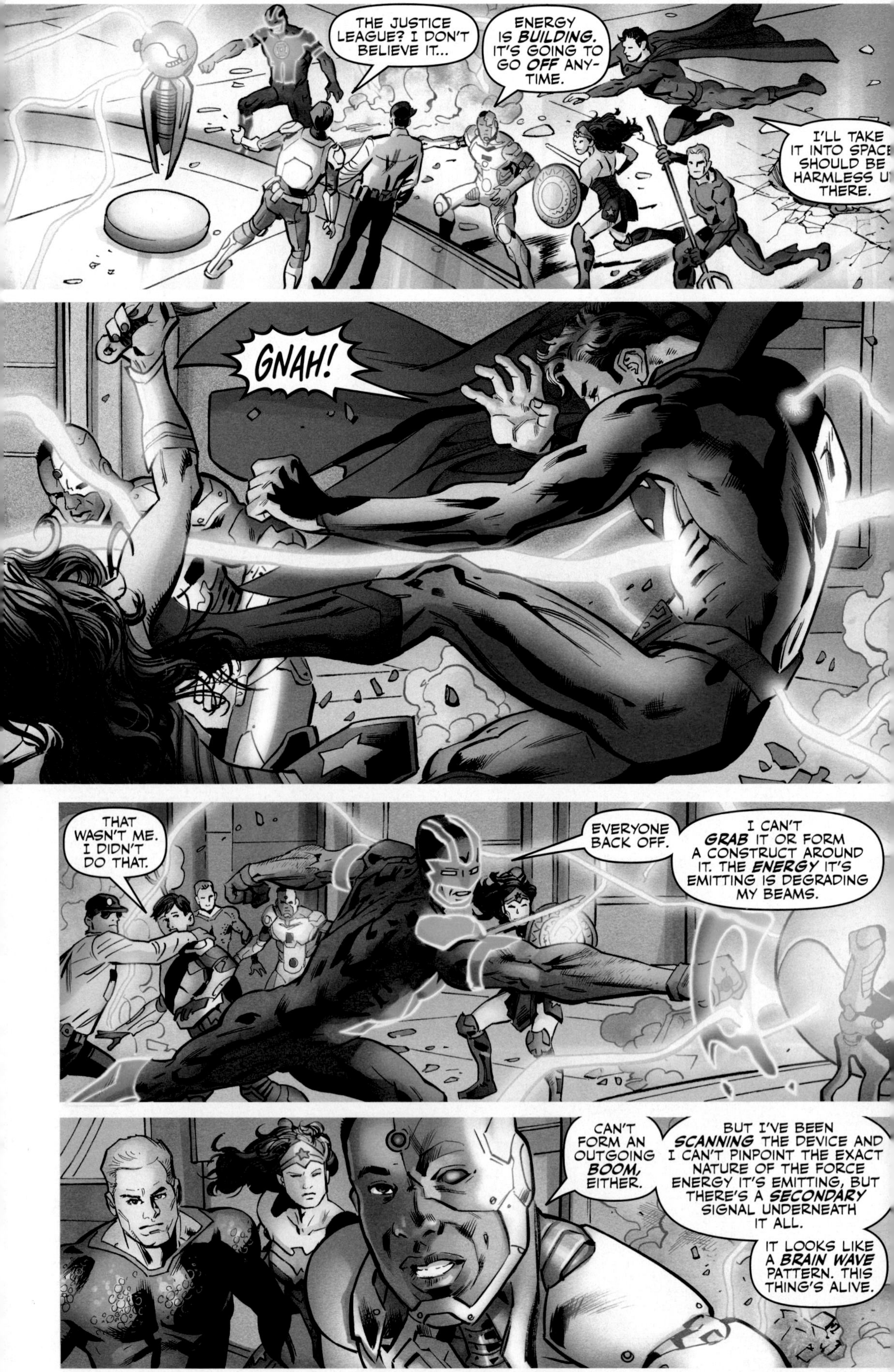
THE JUSTICE LEAGUE? I DON'T BELIEVE IT...
ENERGY IS BUILDING. IT'S GOING TO GO OFF ANY-TIME.
I'LL TAKE IT INTO SPACE SHOULD BE HARMLESS THERE.
GNAH!
THAT WASN'T ME. I DIDN'T DO THAT.
EVERYONE BACK OFF.
I CAN'T GRAB IT OR FORM A CONSTRUCT AROUND IT. THE ENERGY IT'S EMITTING IS DEGRADING MY BEAMS.
CAN'T FORM AN OUTGOING BOOM, EITHER.
BUT I'VE BEEN SCANNING THE DEVICE AND I CAN'T PINPOINT THE EXACT NATURE OF THE FORCE ENERGY IT'S EMITTING, BUT THERE'S A SECONDARY SIGNAL UNDERNEATH IT ALL.
IT LOOKS LIKE A BRAIN WAVE PATTERN. THIS THING'S ALIVE.

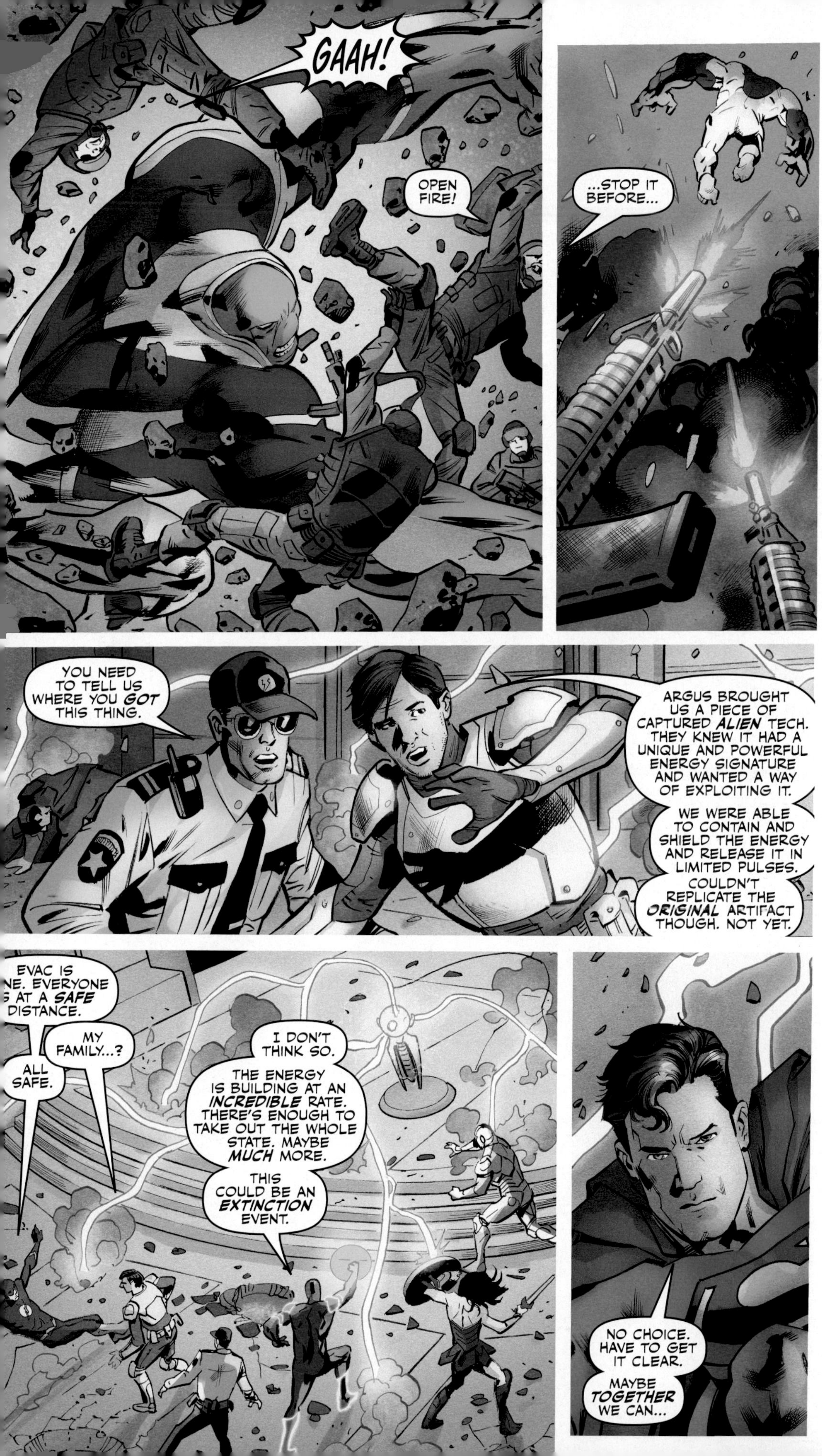
GAAH!
OPEN FIRE!
...STOP IT BEFORE...
YOU NEED TO TELL US WHERE YOU GOT THIS THING.
ARGUS BROUGHT US A PIECE OF CAPTURED ALIEN TECH. THEY KNEW IT HAD A UNIQUE AND POWERFUL ENERGY SIGNATURE AND WANTED A WAY OF EXPLOITING IT.
WE WERE ABLE TO CONTAIN AND SHIELD THE ENERGY AND RELEASE IT IN LIMITED PULSES.
COULDN'T REPLICATE THE ORIGINAL ARTIFACT THOUGH. NOT YET.
EVAC IS NE. EVERYONE S AT A SAFE DISTANCE.
MY FAMILY...?
ALL SAFE.
I DON'T THINK SO.
THE ENERGY IS BUILDING AT AN INCREDIBLE RATE. THERE'S ENOUGH TO TAKE OUT THE WHOLE STATE. MAYBE MUCH MORE.
THIS COULD BE AN EXTINCTION EVENT.
NO CHOICE. HAVE TO GET IT CLEAR.
MAYBE TOGETHER WE CAN...

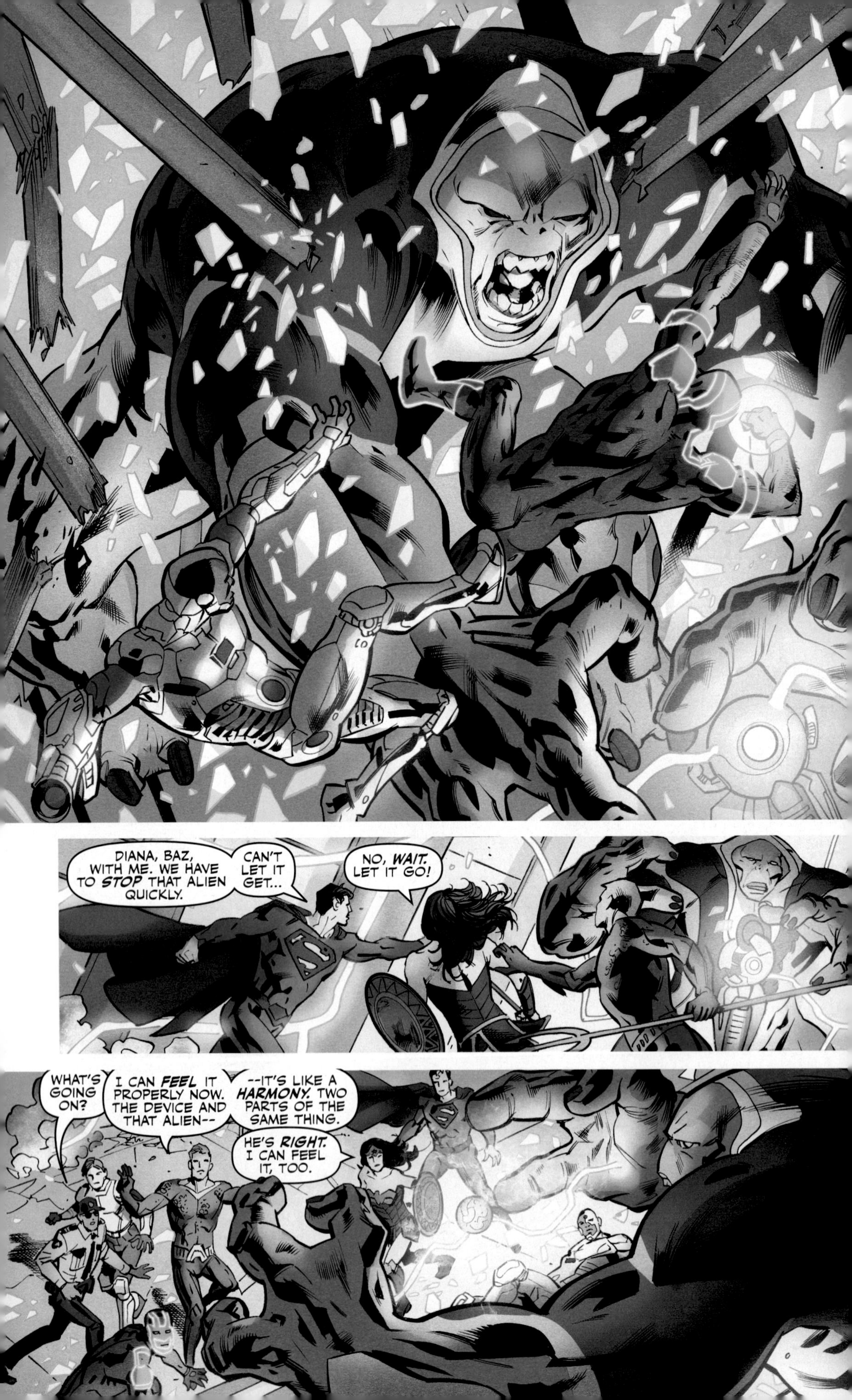
DIANA, BAZ, WITH ME. WE HAVE TO **STOP** THAT ALIEN QUICKLY.
CAN'T LET IT GET...
NO, **WAIT.** LET IT GO!
WHAT'S GOING ON?
I CAN **FEEL** IT PROPERLY NOW. THE DEVICE AND THAT ALIEN--
--IT'S LIKE A **HARMONY.** TWO PARTS OF THE SAME THING.
HE'S **RIGHT.** I CAN FEEL IT, TOO.

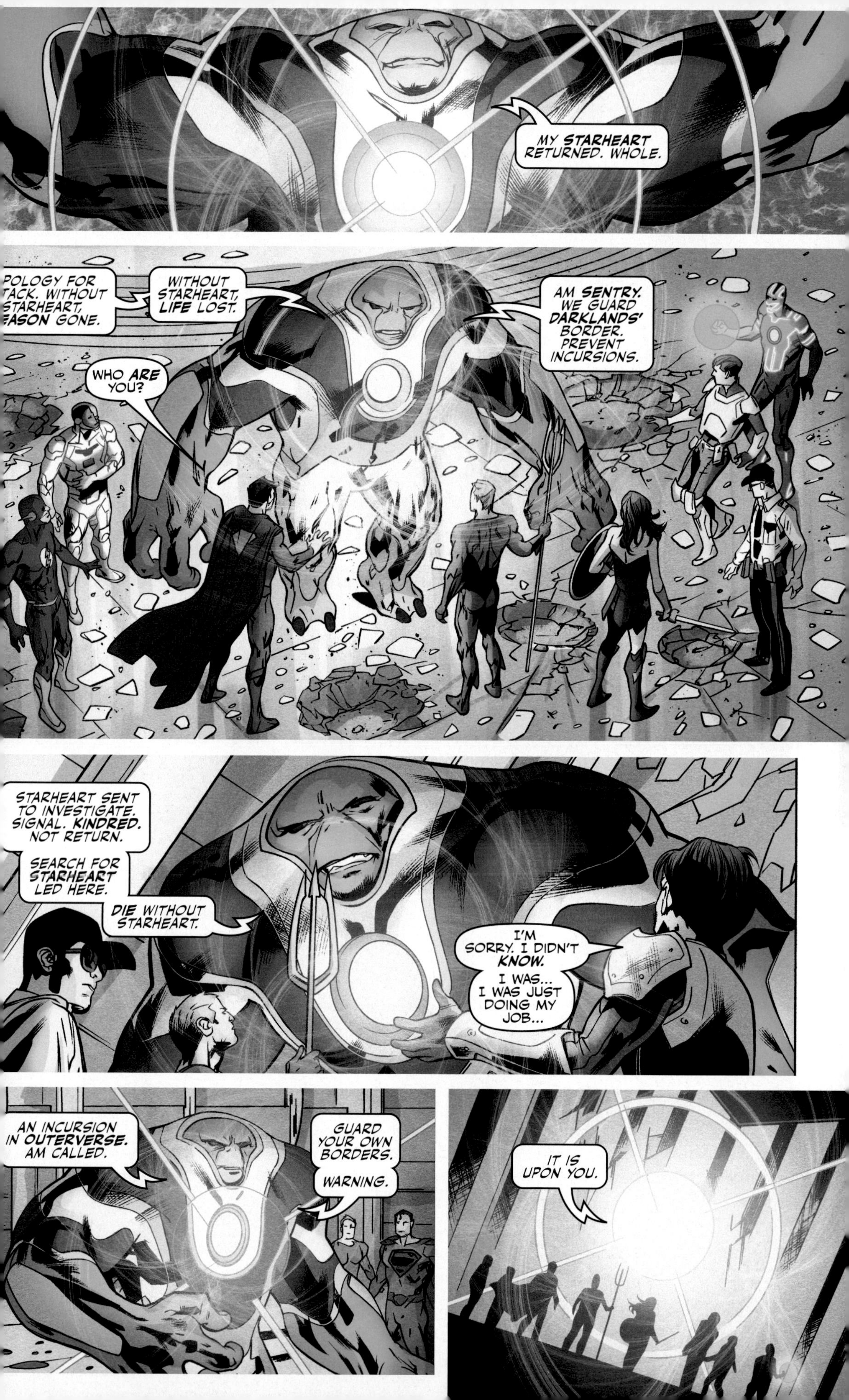
MY STARHEART RETURNED. WHOLE.
POLOGY FOR TACK. WITHOUT STARHEART, EASON GONE.
WITHOUT STARHEART, LIFE LOST.
AM SENTRY. WE GUARD DARKLANDS' BORDER. PREVENT INCURSIONS.
WHO ARE YOU?
STARHEART SENT TO INVESTIGATE. SIGNAL. KINDRED. NOT RETURN.
SEARCH FOR STARHEART LED HERE.
DIE WITHOUT STARHEART.
I'M SORRY. I DIDN'T KNOW.
I WAS... I WAS JUST DOING MY JOB...
AN INCURSION IN OUTERVERSE. AM CALLED.
GUARD YOUR OWN BORDERS.
WARNING.
IT IS UPON YOU.

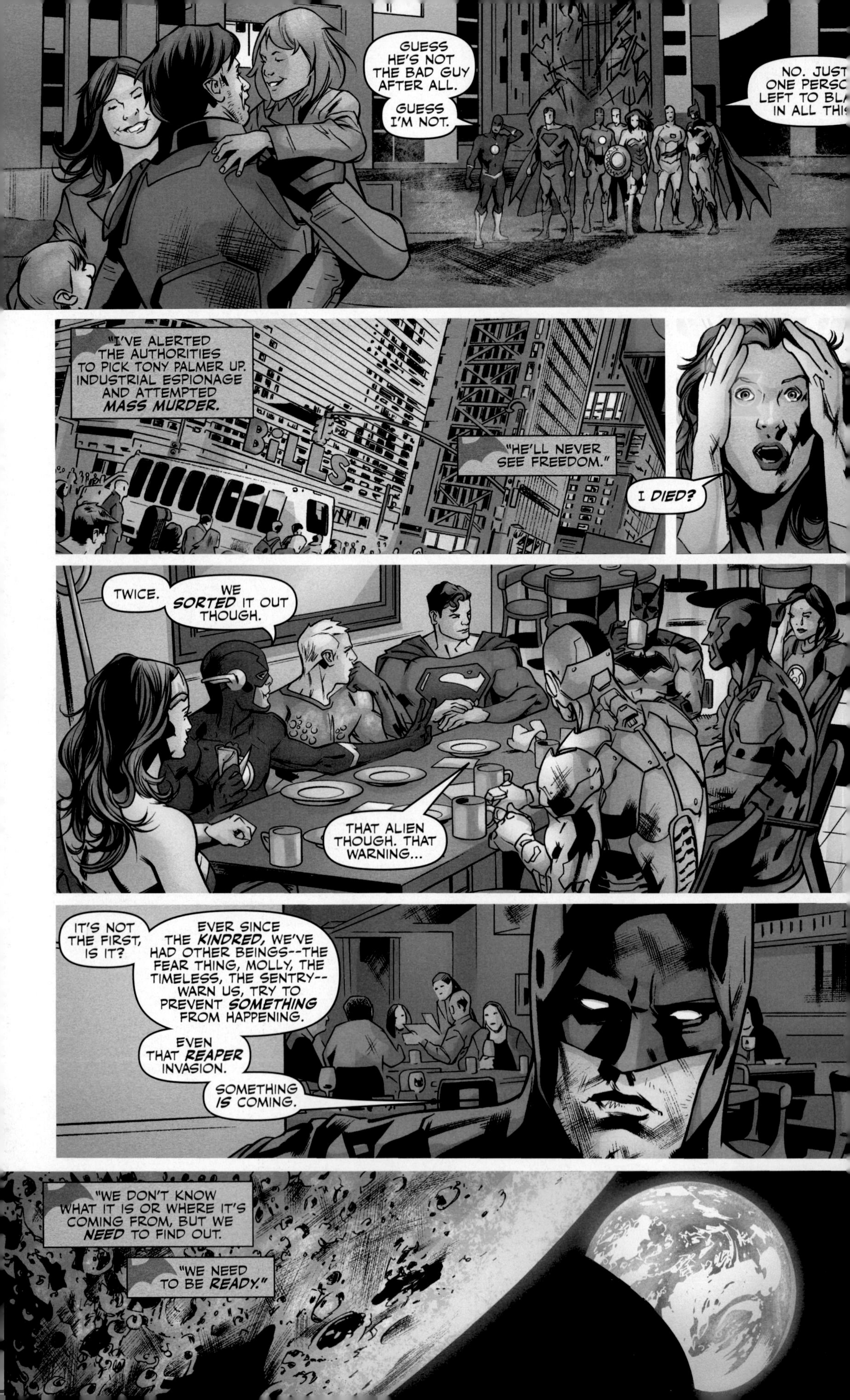

GUESS HE'S NOT THE BAD GUY AFTER ALL.
GUESS I'M NOT.
NO. JUST ONE PERSO LEFT TO BLA IN ALL THI
"I'VE ALERTED THE AUTHORITIES TO PICK TONY PALMER UP. INDUSTRIAL ESPIONAGE AND ATTEMPTED MASS MURDER.
BILLS
"HE'LL NEVER SEE FREEDOM."
I DIED?
TWICE.
WE SORTED IT OUT THOUGH.
THAT ALIEN THOUGH. THAT WARNING...
IT'S NOT THE FIRST, IS IT?
EVER SINCE THE KINDRED, WE'VE HAD OTHER BEINGS--THE FEAR THING, MOLLY, THE TIMELESS, THE SENTRY--WARN US, TRY TO PREVENT SOMETHING FROM HAPPENING.
EVEN THAT REAPER INVASION.
SOMETHING IS COMING.
"WE DON'T KNOW WHAT IT IS OR WHERE IT'S COMING FROM, BUT WE NEED TO FIND OUT.
"WE NEED TO BE READY."

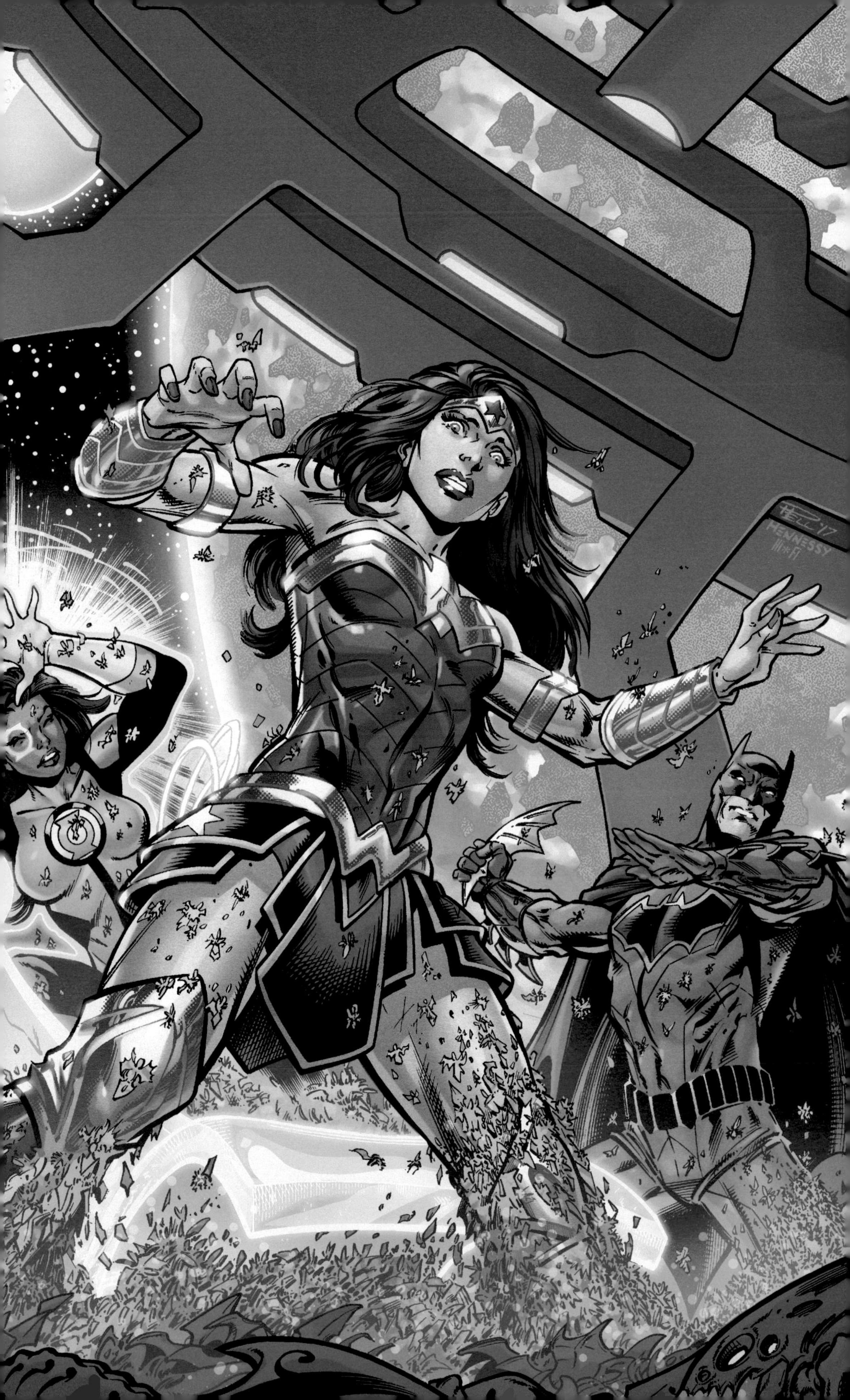
HENNESSY

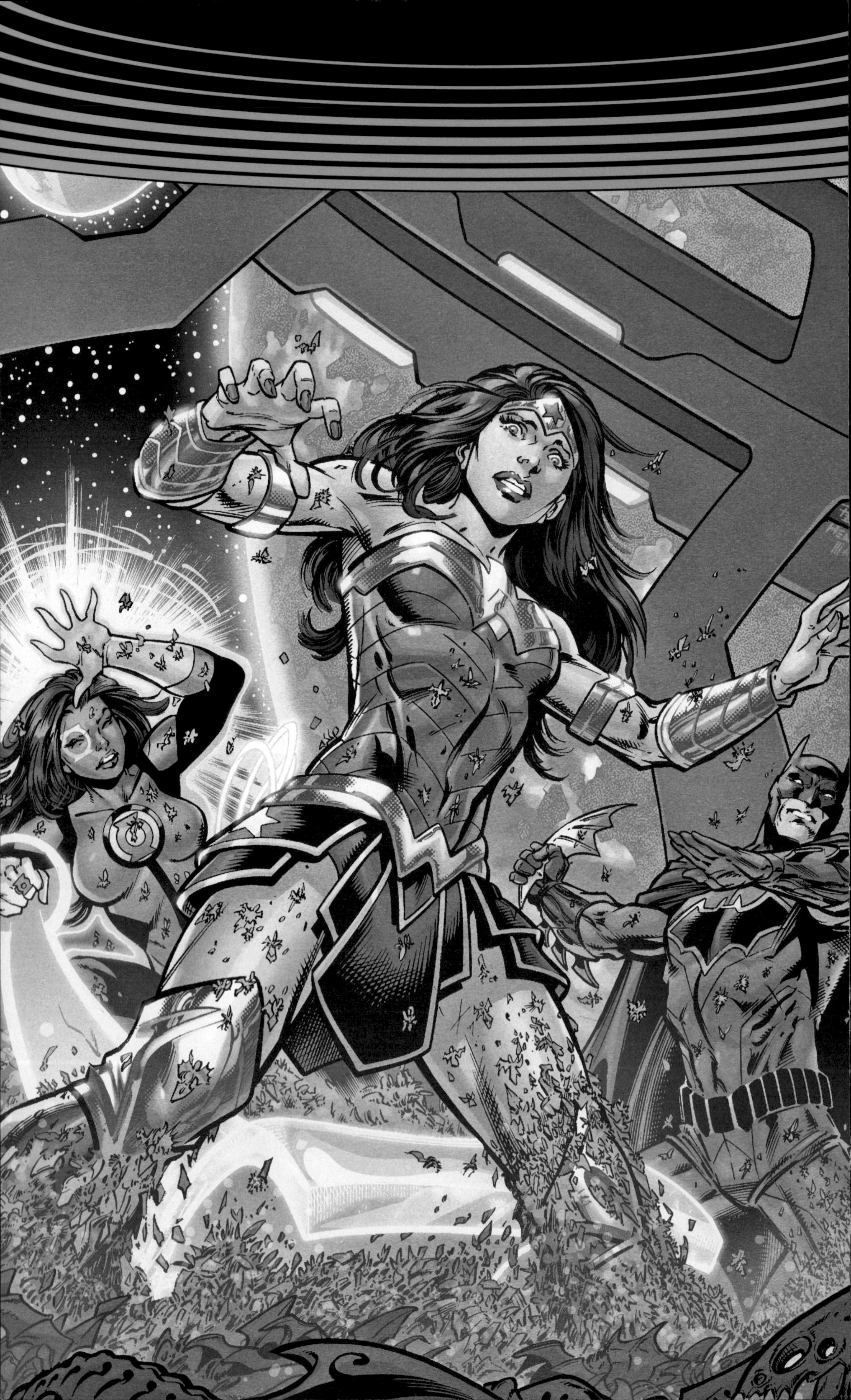

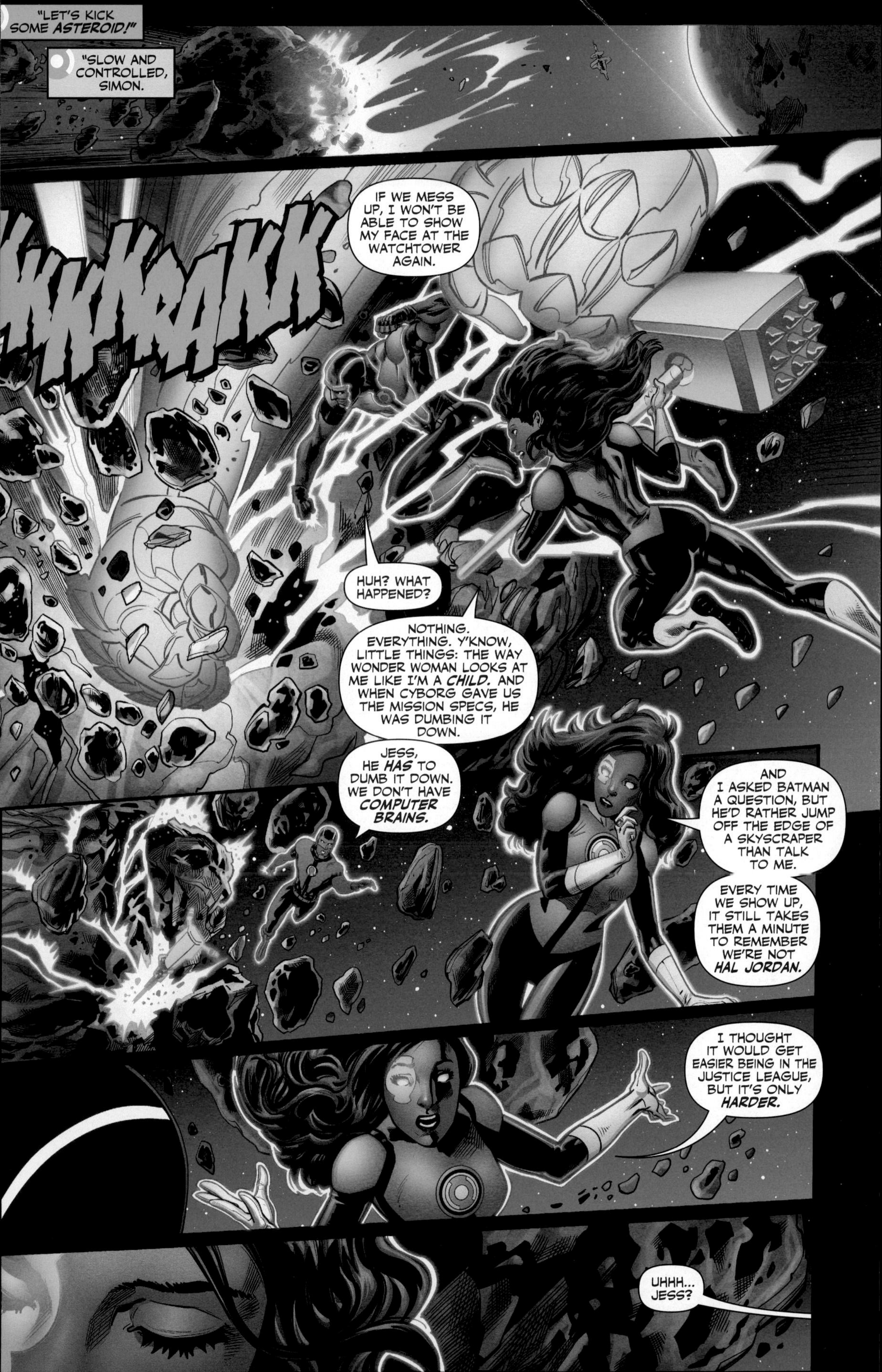
"LET'S KICK SOME ASTEROID!"
"SLOW AND CONTROLLED, SIMON.
KKKRAKK
IF WE MESS UP, I WON'T BE ABLE TO SHOW MY FACE AT THE WATCHTOWER AGAIN.
HUH? WHAT HAPPENED?
NOTHING. EVERYTHING. Y'KNOW, LITTLE THINGS: THE WAY WONDER WOMAN LOOKS AT ME LIKE I'M A CHILD. AND WHEN CYBORG GAVE US THE MISSION SPECS, HE WAS DUMBING IT DOWN.
JESS, HE HAS TO DUMB IT DOWN. WE DON'T HAVE COMPUTER BRAINS.
AND I ASKED BATMAN A QUESTION, BUT HE'D RATHER JUMP OFF THE EDGE OF A SKYSCRAPER THAN TALK TO ME.
EVERY TIME WE SHOW UP, IT STILL TAKES THEM A MINUTE TO REMEMBER WE'RE NOT HAL JORDAN.
I THOUGHT IT WOULD GET EASIER BEING IN THE JUSTICE LEAGUE, BUT IT'S ONLY HARDER.
UHHH... JESS?

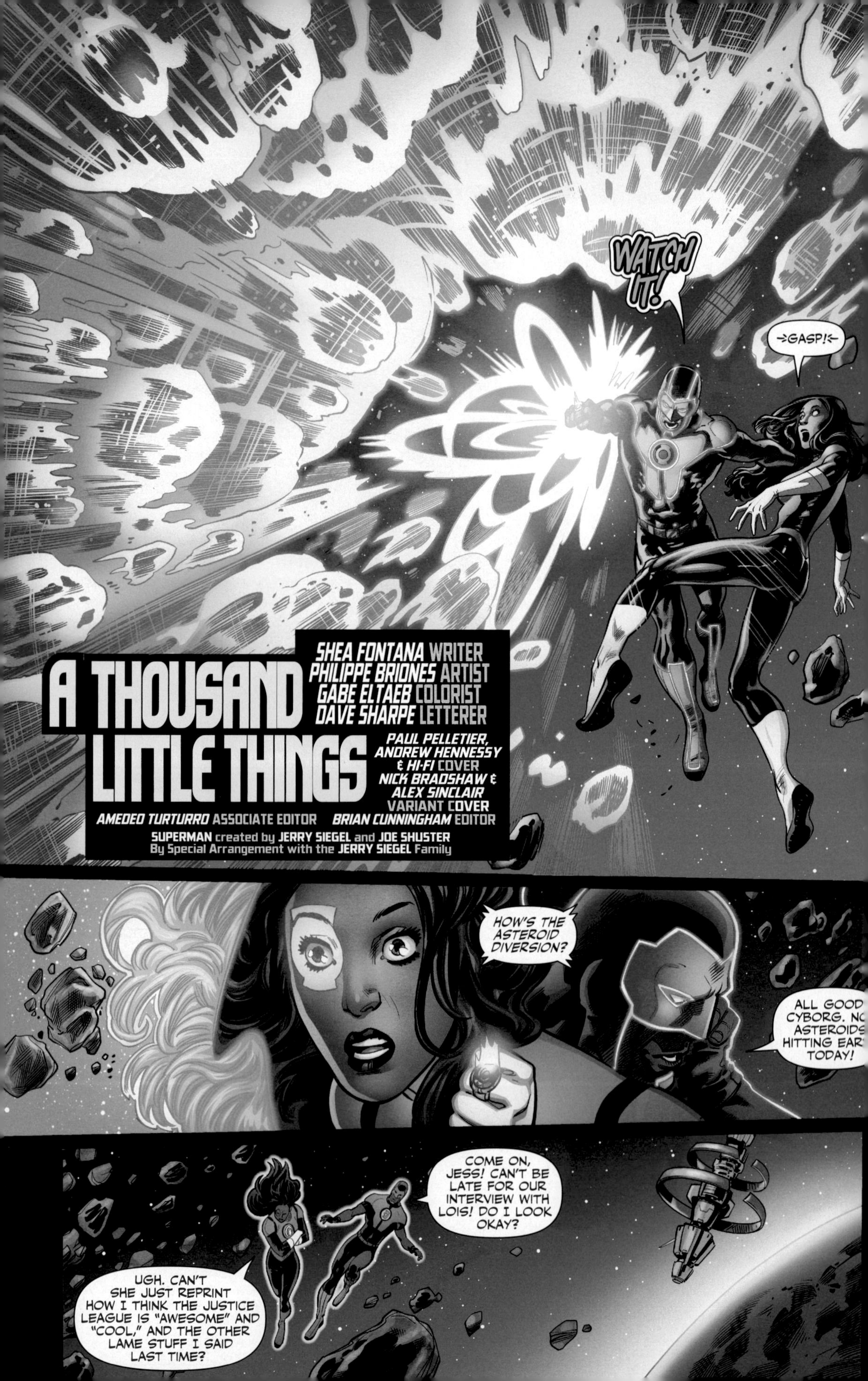
WATCH IT!
>GASP!<
A THOUSAND LITTLE THINGS
SHEA FONTANA WRITER
PHILIPPE BRIONES ARTIST
GABE ELTAEB COLORIST
DAVE SHARPE LETTERER
PAUL PELLETIER, ANDREW HENNESSY & HI-FI COVER
NICK BRADSHAW & ALEX SINCLAIR VARIANT COVER
AMEDEO TURTURRO ASSOCIATE EDITOR BRIAN CUNNINGHAM EDITOR
SUPERMAN created by JERRY SIEGEL and JOE SHUSTER
By Special Arrangement with the JERRY SIEGEL Family
HOW'S THE ASTEROID DIVERSION?
ALL GOOD CYBORG. NO ASTEROIDS HITTING EARTH TODAY!
COME ON, JESS! CAN'T BE LATE FOR OUR INTERVIEW WITH LOIS! DO I LOOK OKAY?
UGH. CAN'T SHE JUST REPRINT HOW I THINK THE JUSTICE LEAGUE IS "AWESOME" AND "COOL," AND THE OTHER LAME STUFF I SAID LAST TIME?

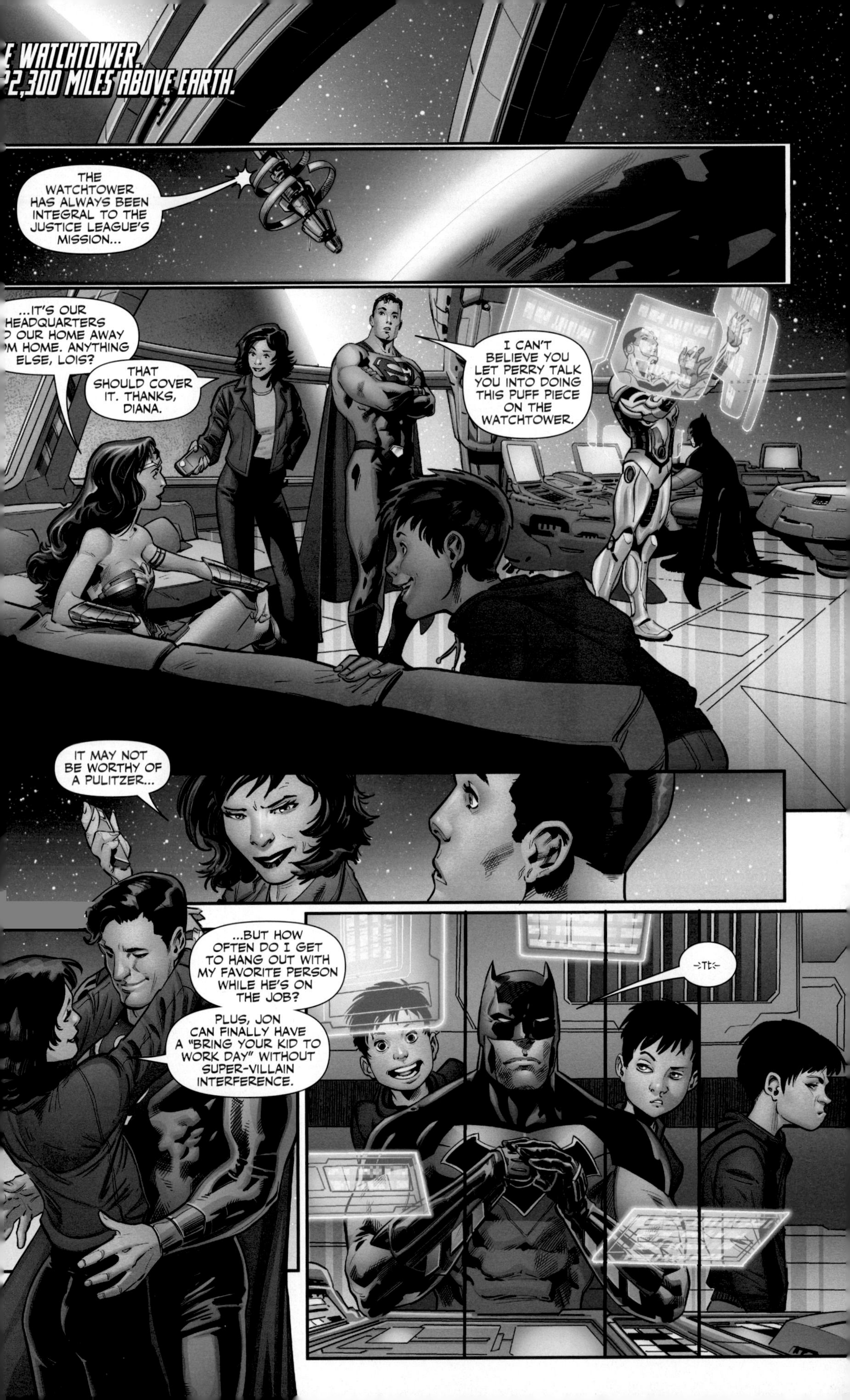
E WATCHTOWER.
2,300 MILES ABOVE EARTH.
THE WATCHTOWER HAS ALWAYS BEEN INTEGRAL TO THE JUSTICE LEAGUE'S MISSION...
...IT'S OUR HEADQUARTERS D OUR HOME AWAY M HOME. ANYTHING ELSE, LOIS?
THAT SHOULD COVER IT. THANKS, DIANA.
I CAN'T BELIEVE YOU LET PERRY TALK YOU INTO DOING THIS PUFF PIECE ON THE WATCHTOWER.
IT MAY NOT BE WORTHY OF A PULITZER...
...BUT HOW OFTEN DO I GET TO HANG OUT WITH MY FAVORITE PERSON WHILE HE'S ON THE JOB?
PLUS, JON CAN FINALLY HAVE A "BRING YOUR KID TO WORK DAY" WITHOUT SUPER-VILLAIN INTERFERENCE.
-TT-

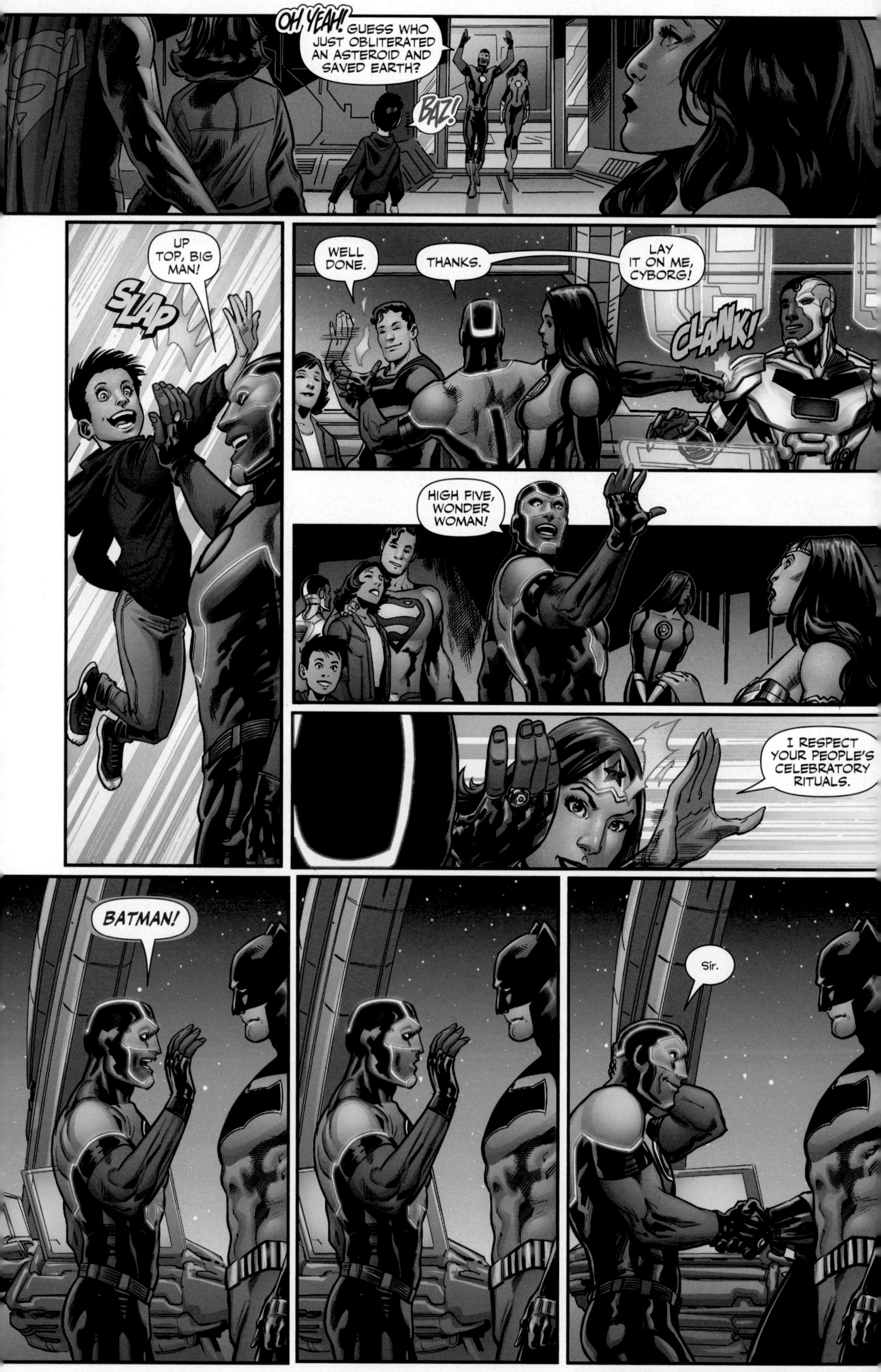
OH YEAH!
GUESS WHO JUST OBLITERATED AN ASTEROID AND SAVED EARTH?
BAZ!
UP TOP, BIG MAN!
SLAP
WELL DONE.
THANKS.
LAY IT ON ME, CYBORG!
CLANK!
HIGH FIVE, WONDER WOMAN!
I RESPECT YOUR PEOPLE'S CELEBRATORY RITUALS.
BATMAN!
Sir.

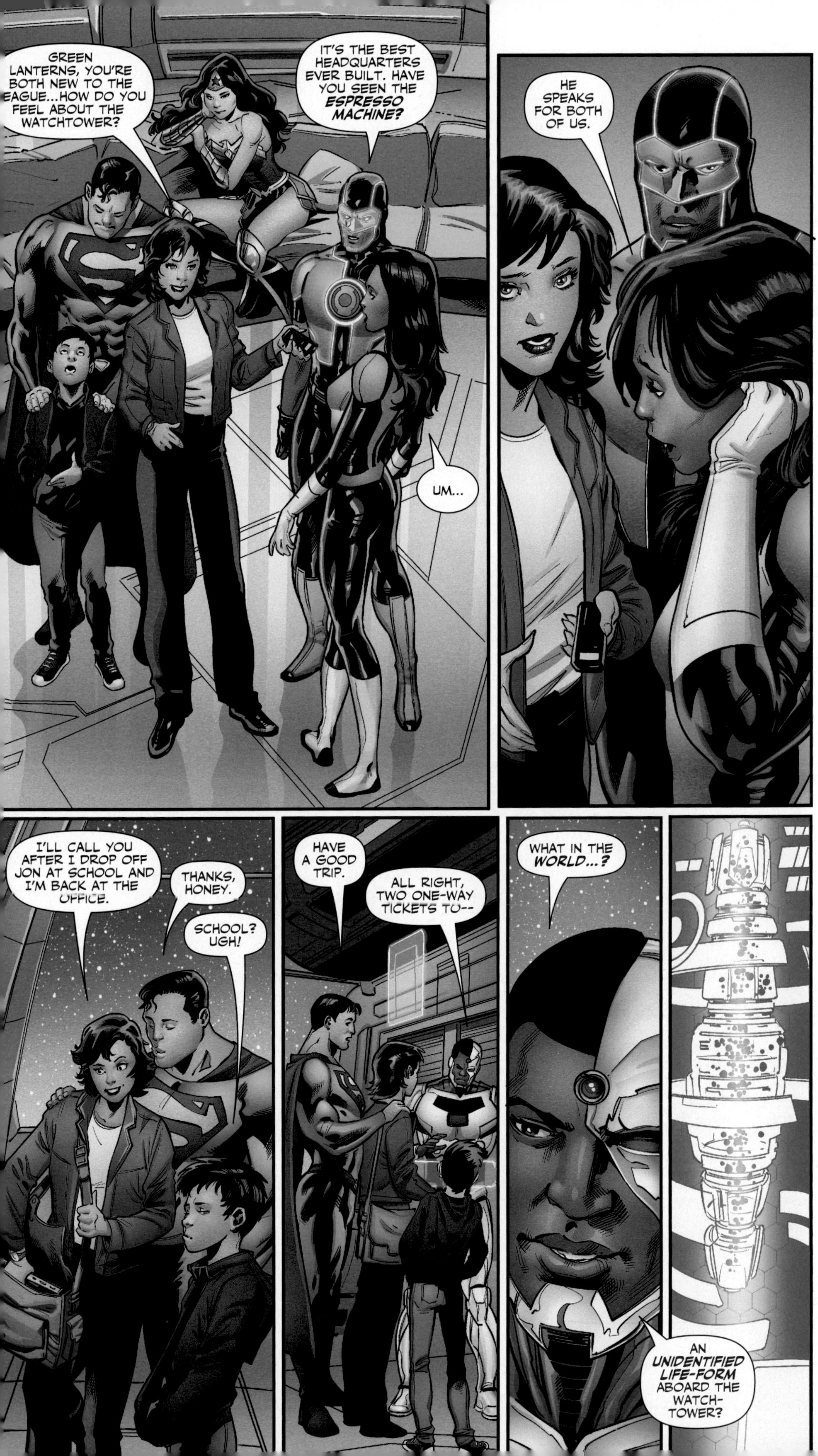
GREEN LANTERNS, YOU'RE BOTH NEW TO THE LEAGUE...HOW DO YOU FEEL ABOUT THE WATCHTOWER?
IT'S THE BEST HEADQUARTERS EVER BUILT. HAVE YOU SEEN THE ESPRESSO MACHINE?
UM...
HE SPEAKS FOR BOTH OF US.
I'LL CALL YOU AFTER I DROP OFF JON AT SCHOOL AND I'M BACK AT THE OFFICE.
THANKS, HONEY.
SCHOOL? UGH!
HAVE A GOOD TRIP.
ALL RIGHT, TWO ONE-WAY TICKETS TO--
WHAT IN THE WORLD...?
AN UNIDENTIFIED LIFE-FORM ABOARD THE WATCH-TOWER?

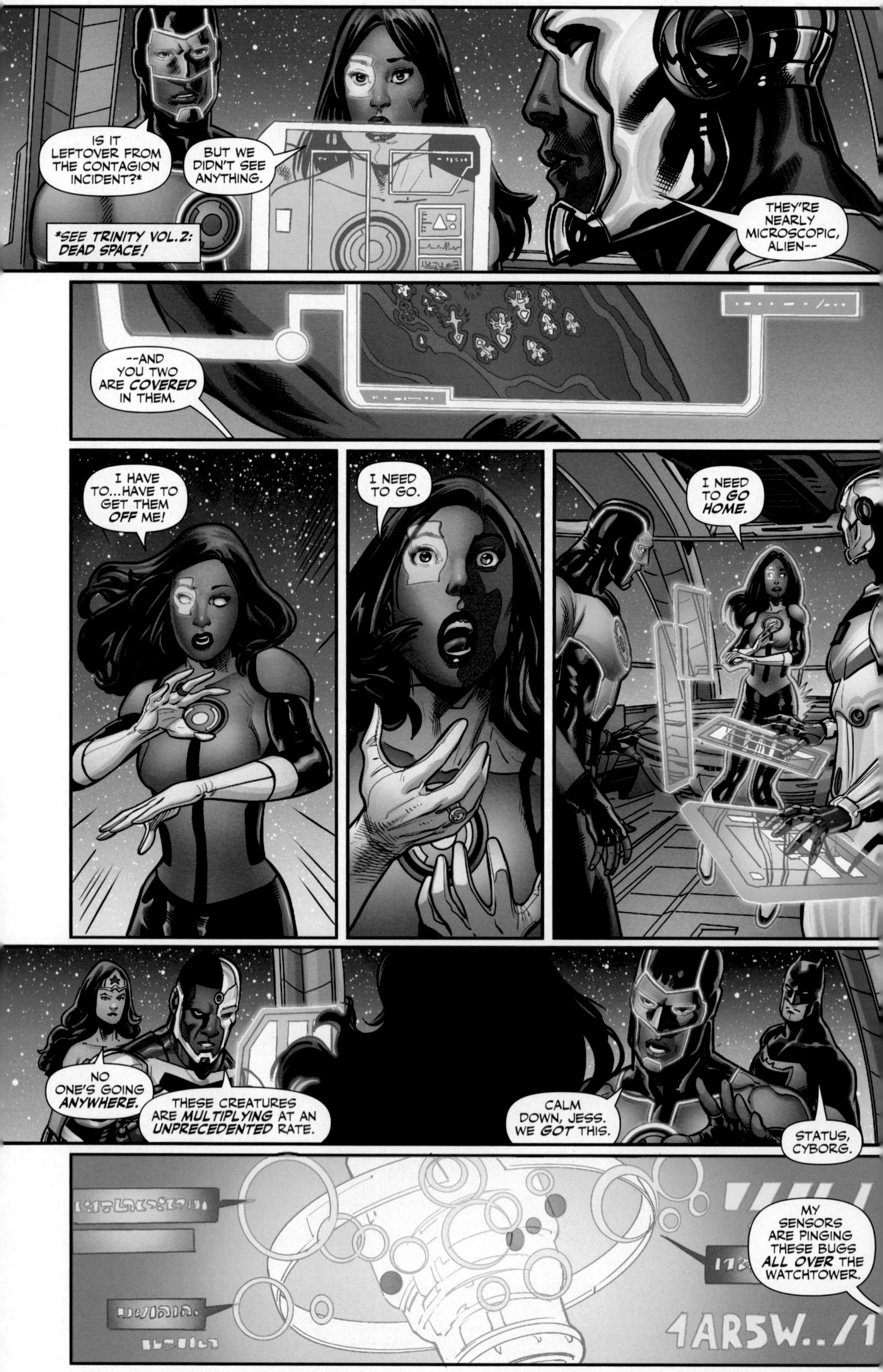
IS IT LEFTOVER FROM THE CONTAGION INCIDENT?*
BUT WE DIDN'T SEE ANYTHING.
*SEE TRINITY VOL.2: DEAD SPACE!
THEY'RE NEARLY MICROSCOPIC, ALIEN--
--AND YOU TWO ARE COVERED IN THEM.
I HAVE TO...HAVE TO GET THEM OFF ME!
I NEED TO GO.
I NEED TO GO HOME.
NO ONE'S GOING ANYWHERE.
THESE CREATURES ARE MULTIPLYING AT AN UNPRECEDENTED RATE.
CALM DOWN, JESS. WE GOT THIS.
STATUS, CYBORG.
MY SENSORS ARE PINGING THESE BUGS ALL OVER THE WATCHTOWER.
4AR5W../1

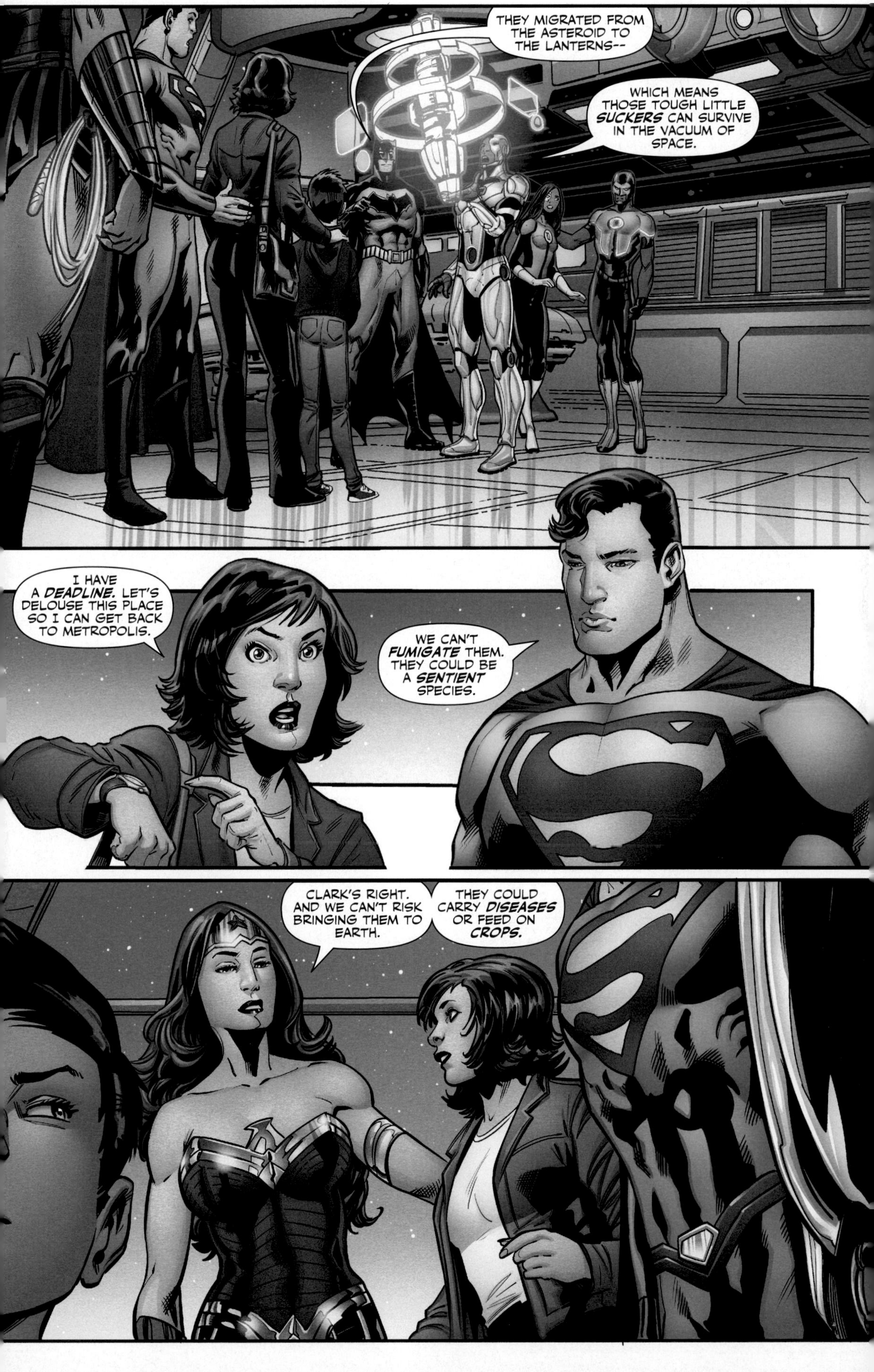

THEY MIGRATED FROM THE ASTEROID TO THE LANTERNS--
WHICH MEANS THOSE TOUGH LITTLE SUCKERS CAN SURVIVE IN THE VACUUM OF SPACE.
I HAVE A DEADLINE. LET'S DELOUSE THIS PLACE SO I CAN GET BACK TO METROPOLIS.
WE CAN'T FUMIGATE THEM. THEY COULD BE A SENTIENT SPECIES.
CLARK'S RIGHT. AND WE CAN'T RISK BRINGING THEM TO EARTH.
THEY COULD CARRY DISEASES OR FEED ON CROPS.

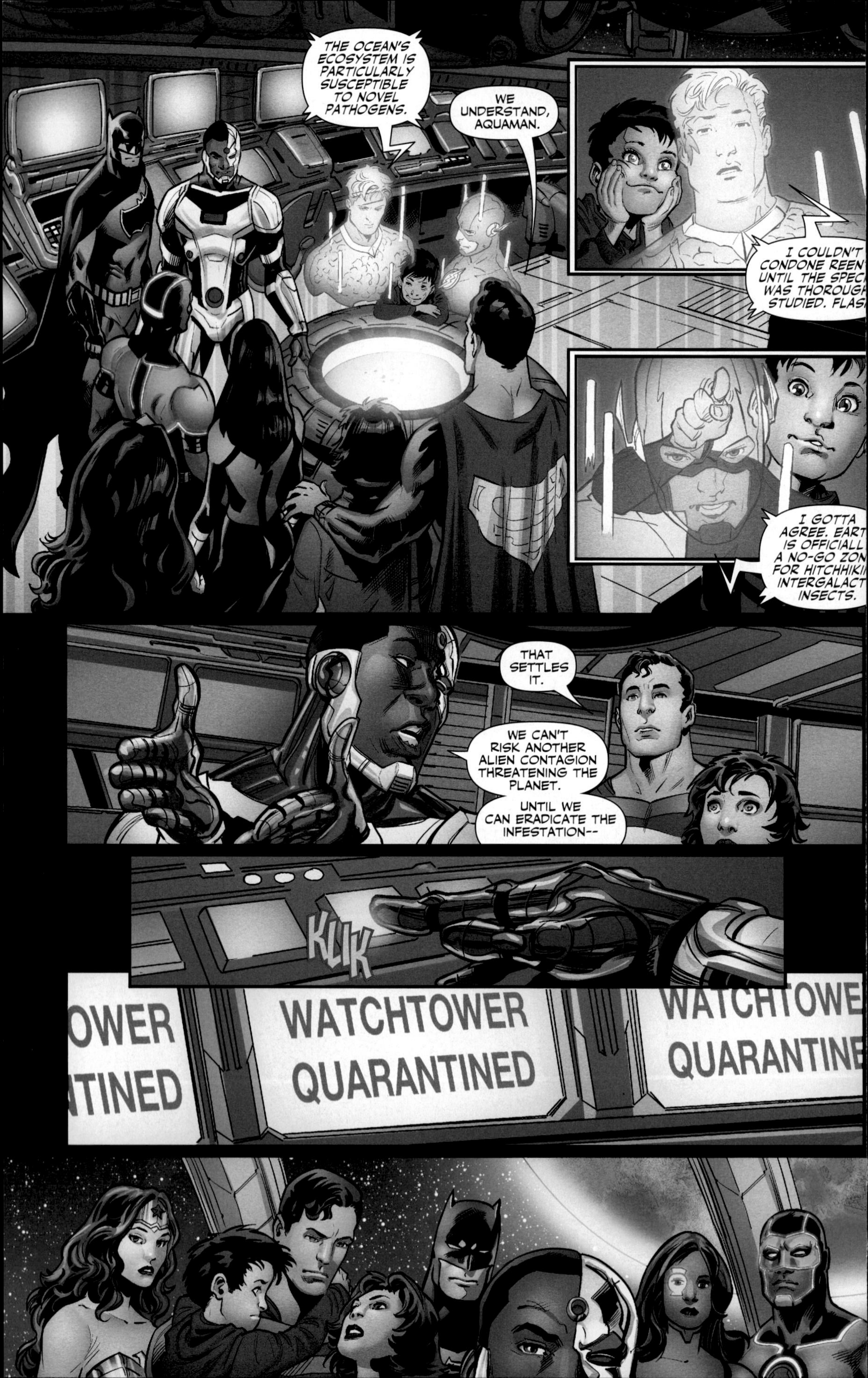

THE OCEAN'S ECOSYSTEM IS PARTICULARLY SUSCEPTIBLE TO NOVEL PATHOGENS.
WE UNDERSTAND, AQUAMAN.
I COULDN'T CONDONE REENT UNTIL THE SPEC WAS THOROUG STUDIED. FLAS
I GOTTA AGREE. EART IS OFFICIALL A NO-GO ZON FOR HITCHHIKI INTERGALACT INSECTS.
THAT SETTLES IT.
WE CAN'T RISK ANOTHER ALIEN CONTAGION THREATENING THE PLANET.
UNTIL WE CAN ERADICATE THE INFESTATION--
KLIK
OWER
NTINED
WATCHTOWER QUARANTINED
WATCHTOWE QUARANTINE

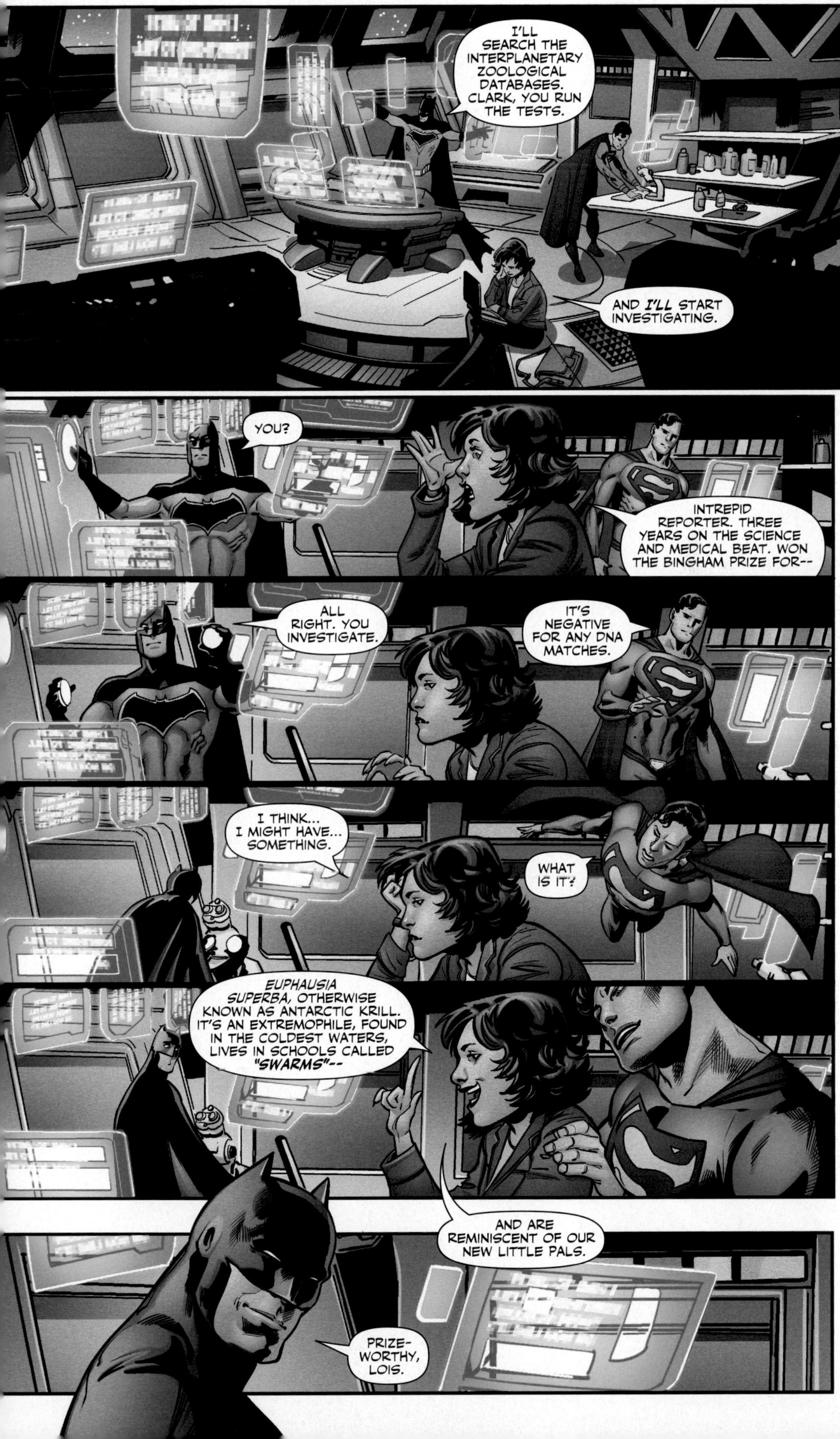
I'LL SEARCH THE INTERPLANETARY ZOOLOGICAL DATABASES. CLARK, YOU RUN THE TESTS.
AND I'LL START INVESTIGATING.
YOU?
INTREPID REPORTER. THREE YEARS ON THE SCIENCE AND MEDICAL BEAT. WON THE BINGHAM PRIZE FOR--
ALL RIGHT. YOU INVESTIGATE.
IT'S NEGATIVE FOR ANY DNA MATCHES.
I THINK... I MIGHT HAVE... SOMETHING.
WHAT IS IT?
EUPHAUSIA SUPERBA, OTHERWISE KNOWN AS ANTARCTIC KRILL. IT'S AN EXTREMOPHILE, FOUND IN THE COLDEST WATERS, LIVES IN SCHOOLS CALLED "SWARMS"--
AND ARE REMINISCENT OF OUR NEW LITTLE PALS.
PRIZE-WORTHY, LOIS.

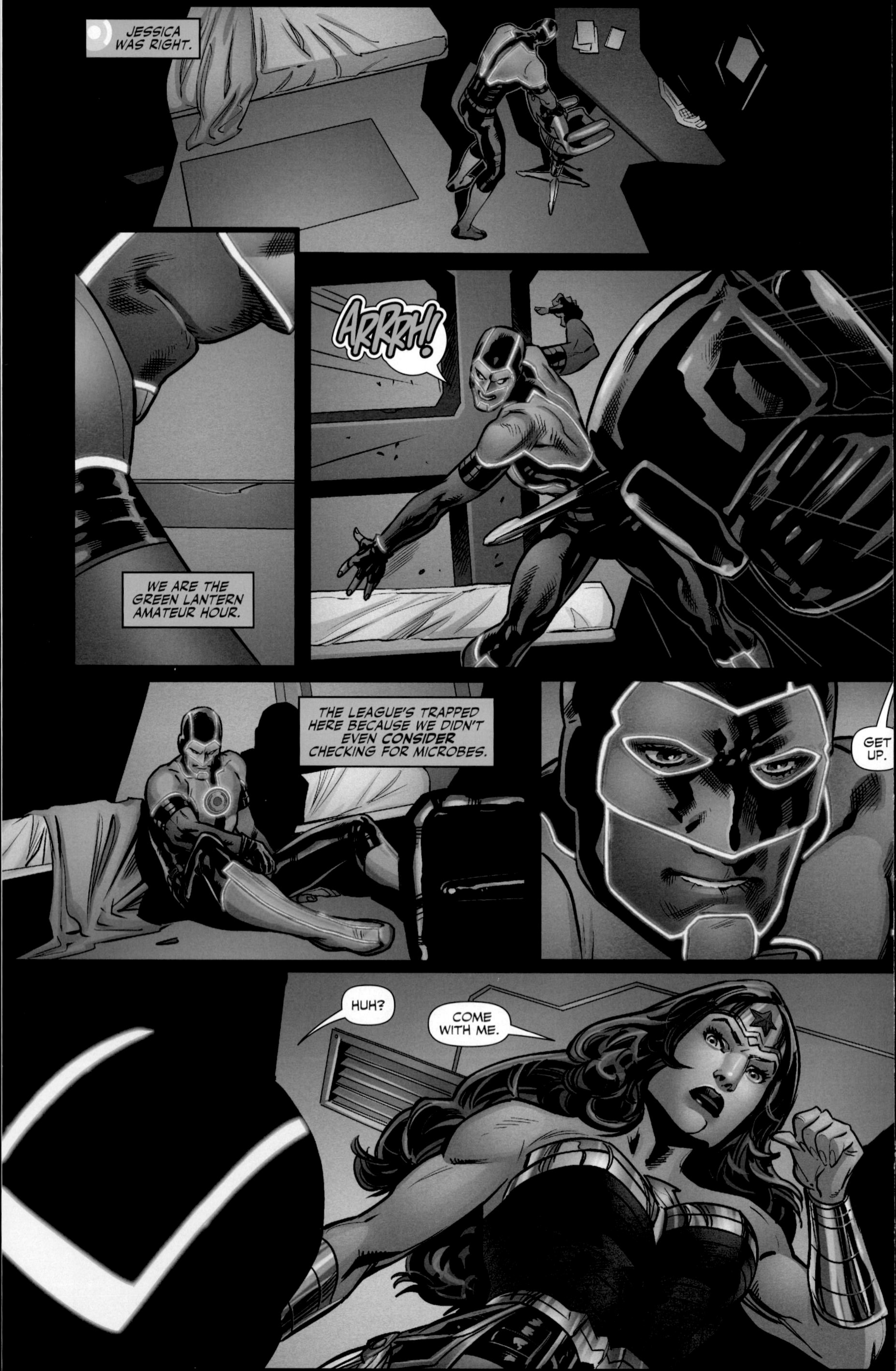

JESSICA WAS RIGHT.
WE ARE THE GREEN LANTERN AMATEUR HOUR.
ARRRH!
THE LEAGUE'S TRAPPED HERE BECAUSE WE DIDN'T EVEN CONSIDER CHECKING FOR MICROBES.
GET UP.
HUH?
COME WITH ME.

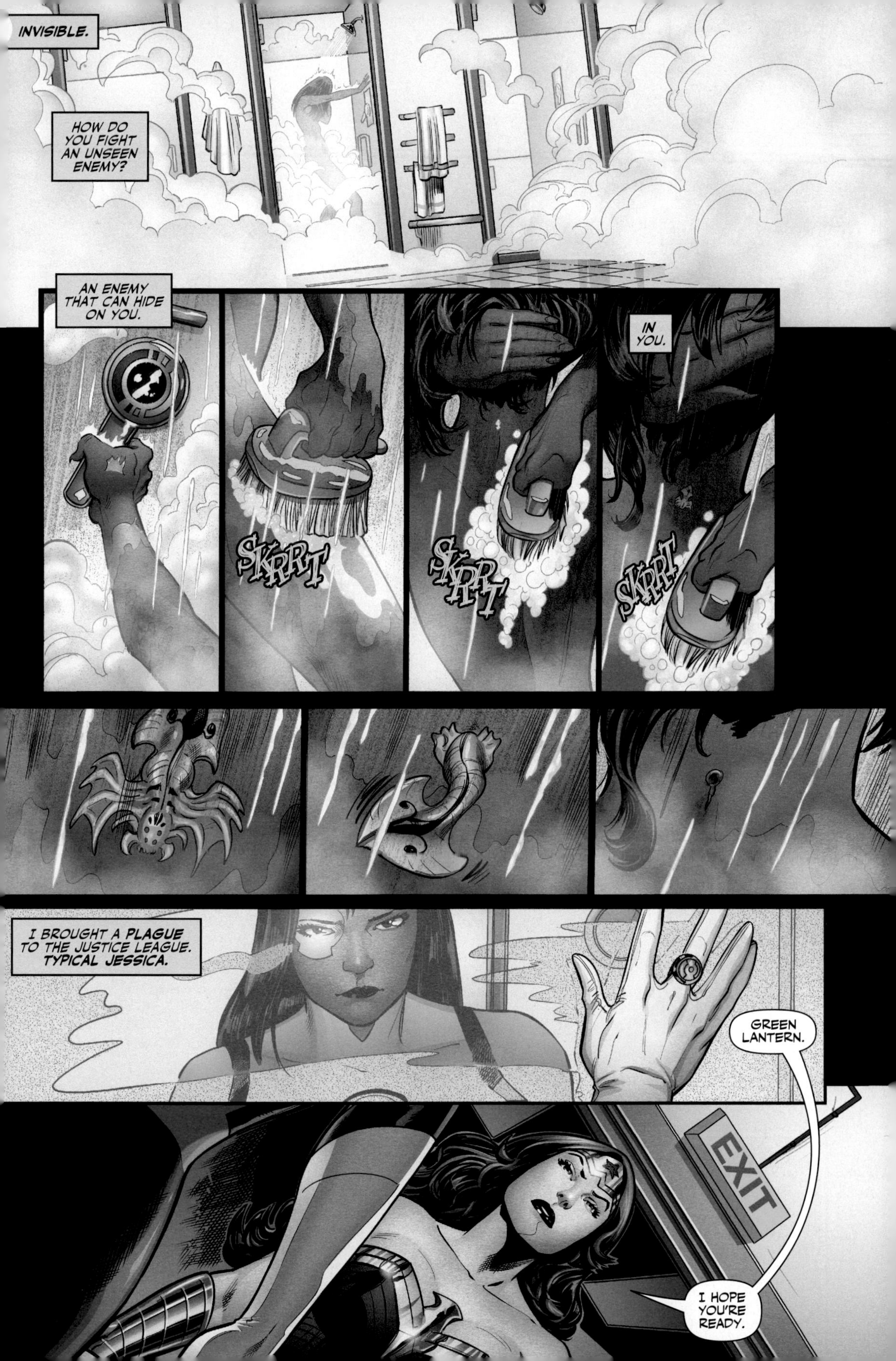
INVISIBLE.
HOW DO YOU FIGHT AN UNSEEN ENEMY?
AN ENEMY THAT CAN HIDE ON YOU.
SKRRT
SKRRT
IN YOU.
SKRRT
I BROUGHT A PLAGUE TO THE JUSTICE LEAGUE. TYPICAL JESSICA.
GREEN LANTERN.
I HOPE YOU'RE READY.
EXIT

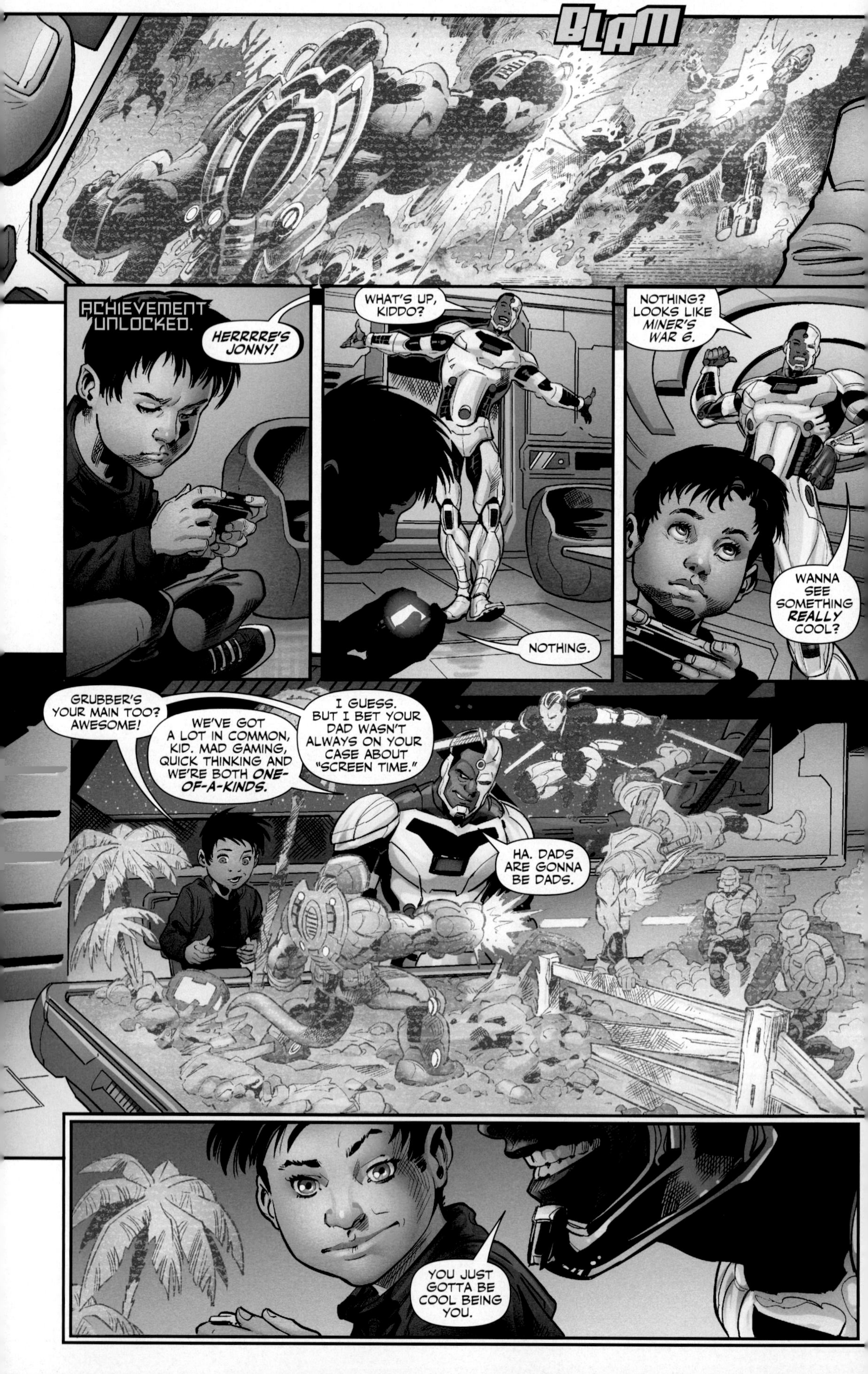
BLAM
ACHIEVEMENT UNLOCKED.
HERRRRE'S JONNY!
WHAT'S UP, KIDDO?
NOTHING.
NOTHING? LOOKS LIKE MINER'S WAR 6.
WANNA SEE SOMETHING REALLY COOL?
GRUBBER'S YOUR MAIN TOO? AWESOME!
WE'VE GOT A LOT IN COMMON, KID. MAD GAMING, QUICK THINKING AND WE'RE BOTH ONE-OF-A-KINDS.
I GUESS. BUT I BET YOUR DAD WASN'T ALWAYS ON YOUR CASE ABOUT "SCREEN TIME."
HA. DADS ARE GONNA BE DADS.
YOU JUST GOTTA BE COOL BEING YOU.

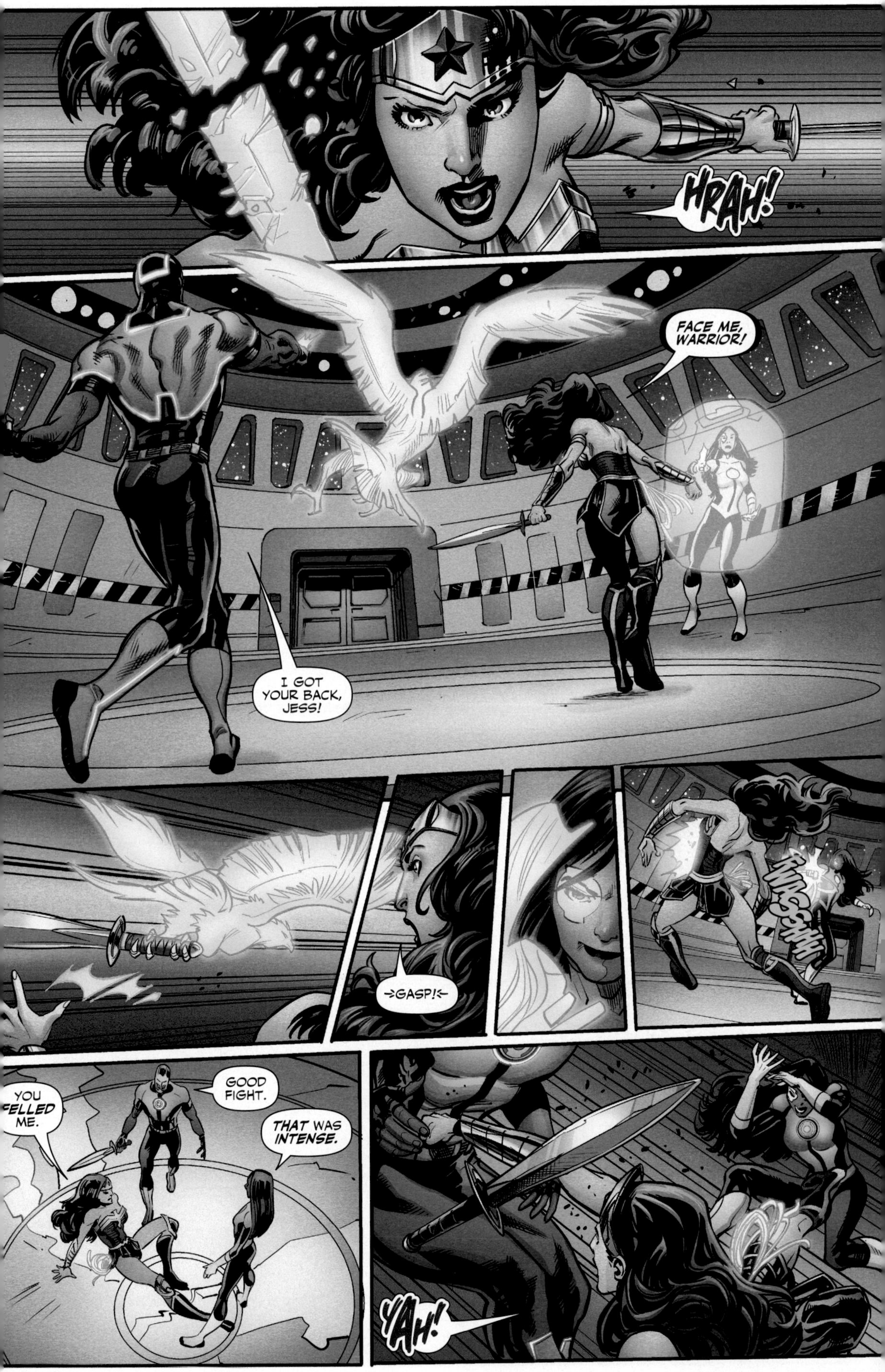
HRAH!
FACE ME, WARRIOR!
I GOT YOUR BACK, JESS!
GASP!
FWASHHH
YOU FELLED ME.
GOOD FIGHT.
THAT WAS INTENSE.
YAH!

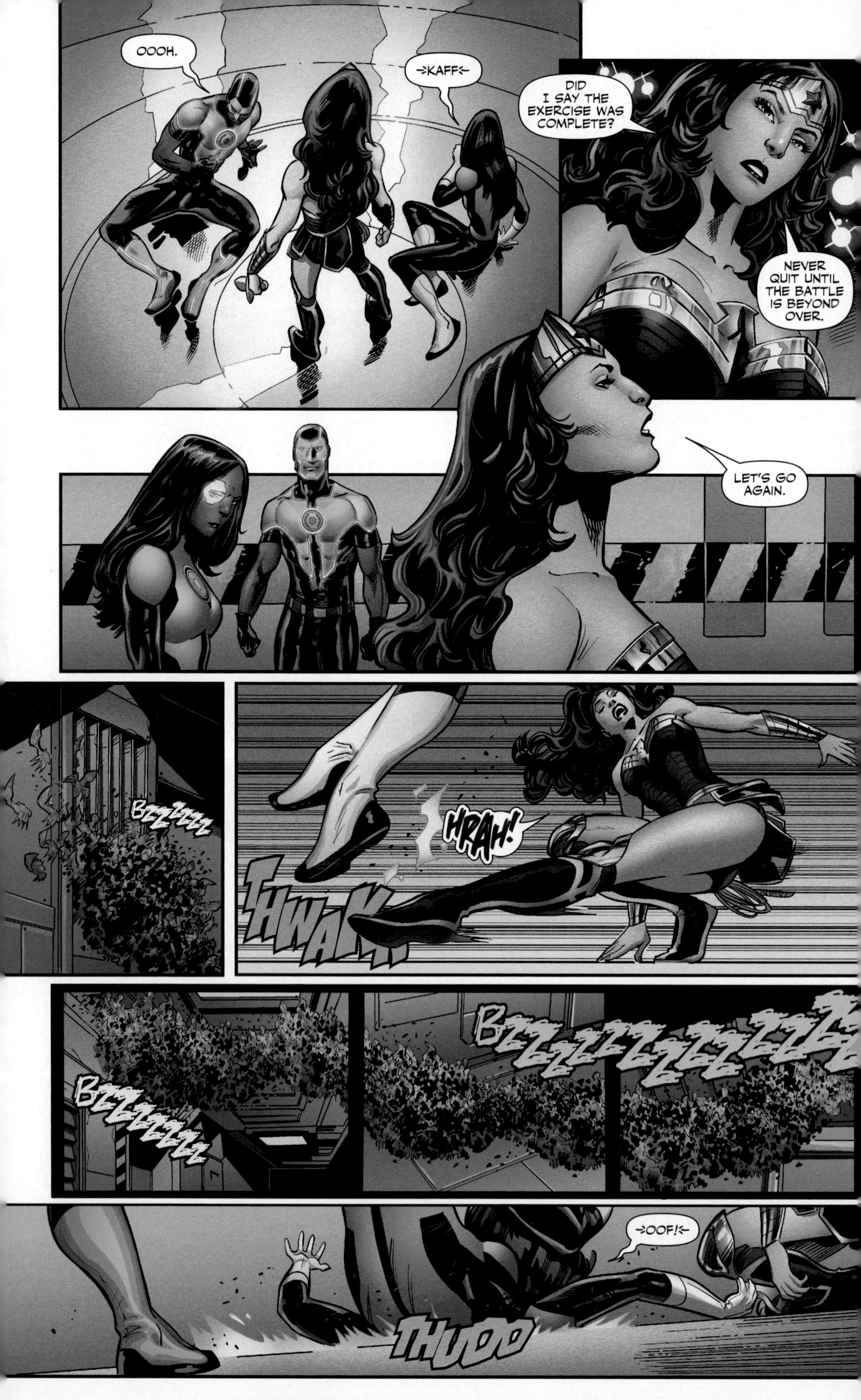
OOOH.
-KAFF-
DID I SAY THE EXERCISE WAS COMPLETE?
NEVER QUIT UNTIL THE BATTLE IS BEYOND OVER.
LET'S GO AGAIN.
BZZZZZZZ
HRAH!
THWAKK!
BZZZZZZZZZ
BZZZZZZZZZZZZZZZZZZ
-OOF!-
THUDD

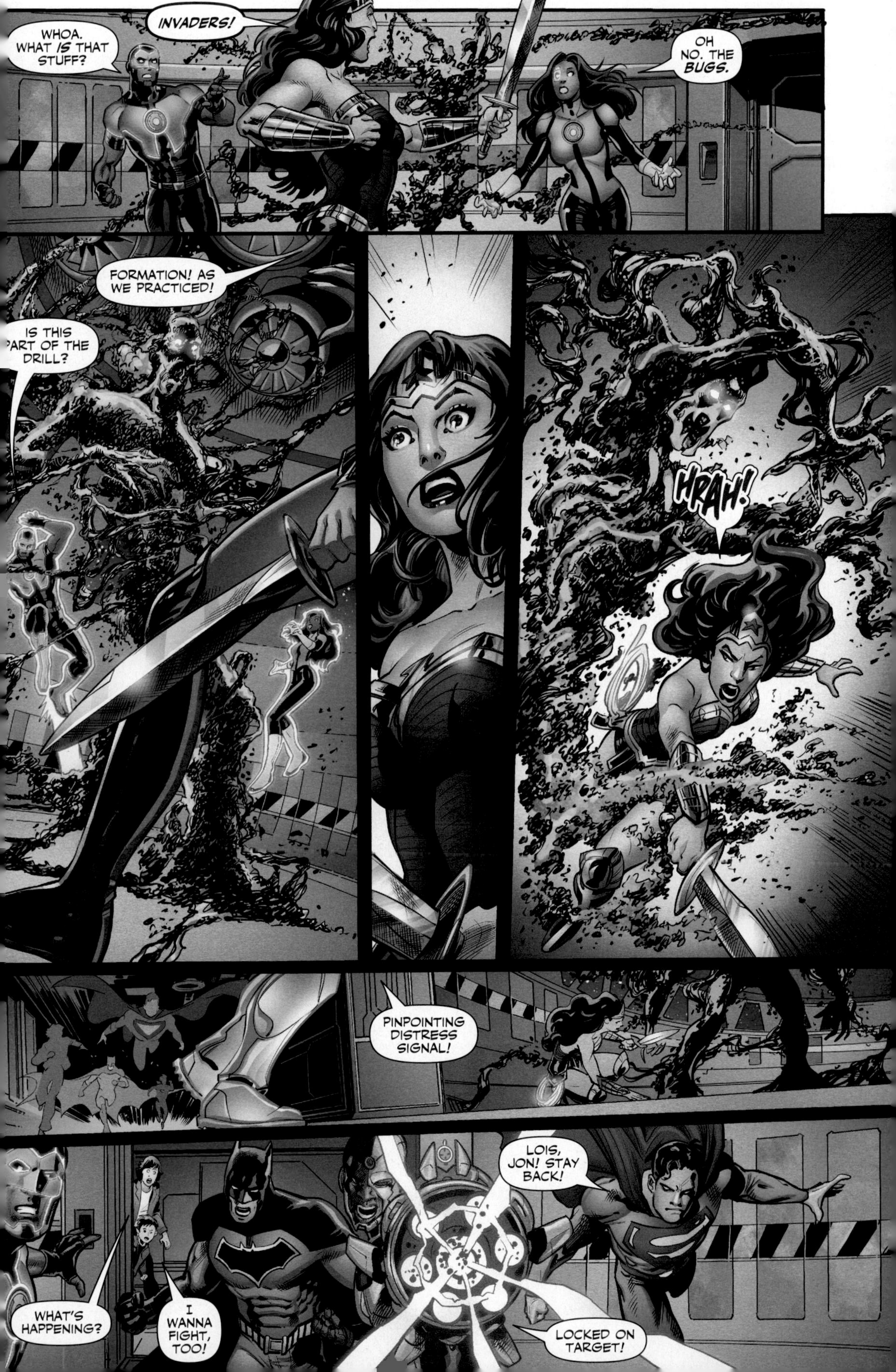

WHOA. WHAT IS THAT STUFF?
INVADERS!
OH NO. THE BUGS.
FORMATION! AS WE PRACTICED!
IS THIS PART OF THE DRILL?
HRAH!
PINPOINTING DISTRESS SIGNAL!
LOIS, JON! STAY BACK!
WHAT'S HAPPENING?
I WANNA FIGHT, TOO!
LOCKED ON TARGET!

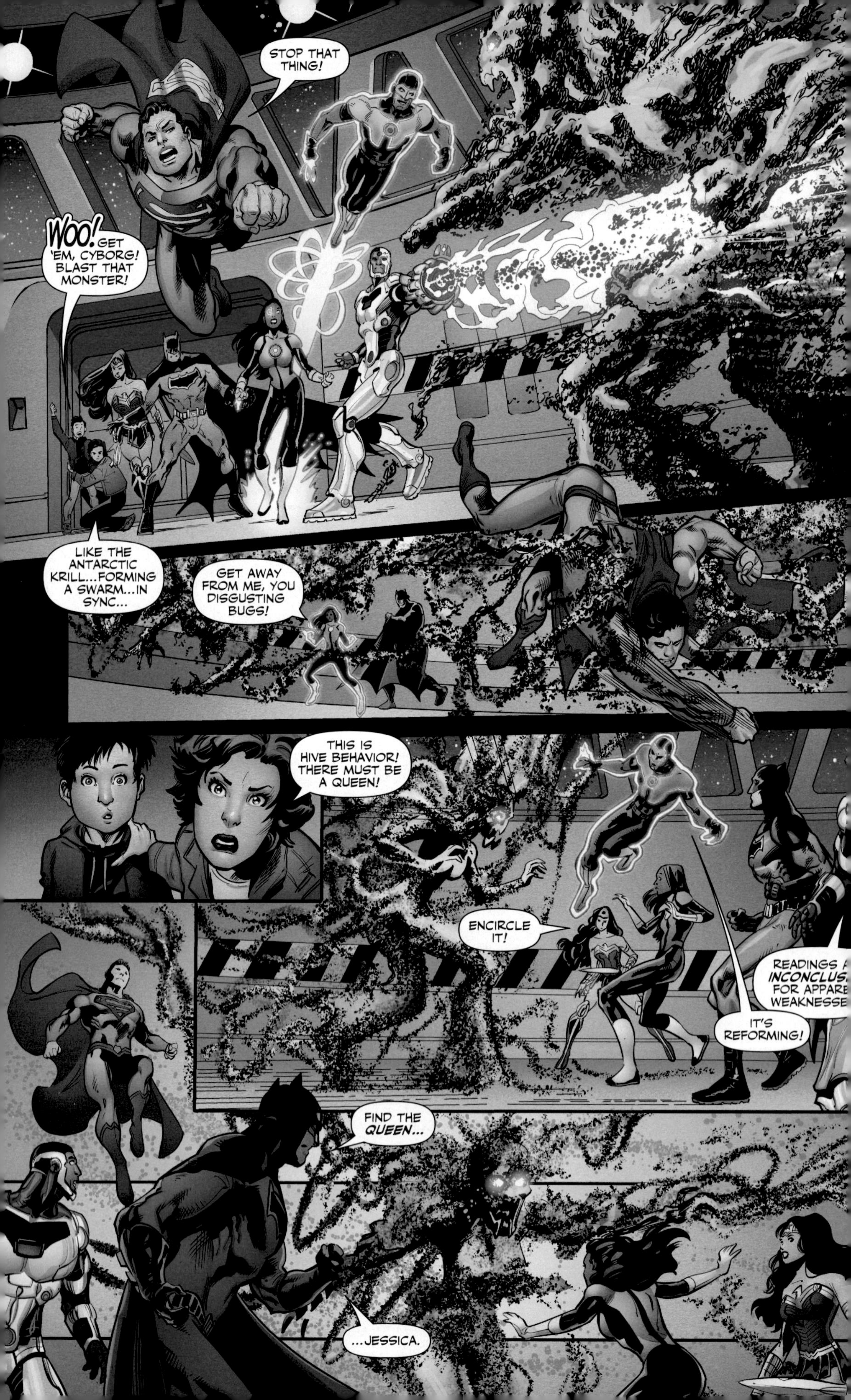
STOP THAT THING!
WOO! GET 'EM, CYBORG! BLAST THAT MONSTER!
LIKE THE ANTARCTIC KRILL...FORMING A SWARM...IN SYNC...
GET AWAY FROM ME, YOU DISGUSTING BUGS!
THIS IS HIVE BEHAVIOR! THERE MUST BE A QUEEN!
ENCIRCLE IT!
IT'S REFORMING!
FIND THE QUEEN...
...JESSICA.

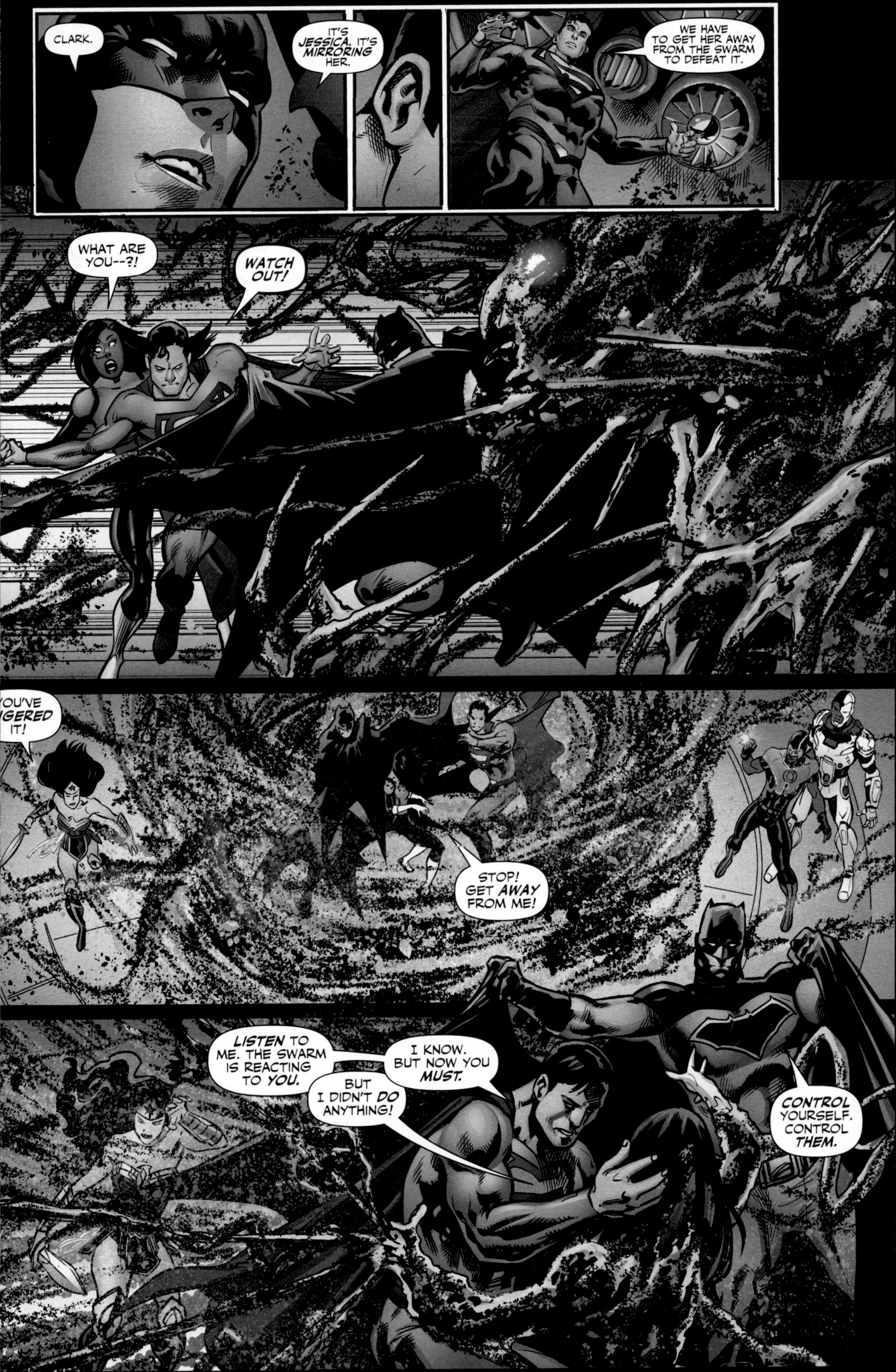
CLARK.
IT'S *JESSICA.* IT'S *MIRRORING* HER.
WE HAVE TO GET HER AWAY FROM THE SWARM TO DEFEAT IT.
WHAT ARE YOU--?!
WATCH OUT!
OU'VE *IGERED* IT!
STOP! GET *AWAY* FROM ME!
LISTEN TO ME. THE SWARM IS REACTING TO *YOU.*
BUT I DIDN'T *DO* ANYTHING!
I KNOW. BUT NOW YOU *MUST.*
CONTROL YOURSELF. CONTROL *THEM.*

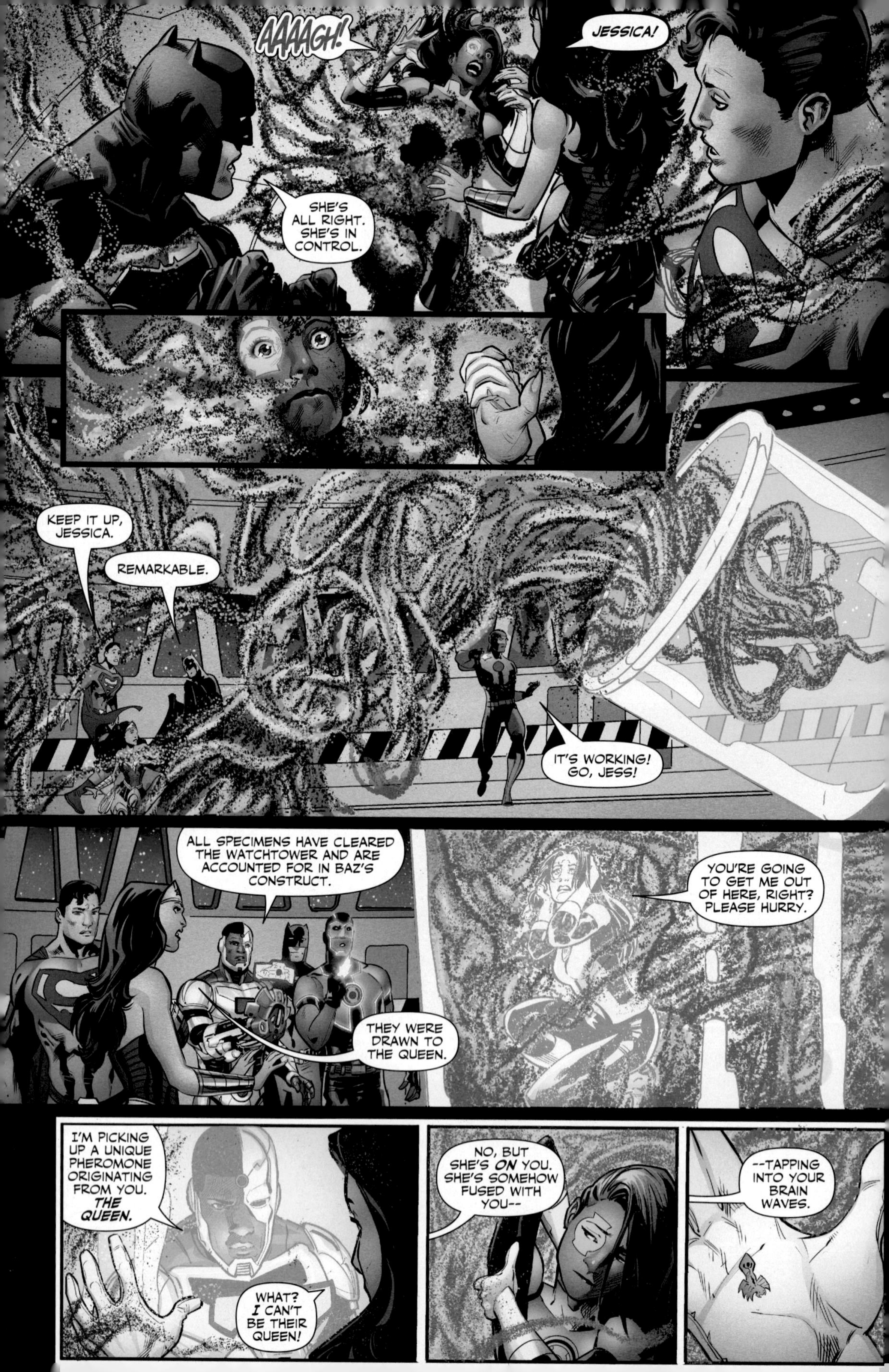
AAAAGH!
JESSICA!
SHE'S ALL RIGHT. SHE'S IN CONTROL.
KEEP IT UP, JESSICA.
REMARKABLE.
IT'S WORKING! GO, JESS!
ALL SPECIMENS HAVE CLEARED THE WATCHTOWER AND ARE ACCOUNTED FOR IN BAZ'S CONSTRUCT.
THEY WERE DRAWN TO THE QUEEN.
YOU'RE GOING TO GET ME OUT OF HERE, RIGHT? PLEASE HURRY.
I'M PICKING UP A UNIQUE PHEROMONE ORIGINATING FROM YOU. THE QUEEN.
WHAT? I CAN'T BE THEIR QUEEN!
NO, BUT SHE'S ON YOU. SHE'S SOMEHOW FUSED WITH YOU--
--TAPPING INTO YOUR BRAIN WAVES.

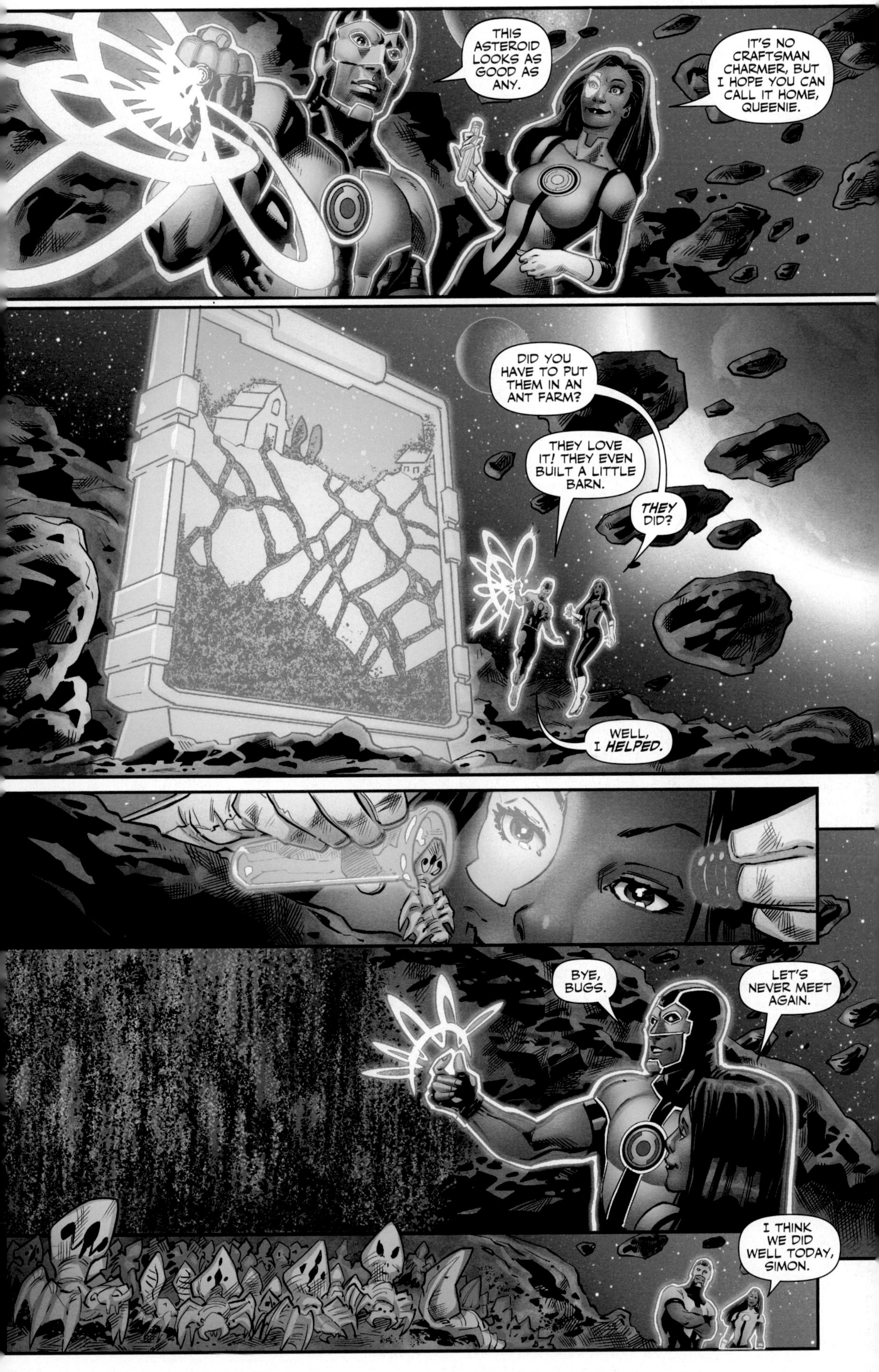
THIS ASTEROID LOOKS AS GOOD AS ANY.
IT'S NO CRAFTSMAN CHARMER, BUT I HOPE YOU CAN CALL IT HOME, QUEENIE.
DID YOU HAVE TO PUT THEM IN AN ANT FARM?
THEY LOVE IT! THEY EVEN BUILT A LITTLE BARN.
THEY DID?
WELL, I HELPED.
BYE, BUGS.
LET'S NEVER MEET AGAIN.
I THINK WE DID WELL TODAY, SIMON.

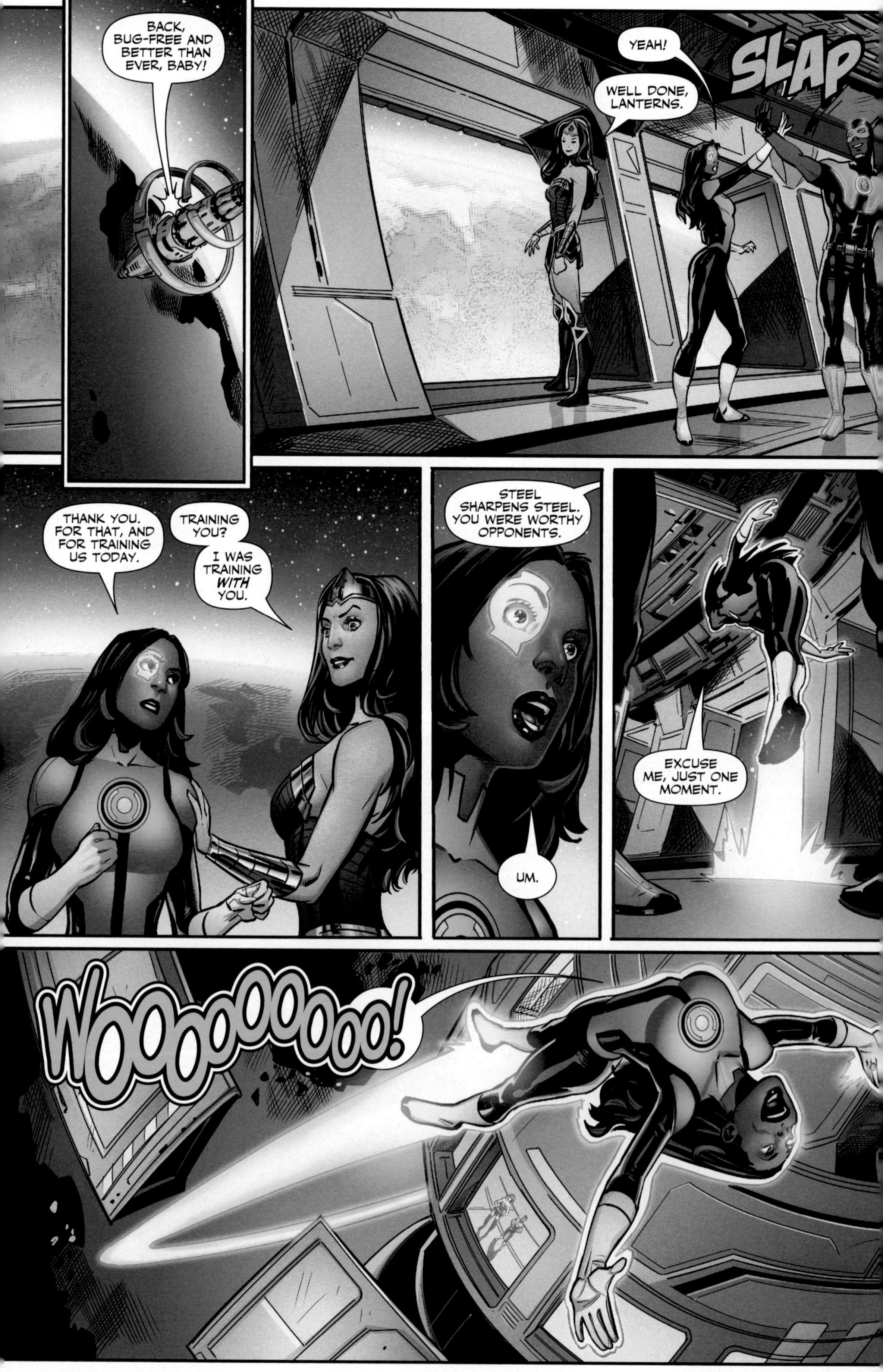
BACK, BUG-FREE AND BETTER THAN EVER, BABY!
YEAH!
WELL DONE, LANTERNS.
SLAP
THANK YOU. FOR THAT, AND FOR TRAINING US TODAY.
TRAINING YOU?
I WAS TRAINING *WITH* YOU.
STEEL SHARPENS STEEL. YOU WERE WORTHY OPPONENTS.
UM.
EXCUSE ME, JUST ONE MOMENT.
WOOOOOOOOO!

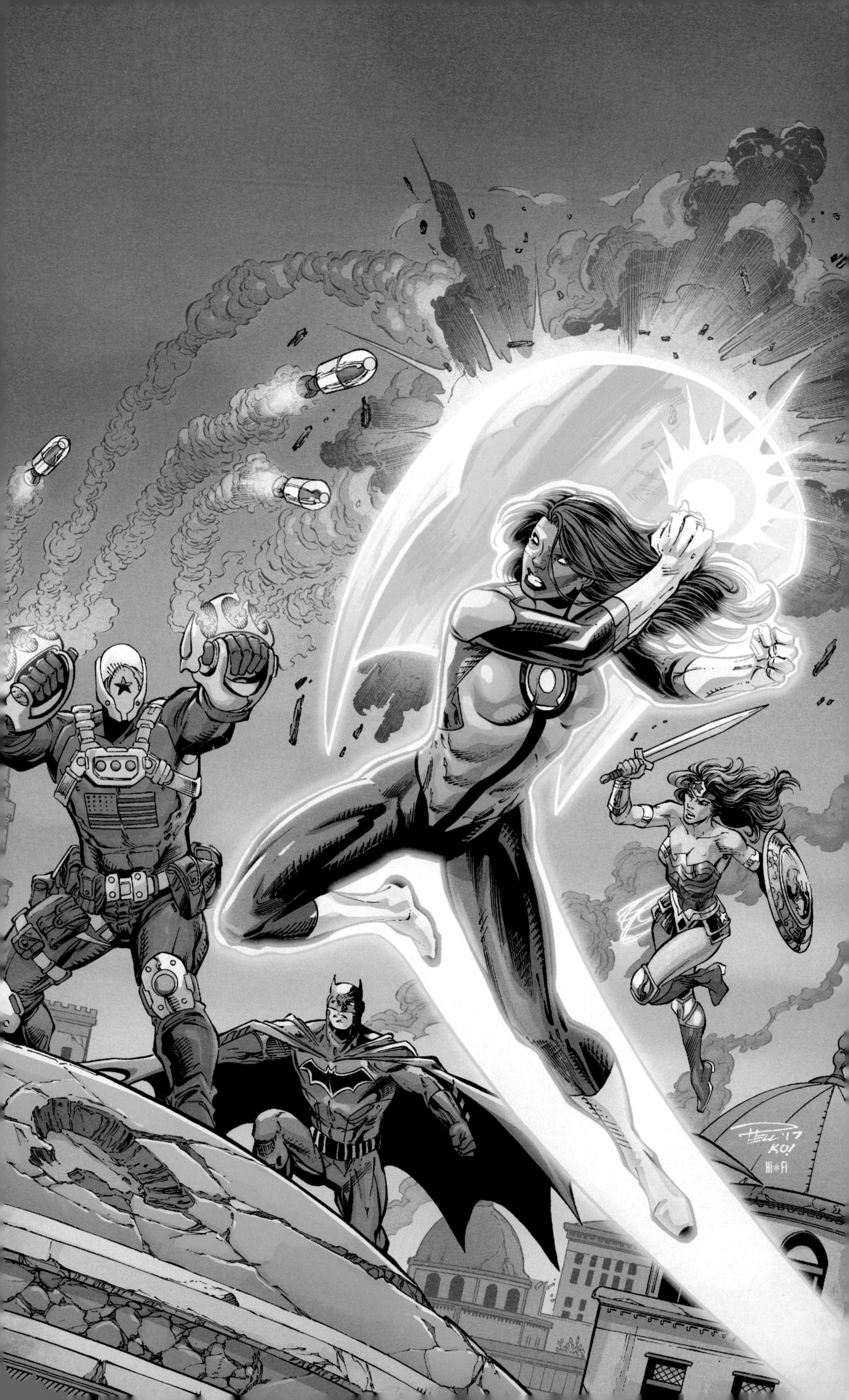

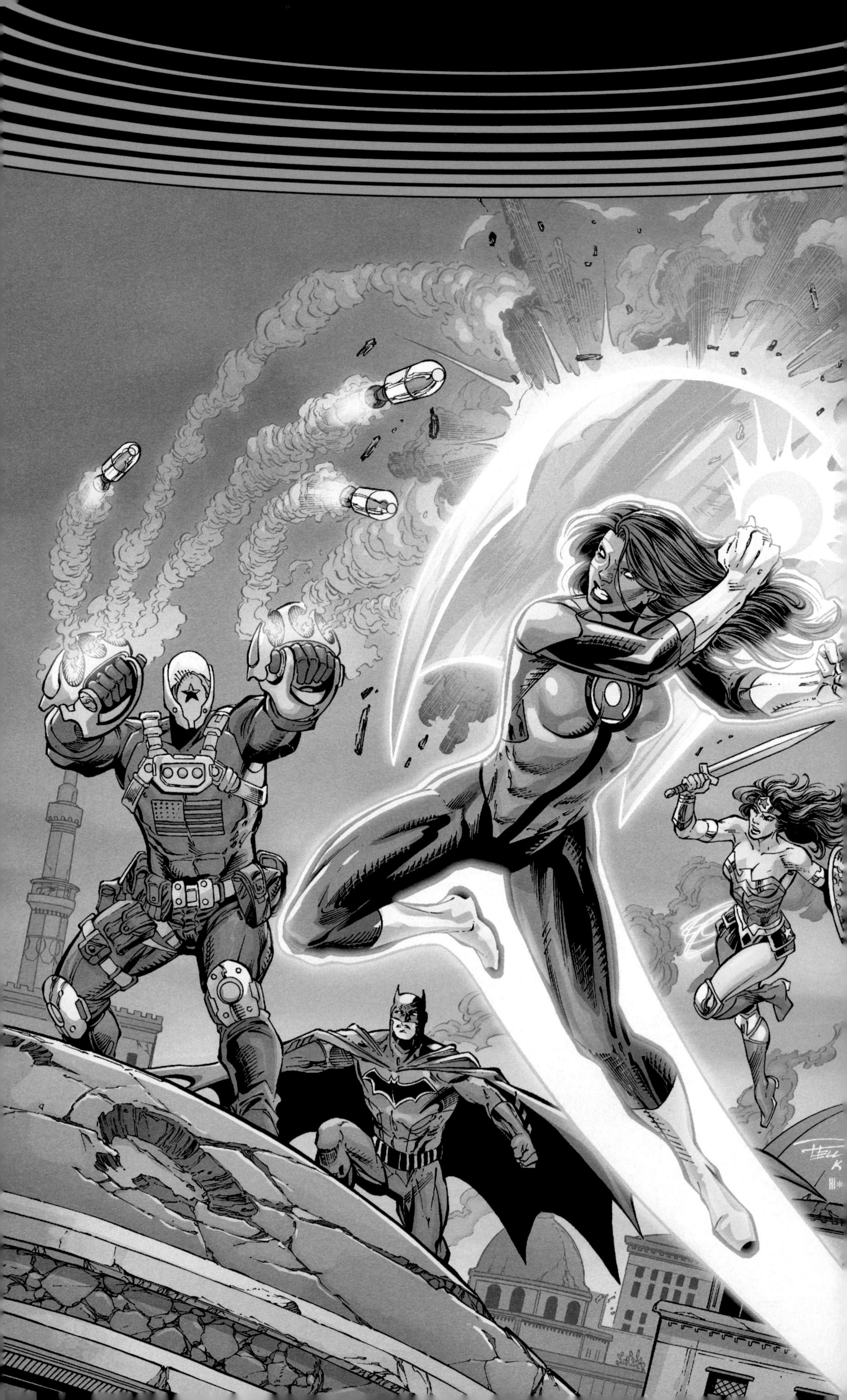

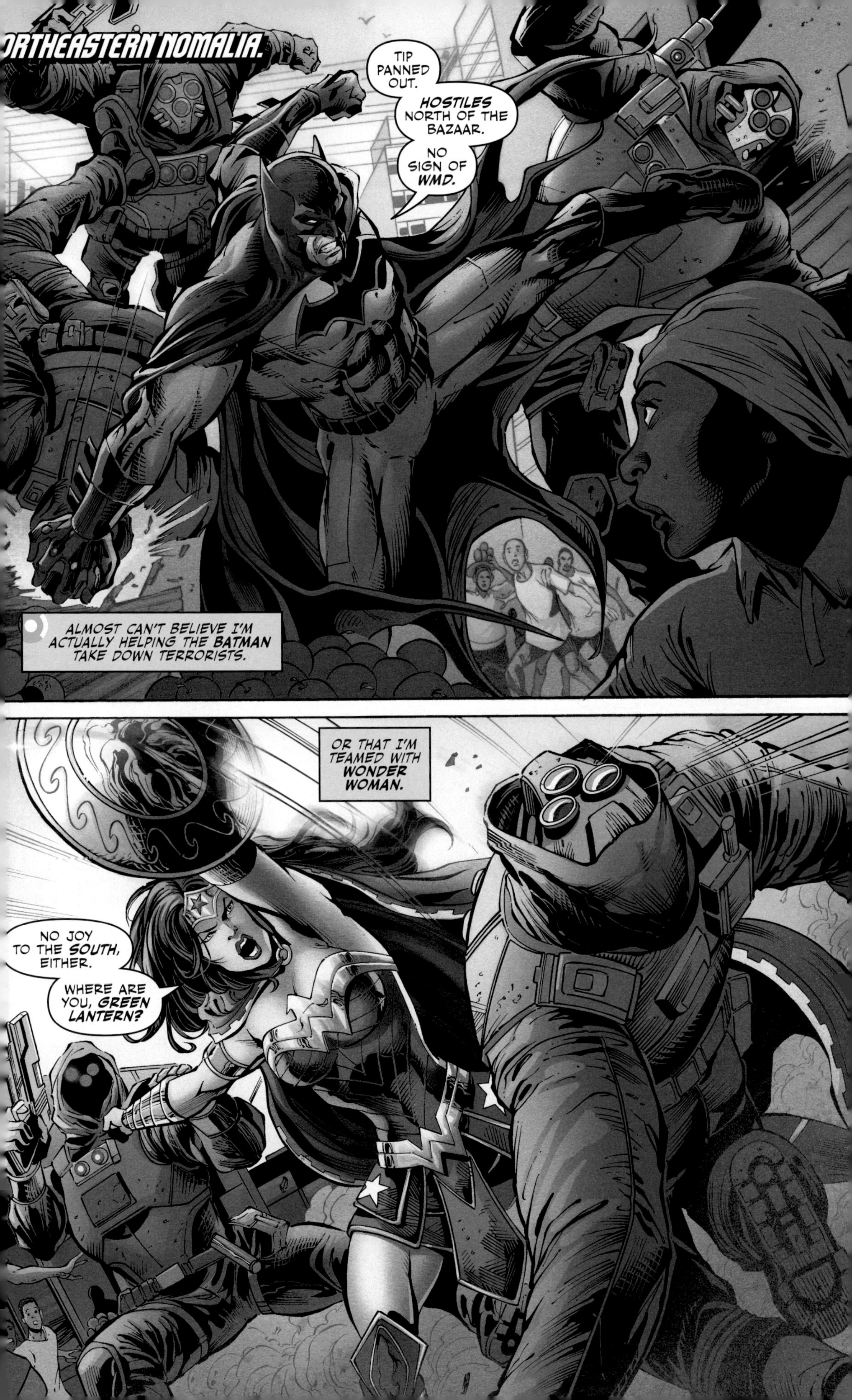
ORTHEASTERN NOMALIA.
TIP PANNED OUT.
HOSTILES NORTH OF THE BAZAAR.
NO SIGN OF WMD.
ALMOST CAN'T BELIEVE I'M ACTUALLY HELPING THE BATMAN TAKE DOWN TERRORISTS.
OR THAT I'M TEAMED WITH WONDER WOMAN.
NO JOY TO THE SOUTH, EITHER.
WHERE ARE YOU, GREEN LANTERN?

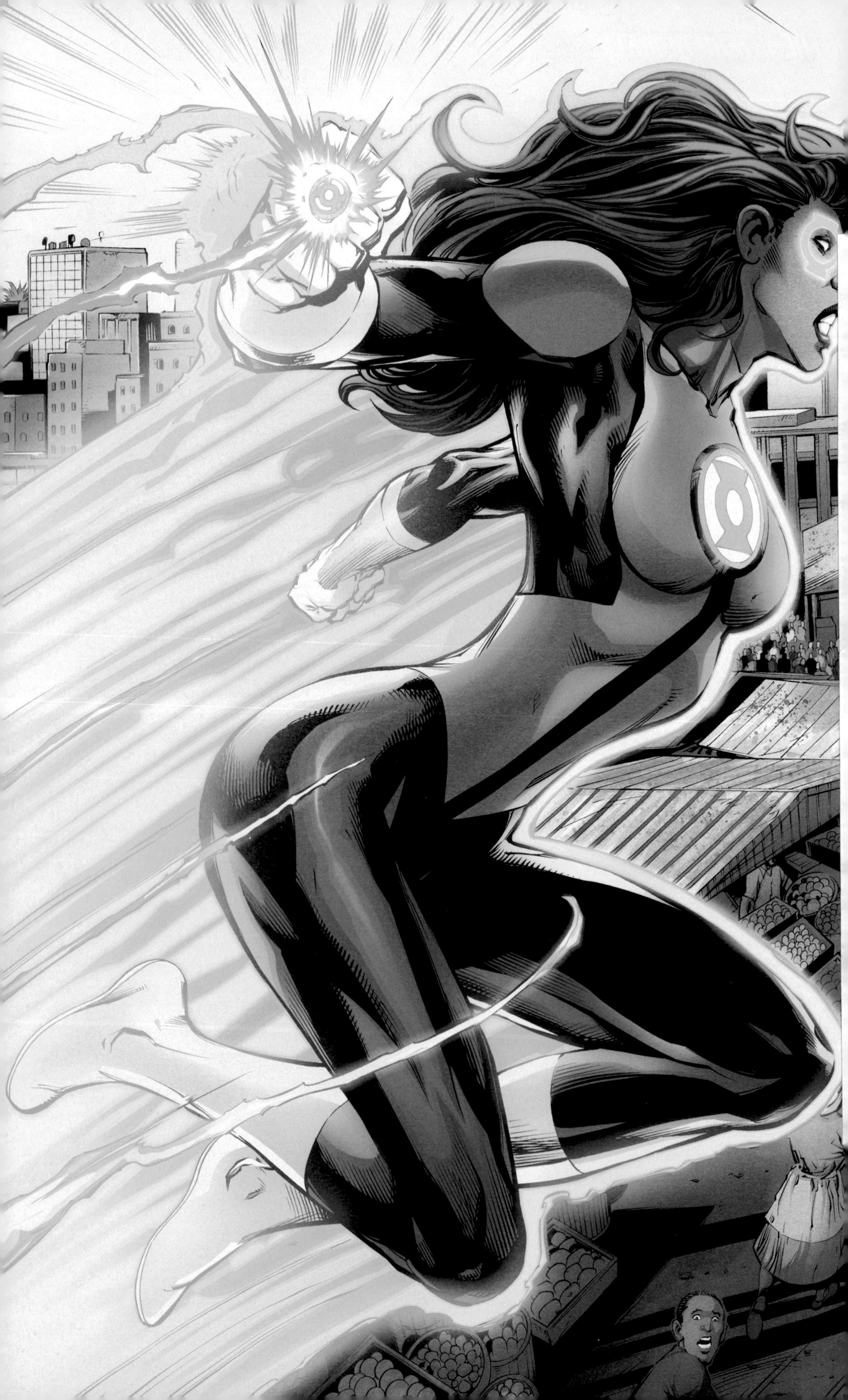

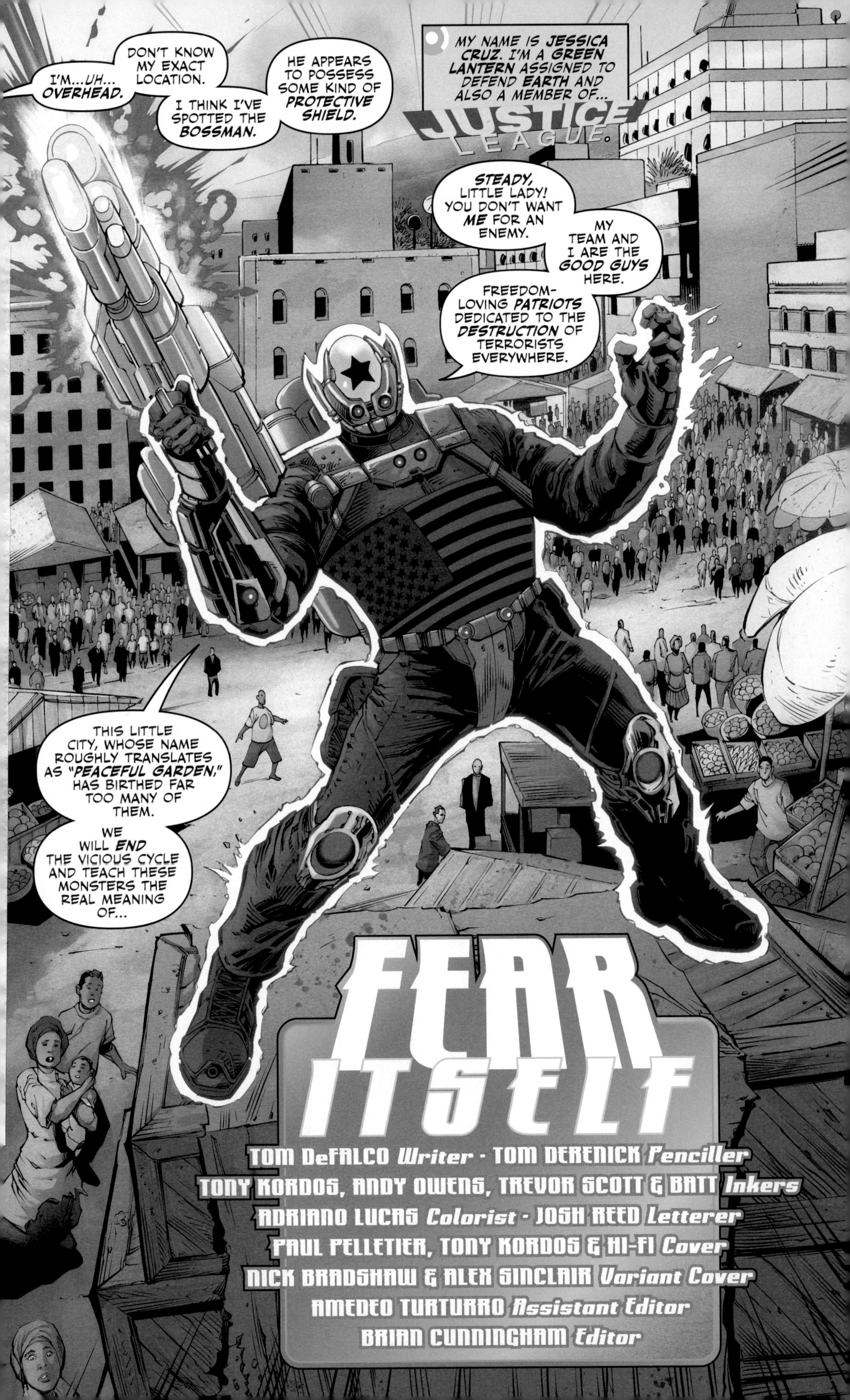
I'M...UH... OVERHEAD.
DON'T KNOW MY EXACT LOCATION.
I THINK I'VE SPOTTED THE BOSSMAN.
HE APPEARS TO POSSESS SOME KIND OF PROTECTIVE SHIELD.
MY NAME IS JESSICA CRUZ. I'M A GREEN LANTERN ASSIGNED TO DEFEND EARTH AND ALSO A MEMBER OF...
JUSTICE LEAGUE.
STEADY, LITTLE LADY! YOU DON'T WANT ME FOR AN ENEMY.
MY TEAM AND I ARE THE GOOD GUYS HERE.
FREEDOM-LOVING PATRIOTS DEDICATED TO THE DESTRUCTION OF TERRORISTS EVERYWHERE.
THIS LITTLE CITY, WHOSE NAME ROUGHLY TRANSLATES AS "PEACEFUL GARDEN," HAS BIRTHED FAR TOO MANY OF THEM.
WE WILL END THE VICIOUS CYCLE AND TEACH THESE MONSTERS THE REAL MEANING OF...
FEAR ITSELF
TOM DeFALCO Writer - TOM DERENICK Penciller
TONY KORDOS, ANDY OWENS, TREVOR SCOTT & BATT Inkers
ADRIANO LUCAS Colorist - JOSH REED Letterer
PAUL PELLETIER, TONY KORDOS & HI-FI Cover
NICK BRADSHAW & ALEX SINCLAIR Variant Cover
AMEDEO TURTURRO Assistant Editor
BRIAN CUNNINGHAM Editor

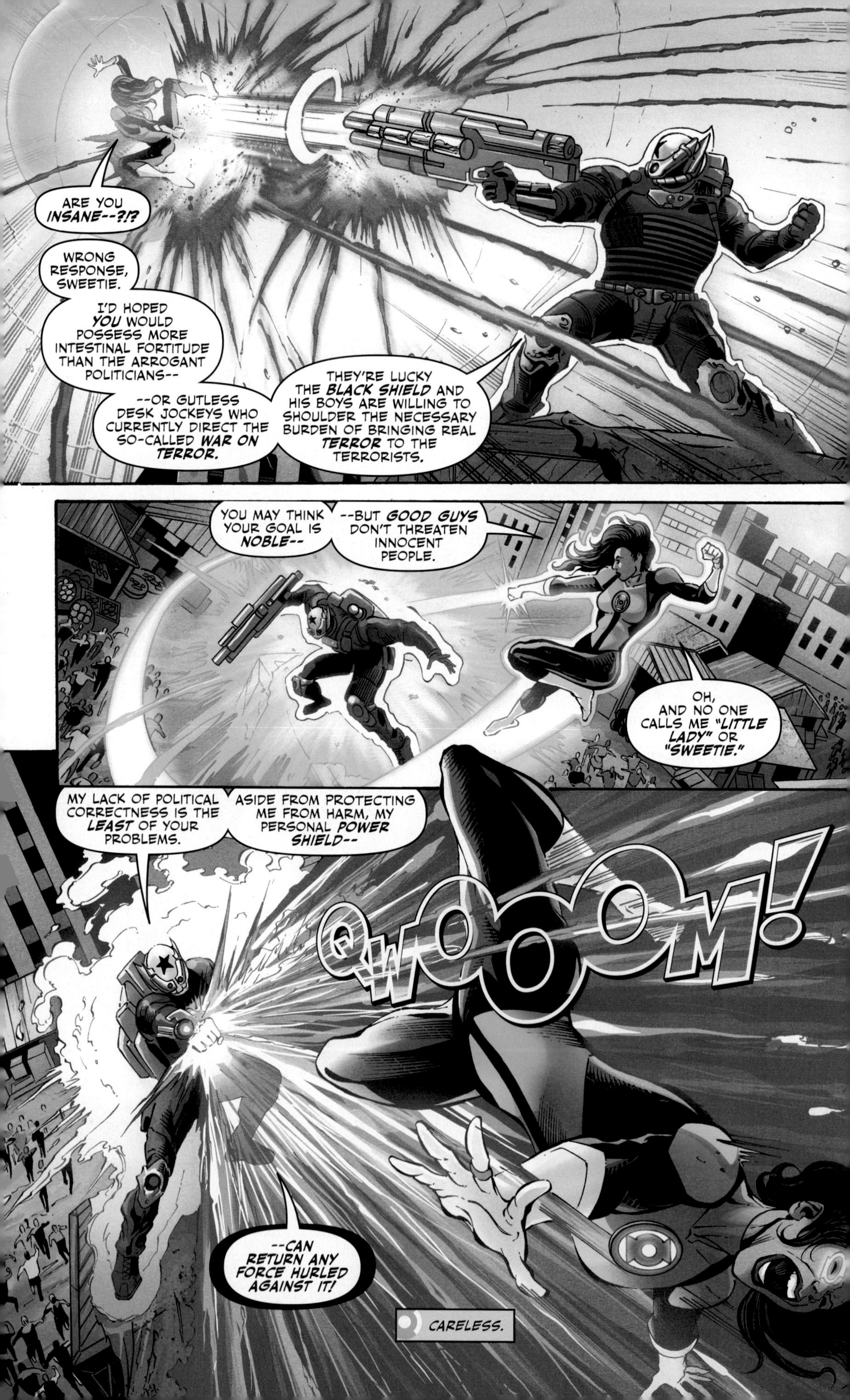
ARE YOU INSANE--?!?
WRONG RESPONSE, SWEETIE.
I'D HOPED YOU WOULD POSSESS MORE INTESTINAL FORTITUDE THAN THE ARROGANT POLITICIANS--
--OR GUTLESS DESK JOCKEYS WHO CURRENTLY DIRECT THE SO-CALLED WAR ON TERROR.
THEY'RE LUCKY THE BLACK SHIELD AND HIS BOYS ARE WILLING TO SHOULDER THE NECESSARY BURDEN OF BRINGING REAL TERROR TO THE TERRORISTS.
YOU MAY THINK YOUR GOAL IS NOBLE--
--BUT GOOD GUYS DON'T THREATEN INNOCENT PEOPLE.
OH, AND NO ONE CALLS ME "LITTLE LADY" OR "SWEETIE."
MY LACK OF POLITICAL CORRECTNESS IS THE LEAST OF YOUR PROBLEMS.
ASIDE FROM PROTECTING ME FROM HARM, MY PERSONAL POWER SHIELD--
QWOOOOM!
--CAN RETURN ANY FORCE HURLED AGAINST IT!
CARELESS.

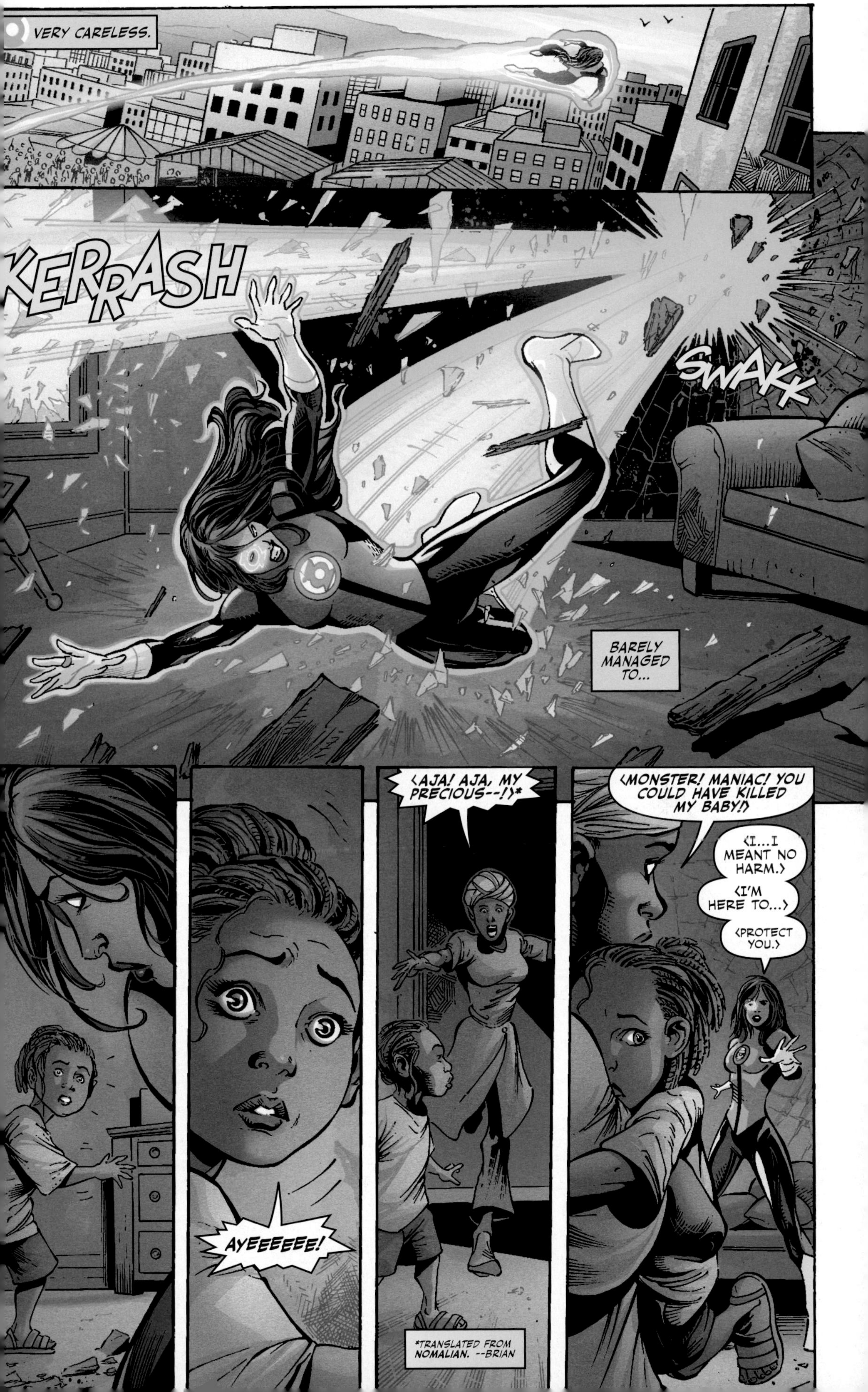
VERY CARELESS.
KERRASH
SWAKK
BARELY MANAGED TO...
AYEEEEEE!
‹AJA! AJA, MY PRECIOUS--!›*
‹MONSTER! MANIAC! YOU COULD HAVE KILLED MY BABY!›
‹I...I MEANT NO HARM.›
‹I'M HERE TO...›
‹PROTECT YOU.›
*TRANSLATED FROM NOMALIAN. --BRIAN

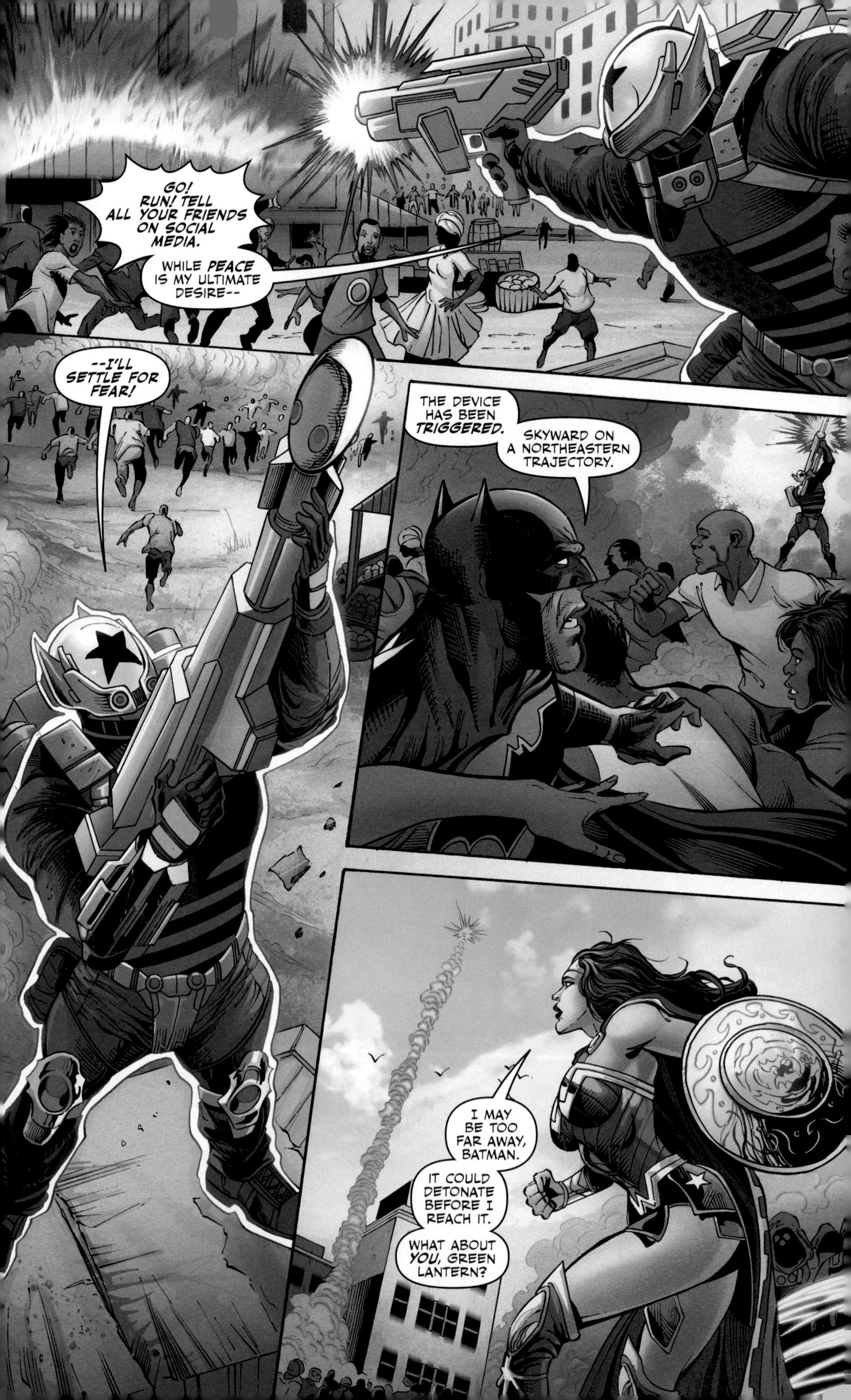
GO! RUN! TELL ALL YOUR FRIENDS ON SOCIAL MEDIA.
WHILE PEACE IS MY ULTIMATE DESIRE--
--I'LL SETTLE FOR FEAR!
THE DEVICE HAS BEEN TRIGGERED.
SKYWARD ON A NORTHEASTERN TRAJECTORY.
I MAY BE TOO FAR AWAY, BATMAN.
IT COULD DETONATE BEFORE I REACH IT.
WHAT ABOUT YOU, GREEN LANTERN?

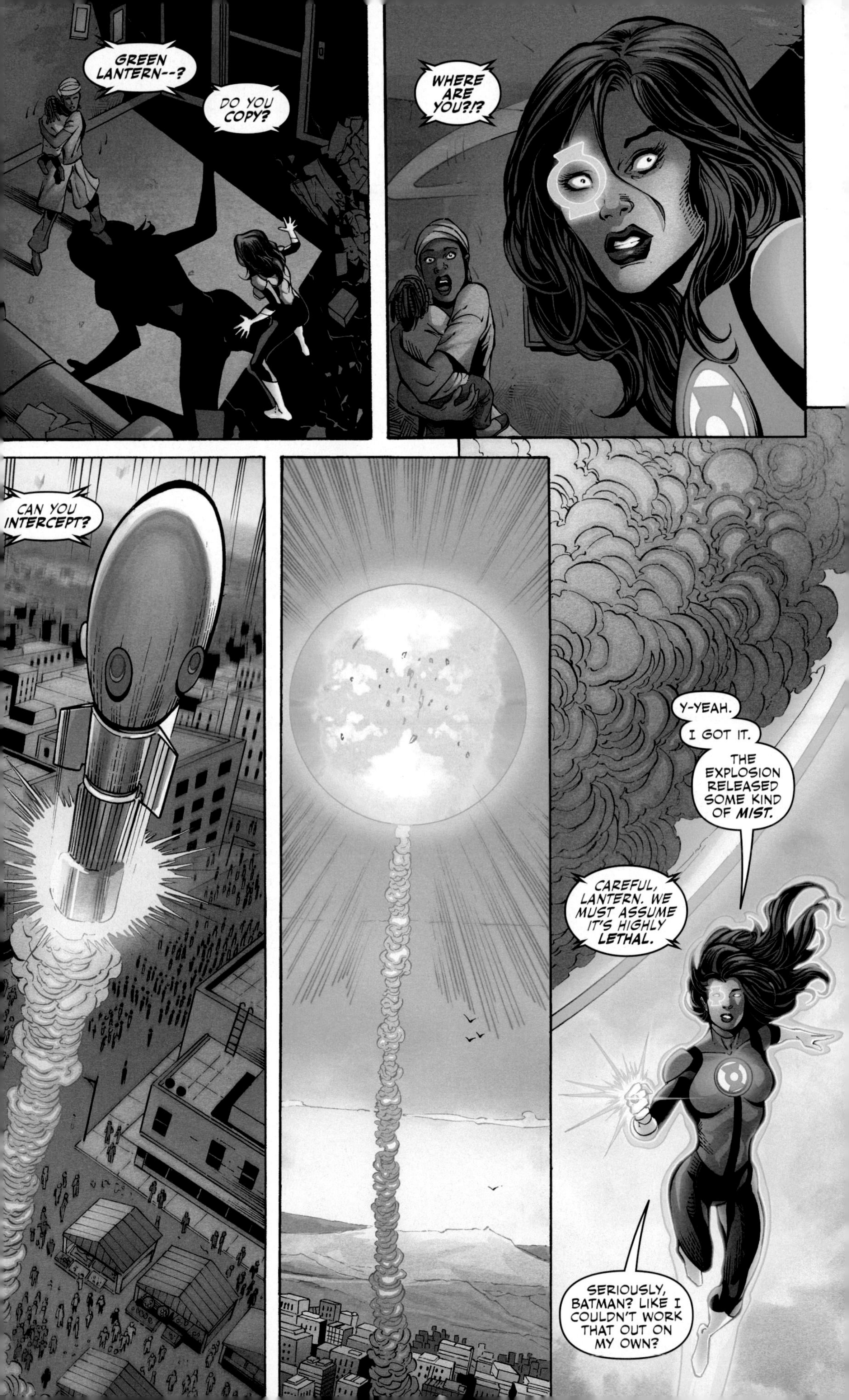
GREEN LANTERN--?
DO YOU COPY?
WHERE ARE YOU?!?
CAN YOU INTERCEPT?
Y-YEAH.
I GOT IT.
THE EXPLOSION RELEASED SOME KIND OF MIST.
CAREFUL, LANTERN. WE MUST ASSUME IT'S HIGHLY LETHAL.
SERIOUSLY, BATMAN? LIKE I COULDN'T WORK THAT OUT ON MY OWN?

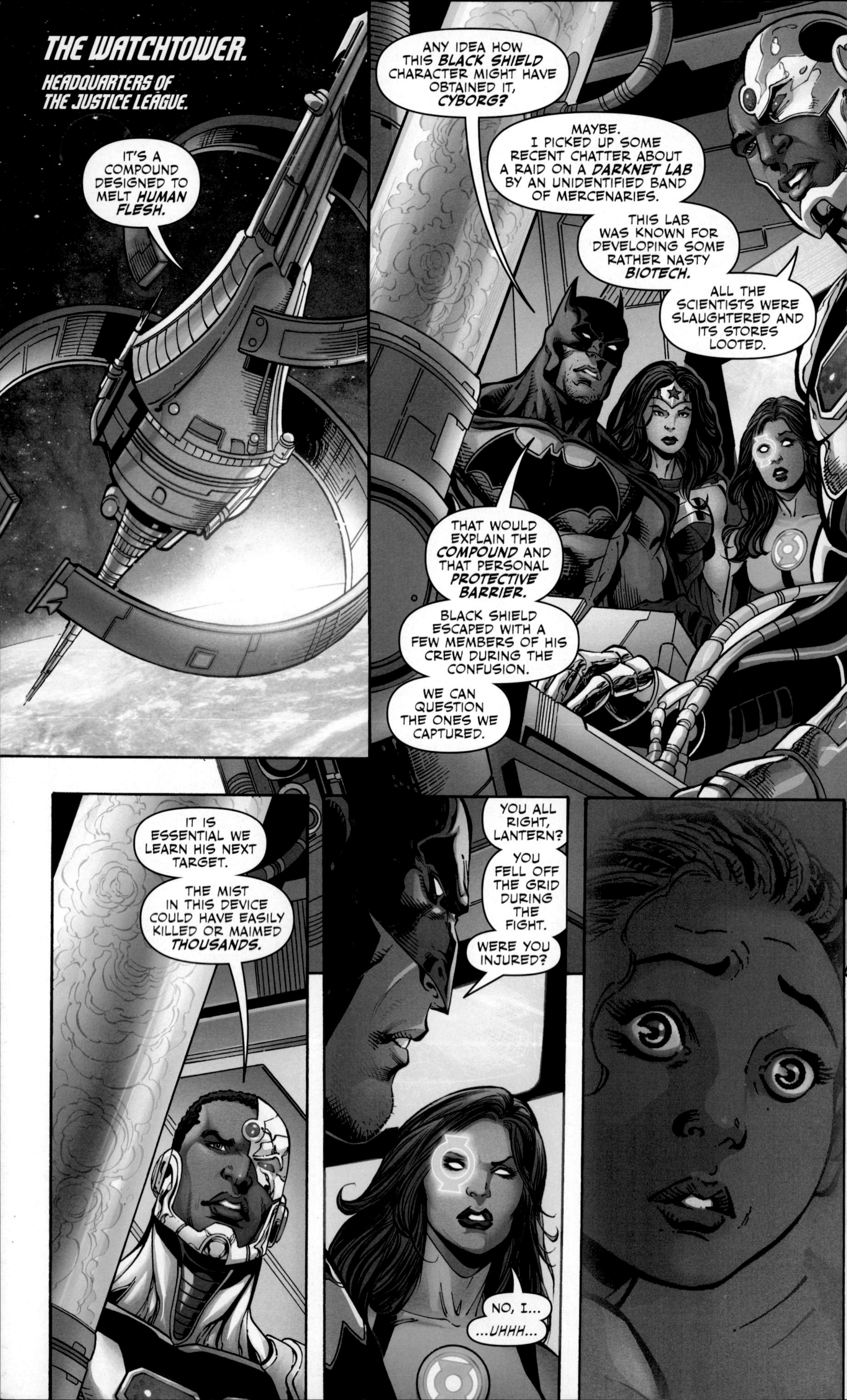
THE WATCHTOWER.
HEADQUARTERS OF THE JUSTICE LEAGUE.
IT'S A COMPOUND DESIGNED TO MELT HUMAN FLESH.
ANY IDEA HOW THIS BLACK SHIELD CHARACTER MIGHT HAVE OBTAINED IT, CYBORG?
MAYBE. I PICKED UP SOME RECENT CHATTER ABOUT A RAID ON A DARKNET LAB BY AN UNIDENTIFIED BAND OF MERCENARIES.
THIS LAB WAS KNOWN FOR DEVELOPING SOME RATHER NASTY BIOTECH.
ALL THE SCIENTISTS WERE SLAUGHTERED AND ITS STORES LOOTED.
THAT WOULD EXPLAIN THE COMPOUND AND THAT PERSONAL PROTECTIVE BARRIER.
BLACK SHIELD ESCAPED WITH A FEW MEMBERS OF HIS CREW DURING THE CONFUSION.
WE CAN QUESTION THE ONES WE CAPTURED.
IT IS ESSENTIAL WE LEARN HIS NEXT TARGET.
THE MIST IN THIS DEVICE COULD HAVE EASILY KILLED OR MAIMED THOUSANDS.
YOU ALL RIGHT, LANTERN?
YOU FELL OFF THE GRID DURING THE FIGHT.
WERE YOU INJURED?
NO, I...
...UHHH...

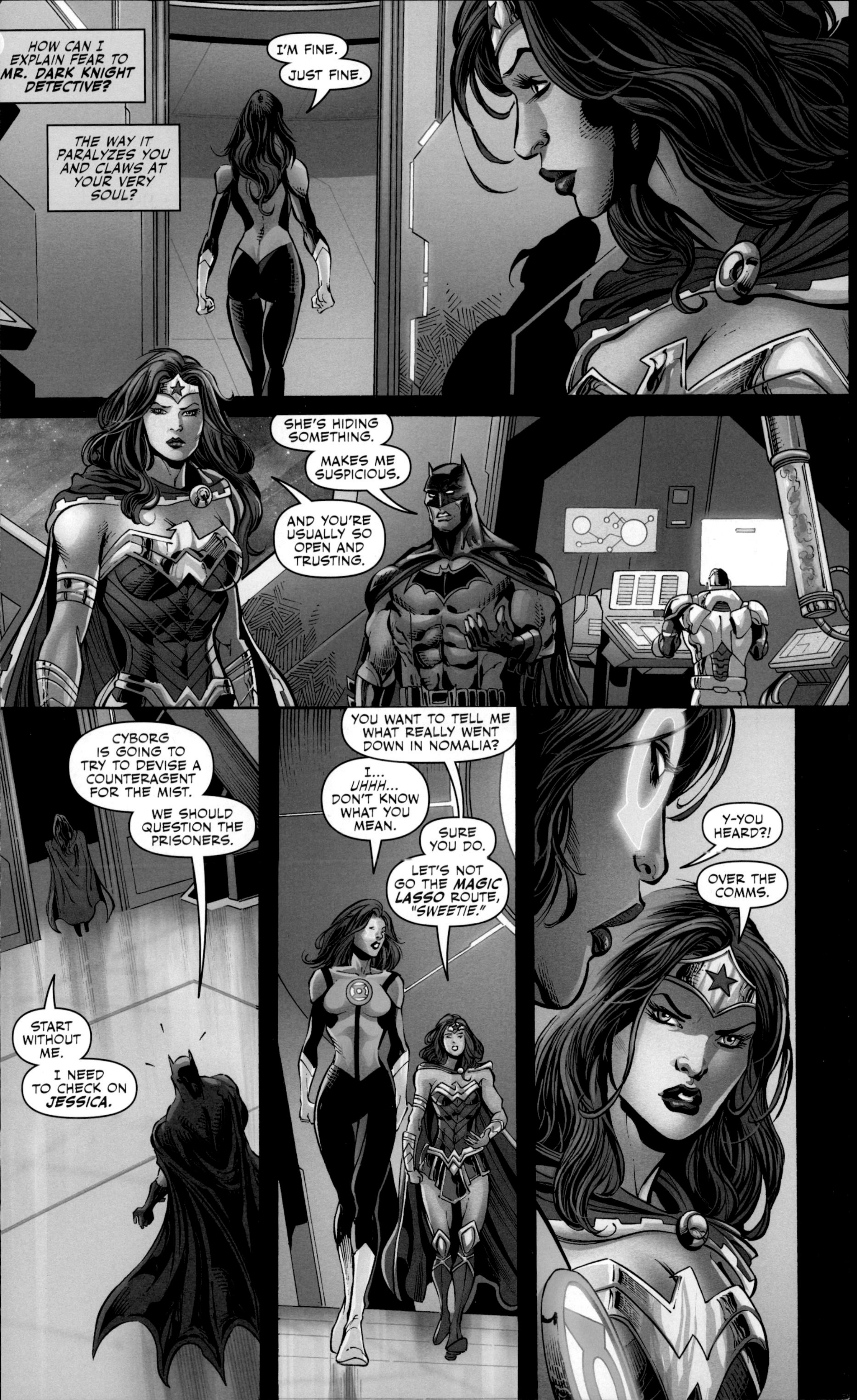

HOW CAN I EXPLAIN FEAR TO MR. DARK KNIGHT DETECTIVE?
I'M FINE.
JUST FINE.
THE WAY IT PARALYZES YOU AND CLAWS AT YOUR VERY SOUL?
SHE'S HIDING SOMETHING.
MAKES ME SUSPICIOUS.
AND YOU'RE USUALLY SO OPEN AND TRUSTING.
CYBORG IS GOING TO TRY TO DEVISE A COUNTERAGENT FOR THE MIST.
WE SHOULD QUESTION THE PRISONERS.
START WITHOUT ME.
I NEED TO CHECK ON JESSICA.
YOU WANT TO TELL ME WHAT REALLY WENT DOWN IN NOMALIA?
I... UHHH... DON'T KNOW WHAT YOU MEAN.
SURE YOU DO.
LET'S NOT GO THE MAGIC LASSO ROUTE, "SWEETIE."
Y-YOU HEARD?!
OVER THE COMMS.

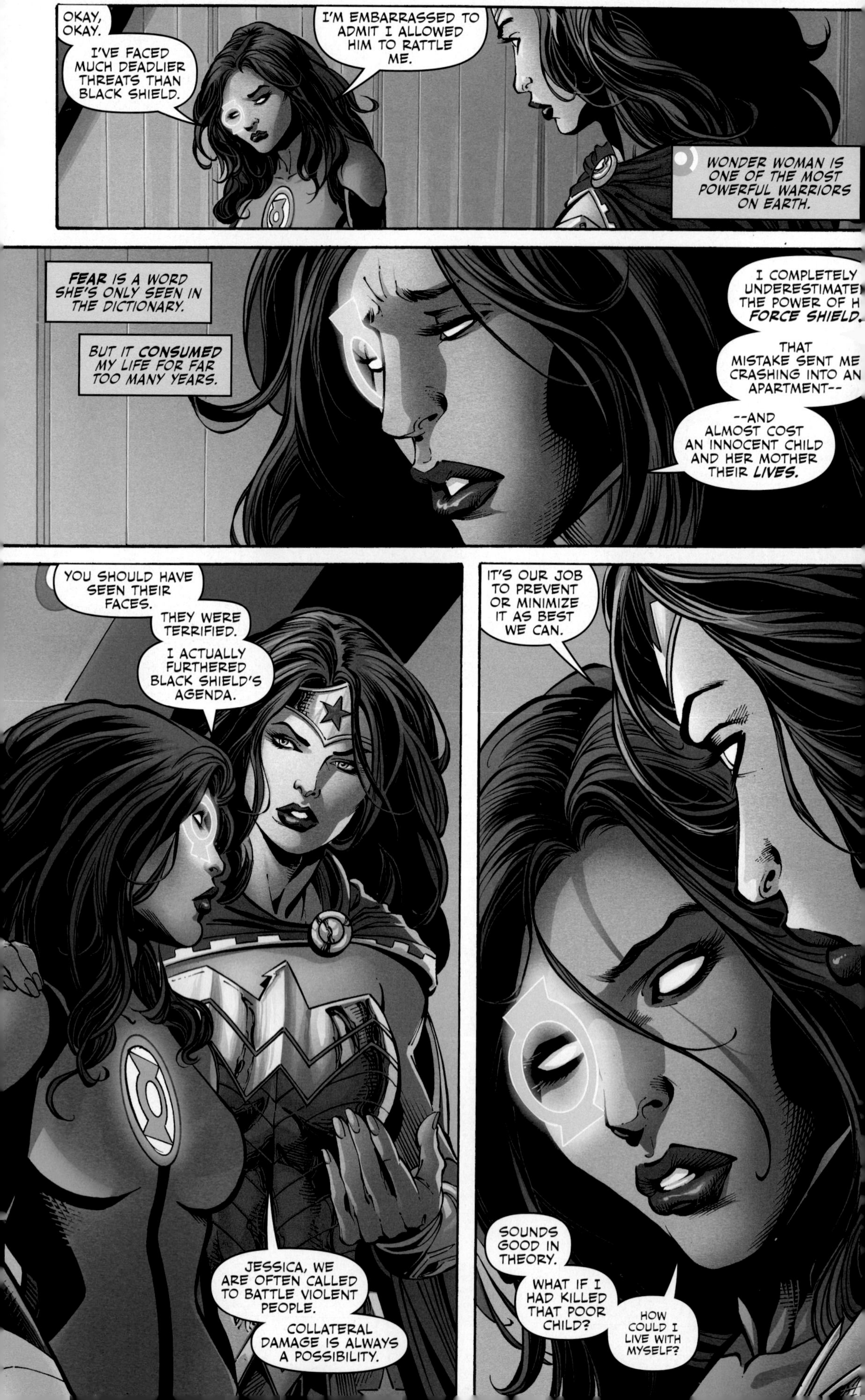
OKAY, OKAY.
I'VE FACED MUCH DEADLIER THREATS THAN BLACK SHIELD.
I'M EMBARRASSED TO ADMIT I ALLOWED HIM TO RATTLE ME.
WONDER WOMAN IS ONE OF THE MOST POWERFUL WARRIORS ON EARTH.
FEAR IS A WORD SHE'S ONLY SEEN IN THE DICTIONARY.
BUT IT CONSUMED MY LIFE FOR FAR TOO MANY YEARS.
I COMPLETELY UNDERESTIMATE THE POWER OF H FORCE SHIELD.
THAT MISTAKE SENT ME CRASHING INTO AN APARTMENT--
--AND ALMOST COST AN INNOCENT CHILD AND HER MOTHER THEIR LIVES.
YOU SHOULD HAVE SEEN THEIR FACES.
THEY WERE TERRIFIED.
I ACTUALLY FURTHERED BLACK SHIELD'S AGENDA.
JESSICA, WE ARE OFTEN CALLED TO BATTLE VIOLENT PEOPLE.
COLLATERAL DAMAGE IS ALWAYS A POSSIBILITY.
IT'S OUR JOB TO PREVENT OR MINIMIZE IT AS BEST WE CAN.
SOUNDS GOOD IN THEORY.
WHAT IF I HAD KILLED THAT POOR CHILD?
HOW COULD I LIVE WITH MYSELF?

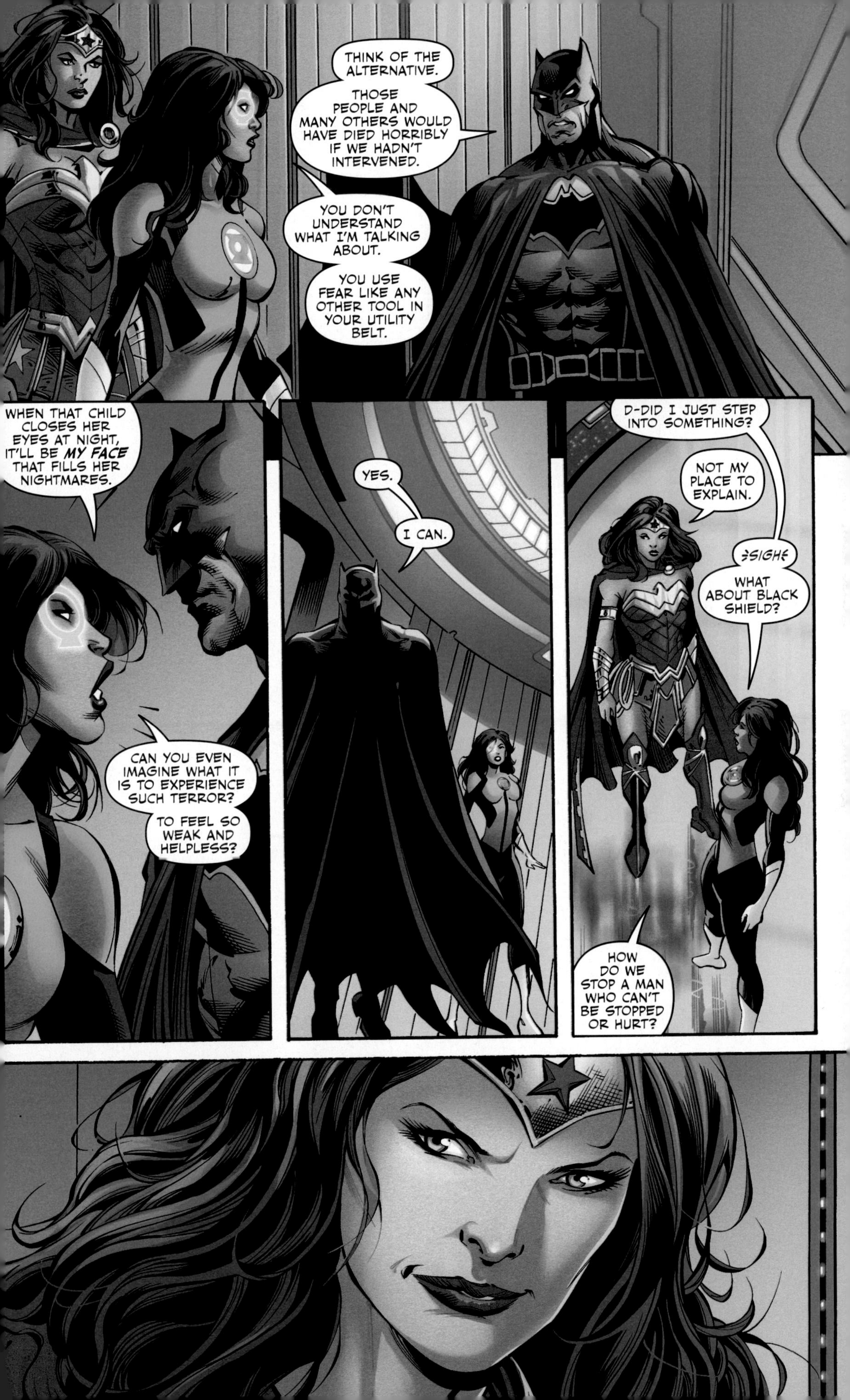
THINK OF THE ALTERNATIVE.
THOSE PEOPLE AND MANY OTHERS WOULD HAVE DIED HORRIBLY IF WE HADN'T INTERVENED.
YOU DON'T UNDERSTAND WHAT I'M TALKING ABOUT.
YOU USE FEAR LIKE ANY OTHER TOOL IN YOUR UTILITY BELT.
WHEN THAT CHILD CLOSES HER EYES AT NIGHT, IT'LL BE *MY FACE* THAT FILLS HER NIGHTMARES.
CAN YOU EVEN IMAGINE WHAT IT IS TO EXPERIENCE SUCH TERROR?
TO FEEL SO WEAK AND HELPLESS?
YES.
I CAN.
D-DID I JUST STEP INTO SOMETHING?
NOT MY PLACE TO EXPLAIN.
SIGH
WHAT ABOUT BLACK SHIELD?
HOW DO WE STOP A MAN WHO CAN'T BE STOPPED OR HURT?

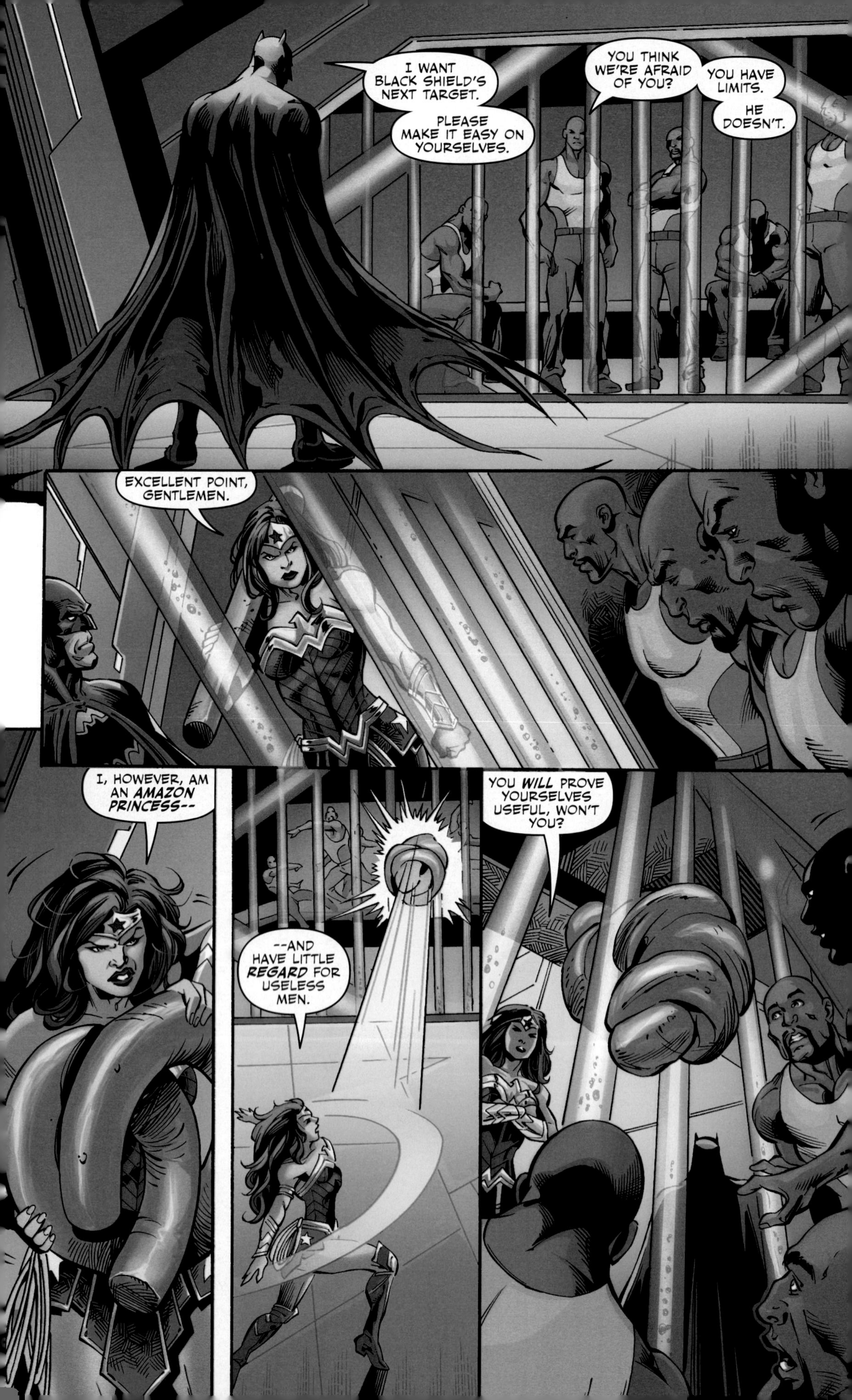
I WANT BLACK SHIELD'S NEXT TARGET.
PLEASE MAKE IT EASY ON YOURSELVES.
YOU THINK WE'RE AFRAID OF YOU?
YOU HAVE LIMITS.
HE DOESN'T.
EXCELLENT POINT, GENTLEMEN.
I, HOWEVER, AM AN *AMAZON PRINCESS*--
--AND HAVE LITTLE *REGARD* FOR USELESS MEN.
YOU *WILL* PROVE YOURSELVES USEFUL, WON'T YOU?

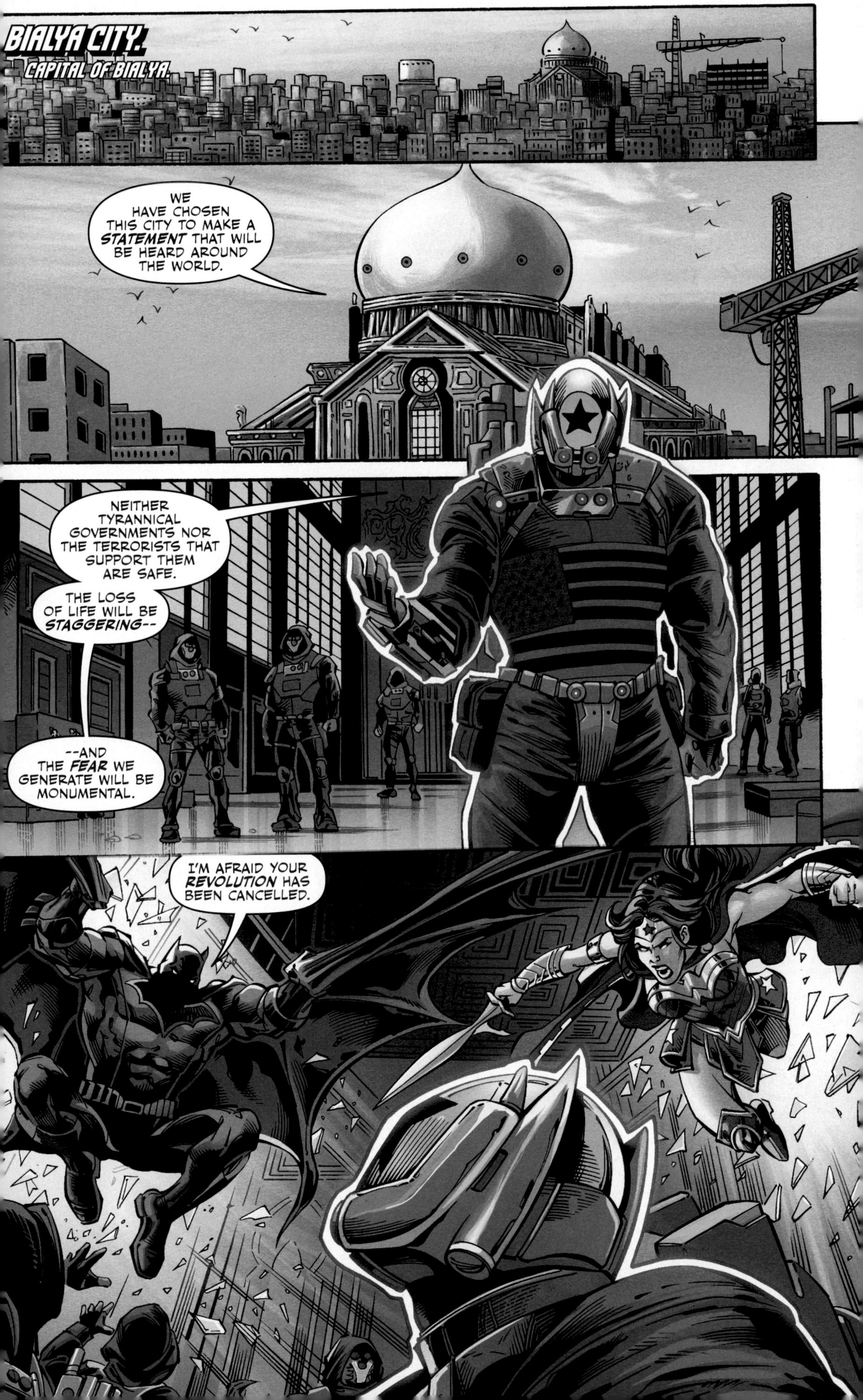
BIALYA CITY.
CAPITAL OF BIALYA.
WE HAVE CHOSEN THIS CITY TO MAKE A STATEMENT THAT WILL BE HEARD AROUND THE WORLD.
NEITHER TYRANNICAL GOVERNMENTS NOR THE TERRORISTS THAT SUPPORT THEM ARE SAFE.
THE LOSS OF LIFE WILL BE STAGGERING--
--AND THE FEAR WE GENERATE WILL BE MONUMENTAL.
I'M AFRAID YOUR REVOLUTION HAS BEEN CANCELLED.

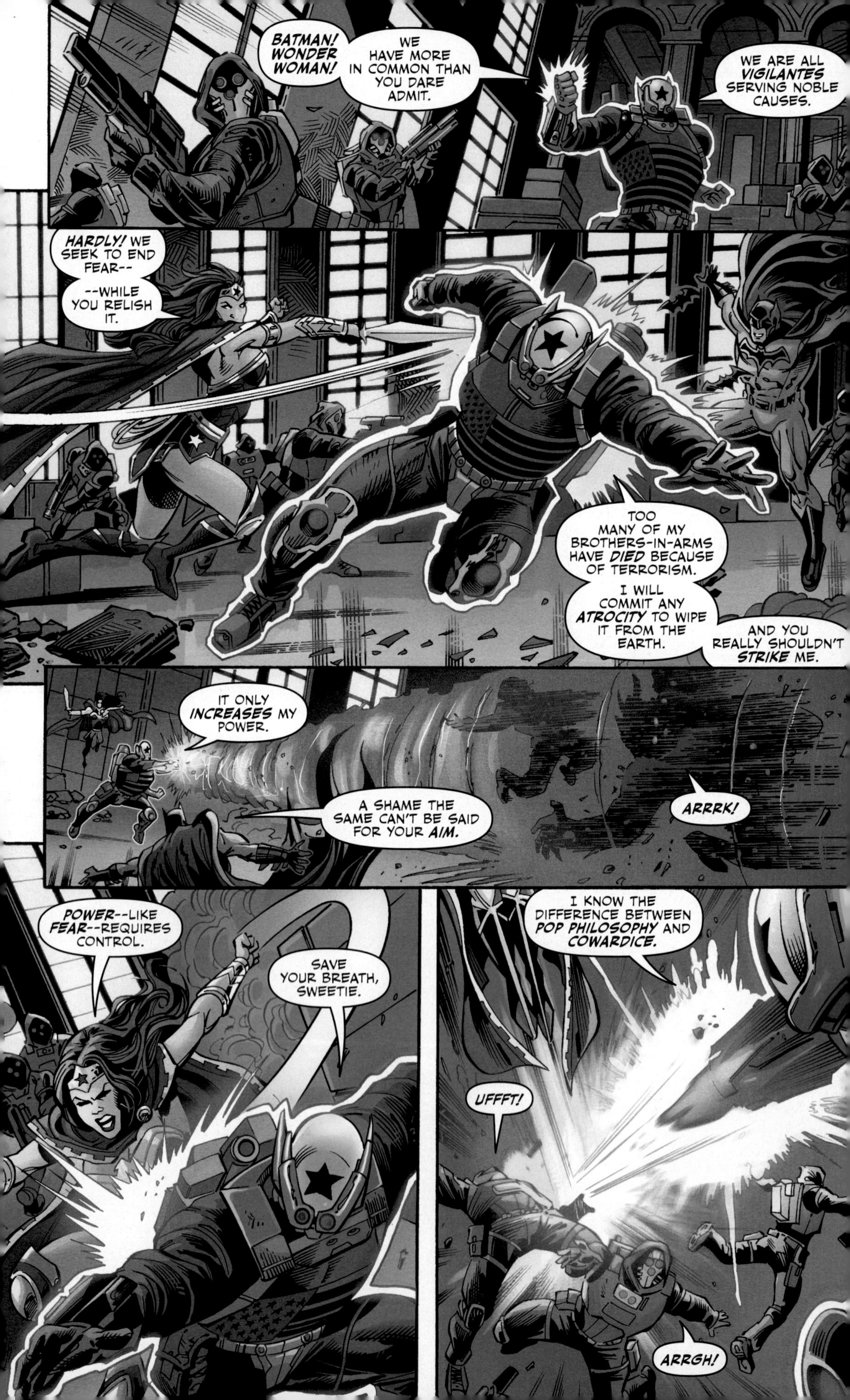
BATMAN! WONDER WOMAN!
WE HAVE MORE IN COMMON THAN YOU DARE ADMIT.
WE ARE ALL VIGILANTES SERVING NOBLE CAUSES.
HARDLY! WE SEEK TO END FEAR--
--WHILE YOU RELISH IT.
TOO MANY OF MY BROTHERS-IN-ARMS HAVE DIED BECAUSE OF TERRORISM.
I WILL COMMIT ANY ATROCITY TO WIPE IT FROM THE EARTH.
AND YOU REALLY SHOULDN'T STRIKE ME.
IT ONLY INCREASES MY POWER.
A SHAME THE SAME CAN'T BE SAID FOR YOUR AIM.
ARRRK!
POWER--LIKE FEAR--REQUIRES CONTROL.
SAVE YOUR BREATH, SWEETIE.
I KNOW THE DIFFERENCE BETWEEN POP PHILOSOPHY AND COWARDICE.
UFFFT!
ARRGH!

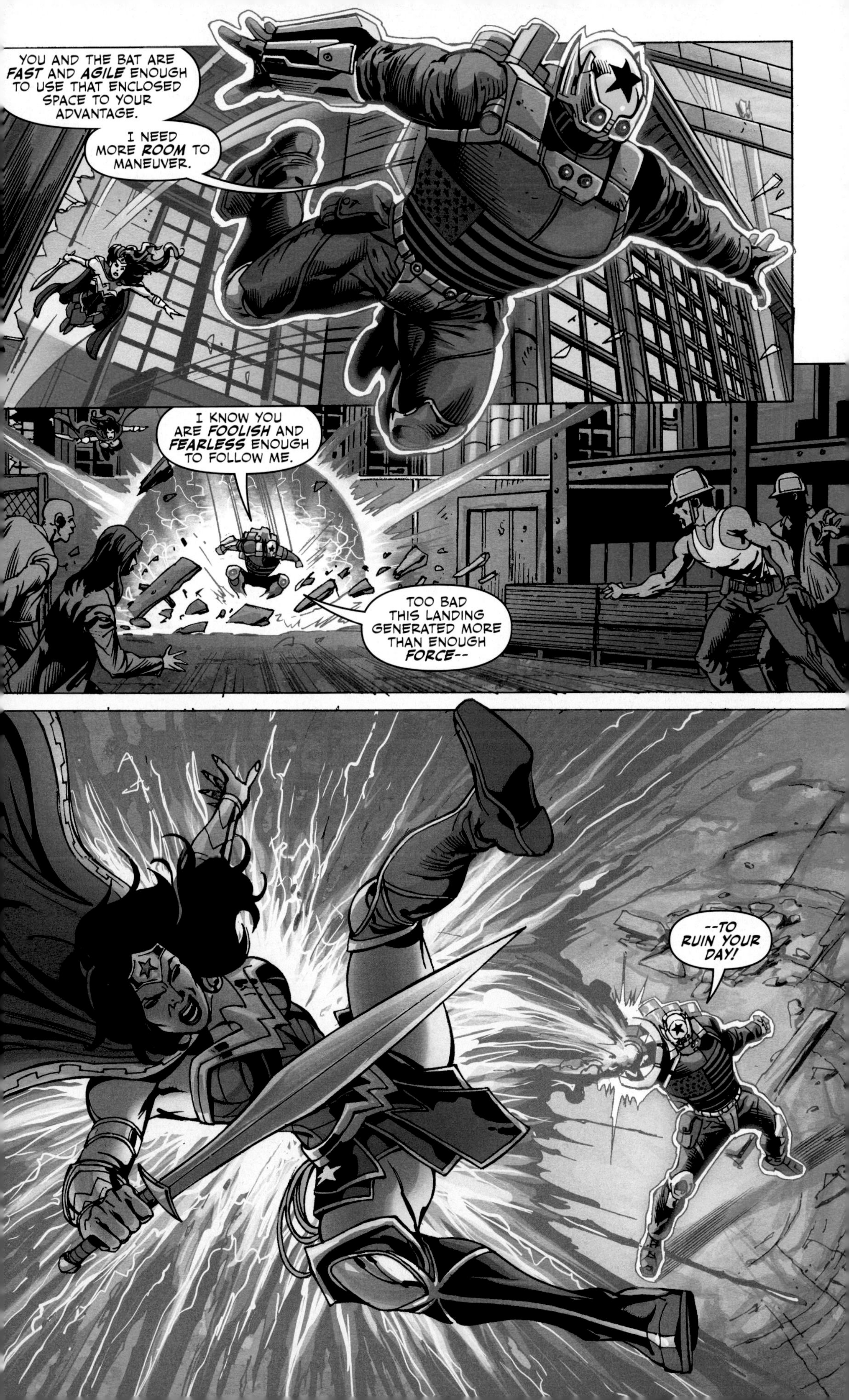
YOU AND THE BAT ARE FAST AND AGILE ENOUGH TO USE THAT ENCLOSED SPACE TO YOUR ADVANTAGE.
I NEED MORE ROOM TO MANEUVER.
I KNOW YOU ARE FOOLISH AND FEARLESS ENOUGH TO FOLLOW ME.
TOO BAD THIS LANDING GENERATED MORE THAN ENOUGH FORCE--
--TO RUIN YOUR DAY!

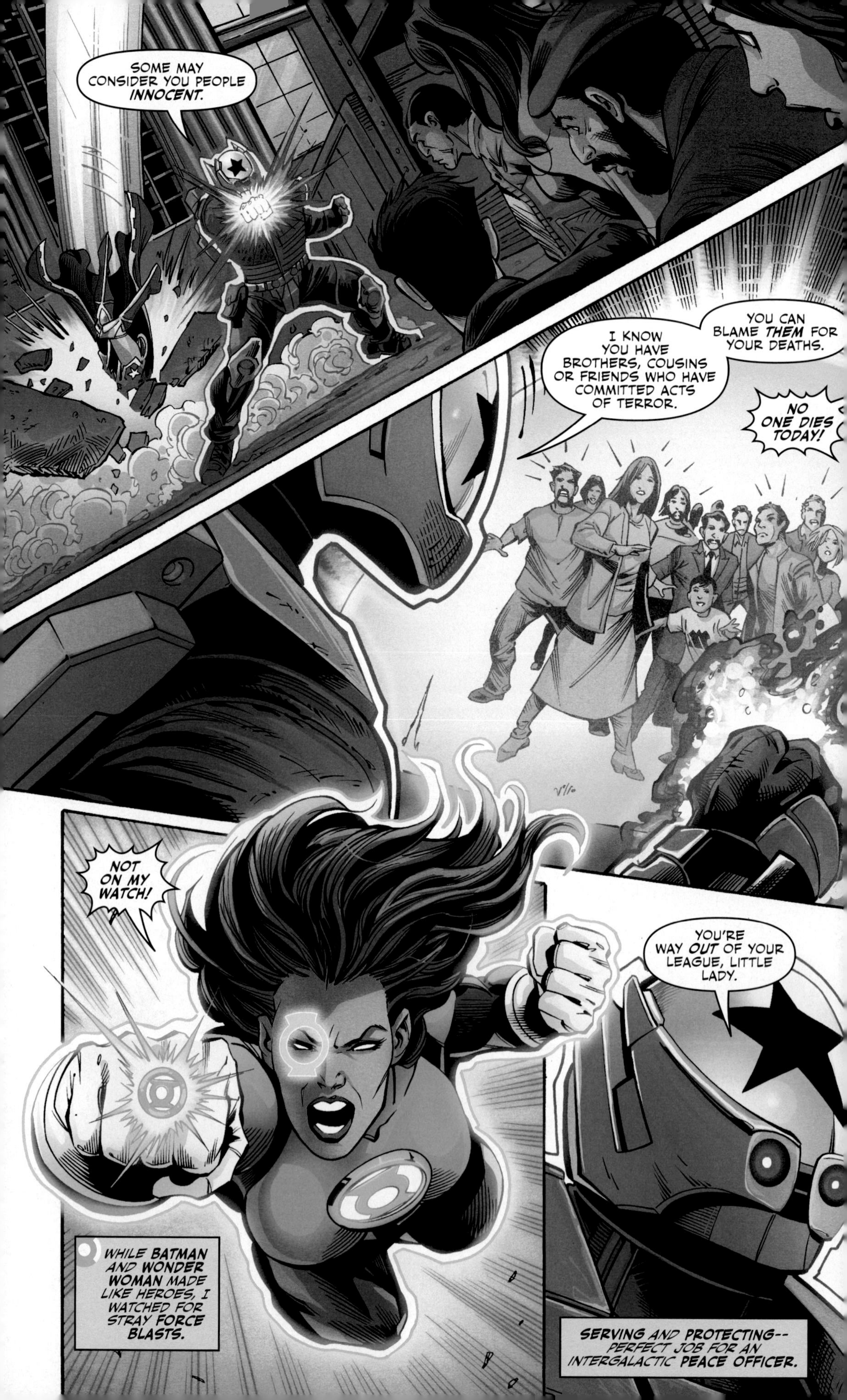
SOME MAY CONSIDER YOU PEOPLE *INNOCENT*.
I KNOW YOU HAVE BROTHERS, COUSINS OR FRIENDS WHO HAVE COMMITTED ACTS OF TERROR.
YOU CAN BLAME *THEM* FOR YOUR DEATHS.
NO ONE DIES TODAY!
NOT ON MY WATCH!
WHILE **BATMAN** AND **WONDER WOMAN** MADE LIKE HEROES, I WATCHED FOR STRAY **FORCE BLASTS**.
YOU'RE WAY *OUT* OF YOUR LEAGUE, LITTLE LADY.
SERVING AND **PROTECTING**-- PERFECT JOB FOR AN INTERGALACTIC **PEACE OFFICER**.

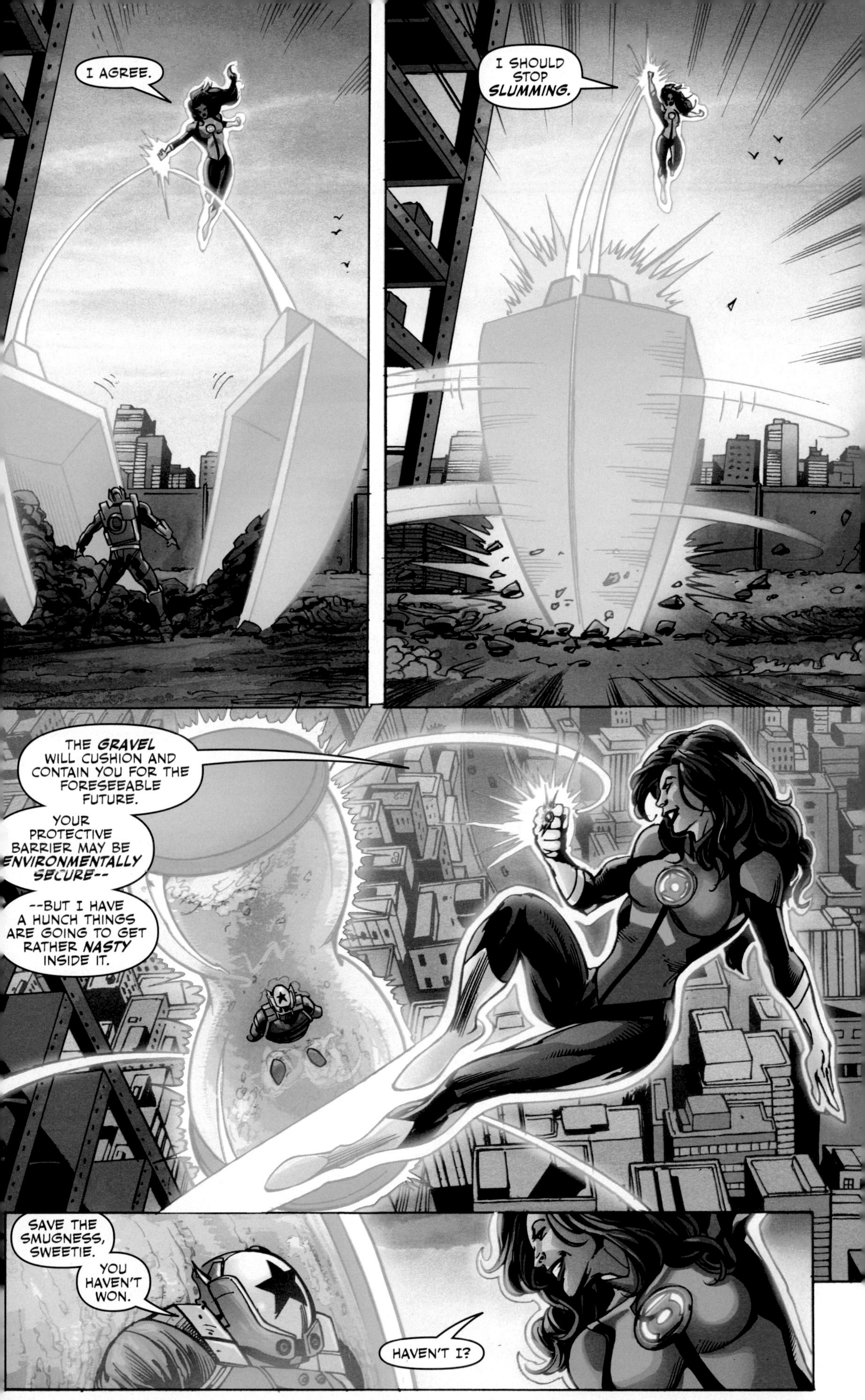
I AGREE.
I SHOULD STOP SLUMMING.
THE GRAVEL WILL CUSHION AND CONTAIN YOU FOR THE FORESEEABLE FUTURE.
YOUR PROTECTIVE BARRIER MAY BE ENVIRONMENTALLY SECURE--
--BUT I HAVE A HUNCH THINGS ARE GOING TO GET RATHER NASTY INSIDE IT.
SAVE THE SMUGNESS, SWEETIE.
YOU HAVEN'T WON.
HAVEN'T I?

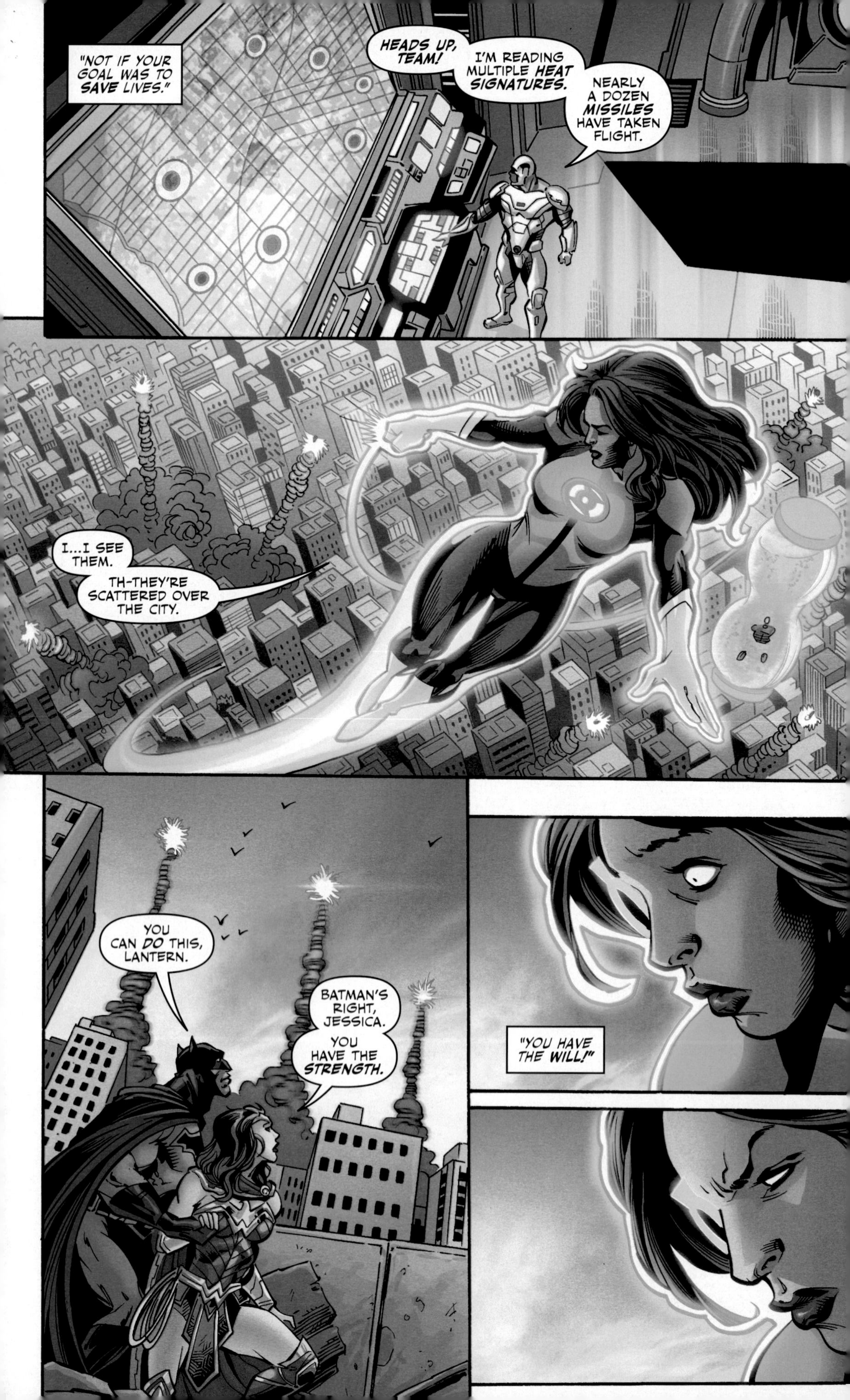
"NOT IF YOUR GOAL WAS TO SAVE LIVES."
HEADS UP, TEAM!
I'M READING MULTIPLE HEAT SIGNATURES.
NEARLY A DOZEN MISSILES HAVE TAKEN FLIGHT.
I...I SEE THEM.
TH-THEY'RE SCATTERED OVER THE CITY.
YOU CAN DO THIS, LANTERN.
BATMAN'S RIGHT, JESSICA.
YOU HAVE THE STRENGTH.
"YOU HAVE THE WILL!"

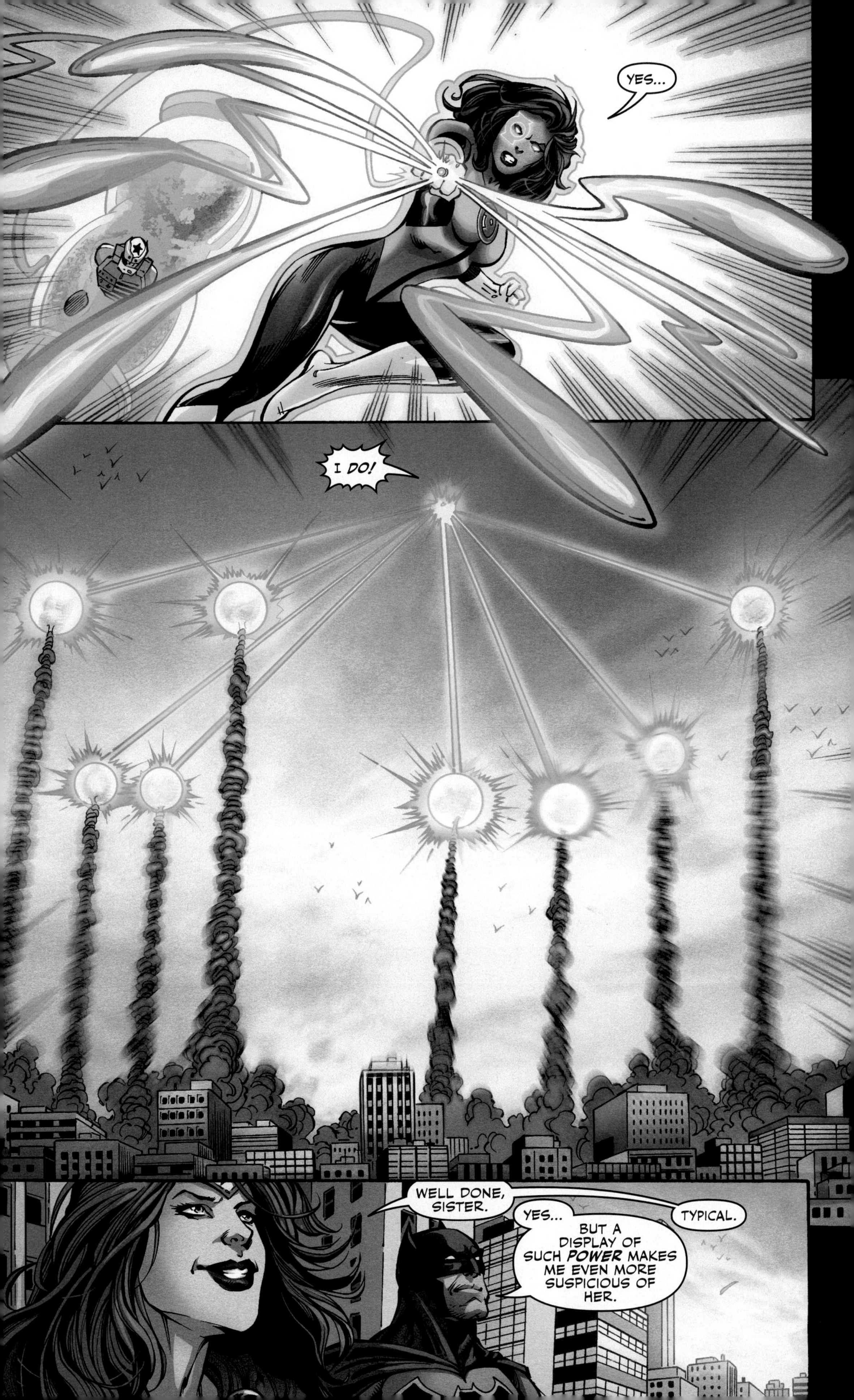

YES...
I DO!
WELL DONE, SISTER.
YES...
TYPICAL.
BUT A DISPLAY OF SUCH POWER MAKES ME EVEN MORE SUSPICIOUS OF HER.

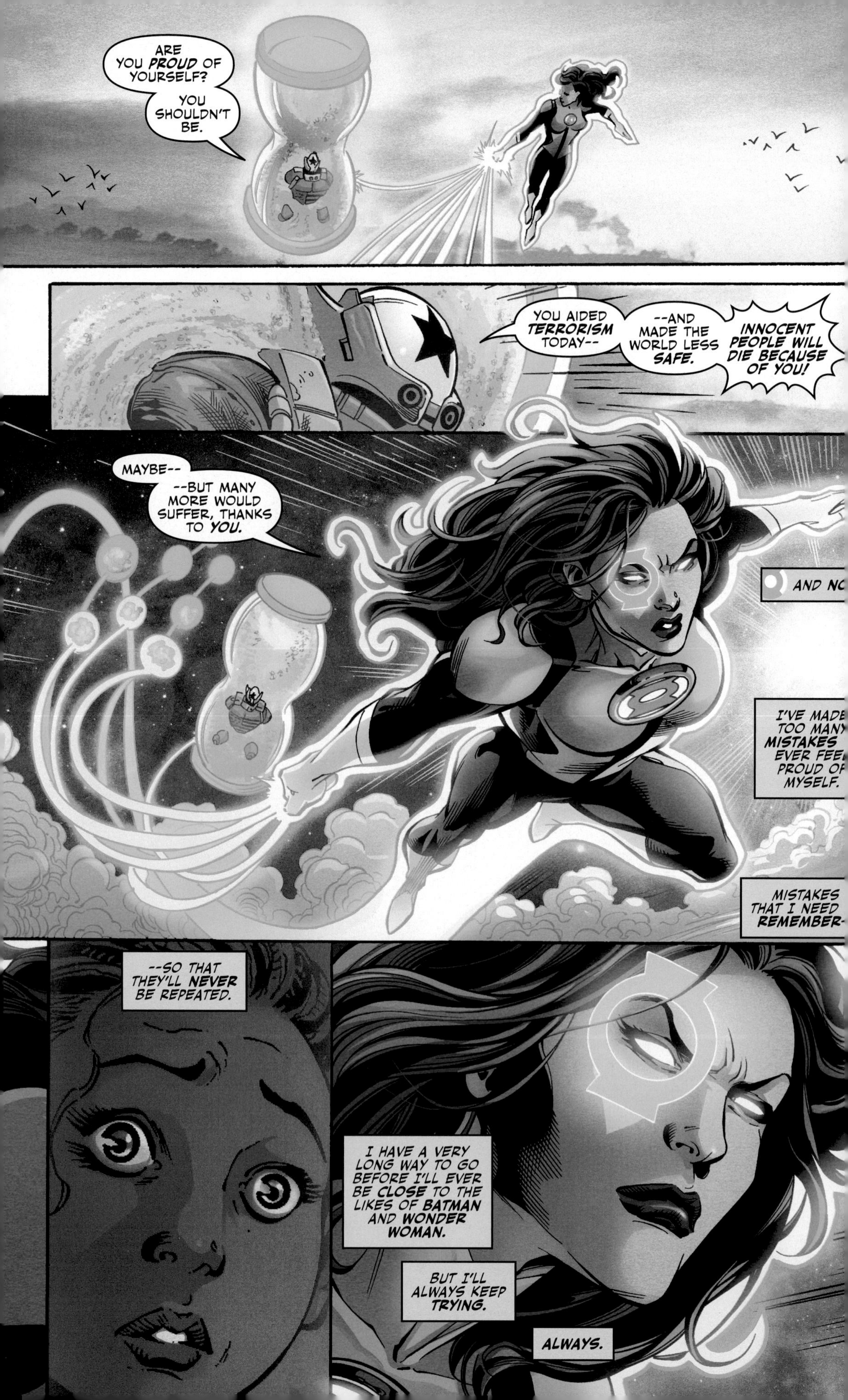
ARE YOU PROUD OF YOURSELF?
YOU SHOULDN'T BE.
YOU AIDED TERRORISM TODAY--
--AND MADE THE WORLD LESS SAFE.
INNOCENT PEOPLE WILL DIE BECAUSE OF YOU!
MAYBE--
--BUT MANY MORE WOULD SUFFER, THANKS TO YOU.
AND
I'VE MADE TOO MANY MISTAKES EVER FEEL PROUD OF MYSELF.
MISTAKES THAT I NEED REMEMBER-
--SO THAT THEY'LL NEVER BE REPEATED.
I HAVE A VERY LONG WAY TO GO BEFORE I'LL EVER BE CLOSE TO THE LIKES OF BATMAN AND WONDER WOMAN.
BUT I'LL ALWAYS KEEP TRYING.
ALWAYS.

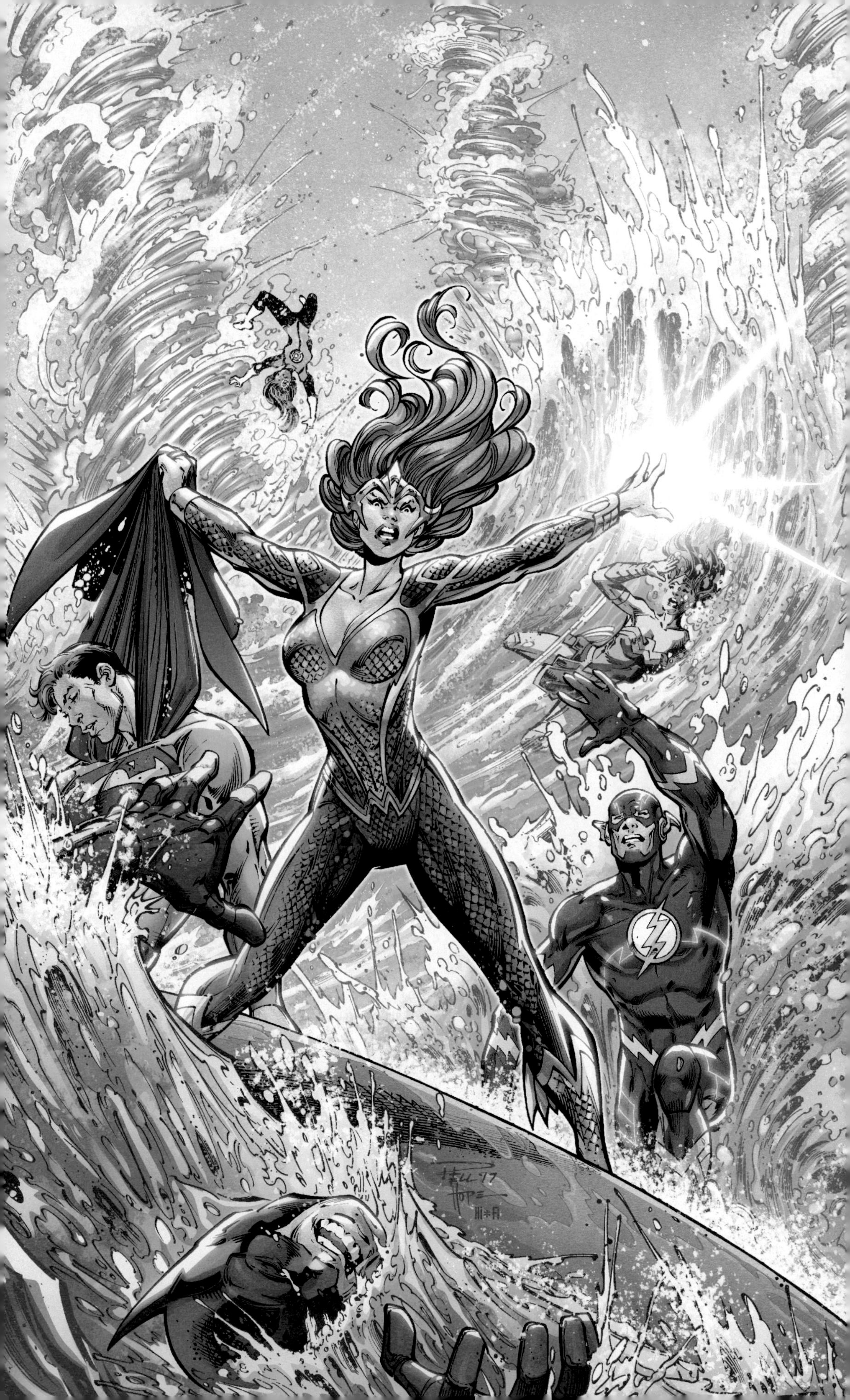
HOPE
Hi*Fi

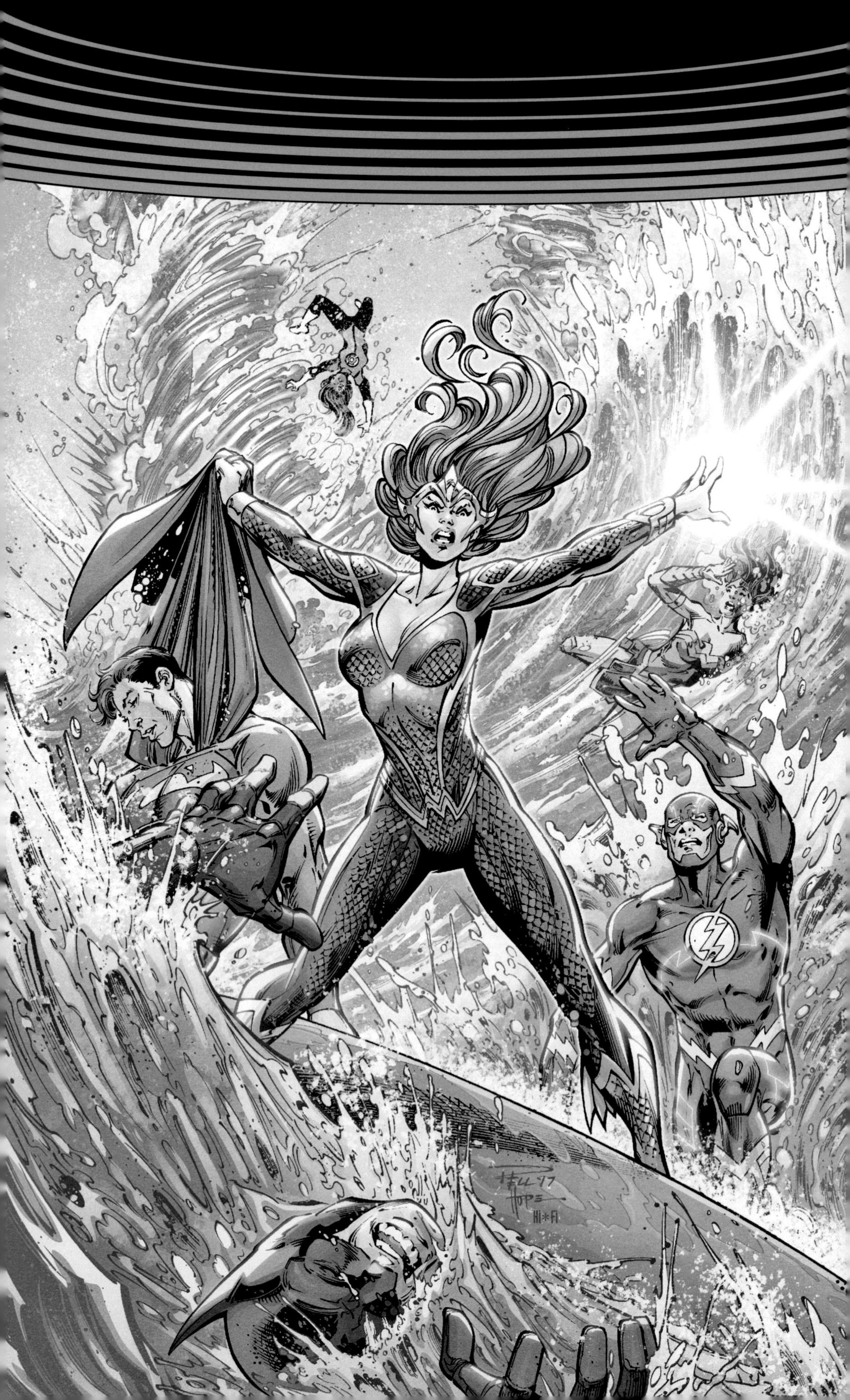

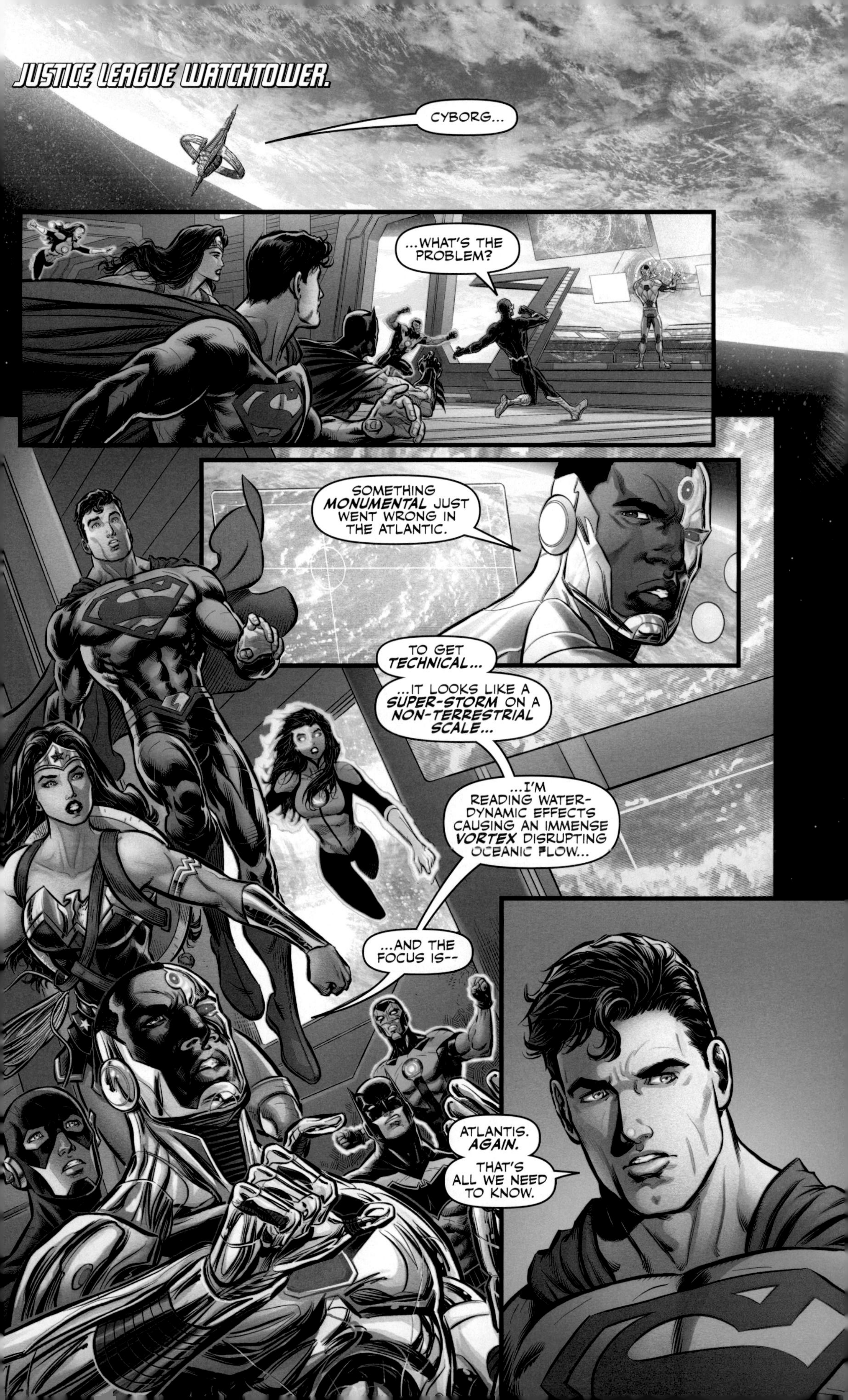
JUSTICE LEAGUE WATCHTOWER.
CYBORG...
...WHAT'S THE PROBLEM?
SOMETHING MONUMENTAL JUST WENT WRONG IN THE ATLANTIC.
TO GET TECHNICAL...
...IT LOOKS LIKE A SUPER-STORM ON A NON-TERRESTRIAL SCALE...
...I'M READING WATER-DYNAMIC EFFECTS CAUSING AN IMMENSE VORTEX DISRUPTING OCEANIC FLOW...
...AND THE FOCUS IS--
ATLANTIS. AGAIN.
THAT'S ALL WE NEED TO KNOW.

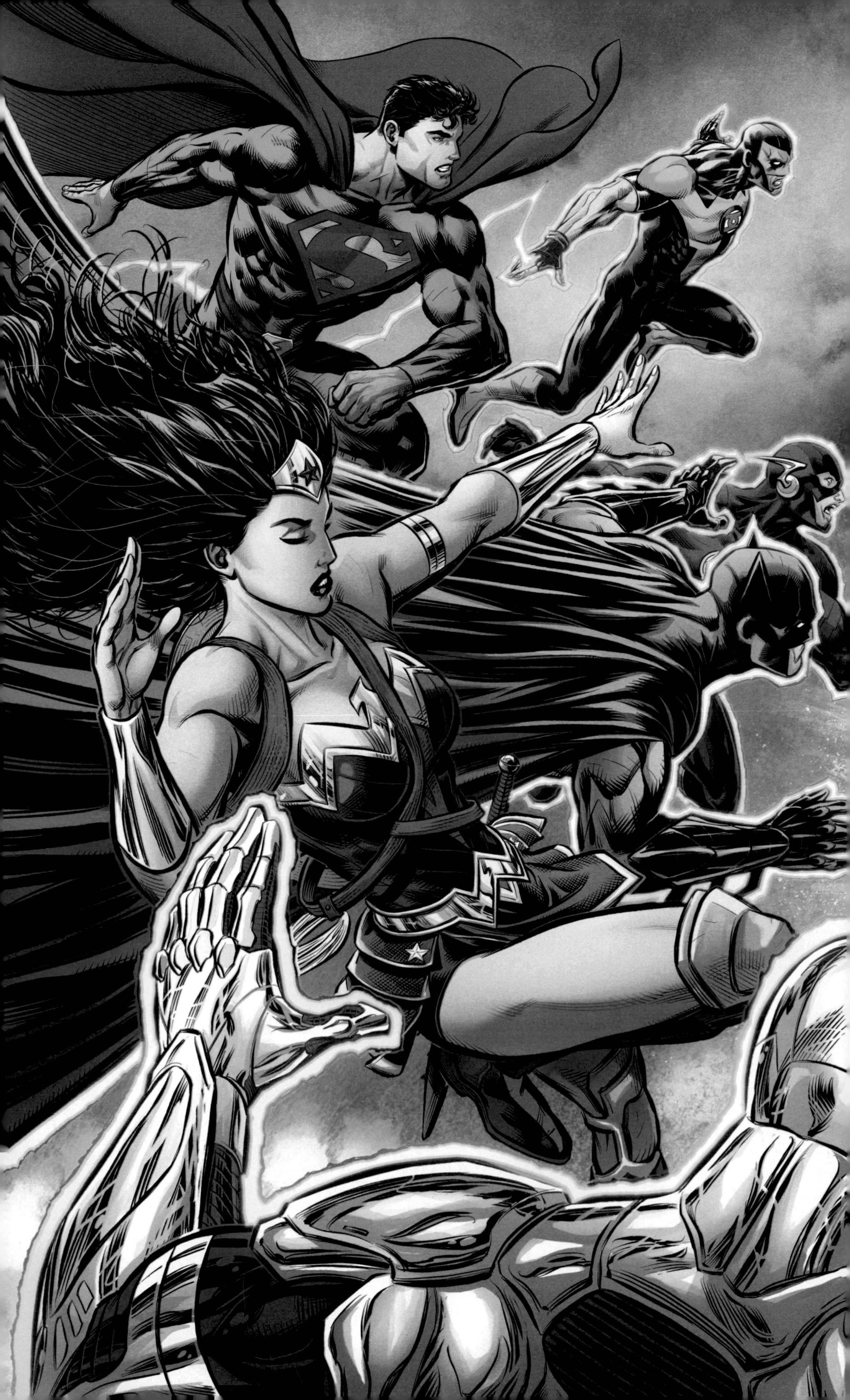

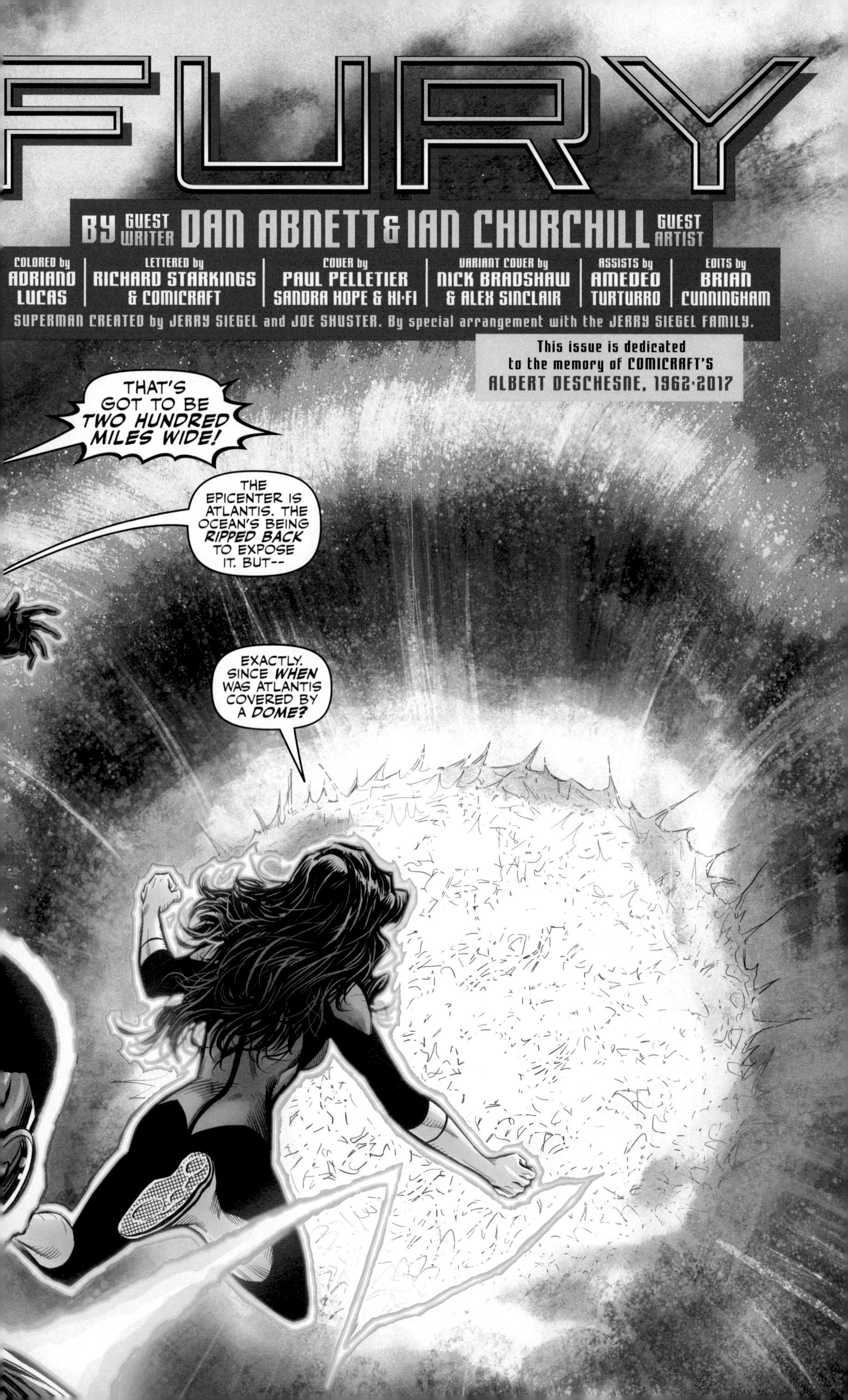
FURY
BY GUEST WRITER DAN ABNETT & IAN CHURCHILL GUEST ARTIST
COLORED by ADRIANO LUCAS
LETTERED by RICHARD STARKINGS & COMICRAFT
COVER by PAUL PELLETIER SANDRA HOPE & HI-FI
VARIANT COVER by NICK BRADSHAW & ALEX SINCLAIR
ASSISTS by AMEDEO TURTURRO
EDITS by BRIAN CUNNINGHAM
SUPERMAN CREATED by JERRY SIEGEL and JOE SHUSTER. By special arrangement with the JERRY SIEGEL FAMILY.
This issue is dedicated to the memory of COMICRAFT'S ALBERT DESCHESNE, 1962-2017
THAT'S GOT TO BE TWO HUNDRED MILES WIDE!
THE EPICENTER IS ATLANTIS. THE OCEAN'S BEING RIPPED BACK TO EXPOSE IT. BUT--
EXACTLY. SINCE WHEN WAS ATLANTIS COVERED BY A DOME?

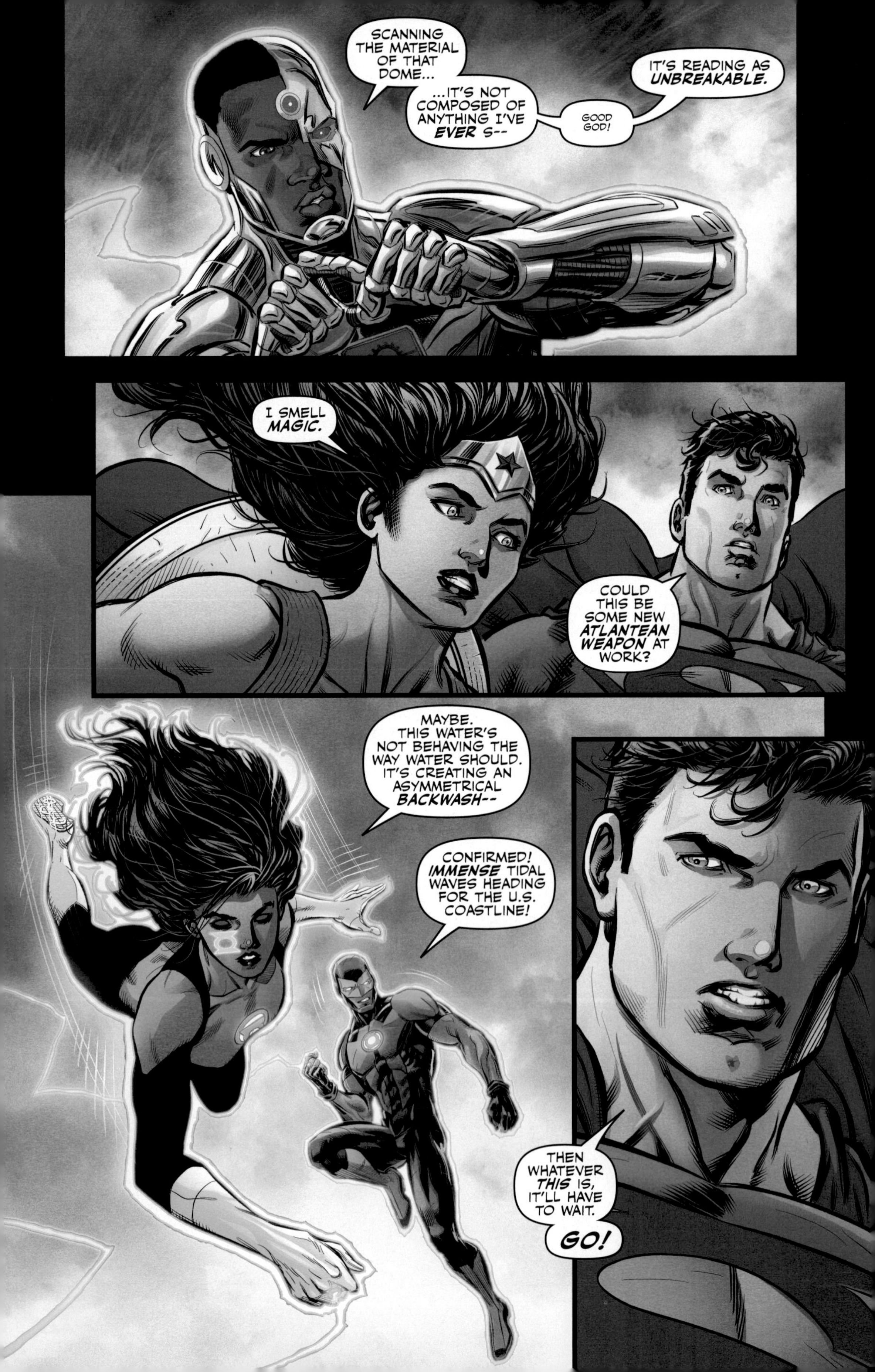
SCANNING THE MATERIAL OF THAT DOME...
...IT'S NOT COMPOSED OF ANYTHING I'VE EVER S--
GOOD GOD!
IT'S READING AS UNBREAKABLE.
I SMELL MAGIC.
COULD THIS BE SOME NEW ATLANTEAN WEAPON AT WORK?
MAYBE. THIS WATER'S NOT BEHAVING THE WAY WATER SHOULD. IT'S CREATING AN ASYMMETRICAL BACKWASH--
CONFIRMED! IMMENSE TIDAL WAVES HEADING FOR THE U.S. COASTLINE!
THEN WHATEVER THIS IS, IT'LL HAVE TO WAIT.
GO!

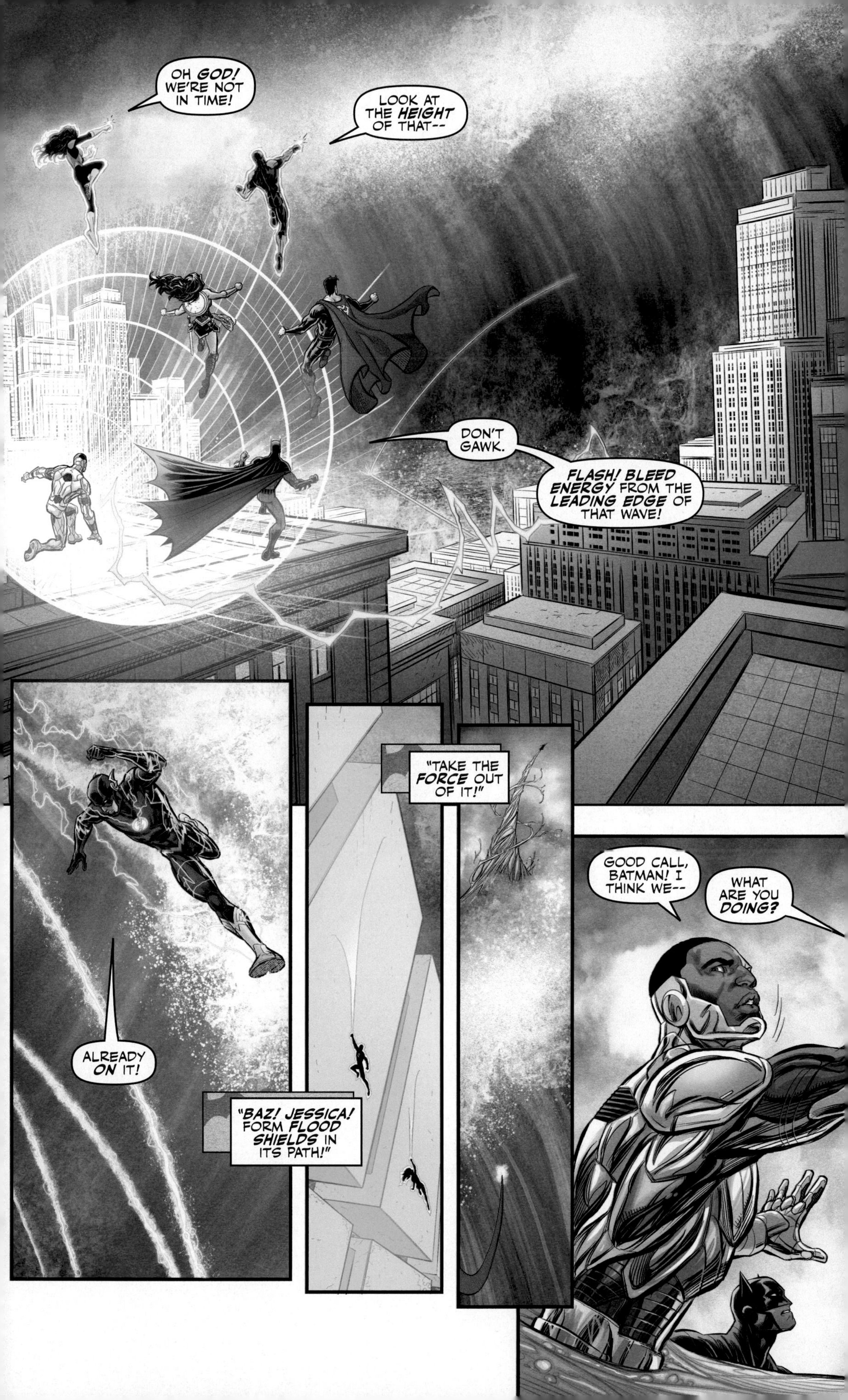

OH GOD! WE'RE NOT IN TIME!
LOOK AT THE HEIGHT OF THAT--
DON'T GAWK.
FLASH! BLEED ENERGY FROM THE LEADING EDGE OF THAT WAVE!
ALREADY ON IT!
"BAZ! JESSICA! FORM FLOOD SHIELDS IN ITS PATH!"
"TAKE THE FORCE OUT OF IT!"
GOOD CALL, BATMAN! I THINK WE--
WHAT ARE YOU DOING?

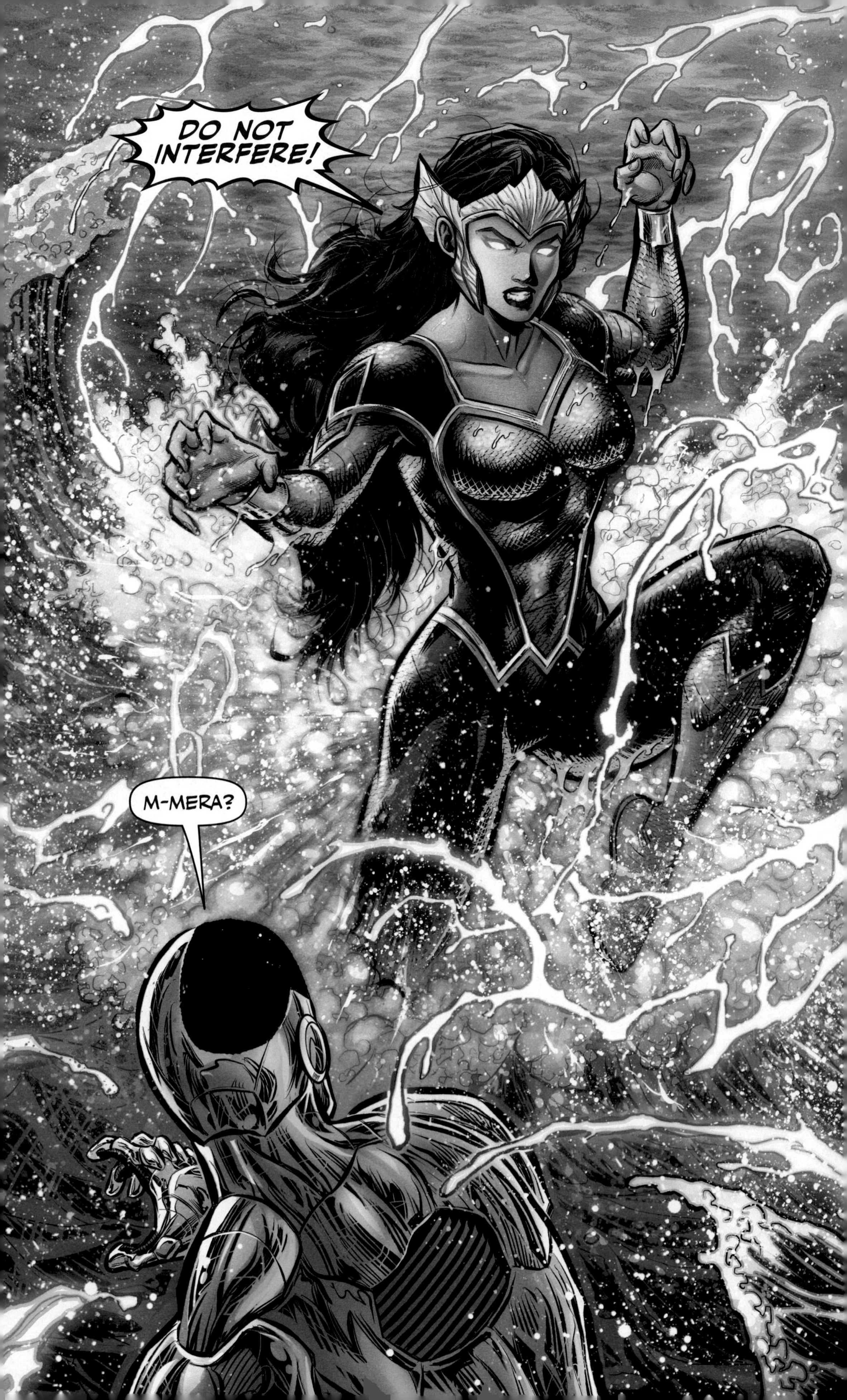
DO NOT INTERFERE!
M-MERA?

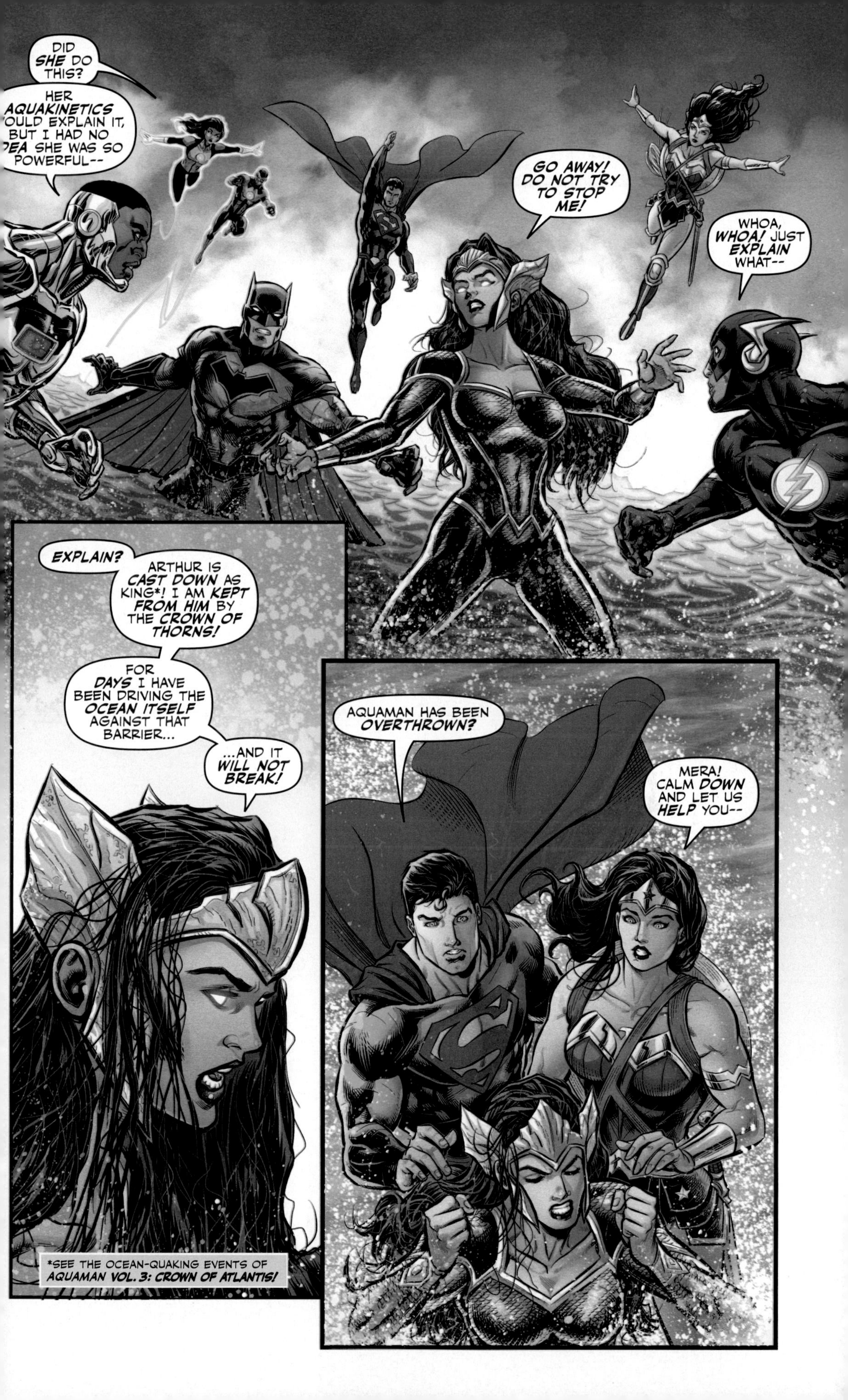
DID SHE DO THIS?
HER AQUAKINETICS OULD EXPLAIN IT, BUT I HAD NO DEA SHE WAS SO POWERFUL--
GO AWAY! DO NOT TRY TO STOP ME!
WHOA, WHOA! JUST EXPLAIN WHAT--
EXPLAIN?
ARTHUR IS CAST DOWN AS KING*! I AM KEPT FROM HIM BY THE CROWN OF THORNS!
FOR DAYS I HAVE BEEN DRIVING THE OCEAN ITSELF AGAINST THAT BARRIER...
...AND IT WILL NOT BREAK!
*SEE THE OCEAN-QUAKING EVENTS OF AQUAMAN VOL. 3: CROWN OF ATLANTIS!
AQUAMAN HAS BEEN OVERTHROWN?
MERA! CALM DOWN AND LET US HELP YOU--

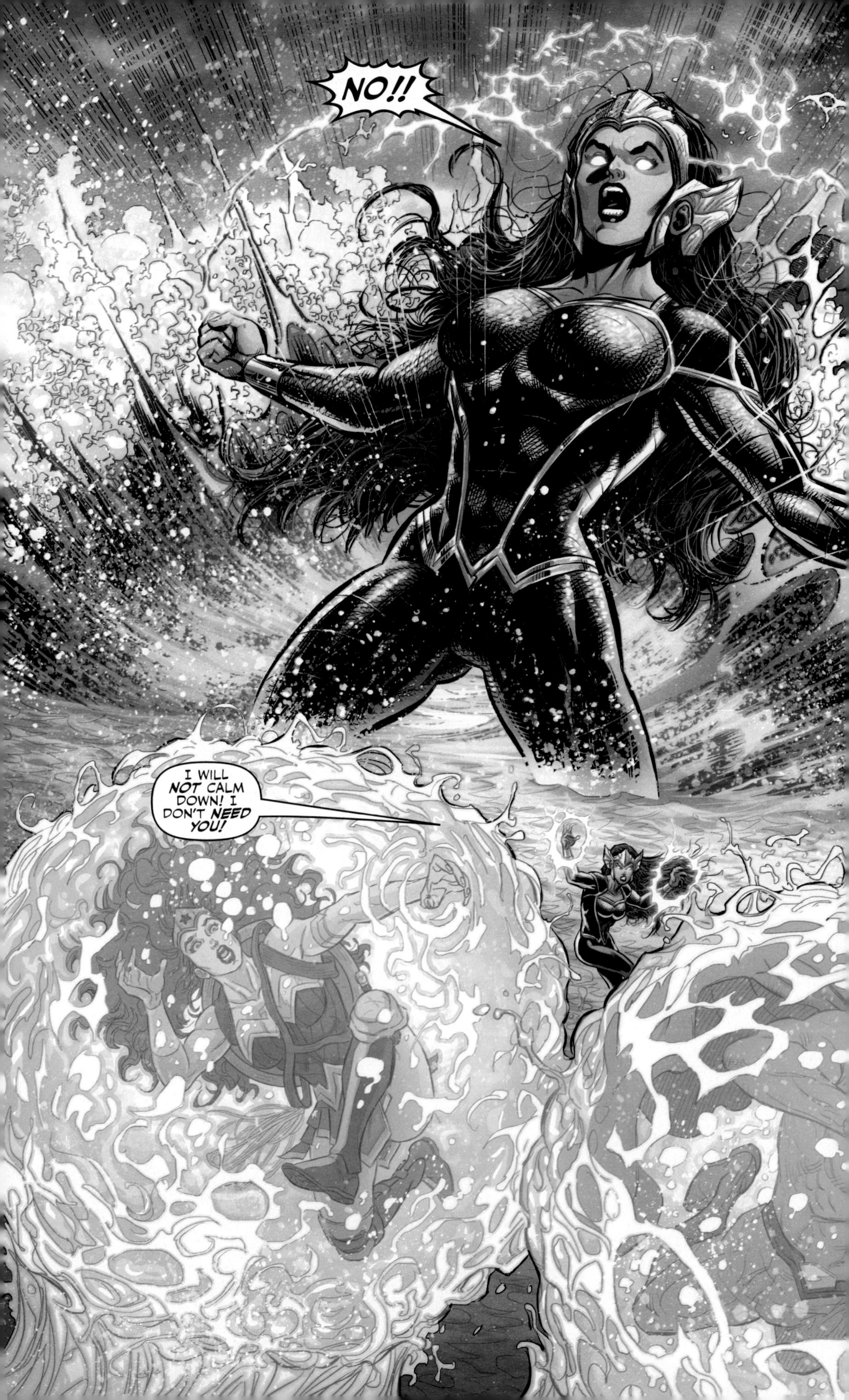
NO!!
I WILL NOT CALM DOWN! I DON'T NEED YOU!

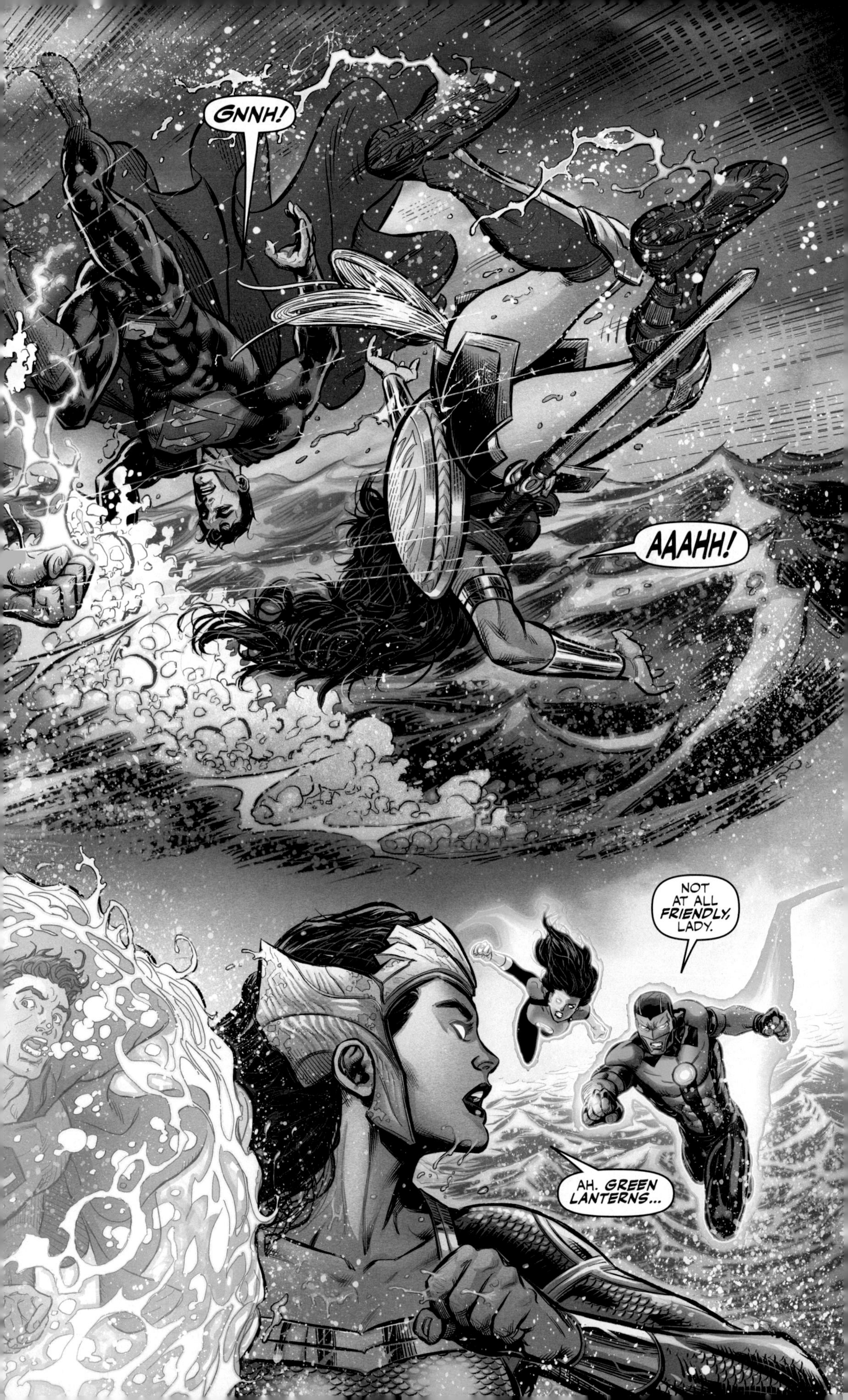
GNNH!
AAAHH!
NOT AT ALL FRIENDLY, LADY.
AH. GREEN LANTERNS...

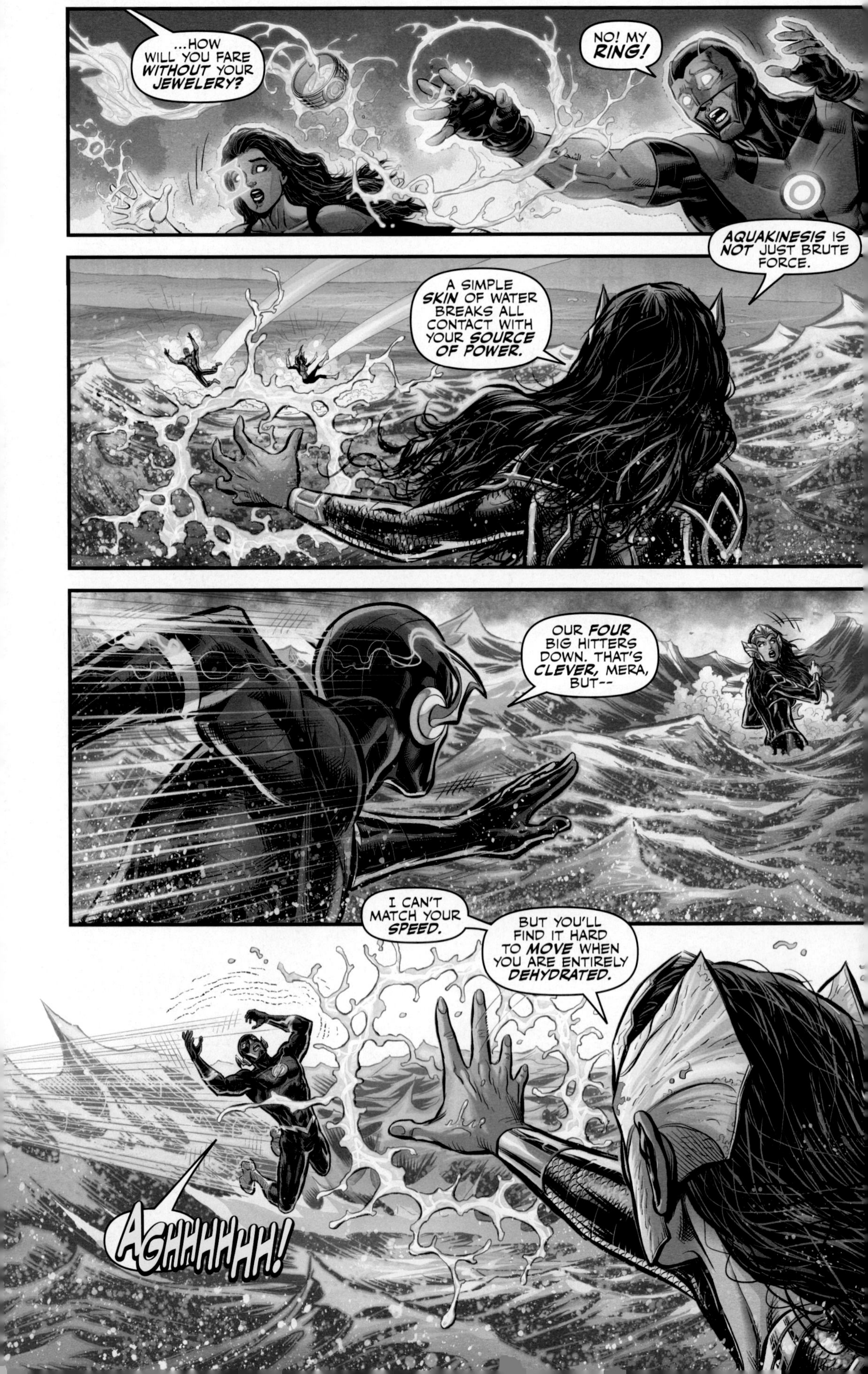
...HOW WILL YOU FARE WITHOUT YOUR JEWELERY?
NO! MY RING!
AQUAKINESIS IS NOT JUST BRUTE FORCE.
A SIMPLE SKIN OF WATER BREAKS ALL CONTACT WITH YOUR SOURCE OF POWER.
OUR FOUR BIG HITTERS DOWN. THAT'S CLEVER, MERA, BUT--
I CAN'T MATCH YOUR SPEED.
BUT YOU'LL FIND IT HARD TO MOVE WHEN YOU ARE ENTIRELY DEHYDRATED.
AGHHHHHH!

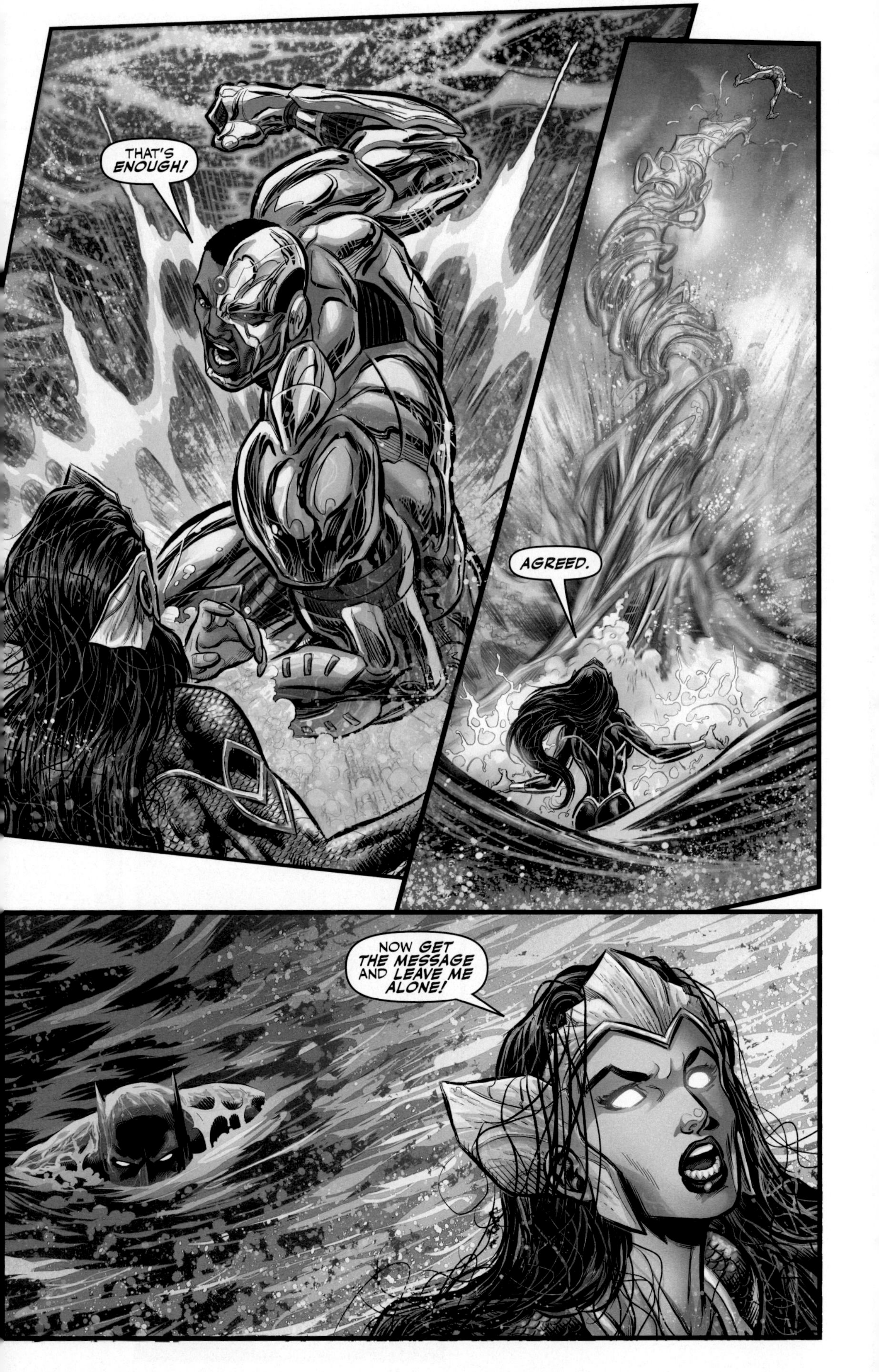
THAT'S ENOUGH!
AGREED.
NOW GET THE MESSAGE AND LEAVE ME ALONE!

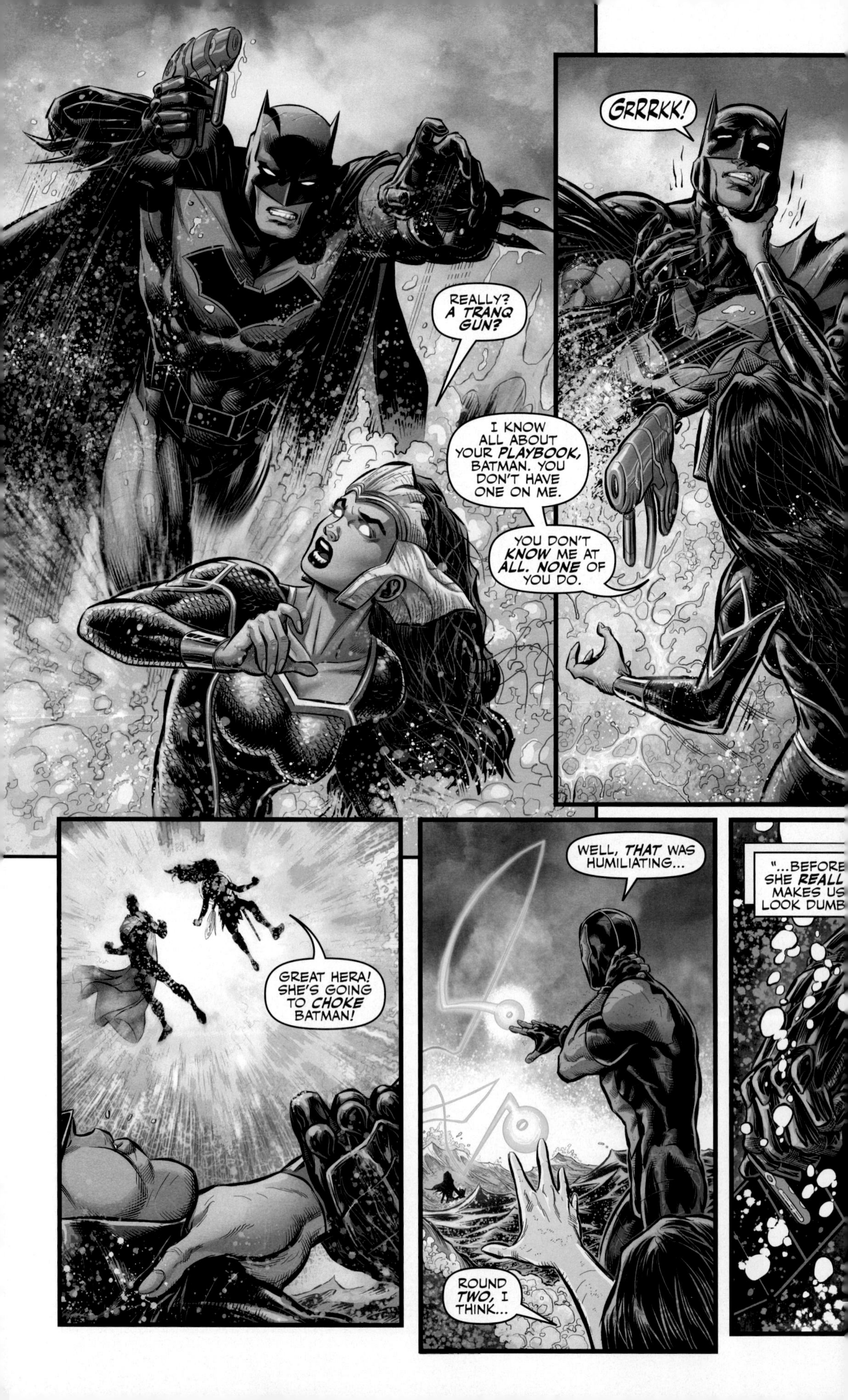
REALLY? A TRANQ GUN?
I KNOW ALL ABOUT YOUR PLAYBOOK, BATMAN. YOU DON'T HAVE ONE ON ME.
YOU DON'T KNOW ME AT ALL. NONE OF YOU DO.
GRRRKK!
GREAT HERA! SHE'S GOING TO CHOKE BATMAN!
WELL, THAT WAS HUMILIATING...
ROUND TWO, I THINK...
"...BEFORE SHE REALL MAKES US LOOK DUMB

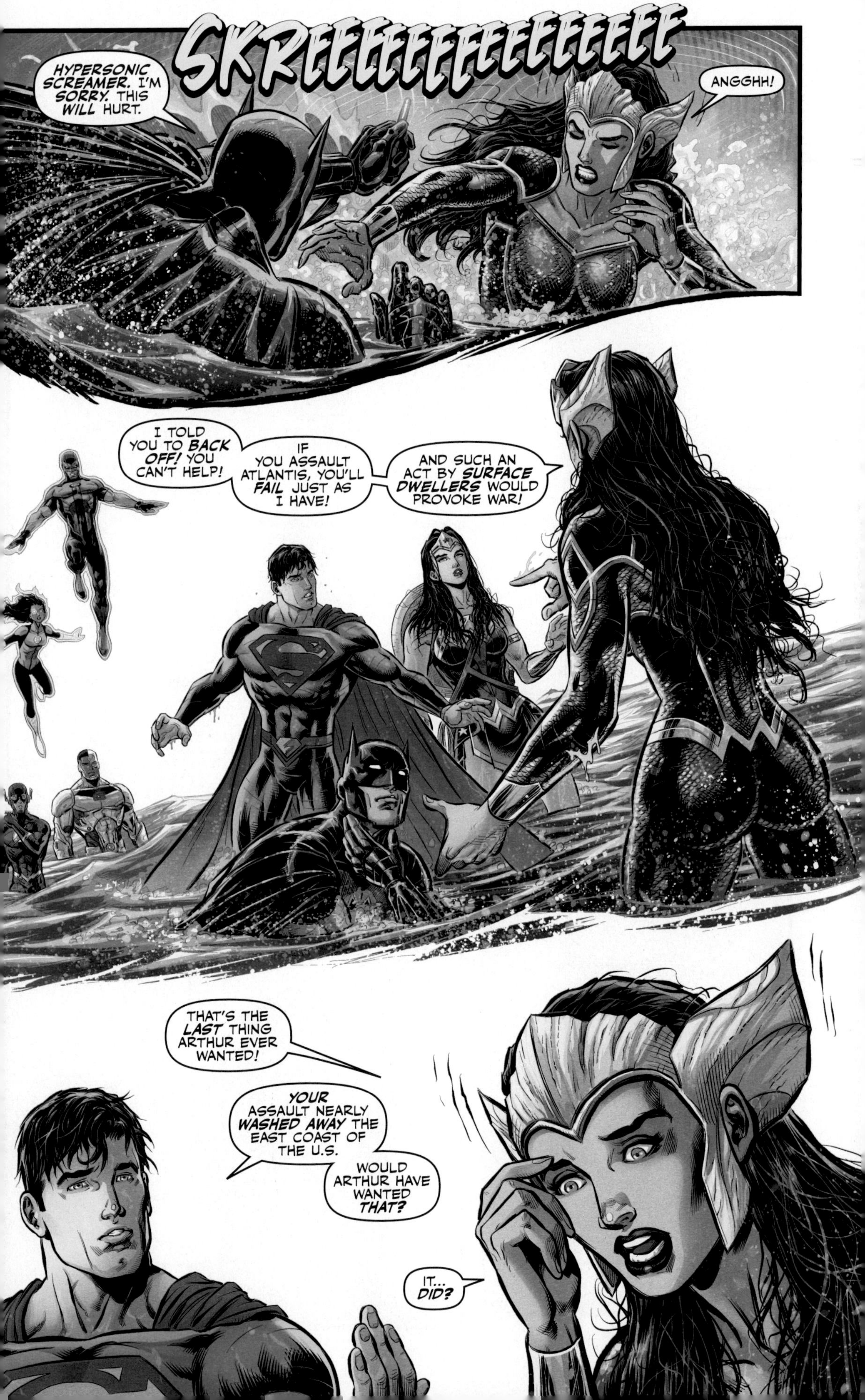
SKREEEEEEEEEEEEEEEE
HYPERSONIC SCREAMER. I'M SORRY. THIS WILL HURT.
ANGGHH!
I TOLD YOU TO BACK OFF! YOU CAN'T HELP!
IF YOU ASSAULT ATLANTIS, YOU'LL FAIL JUST AS I HAVE!
AND SUCH AN ACT BY SURFACE DWELLERS WOULD PROVOKE WAR!
THAT'S THE LAST THING ARTHUR EVER WANTED!
YOUR ASSAULT NEARLY WASHED AWAY THE EAST COAST OF THE U.S.
WOULD ARTHUR HAVE WANTED THAT?
IT... DID?

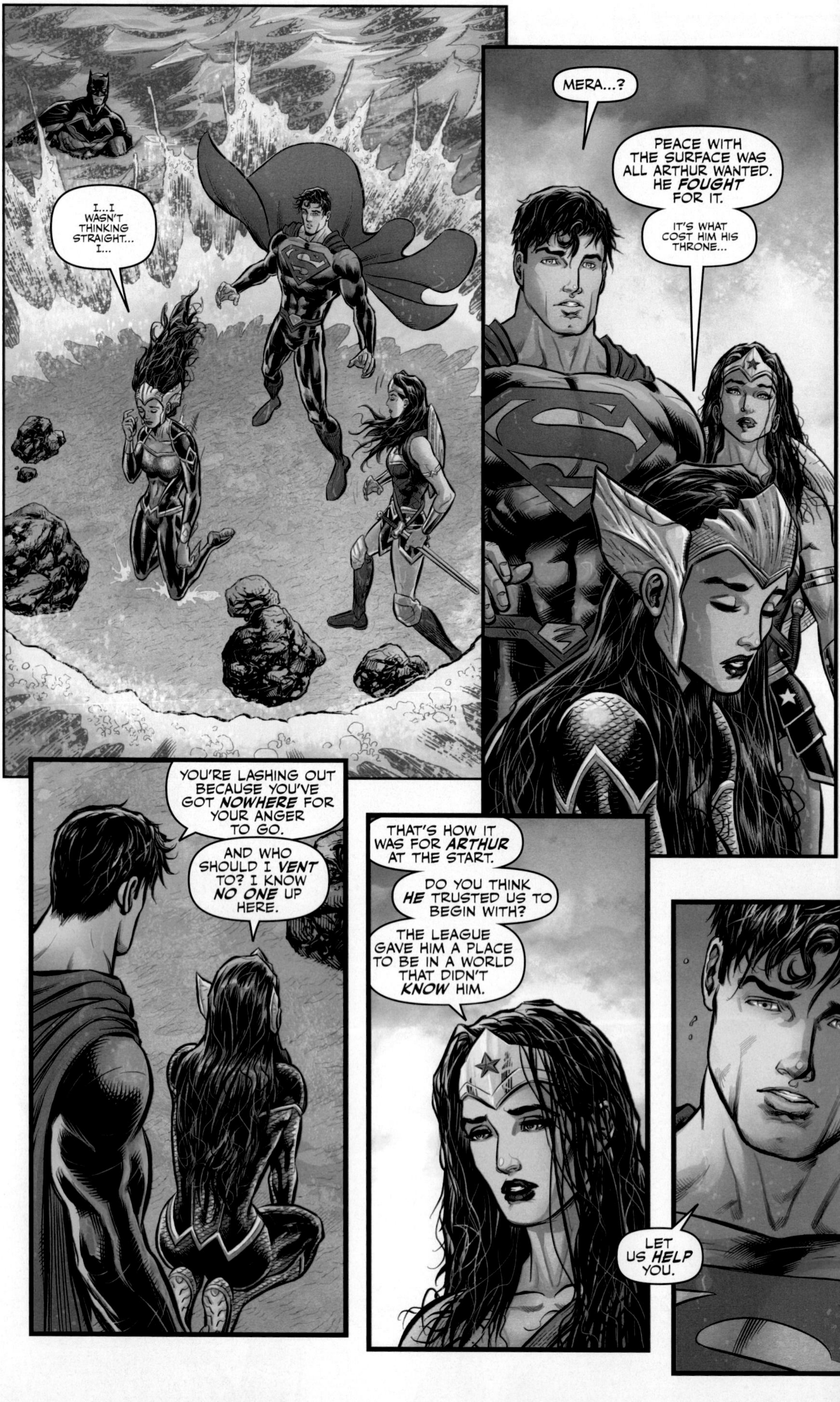
I...I WASN'T THINKING STRAIGHT... I...
MERA...?
PEACE WITH THE SURFACE WAS ALL ARTHUR WANTED. HE FOUGHT FOR IT.
IT'S WHAT COST HIM HIS THRONE...
YOU'RE LASHING OUT BECAUSE YOU'VE GOT NOWHERE FOR YOUR ANGER TO GO.
AND WHO SHOULD I VENT TO? I KNOW NO ONE UP HERE.
THAT'S HOW IT WAS FOR ARTHUR AT THE START.
DO YOU THINK HE TRUSTED US TO BEGIN WITH?
THE LEAGUE GAVE HIM A PLACE TO BE IN A WORLD THAT DIDN'T KNOW HIM.
LET US HELP YOU.

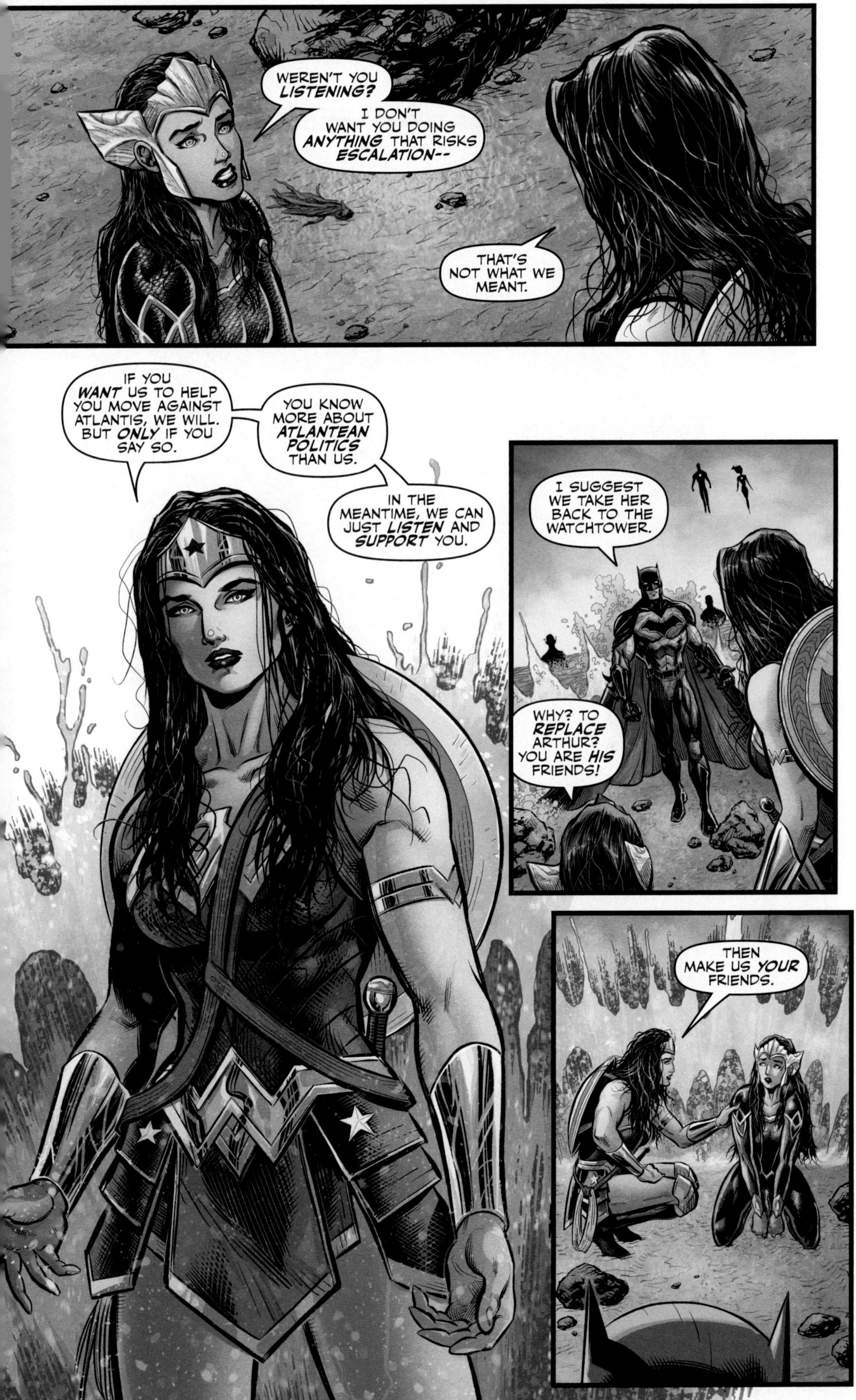
WEREN'T YOU LISTENING?
I DON'T WANT YOU DOING ANYTHING THAT RISKS ESCALATION--
THAT'S NOT WHAT WE MEANT.
IF YOU WANT US TO HELP YOU MOVE AGAINST ATLANTIS, WE WILL. BUT ONLY IF YOU SAY SO.
YOU KNOW MORE ABOUT ATLANTEAN POLITICS THAN US.
IN THE MEANTIME, WE CAN JUST LISTEN AND SUPPORT YOU.
I SUGGEST WE TAKE HER BACK TO THE WATCHTOWER.
WHY? TO REPLACE ARTHUR? YOU ARE HIS FRIENDS!
THEN MAKE US YOUR FRIENDS.

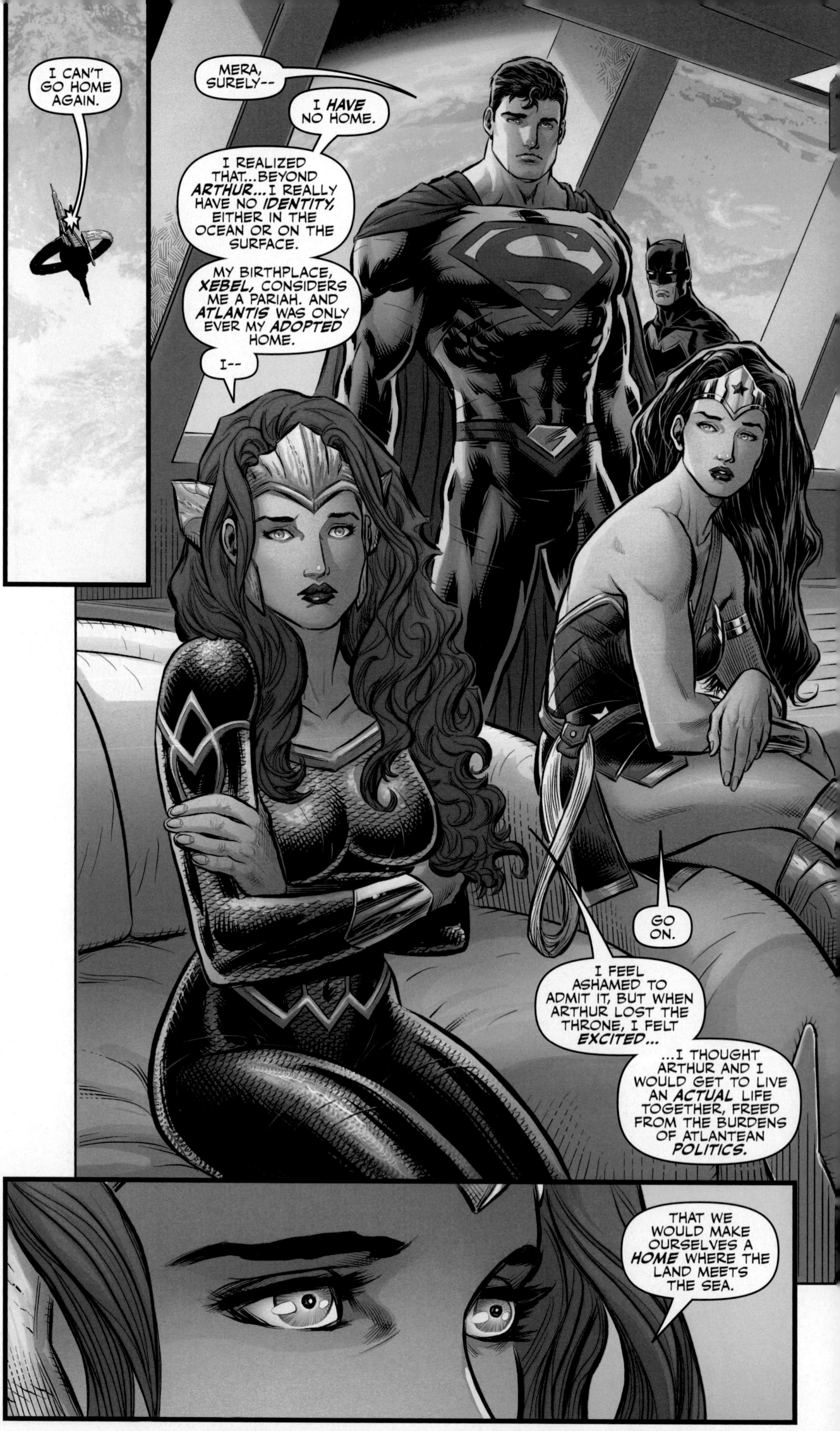
I CAN'T GO HOME AGAIN.
MERA, SURELY--
I *HAVE* NO HOME.
I REALIZED THAT...BEYOND ***ARTHUR...*** I REALLY HAVE NO *IDENTITY,* EITHER IN THE OCEAN OR ON THE SURFACE.
MY BIRTHPLACE, ***XEBEL,*** CONSIDERS ME A PARIAH. AND ***ATLANTIS*** WAS ONLY EVER MY *ADOPTED* HOME.
I--
GO ON.
I FEEL ASHAMED TO ADMIT IT, BUT WHEN ARTHUR LOST THE THRONE, I FELT ***EXCITED...***
...I THOUGHT ARTHUR AND I WOULD GET TO LIVE AN *ACTUAL* LIFE TOGETHER, FREED FROM THE BURDENS OF ATLANTEAN *POLITICS.*
THAT WE WOULD MAKE OURSELVES A ***HOME*** WHERE THE LAND MEETS THE SEA.

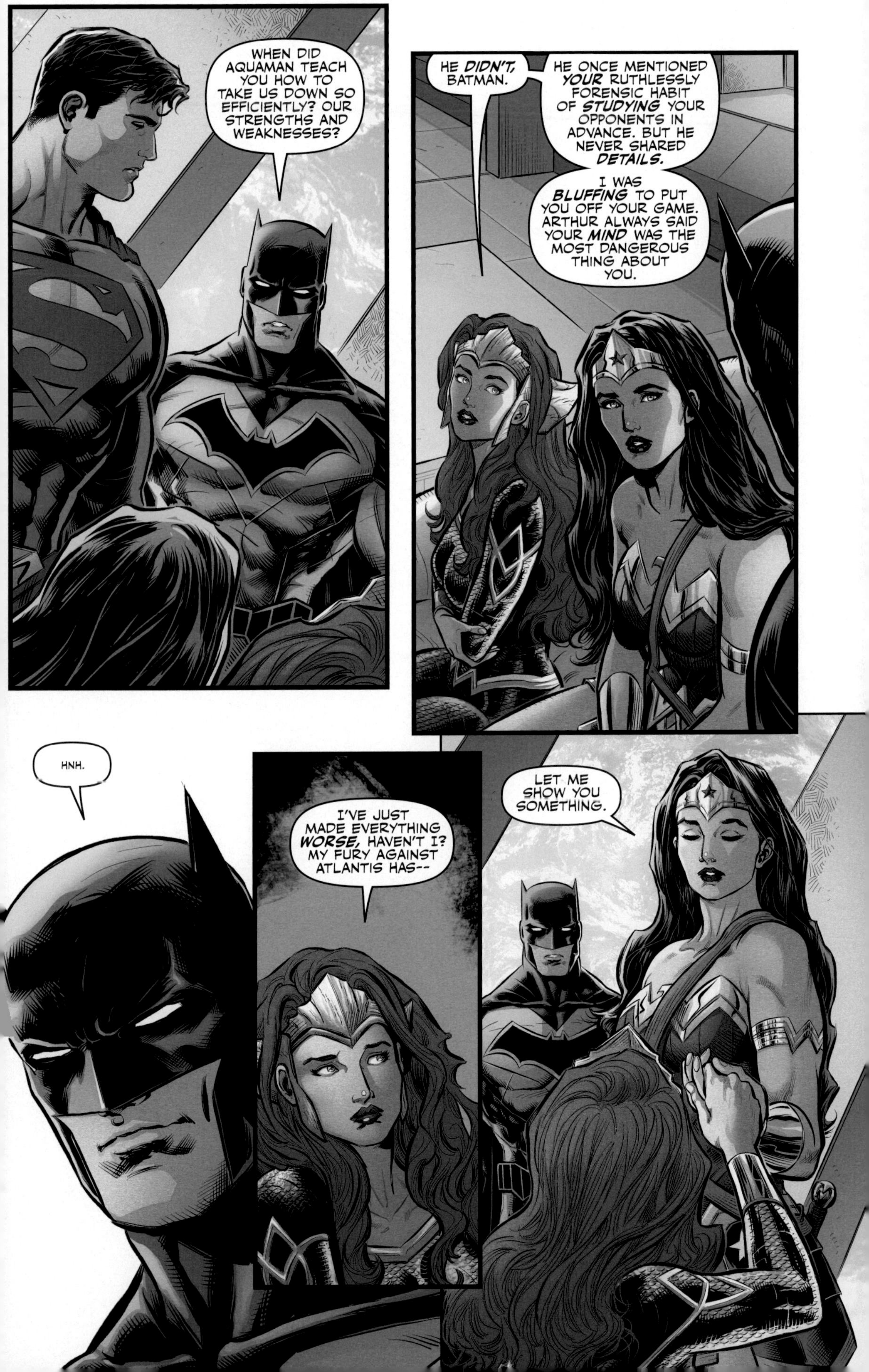
WHEN DID AQUAMAN TEACH YOU HOW TO TAKE US DOWN SO EFFICIENTLY? OUR STRENGTHS AND WEAKNESSES?
HE *DIDN'T,* BATMAN.
HE ONCE MENTIONED *YOUR* RUTHLESSLY FORENSIC HABIT OF *STUDYING* YOUR OPPONENTS IN ADVANCE. BUT HE NEVER SHARED *DETAILS.*
I WAS *BLUFFING* TO PUT YOU OFF YOUR GAME. ARTHUR ALWAYS SAID YOUR *MIND* WAS THE MOST DANGEROUS THING ABOUT YOU.
HNH.
I'VE JUST MADE EVERYTHING *WORSE,* HAVEN'T I? MY FURY AGAINST ATLANTIS HAS--
LET ME SHOW YOU SOMETHING.

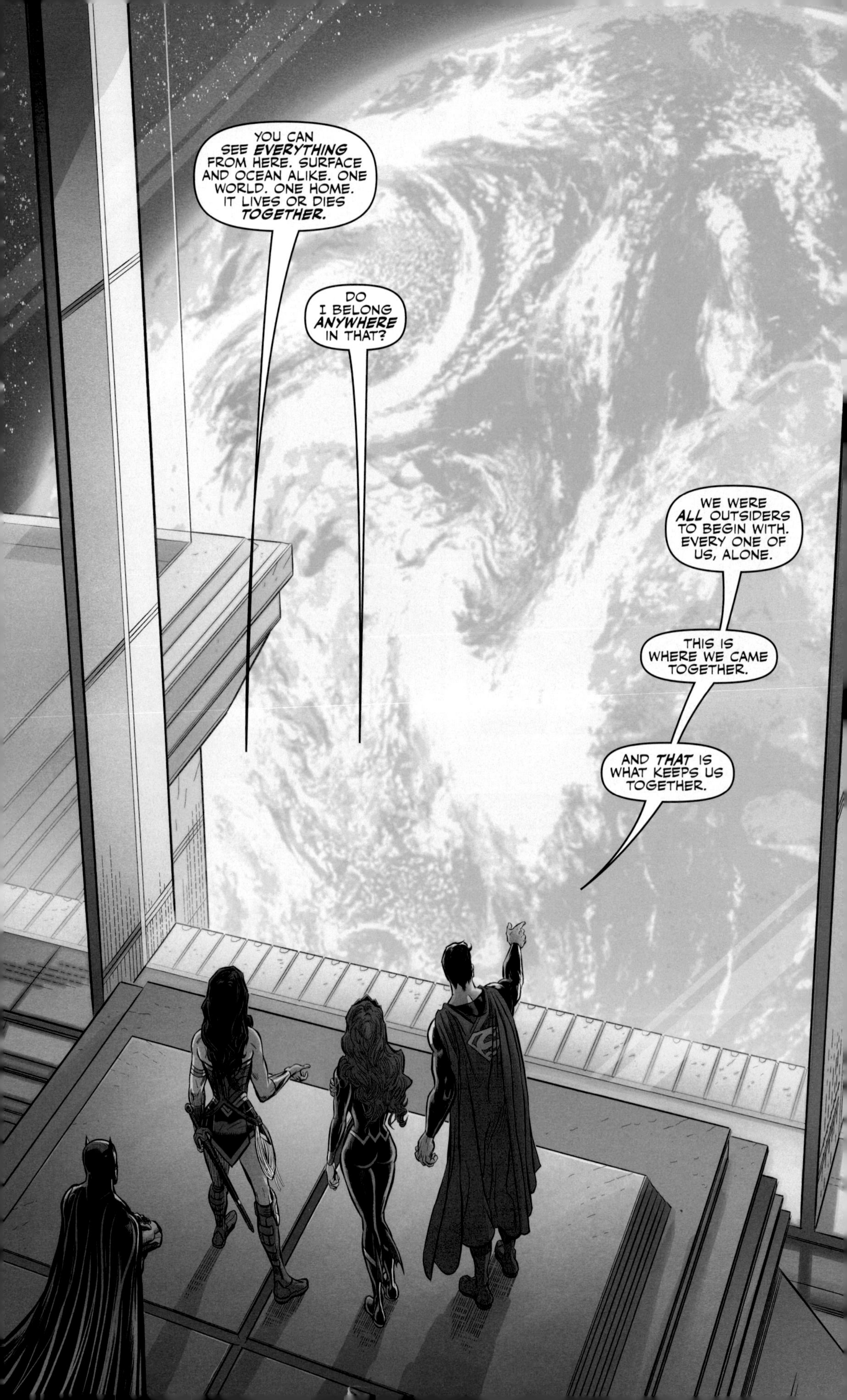
YOU CAN SEE *EVERYTHING* FROM HERE. SURFACE AND OCEAN ALIKE. ONE WORLD. ONE HOME. IT LIVES OR DIES *TOGETHER.*
DO I BELONG *ANYWHERE* IN THAT?
WE WERE *ALL* OUTSIDERS TO BEGIN WITH. EVERY ONE OF US, ALONE.
THIS IS WHERE WE CAME TOGETHER.
AND *THAT* IS WHAT KEEPS US TOGETHER.

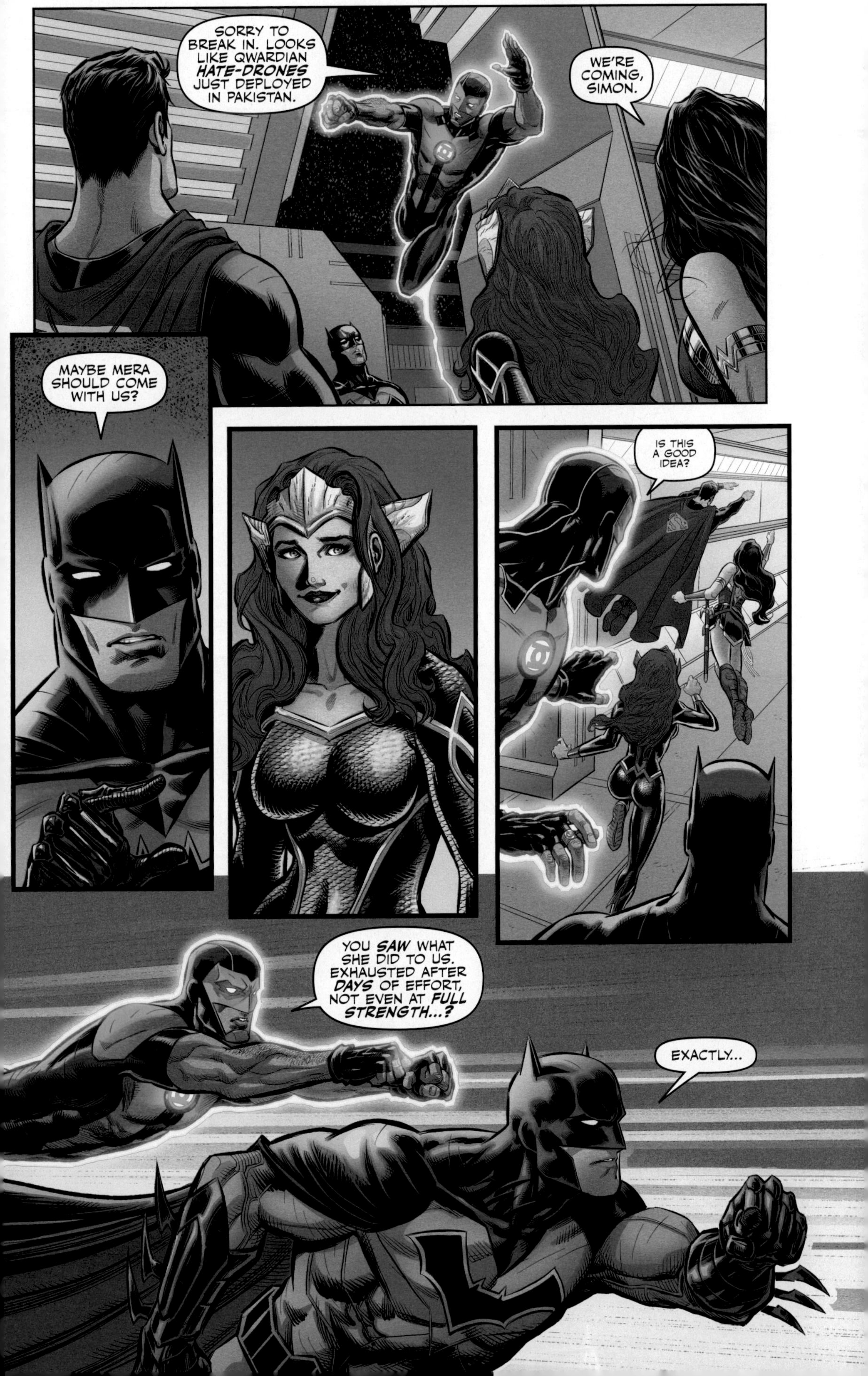
SORRY TO BREAK IN. LOOKS LIKE QWARDIAN HATE-DRONES JUST DEPLOYED IN PAKISTAN.
WE'RE COMING, SIMON.
MAYBE MERA SHOULD COME WITH US?
IS THIS A GOOD IDEA?
YOU SAW WHAT SHE DID TO US. EXHAUSTED AFTER DAYS OF EFFORT, NOT EVEN AT FULL STRENGTH...?
EXACTLY...

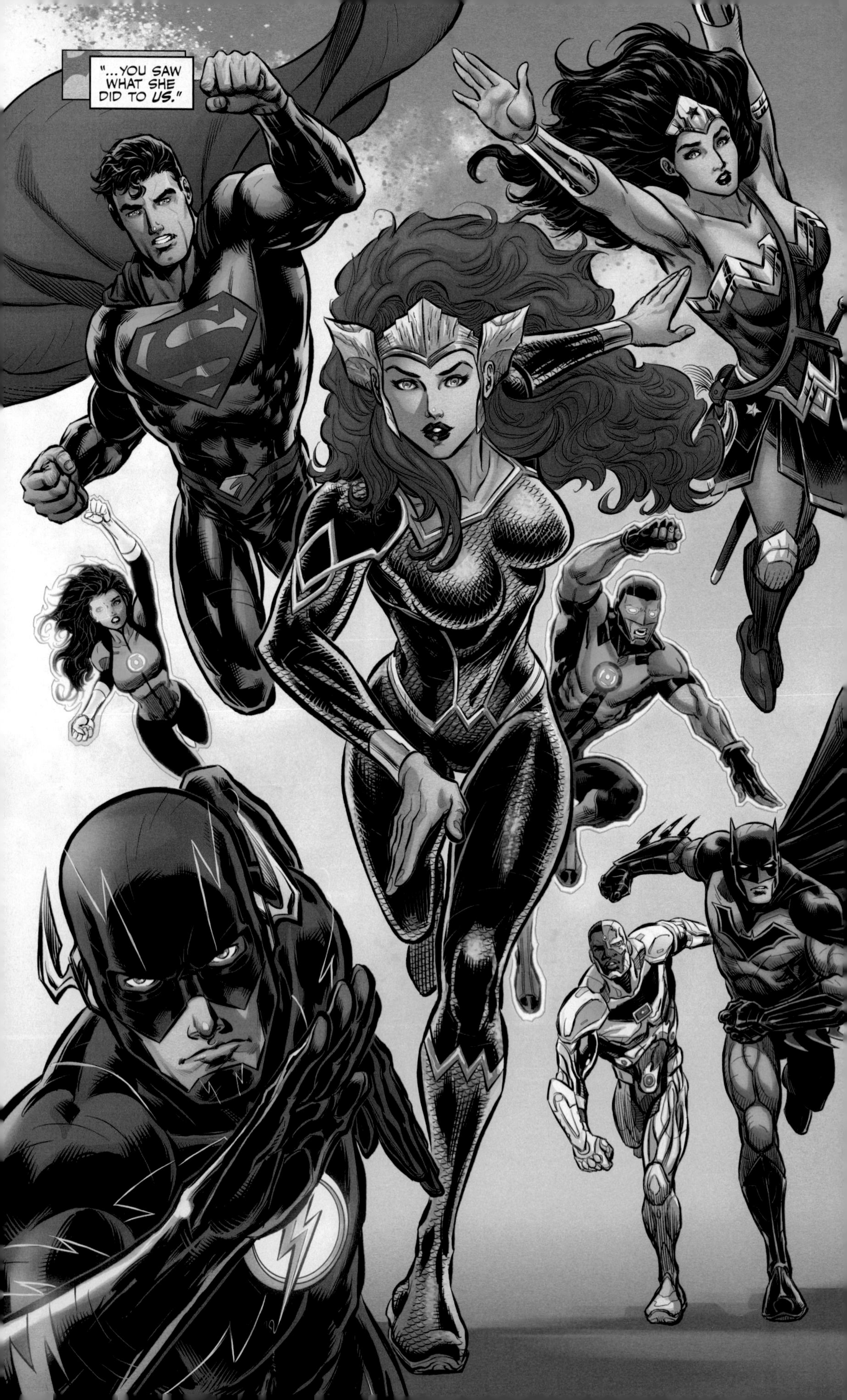
"...YOU SAW WHAT SHE DID TO *US*."

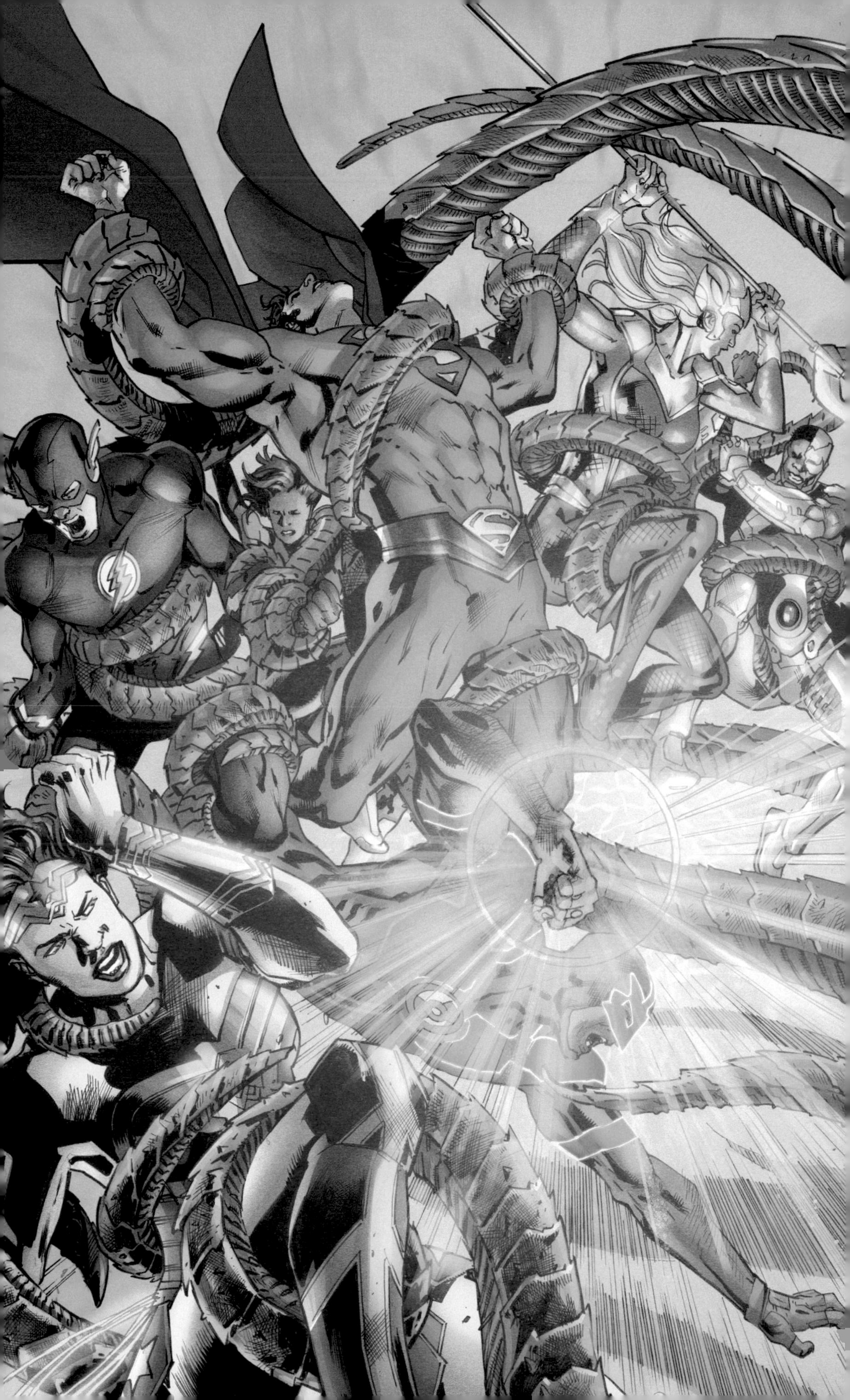

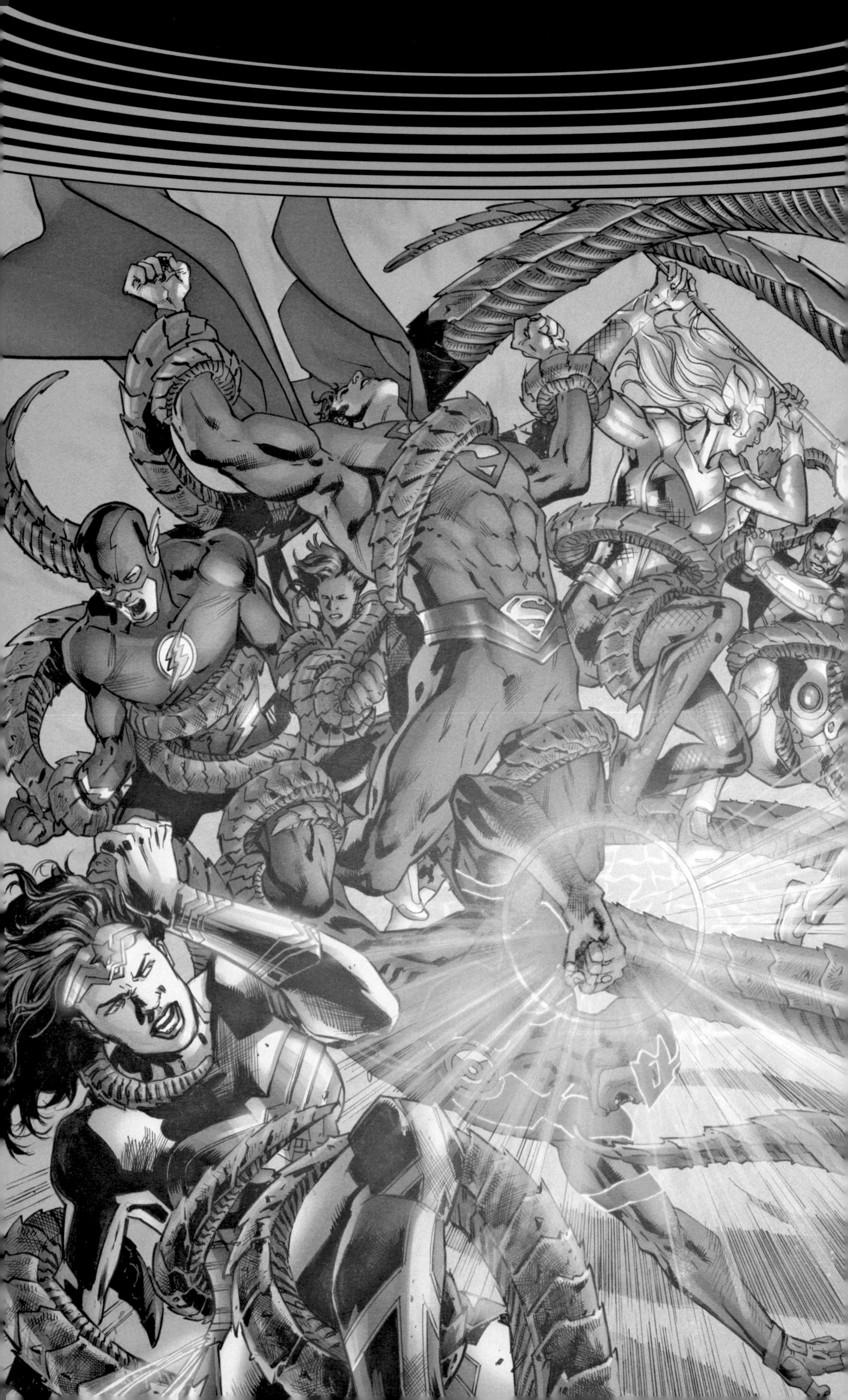

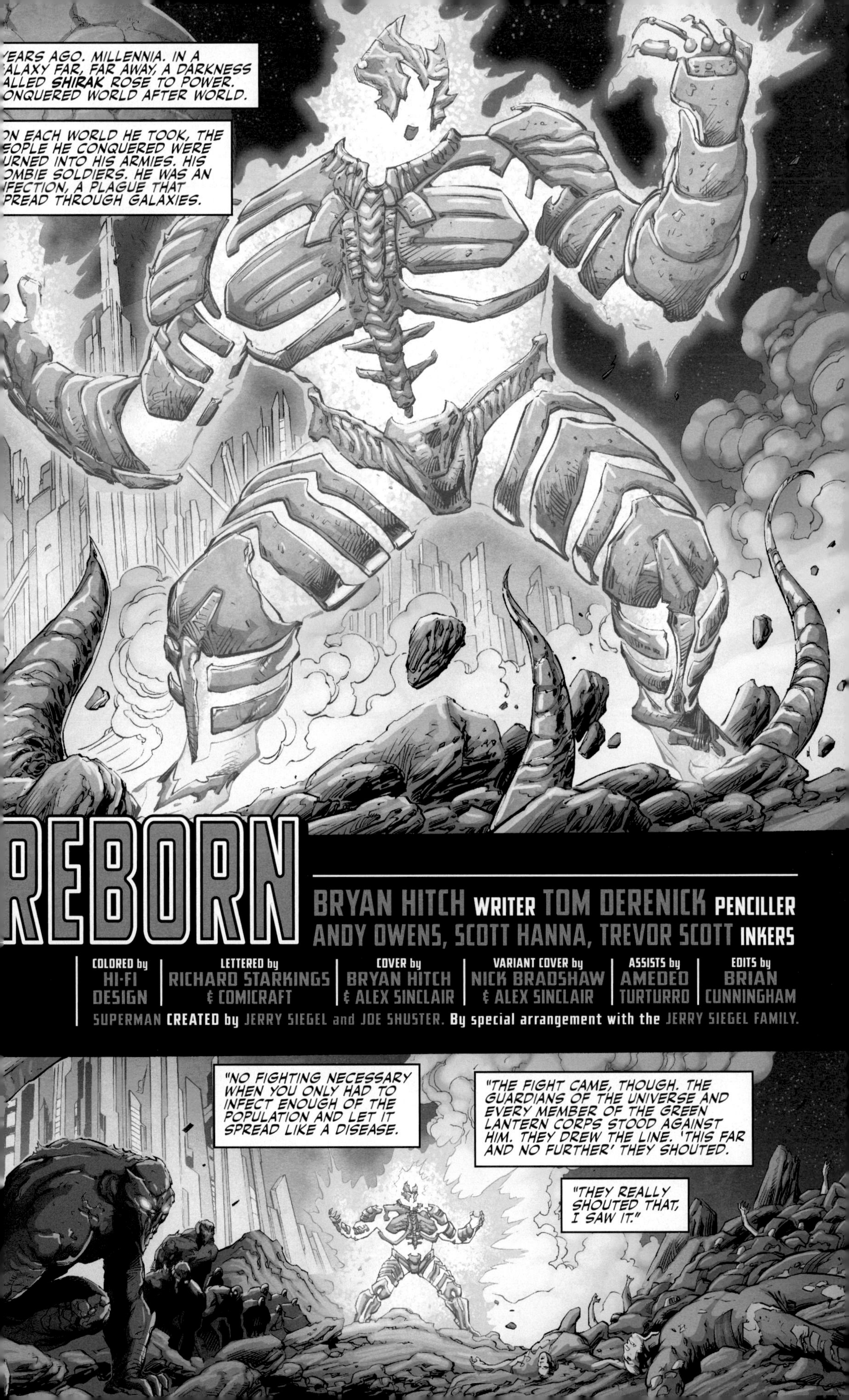
EARS AGO. MILLENNIA. IN A ALAXY FAR, FAR AWAY, A DARKNESS ALLED SHIRAK ROSE TO POWER. ONQUERED WORLD AFTER WORLD.
ON EACH WORLD HE TOOK, THE EOPLE HE CONQUERED WERE URNED INTO HIS ARMIES. HIS OMBIE SOLDIERS. HE WAS AN NFECTION, A PLAGUE THAT PREAD THROUGH GALAXIES.
REBORN
BRYAN HITCH WRITER TOM DERENICK PENCILLER
ANDY OWENS, SCOTT HANNA, TREVOR SCOTT INKERS
COLORED by HI-FI DESIGN
LETTERED by RICHARD STARKINGS & COMICRAFT
COVER by BRYAN HITCH & ALEX SINCLAIR
VARIANT COVER by NICK BRADSHAW & ALEX SINCLAIR
ASSISTS by AMEDEO TURTURRO
EDITS by BRIAN CUNNINGHAM
SUPERMAN CREATED by JERRY SIEGEL and JOE SHUSTER. By special arrangement with the JERRY SIEGEL FAMILY.
"NO FIGHTING NECESSARY WHEN YOU ONLY HAD TO INFECT ENOUGH OF THE POPULATION AND LET IT SPREAD LIKE A DISEASE.
"THE FIGHT CAME, THOUGH. THE GUARDIANS OF THE UNIVERSE AND EVERY MEMBER OF THE GREEN LANTERN CORPS STOOD AGAINST HIM. THEY DREW THE LINE. 'THIS FAR AND NO FURTHER' THEY SHOUTED.
"THEY REALLY SHOUTED THAT, I SAW IT."

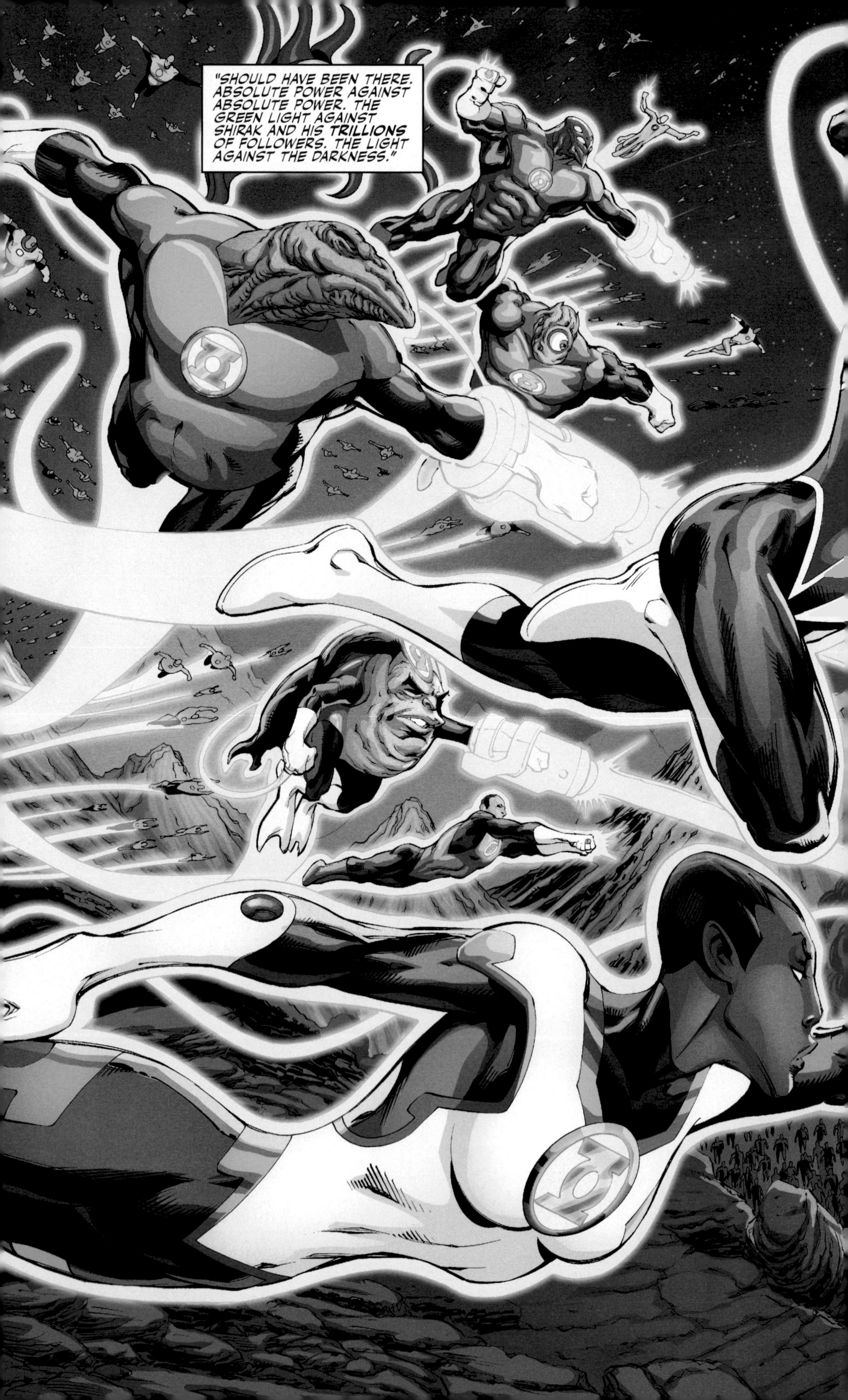
"SHOULD HAVE BEEN THERE. ABSOLUTE POWER AGAINST ABSOLUTE POWER. THE GREEN LIGHT AGAINST SHIRAK AND HIS **TRILLIONS** OF FOLLOWERS. THE LIGHT AGAINST THE DARKNESS."

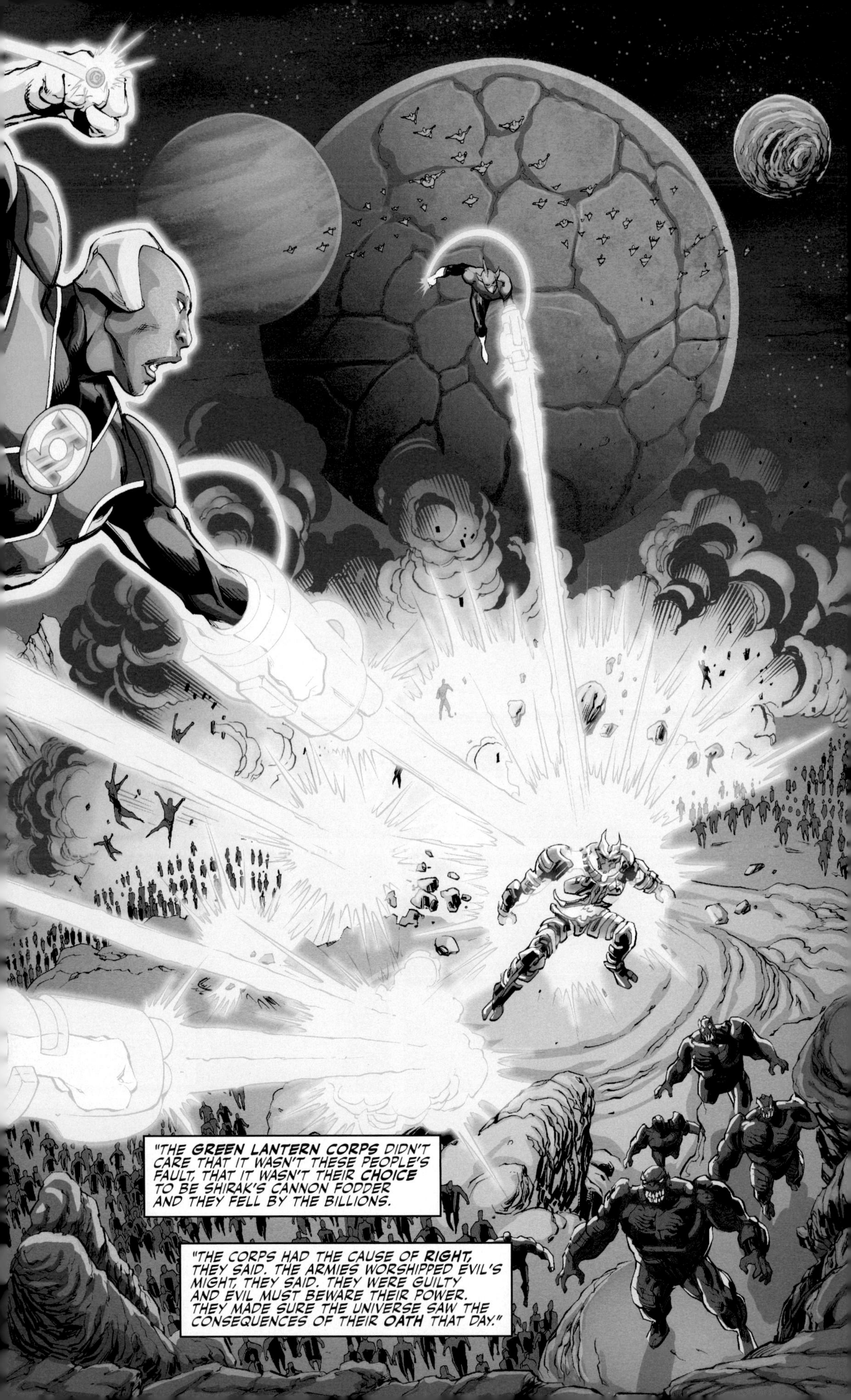
"THE GREEN LANTERN CORPS DIDN'T CARE THAT IT WASN'T THESE PEOPLE'S FAULT, THAT IT WASN'T THEIR CHOICE TO BE SHIRAK'S CANNON FODDER AND THEY FELL BY THE BILLIONS.
"THE CORPS HAD THE CAUSE OF RIGHT, THEY SAID. THE ARMIES WORSHIPPED EVIL'S MIGHT, THEY SAID. THEY WERE GUILTY AND EVIL MUST BEWARE THEIR POWER. THEY MADE SURE THE UNIVERSE SAW THE CONSEQUENCES OF THEIR OATH THAT DAY."

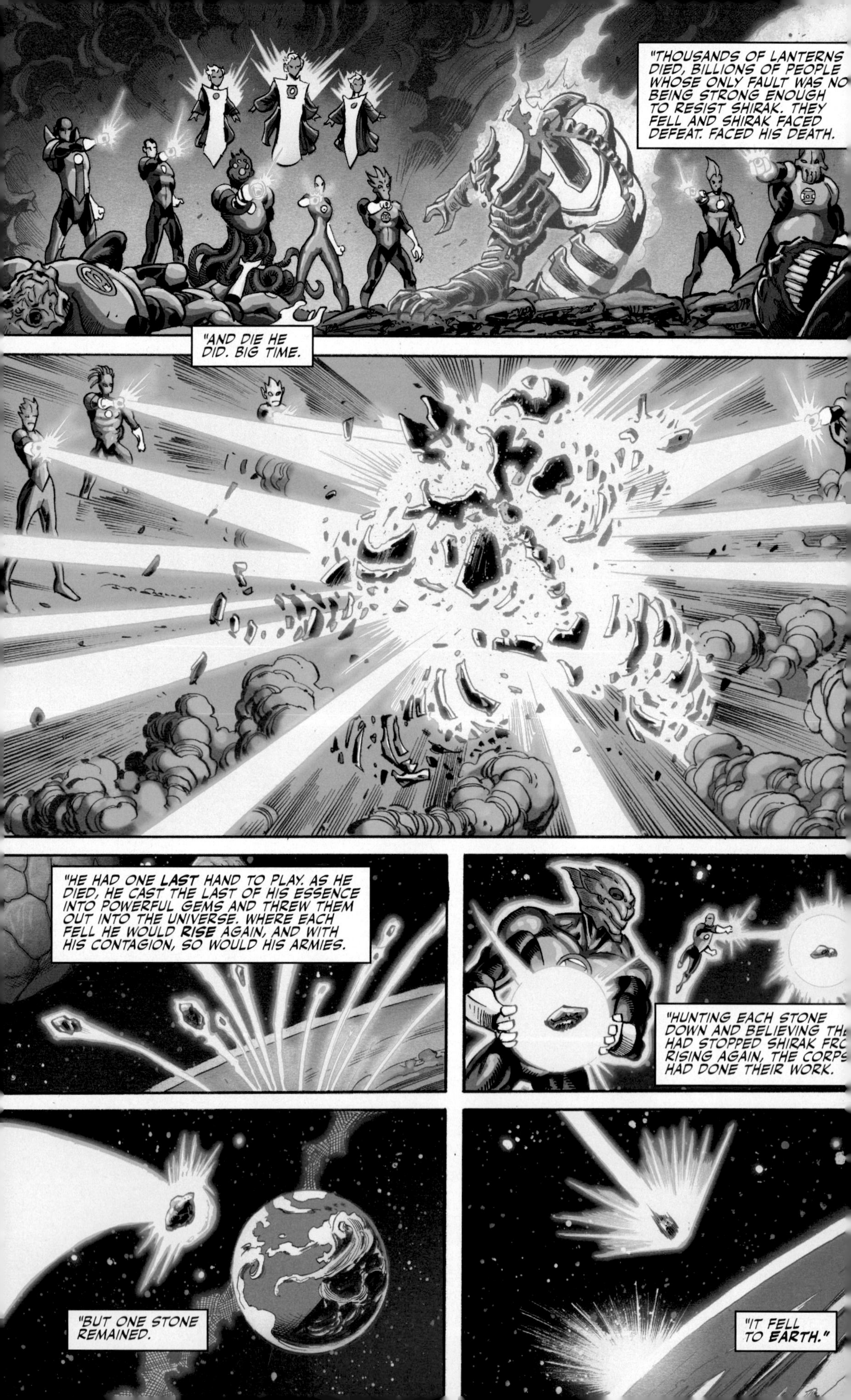
"THOUSANDS OF LANTERNS DIED. BILLIONS OF PEOPLE WHOSE ONLY FAULT WAS NO BEING STRONG ENOUGH TO RESIST SHIRAK. THEY FELL AND SHIRAK FACED DEFEAT. FACED HIS DEATH.
"AND DIE HE DID. BIG TIME.
"HE HAD ONE LAST HAND TO PLAY. AS HE DIED, HE CAST THE LAST OF HIS ESSENCE INTO POWERFUL GEMS AND THREW THEM OUT INTO THE UNIVERSE. WHERE EACH FELL HE WOULD RISE AGAIN, AND WITH HIS CONTAGION, SO WOULD HIS ARMIES.
"HUNTING EACH STONE DOWN AND BELIEVING THE HAD STOPPED SHIRAK FRO RISING AGAIN, THE CORPS HAD DONE THEIR WORK.
"BUT ONE STONE REMAINED.
"IT FELL TO EARTH."

WHY ARE YOU TELLING *ME* THIS?

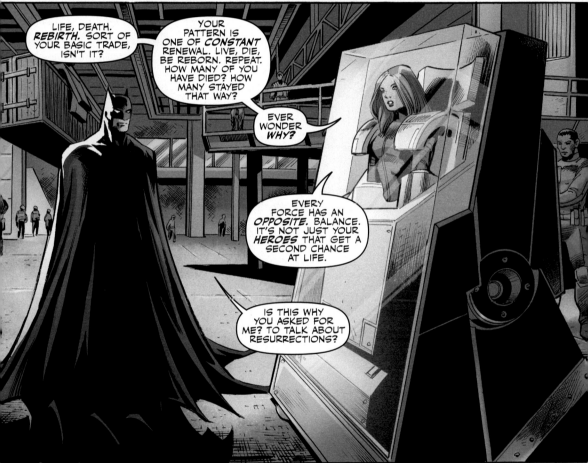

LIFE, DEATH. *REBIRTH.* SORT OF YOUR BASIC TRADE, ISN'T IT?

YOUR PATTERN IS ONE OF *CONSTANT* RENEWAL. LIVE, DIE, BE REBORN. REPEAT. HOW MANY OF YOU HAVE DIED? HOW MANY STAYED THAT WAY?

EVER WONDER *WHY?*

EVERY FORCE HAS AN *OPPOSITE.* BALANCE. IT'S NOT JUST YOUR *HEROES* THAT GET A SECOND CHANCE AT LIFE.

IS THIS WHY YOU ASKED FOR ME? TO TALK ABOUT RESURRECTIONS?

I ASKED FOR YOU BECAUSE THE END IS COMING. I COULDN'T *STOP* IT, THE *TIMELESS* COULDN'T. THE WORLD BREAKERS DIDN'T AND THE PURGE FAILED.

I DON'T KNOW WHAT IT IS EXACTLY, *NOBODY* DOES. BUT WE ALL KNOW IT'S COMING, THAT IT STARTS ON EARTH AND WHAT IT MEANS FOR *EVERY-THING* ELSE.

IT'S GOING TO BE DOWN TO YOU AND THE OTHERS TO STOP IT, SO BEFORE THEY LOCK ME AWAY ON *CERES* FOREVER I'M GOING TO TELL YOU EVERYTHING I KNOW.

IT'S ALL ABOUT *REBIRTH.*

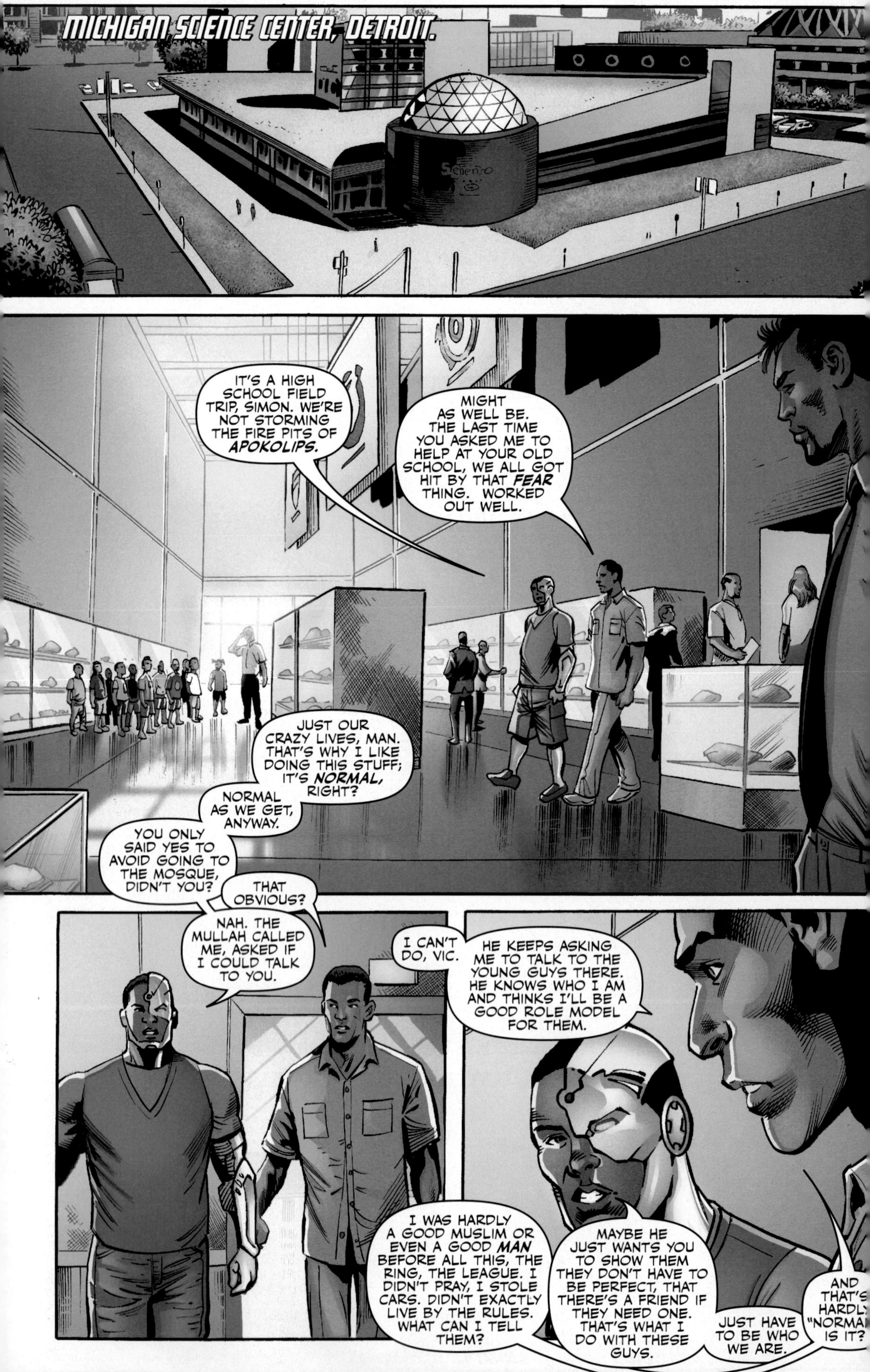
MICHIGAN SCIENCE CENTER, DETROIT.
IT'S A HIGH SCHOOL FIELD TRIP, SIMON. WE'RE NOT STORMING THE FIRE PITS OF APOKOLIPS.
MIGHT AS WELL BE. THE LAST TIME YOU ASKED ME TO HELP AT YOUR OLD SCHOOL, WE ALL GOT HIT BY THAT FEAR THING. WORKED OUT WELL.
JUST OUR CRAZY LIVES, MAN. THAT'S WHY I LIKE DOING THIS STUFF; IT'S NORMAL, RIGHT?
NORMAL AS WE GET, ANYWAY.
YOU ONLY SAID YES TO AVOID GOING TO THE MOSQUE, DIDN'T YOU?
THAT OBVIOUS?
NAH. THE MULLAH CALLED ME, ASKED IF I COULD TALK TO YOU.
I CAN'T DO, VIC.
HE KEEPS ASKING ME TO TALK TO THE YOUNG GUYS THERE. HE KNOWS WHO I AM AND THINKS I'LL BE A GOOD ROLE MODEL FOR THEM.
I WAS HARDLY A GOOD MUSLIM OR EVEN A GOOD MAN BEFORE ALL THIS, THE RING, THE LEAGUE. I DIDN'T PRAY, I STOLE CARS. DIDN'T EXACTLY LIVE BY THE RULES. WHAT CAN I TELL THEM?
MAYBE HE JUST WANTS YOU TO SHOW THEM THEY DON'T HAVE TO BE PERFECT, THAT THERE'S A FRIEND IF THEY NEED ONE. THAT'S WHAT I DO WITH THESE GUYS.
JUST HAVE TO BE WHO WE ARE.
AND THAT'S HARDLY "NORMA IS IT?

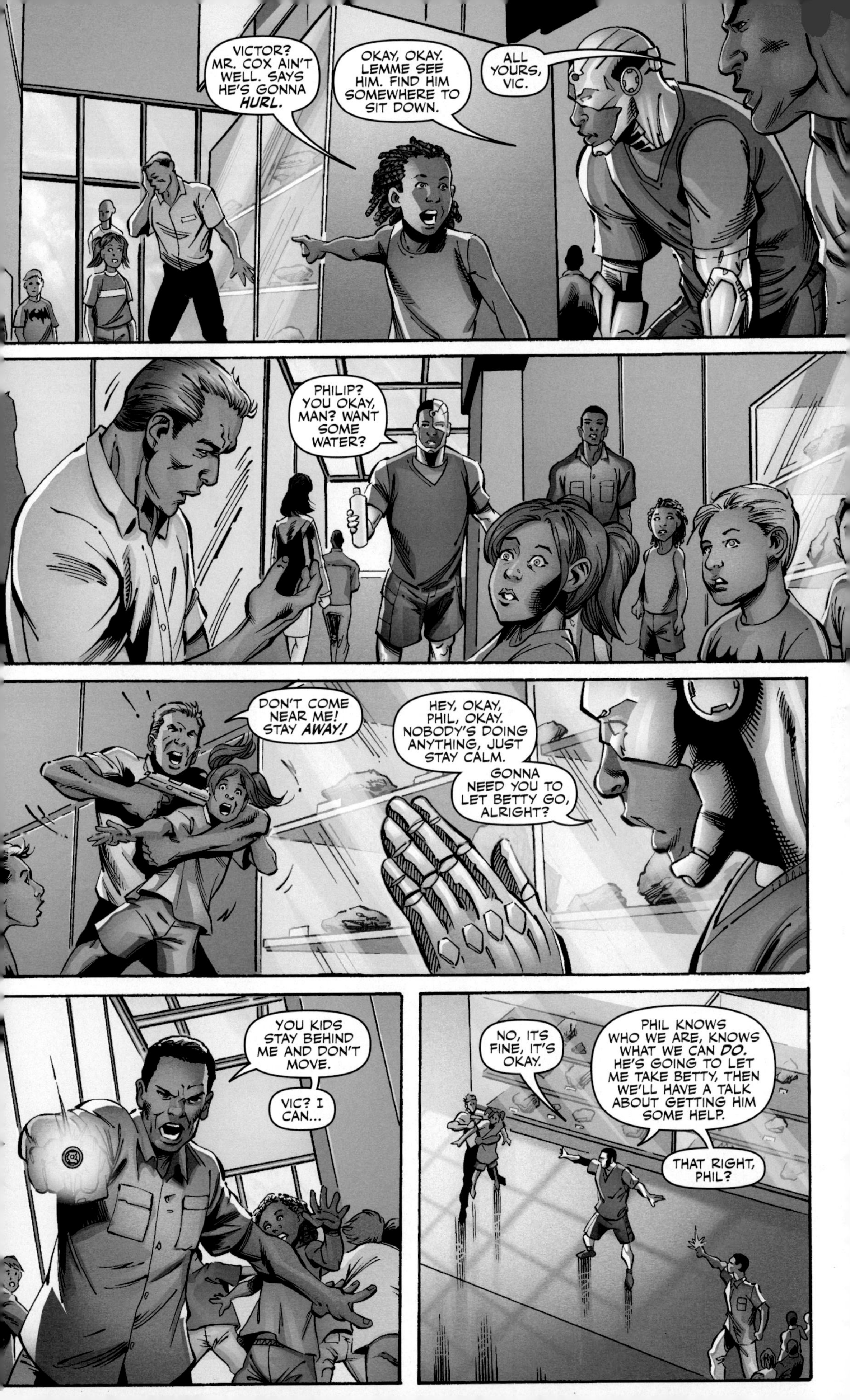
VICTOR? MR. COX AIN'T WELL. SAYS HE'S GONNA *HURL.*
OKAY, OKAY. LEMME SEE HIM. FIND HIM SOMEWHERE TO SIT DOWN.
ALL YOURS, VIC.
PHILIP? YOU OKAY, MAN? WANT SOME WATER?
DON'T COME NEAR ME! STAY *AWAY!*
HEY, OKAY, PHIL, OKAY. NOBODY'S DOING ANYTHING, JUST STAY CALM.
GONNA NEED YOU TO LET BETTY GO, ALRIGHT?
YOU KIDS STAY BEHIND ME AND DON'T MOVE.
VIC? I CAN...
NO, ITS FINE, IT'S OKAY.
PHIL KNOWS WHO WE ARE, KNOWS WHAT WE CAN *DO.* HE'S GOING TO LET ME TAKE BETTY, THEN WE'LL HAVE A TALK ABOUT GETTING HIM SOME HELP.
THAT RIGHT, PHIL?

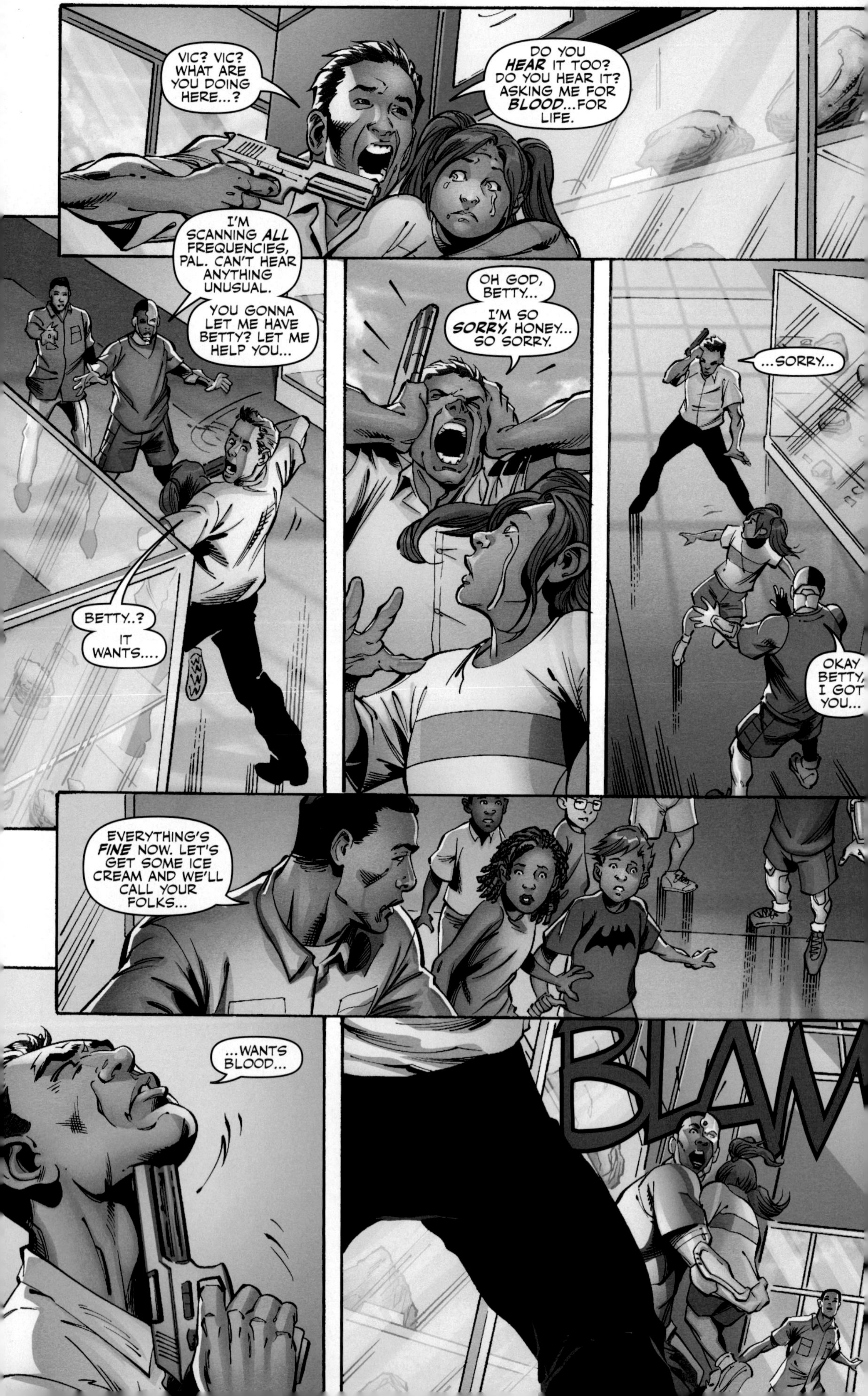
VIC? VIC? WHAT ARE YOU DOING HERE...?
DO YOU HEAR IT TOO? DO YOU HEAR IT? ASKING ME FOR BLOOD...FOR LIFE.
I'M SCANNING ALL FREQUENCIES, PAL. CAN'T HEAR ANYTHING UNUSUAL.
YOU GONNA LET ME HAVE BETTY? LET ME HELP YOU...
BETTY..?
IT WANTS....
OH GOD, BETTY...
I'M SO SORRY, HONEY... SO SORRY.
...SORRY...
OKAY BETTY, I GOT YOU...
EVERYTHING'S FINE NOW. LET'S GET SOME ICE CREAM AND WE'LL CALL YOUR FOLKS...
...WANTS BLOOD...
BLAM

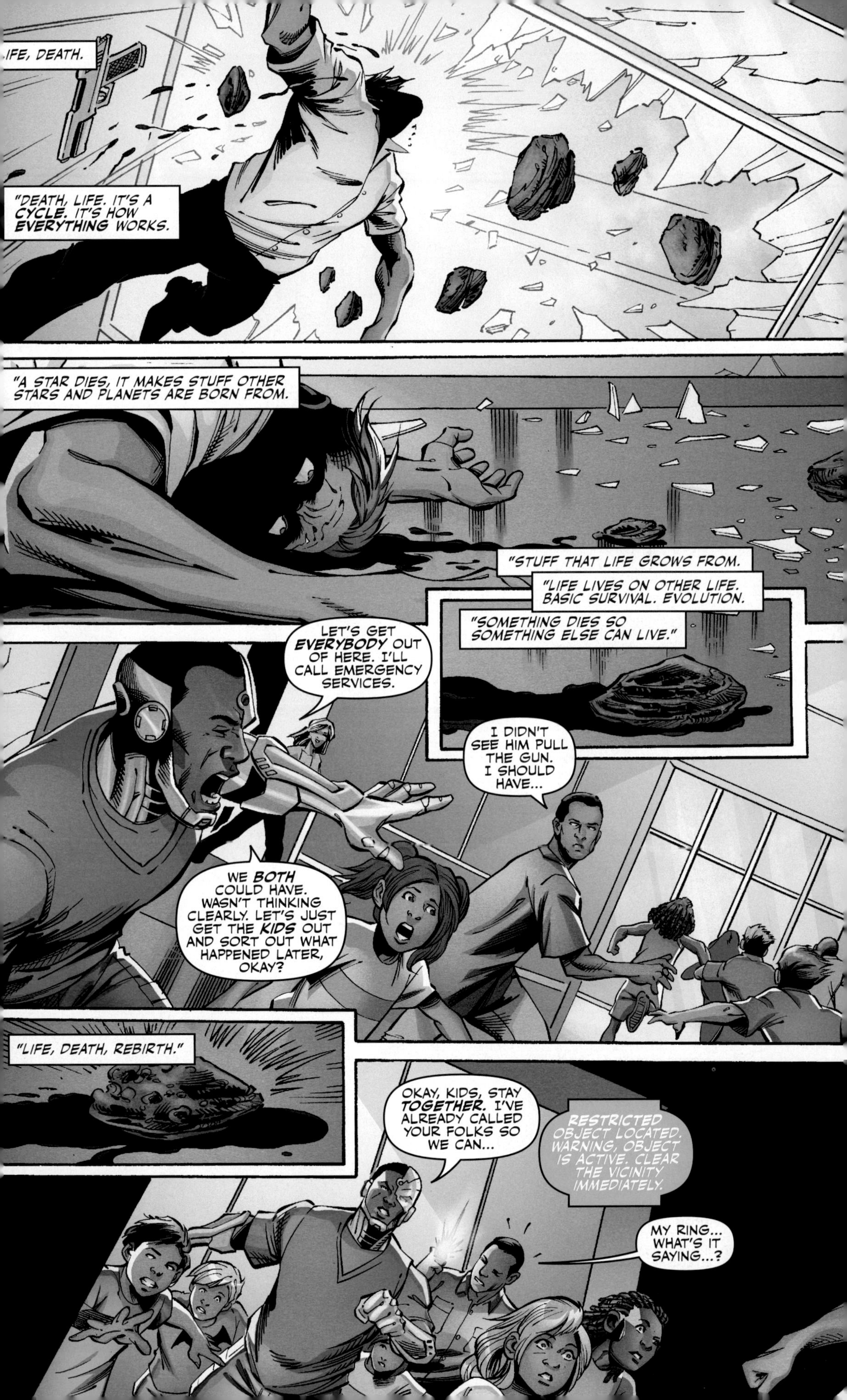

LIFE, DEATH.
"DEATH, LIFE. IT'S A CYCLE. IT'S HOW EVERYTHING WORKS.
"A STAR DIES, IT MAKES STUFF OTHER STARS AND PLANETS ARE BORN FROM.
"STUFF THAT LIFE GROWS FROM.
"LIFE LIVES ON OTHER LIFE. BASIC SURVIVAL. EVOLUTION.
"SOMETHING DIES SO SOMETHING ELSE CAN LIVE."
LET'S GET EVERYBODY OUT OF HERE. I'LL CALL EMERGENCY SERVICES.
I DIDN'T SEE HIM PULL THE GUN. I SHOULD HAVE...
WE BOTH COULD HAVE. WASN'T THINKING CLEARLY. LET'S JUST GET THE KIDS OUT AND SORT OUT WHAT HAPPENED LATER, OKAY?
"LIFE, DEATH, REBIRTH."
OKAY, KIDS, STAY TOGETHER. I'VE ALREADY CALLED YOUR FOLKS SO WE CAN...
RESTRICTED OBJECT LOCATED. WARNING, OBJECT IS ACTIVE. CLEAR THE VICINITY IMMEDIATELY.
MY RING... WHAT'S IT SAYING...?

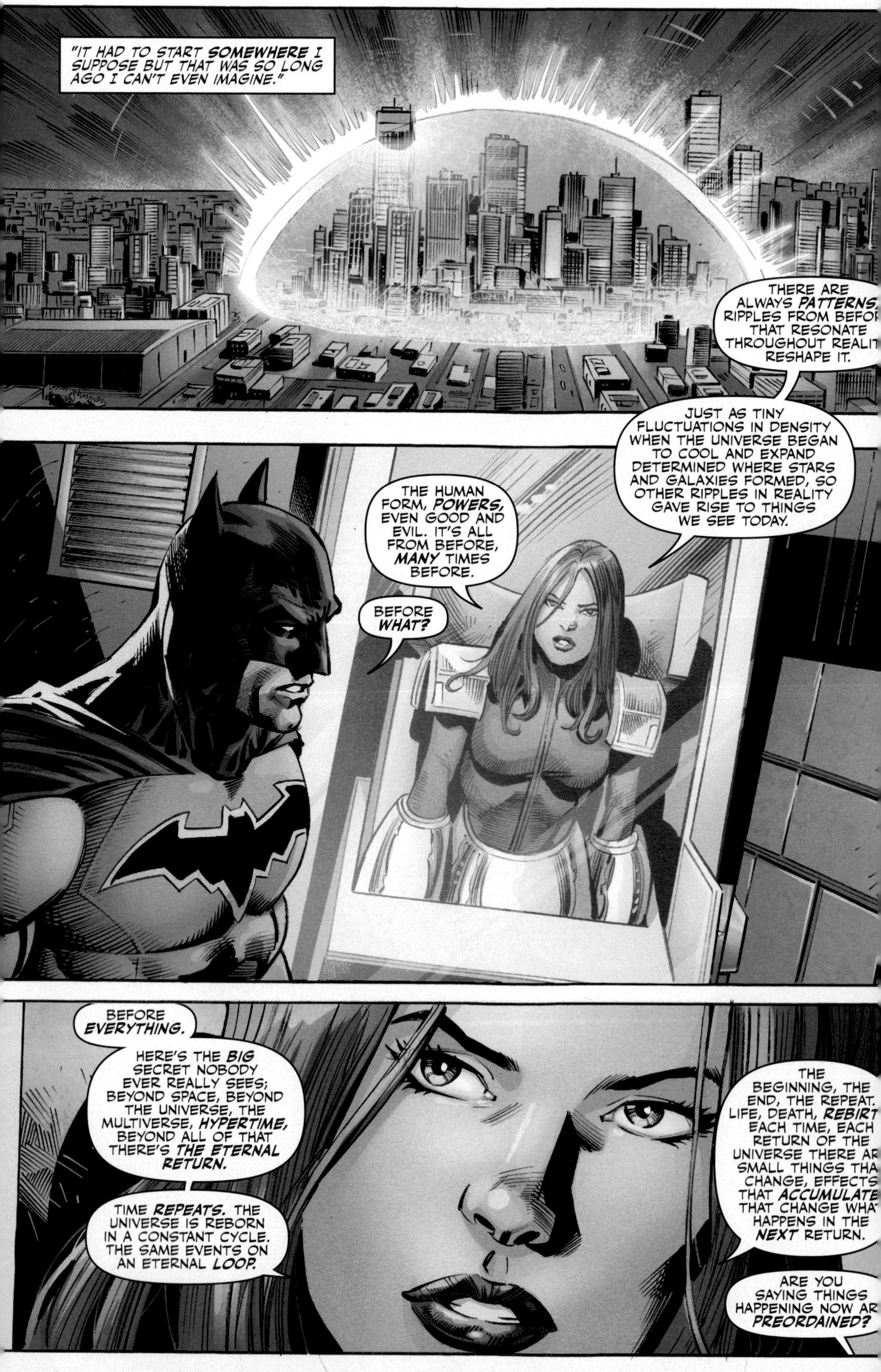
"IT HAD TO START SOMEWHERE I SUPPOSE BUT THAT WAS SO LONG AGO I CAN'T EVEN IMAGINE."
THERE ARE ALWAYS PATTERNS, RIPPLES FROM BEFOR THAT RESONATE THROUGHOUT REALIT RESHAPE IT.
JUST AS TINY FLUCTUATIONS IN DENSITY WHEN THE UNIVERSE BEGAN TO COOL AND EXPAND DETERMINED WHERE STARS AND GALAXIES FORMED, SO OTHER RIPPLES IN REALITY GAVE RISE TO THINGS WE SEE TODAY.
THE HUMAN FORM, POWERS, EVEN GOOD AND EVIL. IT'S ALL FROM BEFORE, MANY TIMES BEFORE.
BEFORE WHAT?
BEFORE EVERYTHING.
HERE'S THE BIG SECRET NOBODY EVER REALLY SEES; BEYOND SPACE, BEYOND THE UNIVERSE, THE MULTIVERSE, HYPERTIME, BEYOND ALL OF THAT THERE'S THE ETERNAL RETURN.
TIME REPEATS. THE UNIVERSE IS REBORN IN A CONSTANT CYCLE. THE SAME EVENTS ON AN ETERNAL LOOP.
THE BEGINNING, THE END, THE REPEAT. LIFE, DEATH, REBIRT EACH TIME, EACH RETURN OF THE UNIVERSE THERE AR SMALL THINGS THA CHANGE, EFFECTS THAT ACCUMULATE THAT CHANGE WHA HAPPENS IN THE NEXT RETURN.
ARE YOU SAYING THINGS HAPPENING NOW AR PREORDAINED?

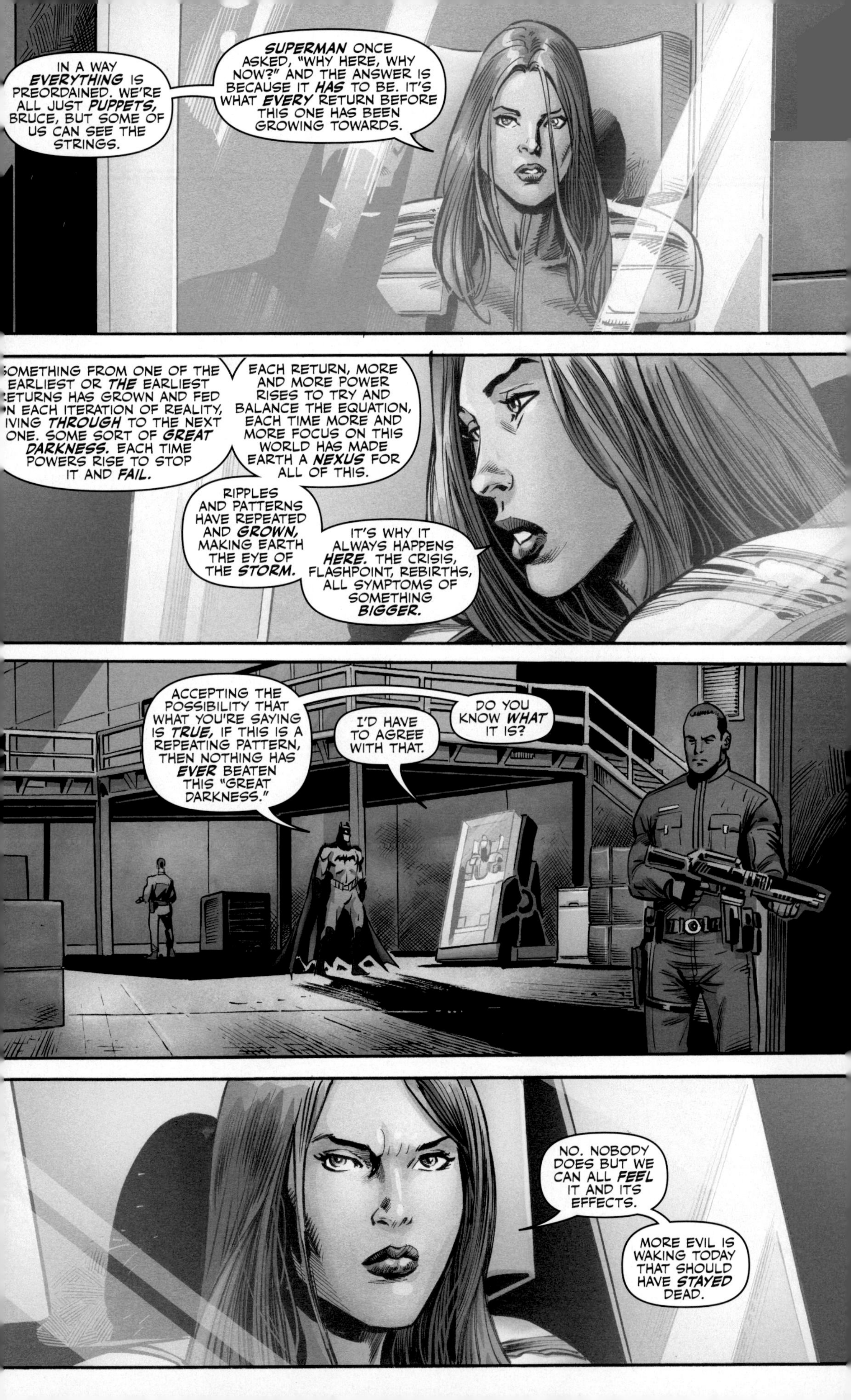
IN A WAY EVERYTHING IS PREORDAINED. WE'RE ALL JUST PUPPETS, BRUCE, BUT SOME OF US CAN SEE THE STRINGS.
SUPERMAN ONCE ASKED, "WHY HERE, WHY NOW?" AND THE ANSWER IS BECAUSE IT HAS TO BE. IT'S WHAT EVERY RETURN BEFORE THIS ONE HAS BEEN GROWING TOWARDS.
OMETHING FROM ONE OF THE EARLIEST OR THE EARLIEST ETURNS HAS GROWN AND FED N EACH ITERATION OF REALITY, IVING THROUGH TO THE NEXT ONE. SOME SORT OF GREAT DARKNESS. EACH TIME POWERS RISE TO STOP IT AND FAIL.
EACH RETURN, MORE AND MORE POWER RISES TO TRY AND BALANCE THE EQUATION, EACH TIME MORE AND MORE FOCUS ON THIS WORLD HAS MADE EARTH A NEXUS FOR ALL OF THIS.
RIPPLES AND PATTERNS HAVE REPEATED AND GROWN, MAKING EARTH THE EYE OF THE STORM.
IT'S WHY IT ALWAYS HAPPENS HERE. THE CRISIS, FLASHPOINT, REBIRTHS, ALL SYMPTOMS OF SOMETHING BIGGER.
ACCEPTING THE POSSIBILITY THAT WHAT YOU'RE SAYING IS TRUE, IF THIS IS A REPEATING PATTERN, THEN NOTHING HAS EVER BEATEN THIS "GREAT DARKNESS."
I'D HAVE TO AGREE WITH THAT.
DO YOU KNOW WHAT IT IS?
NO. NOBODY DOES BUT WE CAN ALL FEEL IT AND ITS EFFECTS.
MORE EVIL IS WAKING TODAY THAT SHOULD HAVE STAYED DEAD.

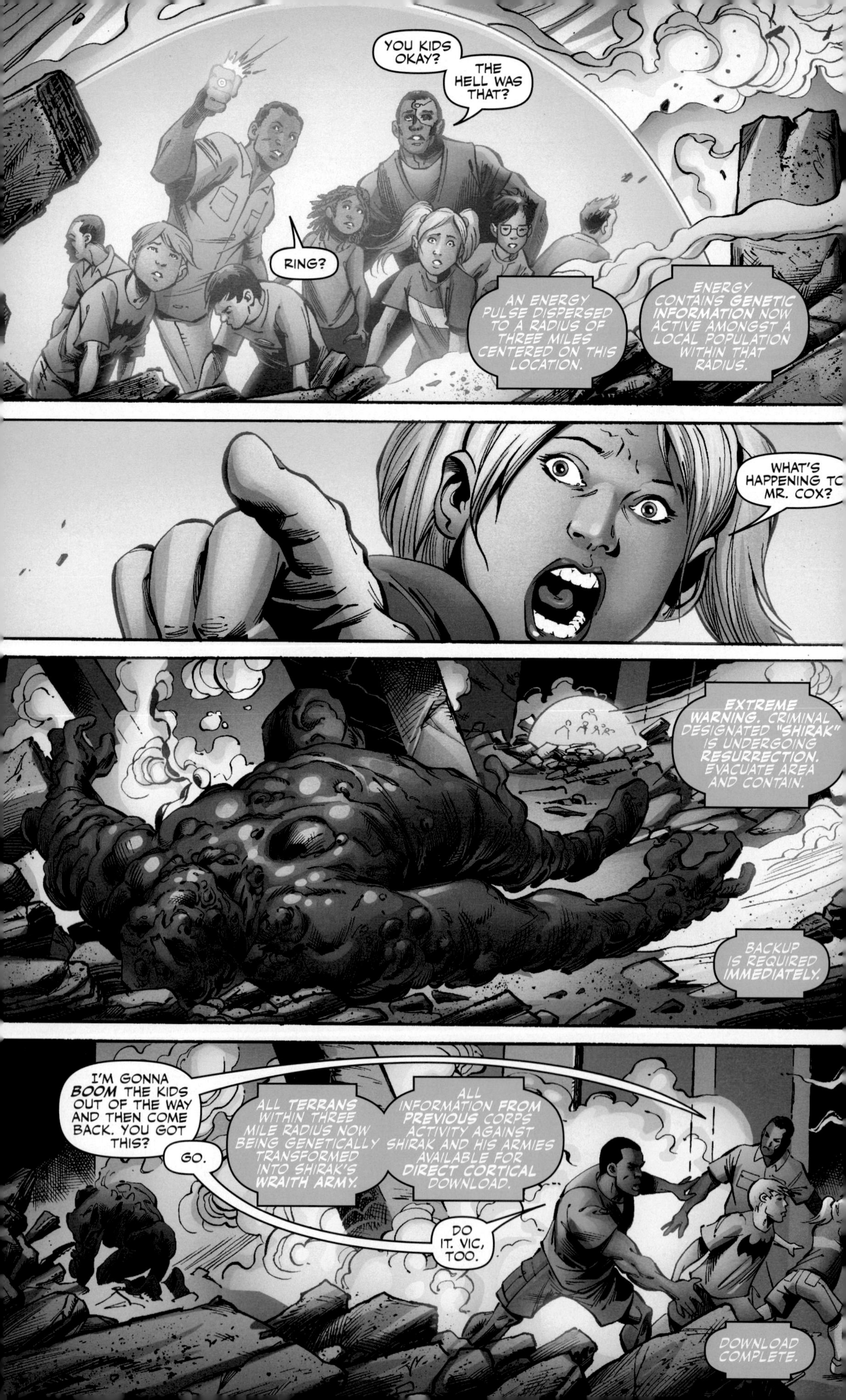
YOU KIDS OKAY?
THE HELL WAS THAT?
RING?
AN ENERGY PULSE DISPERSED TO A RADIUS OF THREE MILES CENTERED ON THIS LOCATION.
ENERGY CONTAINS GENETIC INFORMATION NOW ACTIVE AMONGST A LOCAL POPULATION WITHIN THAT RADIUS.
WHAT'S HAPPENING TO MR. COX?
EXTREME WARNING. CRIMINAL DESIGNATED "SHIRAK" IS UNDERGOING RESURRECTION. EVACUATE AREA AND CONTAIN.
BACKUP IS REQUIRED IMMEDIATELY.
I'M GONNA BOOM THE KIDS OUT OF THE WAY AND THEN COME BACK. YOU GOT THIS?
GO.
ALL TERRANS WITHIN THREE MILE RADIUS NOW BEING GENETICALLY TRANSFORMED INTO SHIRAK'S WRAITH ARMY.
ALL INFORMATION FROM PREVIOUS CORPS ACTIVITY AGAINST SHIRAK AND HIS ARMIES AVAILABLE FOR DIRECT CORTICAL DOWNLOAD.
DO IT. VIC, TOO.
DOWNLOAD COMPLETE.

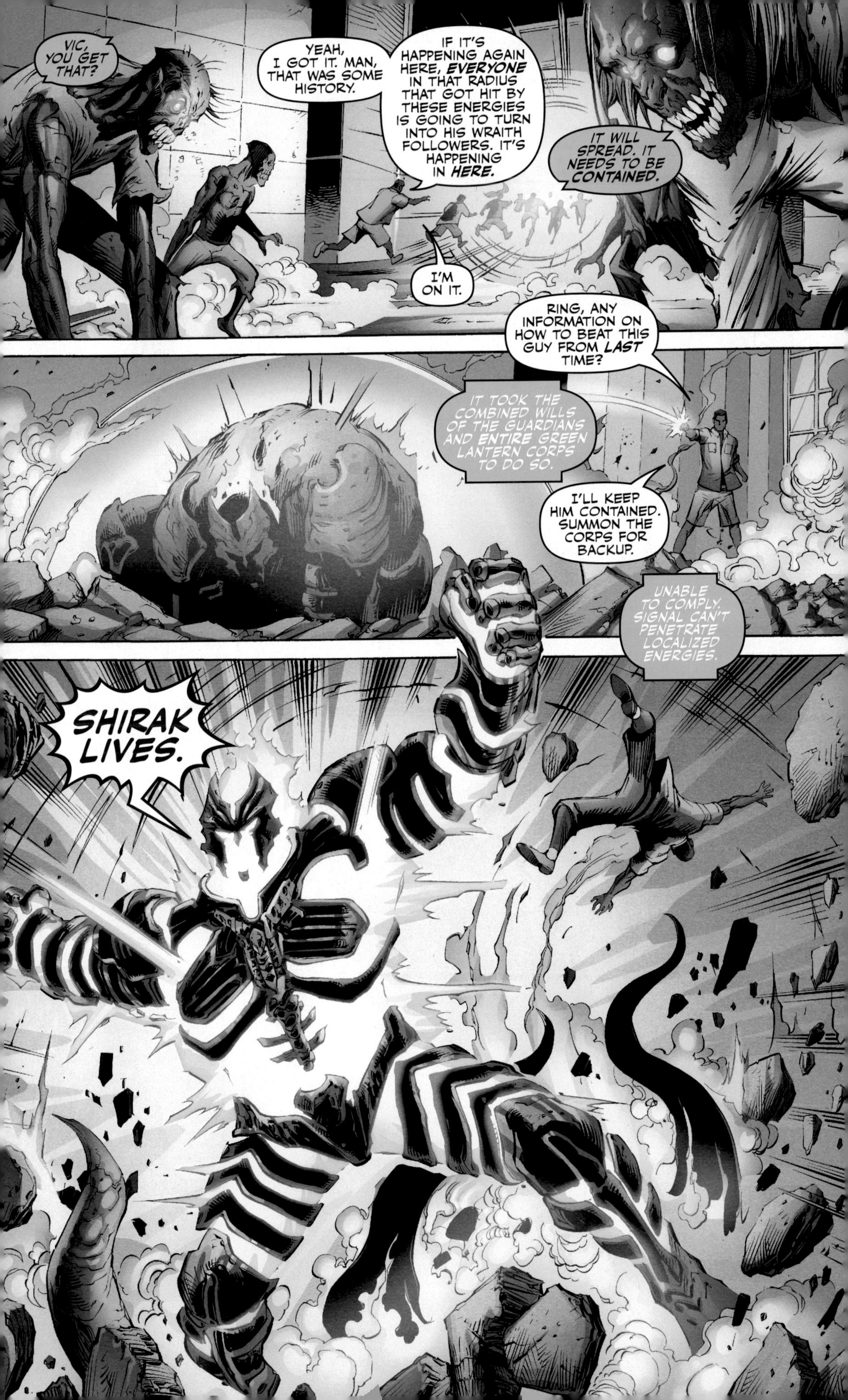
VIC, YOU GET THAT?
YEAH, I GOT IT. MAN, THAT WAS SOME HISTORY.
IF IT'S HAPPENING AGAIN HERE, EVERYONE IN THAT RADIUS THAT GOT HIT BY THESE ENERGIES IS GOING TO TURN INTO HIS WRAITH FOLLOWERS. IT'S HAPPENING IN HERE.
IT WILL SPREAD. IT NEEDS TO BE CONTAINED.
I'M ON IT.
RING, ANY INFORMATION ON HOW TO BEAT THIS GUY FROM LAST TIME?
IT TOOK THE COMBINED WILLS OF THE GUARDIANS AND ENTIRE GREEN LANTERN CORPS TO DO SO.
I'LL KEEP HIM CONTAINED. SUMMON THE CORPS FOR BACKUP.
UNABLE TO COMPLY. SIGNAL CAN'T PENETRATE LOCALIZED ENERGIES.
SHIRAK LIVES.

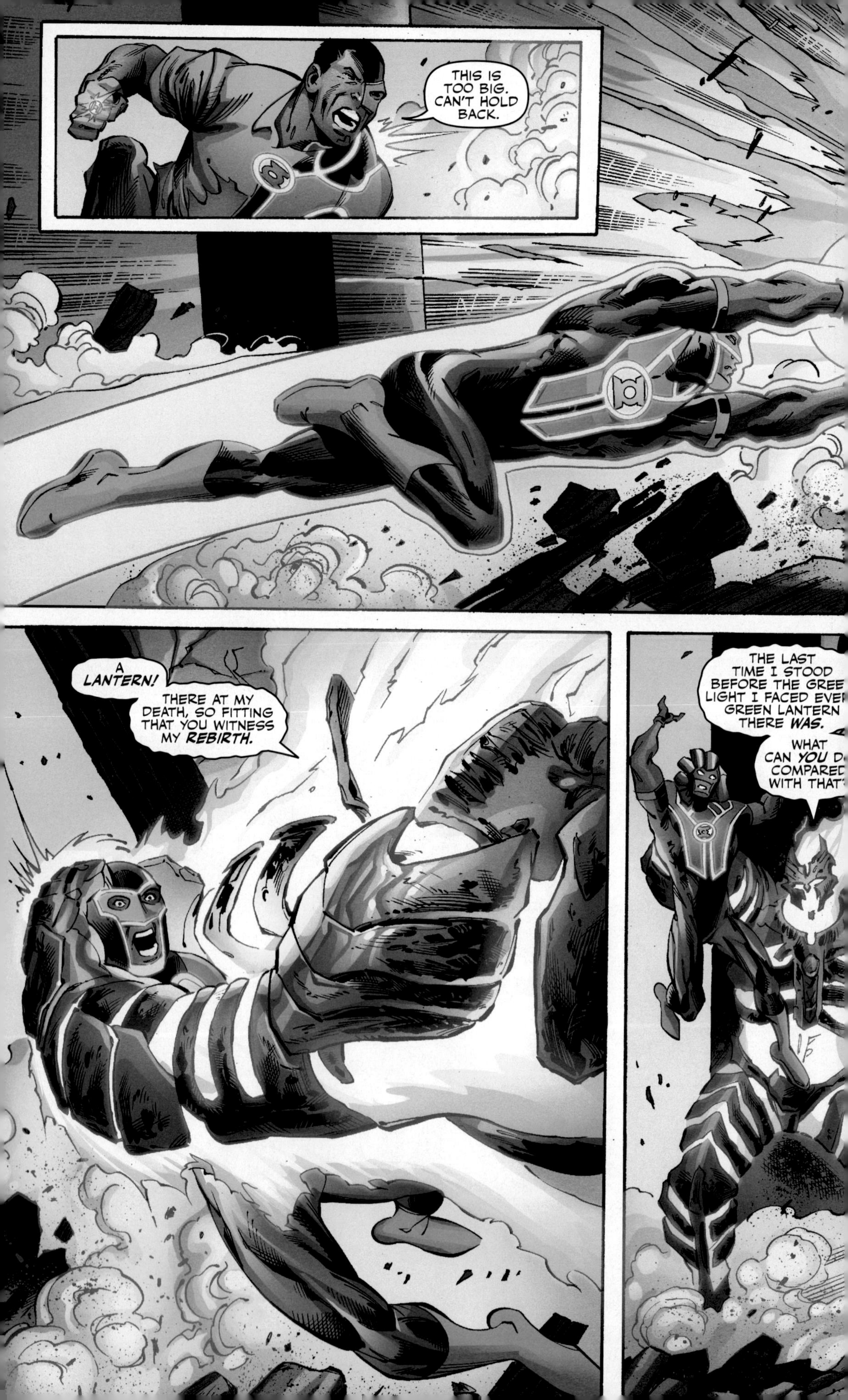
THIS IS TOO BIG. CAN'T HOLD BACK.
A LANTERN!
THERE AT MY DEATH, SO FITTING THAT YOU WITNESS MY REBIRTH.
THE LAST TIME I STOOD BEFORE THE GREE LIGHT I FACED EVER GREEN LANTERN THERE WAS.
WHAT CAN YOU D COMPARED WITH THAT

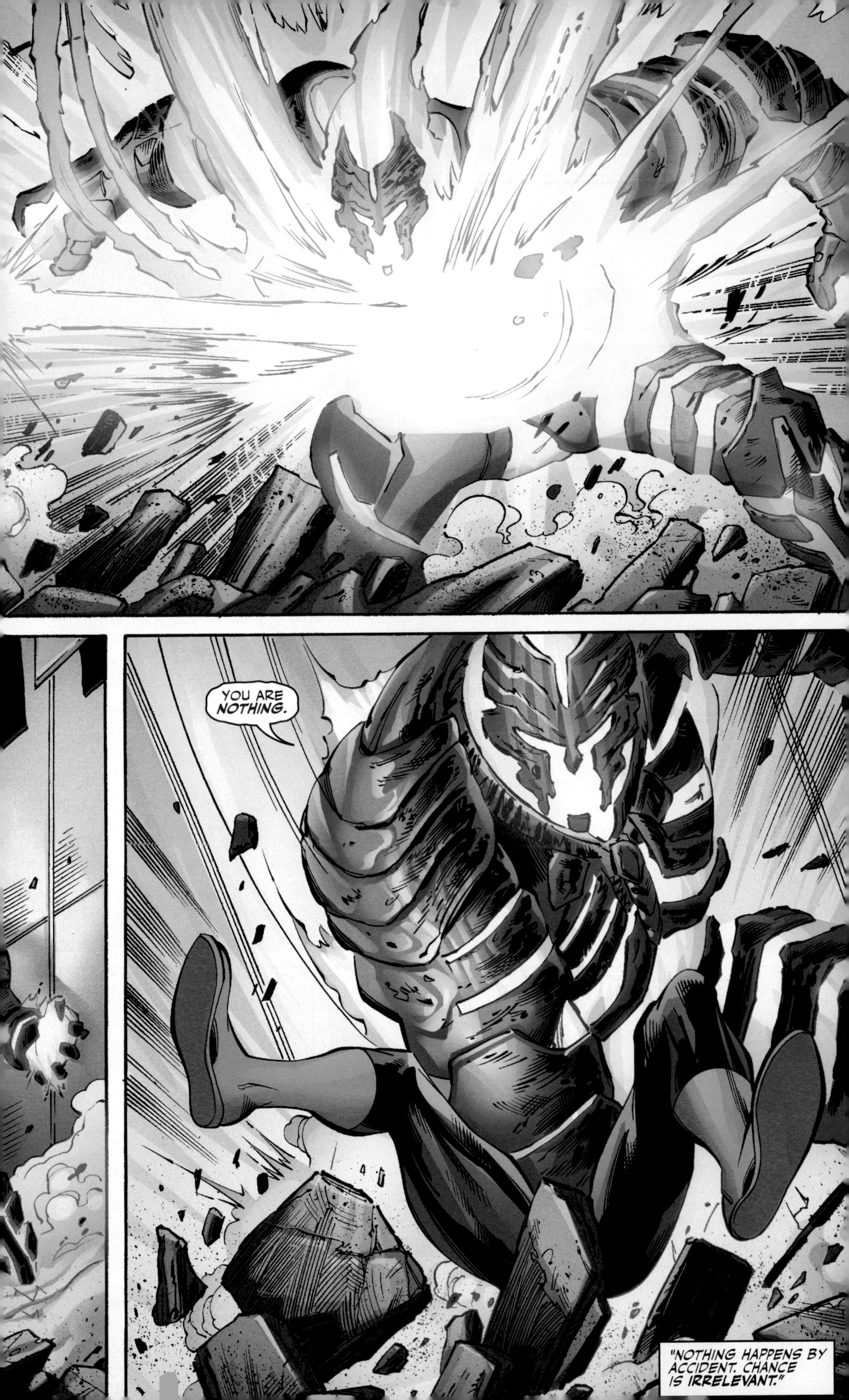
YOU ARE NOTHING.
"NOTHING HAPPENS BY ACCIDENT. CHANCE IS IRRELEVANT."

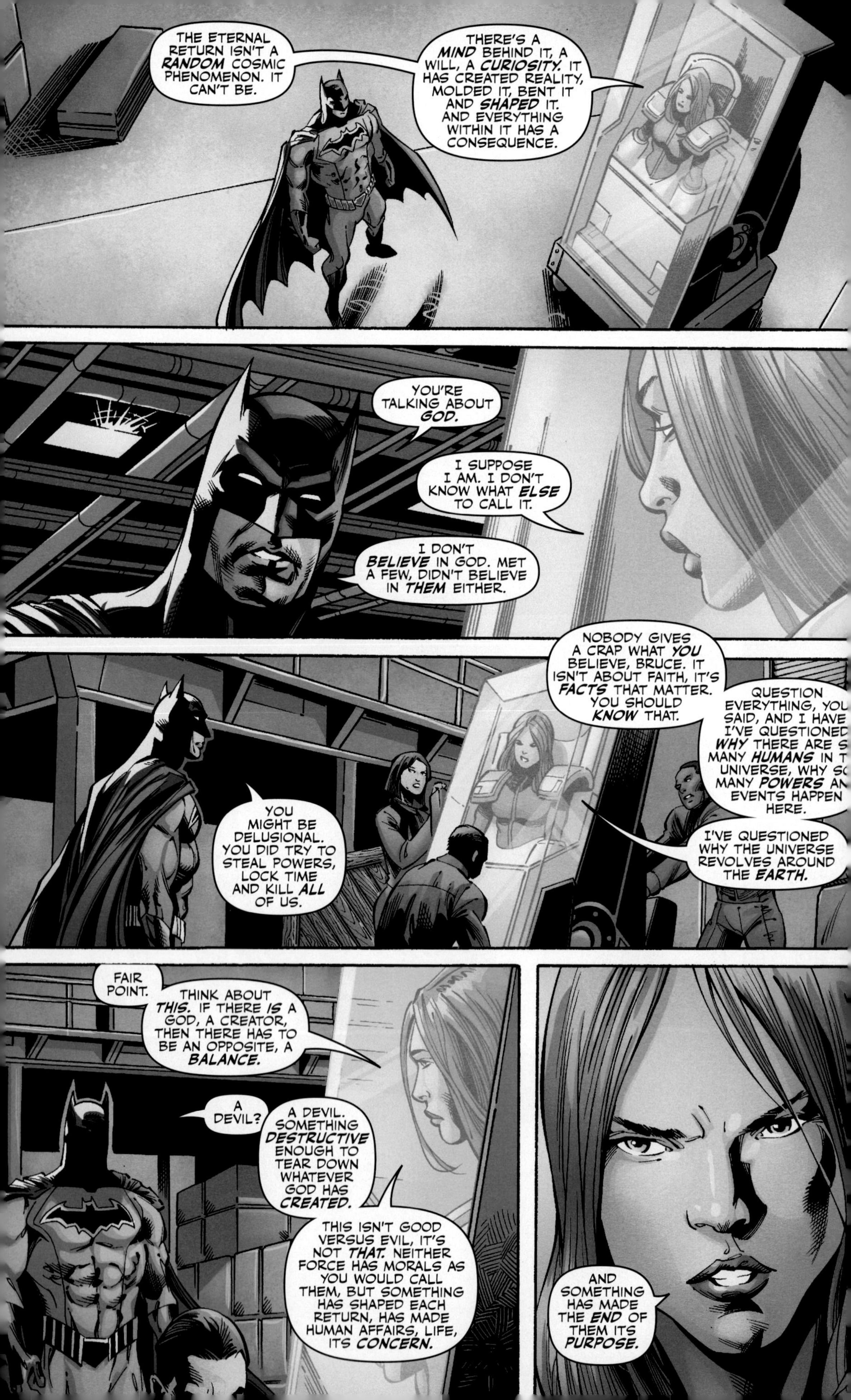
THE ETERNAL RETURN ISN'T A RANDOM COSMIC PHENOMENON. IT CAN'T BE.
THERE'S A MIND BEHIND IT, A WILL, A CURIOSITY. IT HAS CREATED REALITY, MOLDED IT, BENT IT AND SHAPED IT. AND EVERYTHING WITHIN IT HAS A CONSEQUENCE.
YOU'RE TALKING ABOUT GOD.
I SUPPOSE I AM. I DON'T KNOW WHAT ELSE TO CALL IT.
I DON'T BELIEVE IN GOD. MET A FEW, DIDN'T BELIEVE IN THEM EITHER.
NOBODY GIVES A CRAP WHAT YOU BELIEVE, BRUCE. IT ISN'T ABOUT FAITH, IT'S FACTS THAT MATTER. YOU SHOULD KNOW THAT.
YOU MIGHT BE DELUSIONAL. YOU DID TRY TO STEAL POWERS, LOCK TIME AND KILL ALL OF US.
QUESTION EVERYTHING, YOU SAID, AND I HAVE. I'VE QUESTIONED WHY THERE ARE S MANY HUMANS IN T UNIVERSE, WHY S MANY POWERS AN EVENTS HAPPEN HERE.
I'VE QUESTIONED WHY THE UNIVERSE REVOLVES AROUND THE EARTH.
FAIR POINT.
THINK ABOUT THIS. IF THERE IS A GOD, A CREATOR, THEN THERE HAS TO BE AN OPPOSITE, A BALANCE.
A DEVIL?
A DEVIL. SOMETHING DESTRUCTIVE ENOUGH TO TEAR DOWN WHATEVER GOD HAS CREATED.
THIS ISN'T GOOD VERSUS EVIL, IT'S NOT THAT. NEITHER FORCE HAS MORALS AS YOU WOULD CALL THEM, BUT SOMETHING HAS SHAPED EACH RETURN, HAS MADE HUMAN AFFAIRS, LIFE, ITS CONCERN.
AND SOMETHING HAS MADE THE END OF THEM ITS PURPOSE.

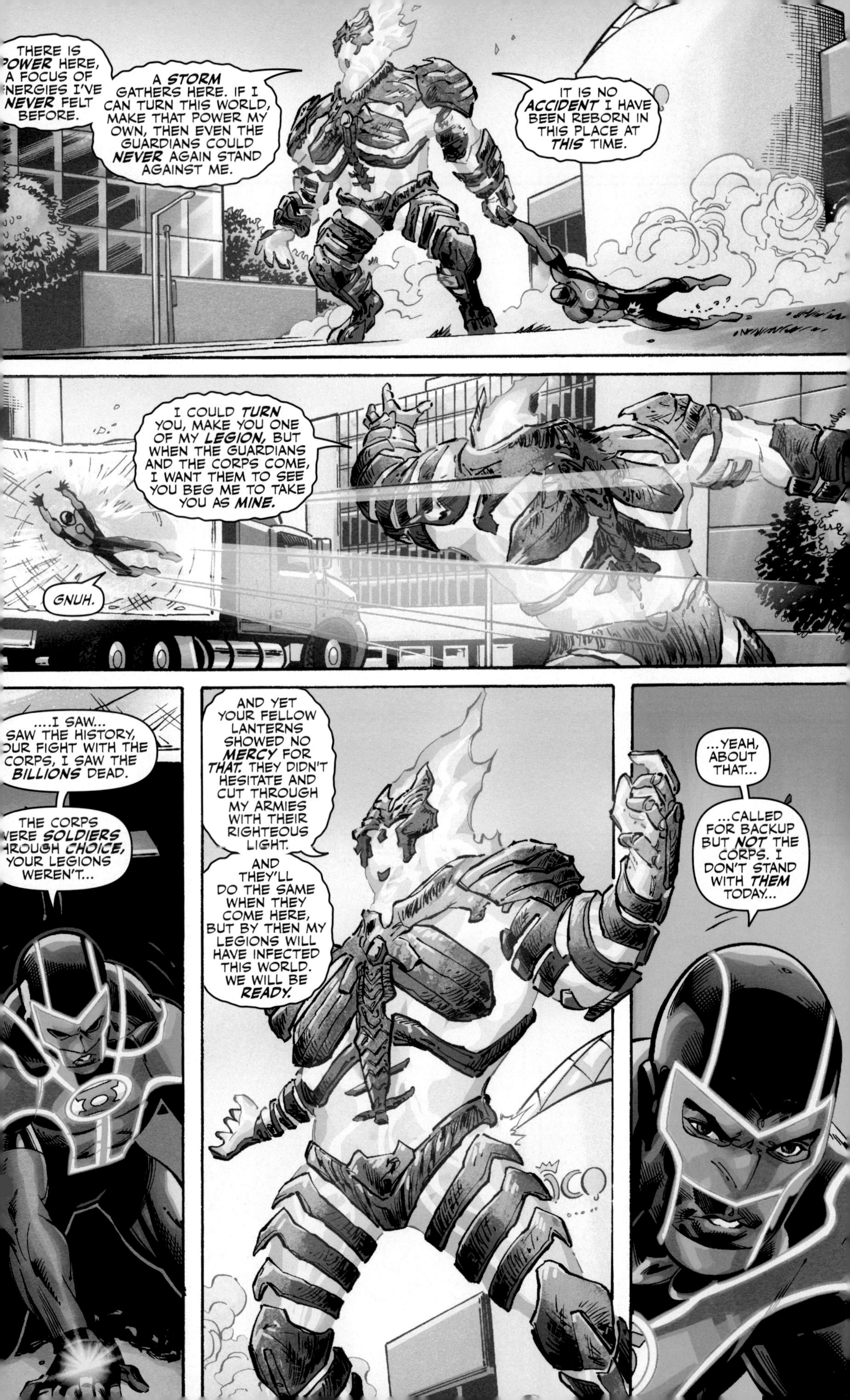
THERE IS POWER HERE, A FOCUS OF ENERGIES I'VE NEVER FELT BEFORE.
A STORM GATHERS HERE. IF I CAN TURN THIS WORLD, MAKE THAT POWER MY OWN, THEN EVEN THE GUARDIANS COULD NEVER AGAIN STAND AGAINST ME.
IT IS NO ACCIDENT I HAVE BEEN REBORN IN THIS PLACE AT THIS TIME.
I COULD TURN YOU, MAKE YOU ONE OF MY LEGION, BUT WHEN THE GUARDIANS AND THE CORPS COME, I WANT THEM TO SEE YOU BEG ME TO TAKE YOU AS MINE.
GNUH.
....I SAW... SAW THE HISTORY, YOUR FIGHT WITH THE CORPS, I SAW THE BILLIONS DEAD.
THE CORPS WERE SOLDIERS THROUGH CHOICE, YOUR LEGIONS WEREN'T...
AND YET YOUR FELLOW LANTERNS SHOWED NO MERCY FOR THAT. THEY DIDN'T HESITATE AND CUT THROUGH MY ARMIES WITH THEIR RIGHTEOUS LIGHT.
AND THEY'LL DO THE SAME WHEN THEY COME HERE, BUT BY THEN MY LEGIONS WILL HAVE INFECTED THIS WORLD. WE WILL BE READY.
...YEAH, ABOUT THAT...
...CALLED FOR BACKUP BUT NOT THE CORPS. I DON'T STAND WITH THEM TODAY...

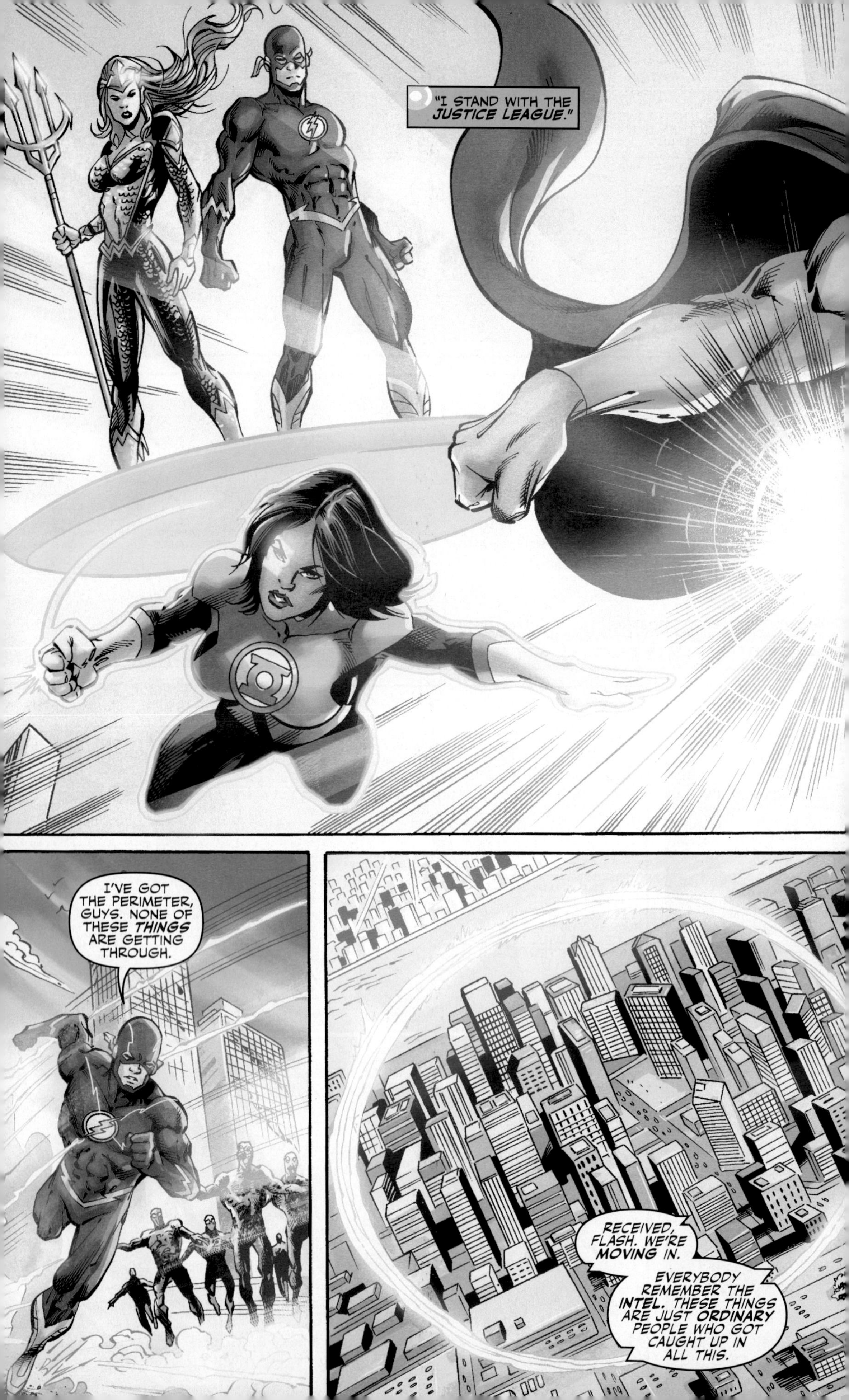
"I STAND WITH THE JUSTICE LEAGUE."
I'VE GOT THE PERIMETER, GUYS. NONE OF THESE THINGS ARE GETTING THROUGH.
RECEIVED, FLASH. WE'RE MOVING IN.
EVERYBODY REMEMBER THE INTEL. THESE THINGS ARE JUST ORDINARY PEOPLE WHO GOT CAUGHT UP IN ALL THIS.

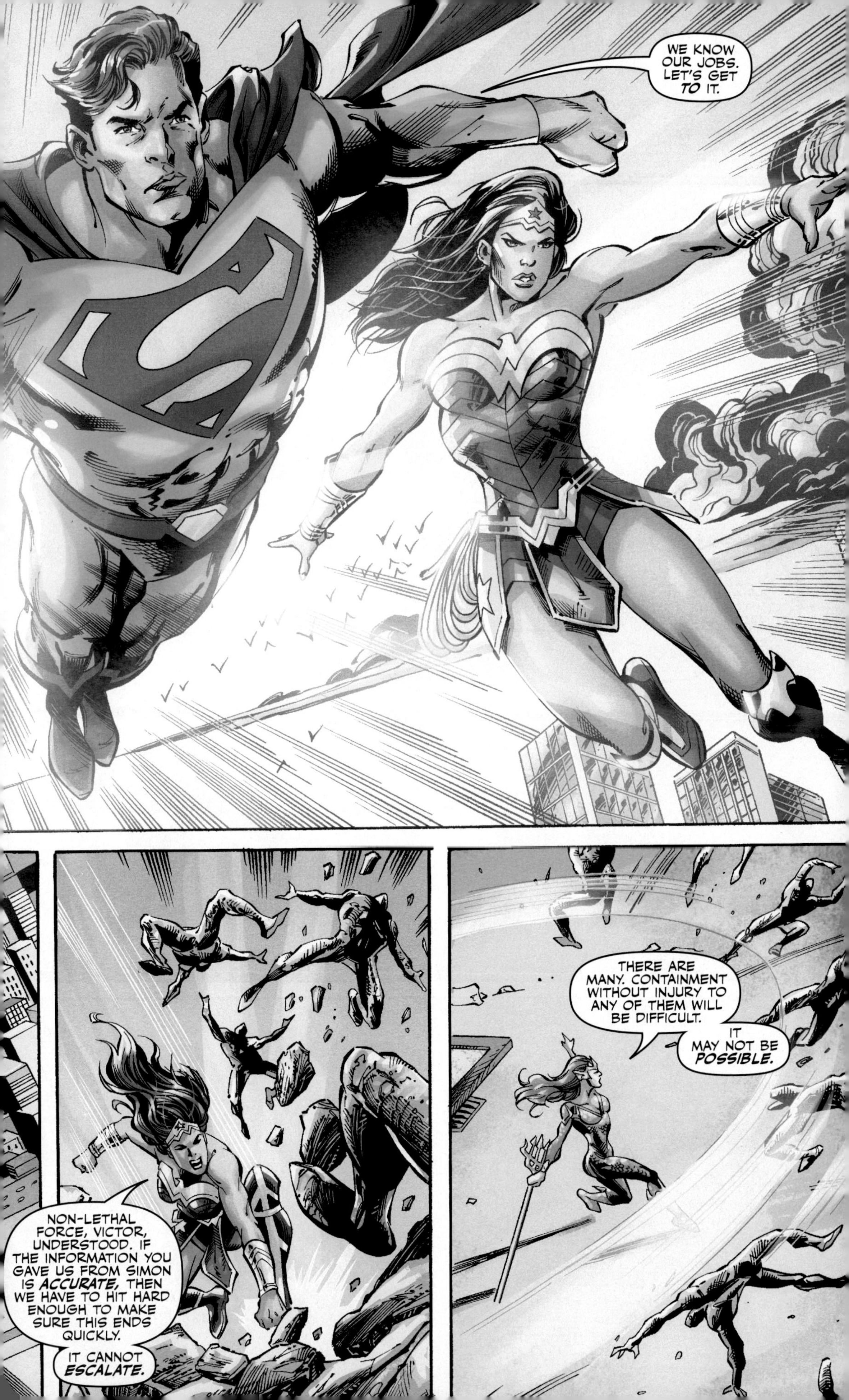
WE KNOW OUR JOBS. LET'S GET *TO* IT.
NON-LETHAL FORCE, VICTOR, UNDERSTOOD. IF THE INFORMATION YOU GAVE US FROM SIMON IS *ACCURATE,* THEN WE HAVE TO HIT HARD ENOUGH TO MAKE SURE THIS ENDS QUICKLY.
IT CANNOT *ESCALATE.*
THERE ARE MANY. CONTAINMENT WITHOUT INJURY TO ANY OF THEM WILL BE DIFFICULT.
IT MAY NOT BE *POSSIBLE.*

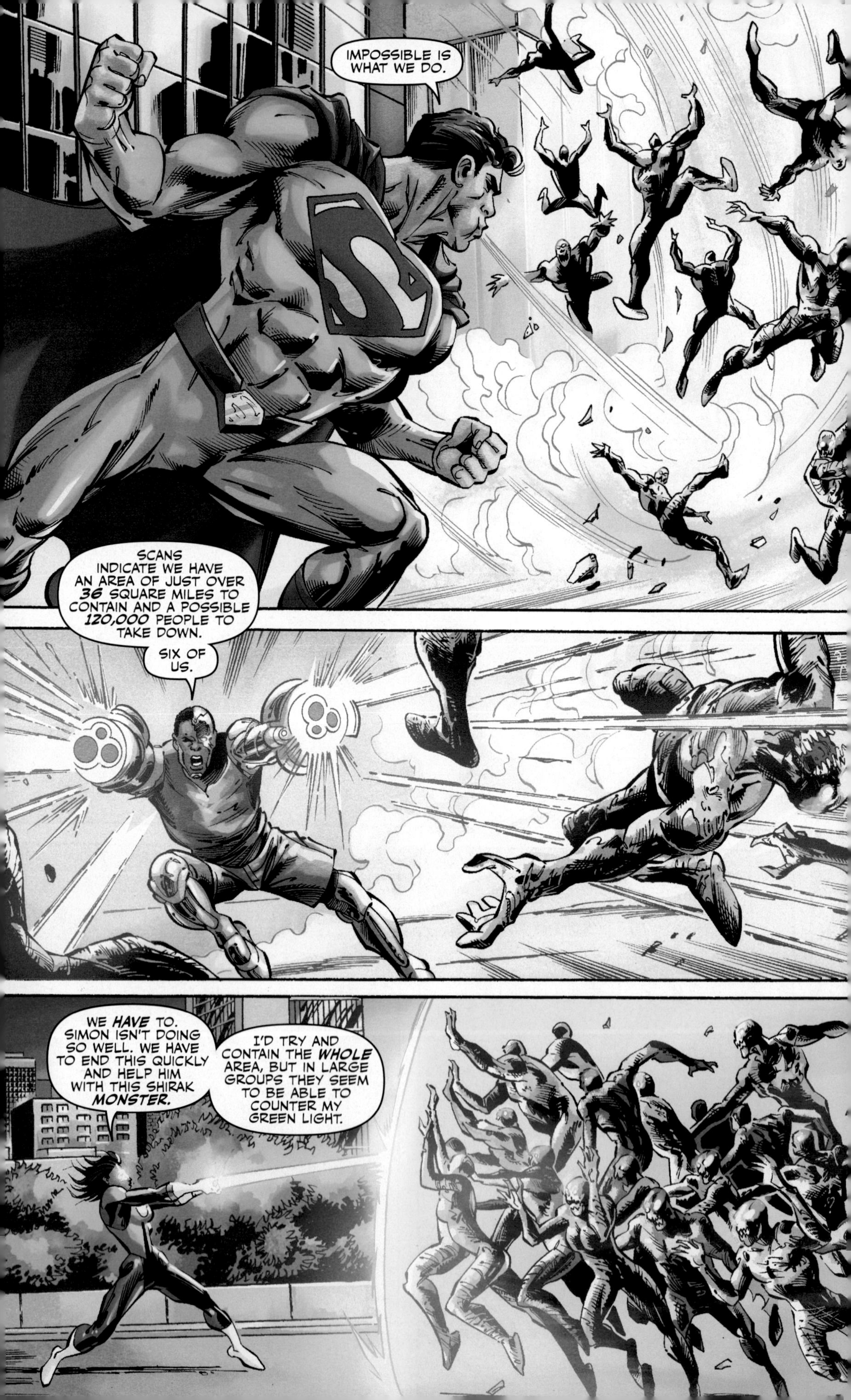
IMPOSSIBLE IS WHAT WE DO.
SCANS INDICATE WE HAVE AN AREA OF JUST OVER 36 SQUARE MILES TO CONTAIN AND A POSSIBLE 120,000 PEOPLE TO TAKE DOWN.
SIX OF US.
WE HAVE TO. SIMON ISN'T DOING SO WELL. WE HAVE TO END THIS QUICKLY AND HELP HIM WITH THIS SHIRAK MONSTER.
I'D TRY AND CONTAIN THE WHOLE AREA, BUT IN LARGE GROUPS THEY SEEM TO BE ABLE TO COUNTER MY GREEN LIGHT.

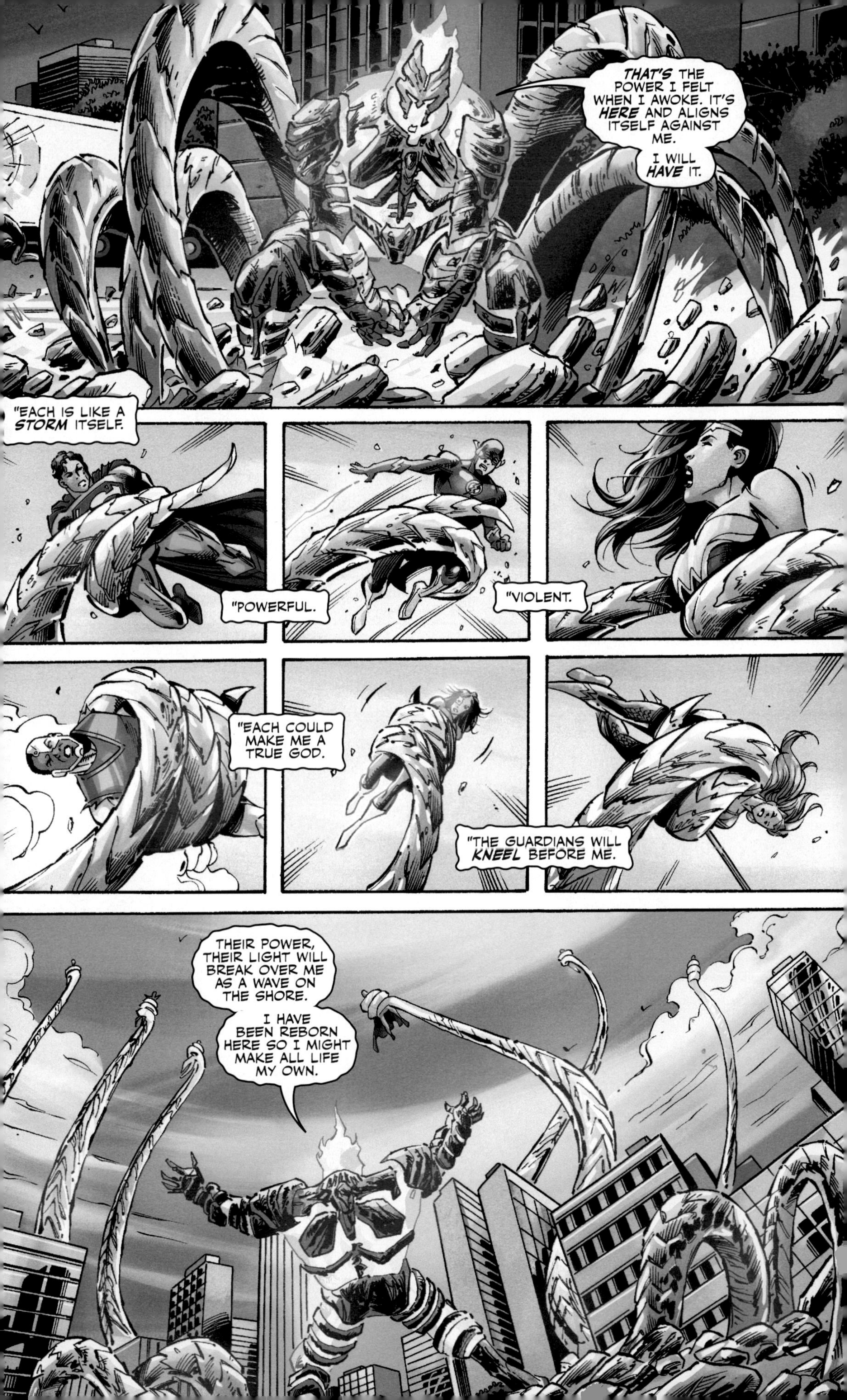
THAT'S THE POWER I FELT WHEN I AWOKE. IT'S HERE AND ALIGNS ITSELF AGAINST ME.
I WILL HAVE IT.
"EACH IS LIKE A STORM ITSELF.
"POWERFUL.
"VIOLENT.
"EACH COULD MAKE ME A TRUE GOD.
"THE GUARDIANS WILL KNEEL BEFORE ME.
THEIR POWER, THEIR LIGHT WILL BREAK OVER ME AS A WAVE ON THE SHORE.
I HAVE BEEN REBORN HERE SO I MIGHT MAKE ALL LIFE MY OWN.

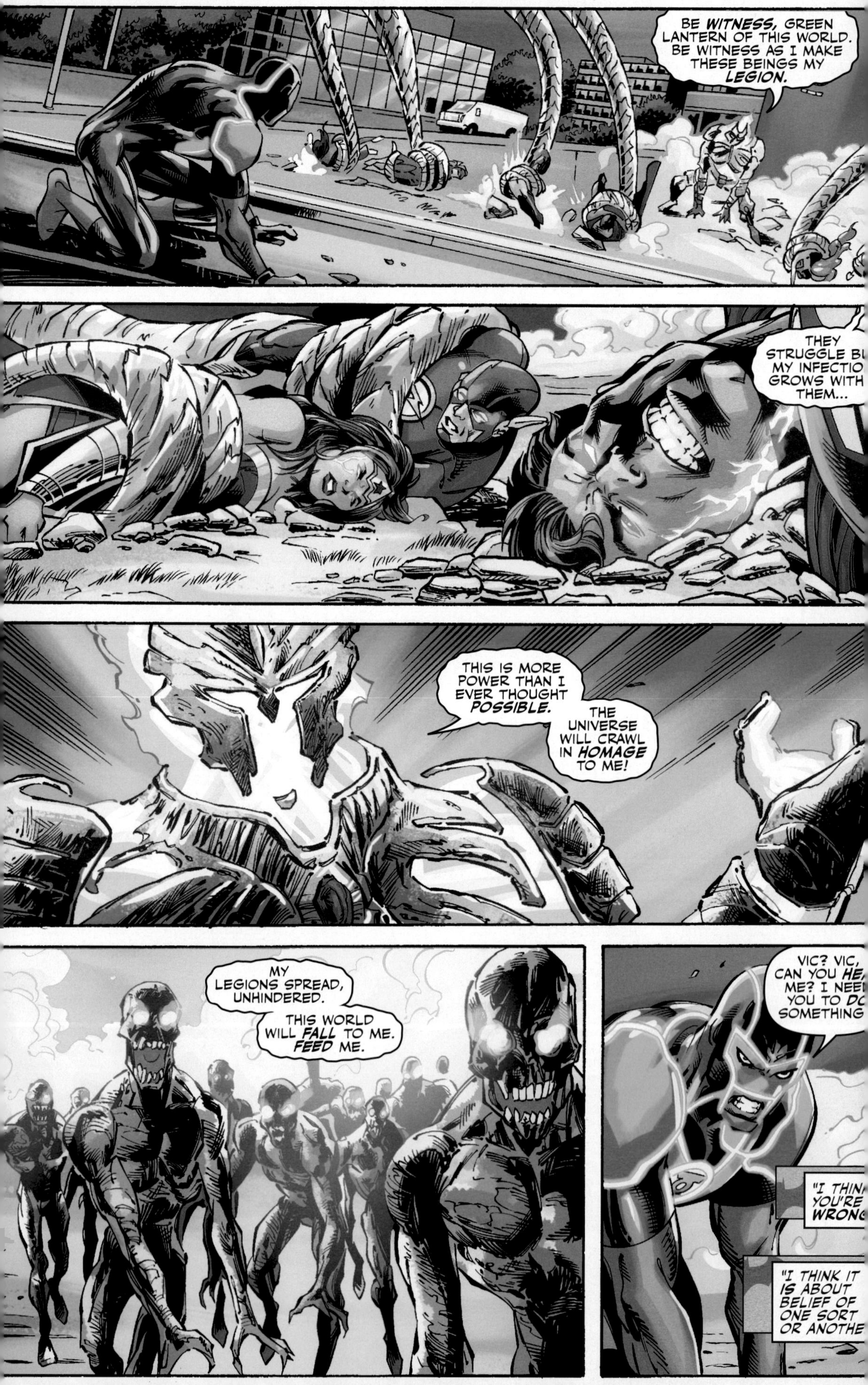
BE WITNESS, GREEN LANTERN OF THIS WORLD. BE WITNESS AS I MAKE THESE BEINGS MY LEGION.
THIS IS MORE POWER THAN I EVER THOUGHT POSSIBLE.
THE UNIVERSE WILL CRAWL IN HOMAGE TO ME!
MY LEGIONS SPREAD, UNHINDERED.
THIS WORLD WILL FALL TO ME. FEED ME.
"I THINK IT IS ABOUT BELIEF OF ONE SORT OR ANOTHE

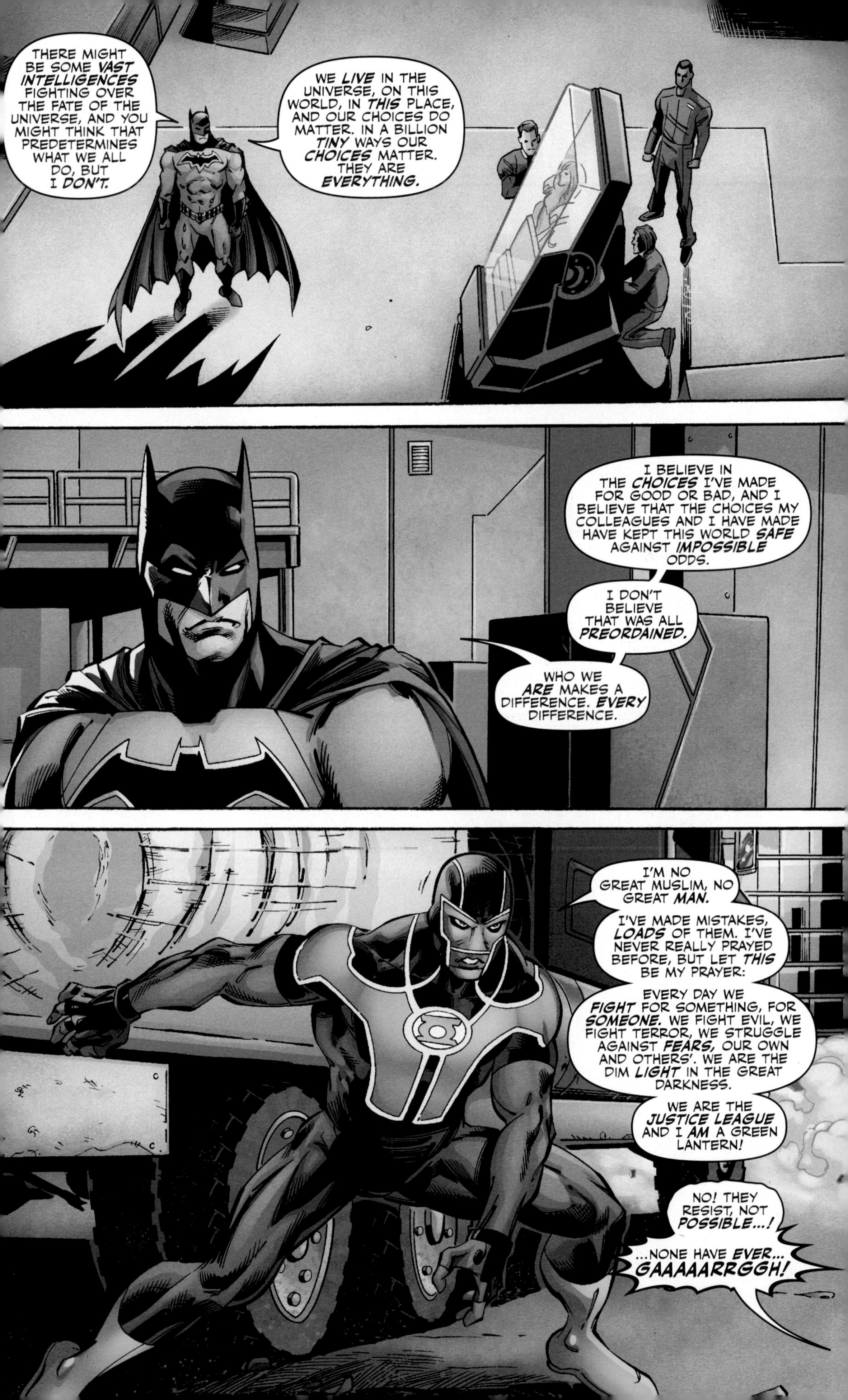

THERE MIGHT BE SOME VAST INTELLIGENCES FIGHTING OVER THE FATE OF THE UNIVERSE, AND YOU MIGHT THINK THAT PREDETERMINES WHAT WE ALL DO, BUT I DON'T.
WE LIVE IN THE UNIVERSE, ON THIS WORLD, IN THIS PLACE, AND OUR CHOICES DO MATTER. IN A BILLION TINY WAYS OUR CHOICES MATTER. THEY ARE EVERYTHING.
I BELIEVE IN THE CHOICES I'VE MADE FOR GOOD OR BAD, AND I BELIEVE THAT THE CHOICES MY COLLEAGUES AND I HAVE MADE HAVE KEPT THIS WORLD SAFE AGAINST IMPOSSIBLE ODDS.
I DON'T BELIEVE THAT WAS ALL PREORDAINED.
WHO WE ARE MAKES A DIFFERENCE. EVERY DIFFERENCE.
I'M NO GREAT MUSLIM, NO GREAT MAN.
I'VE MADE MISTAKES, LOADS OF THEM. I'VE NEVER REALLY PRAYED BEFORE, BUT LET THIS BE MY PRAYER:
EVERY DAY WE FIGHT FOR SOMETHING, FOR SOMEONE. WE FIGHT EVIL, WE FIGHT TERROR, WE STRUGGLE AGAINST FEARS, OUR OWN AND OTHERS'. WE ARE THE DIM LIGHT IN THE GREAT DARKNESS.
WE ARE THE JUSTICE LEAGUE AND I AM A GREEN LANTERN!
NO! THEY RESIST, NOT POSSIBLE...!
...NONE HAVE EVER... GAAAAARRGGH!

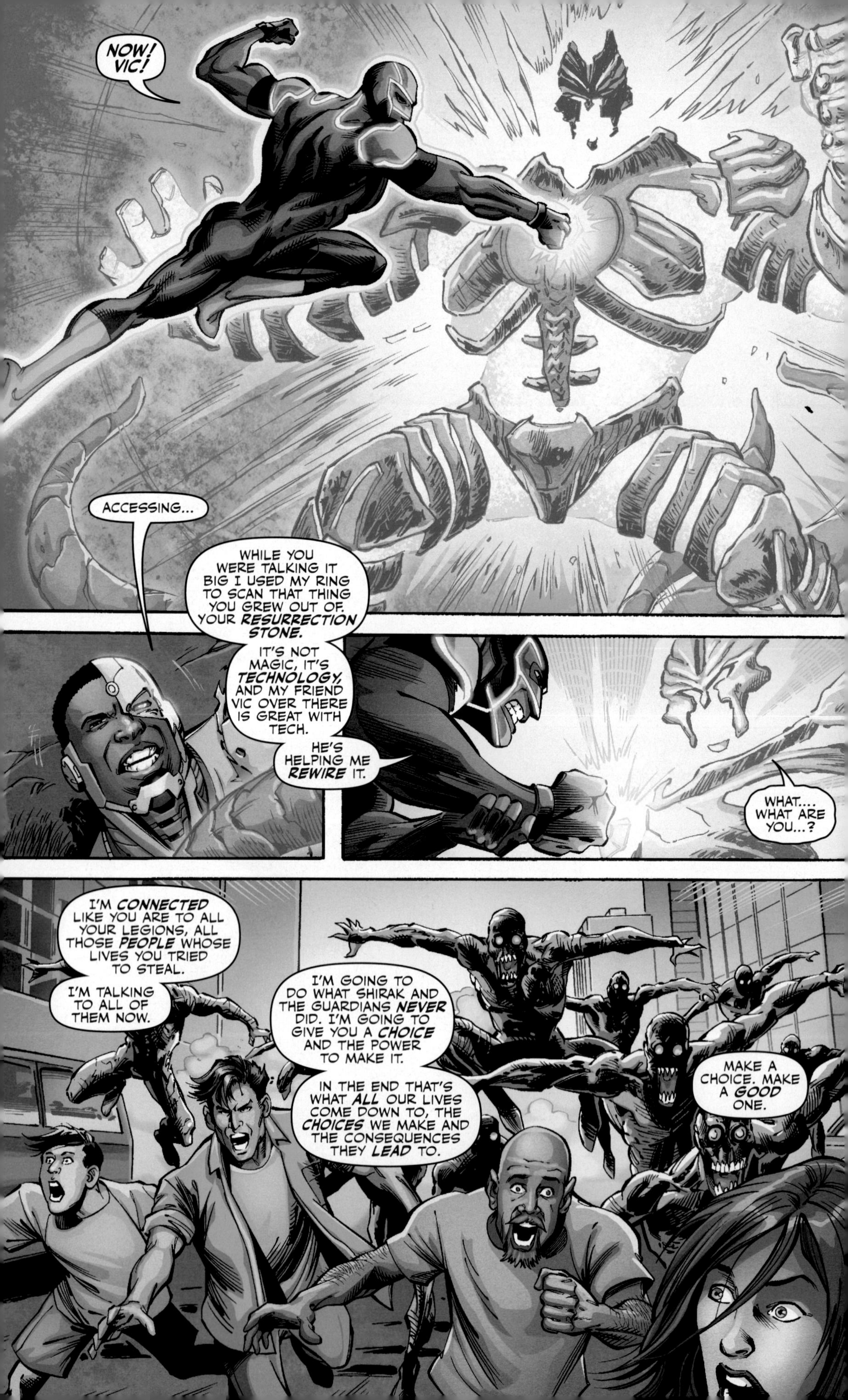
NOW! VIC!
ACCESSING...
WHILE YOU WERE TALKING IT BIG I USED MY RING TO SCAN THAT THING YOU GREW OUT OF. YOUR RESURRECTION STONE.
IT'S NOT MAGIC, IT'S TECHNOLOGY, AND MY FRIEND VIC OVER THERE IS GREAT WITH TECH.
HE'S HELPING ME REWIRE IT.
WHAT.... WHAT ARE YOU...?
I'M CONNECTED LIKE YOU ARE TO ALL YOUR LEGIONS, ALL THOSE PEOPLE WHOSE LIVES YOU TRIED TO STEAL.
I'M TALKING TO ALL OF THEM NOW.
I'M GOING TO DO WHAT SHIRAK AND THE GUARDIANS NEVER DID. I'M GOING TO GIVE YOU A CHOICE AND THE POWER TO MAKE IT.
IN THE END THAT'S WHAT ALL OUR LIVES COME DOWN TO, THE CHOICES WE MAKE AND THE CONSEQUENCES THEY LEAD TO.
MAKE A CHOICE. MAKE A GOOD ONE.

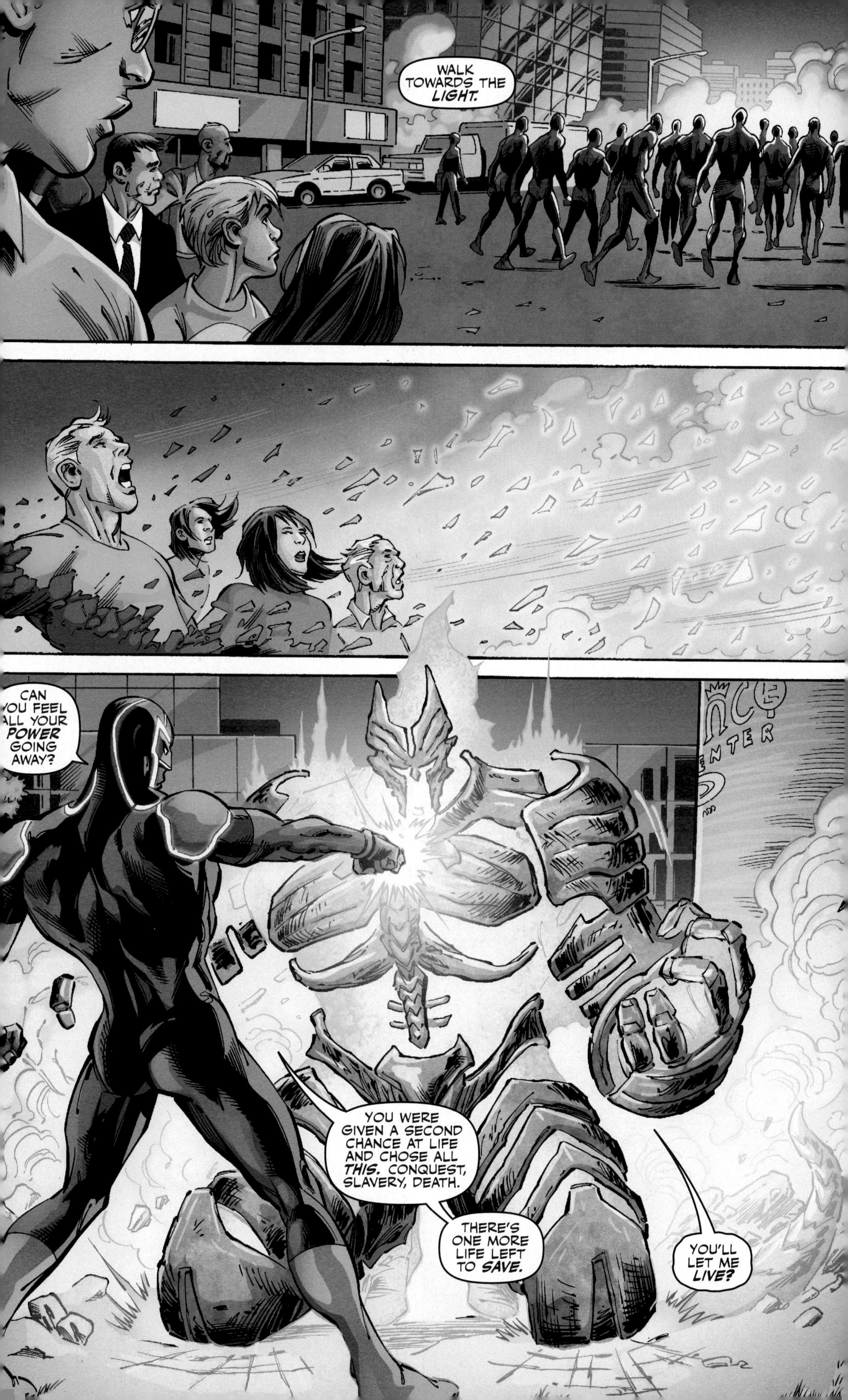
WALK TOWARDS THE LIGHT.
CAN YOU FEEL ALL YOUR POWER GOING AWAY?
YOU WERE GIVEN A SECOND CHANCE AT LIFE AND CHOSE ALL THIS. CONQUEST, SLAVERY, DEATH.
THERE'S ONE MORE LIFE LEFT TO SAVE.
YOU'LL LET ME LIVE?

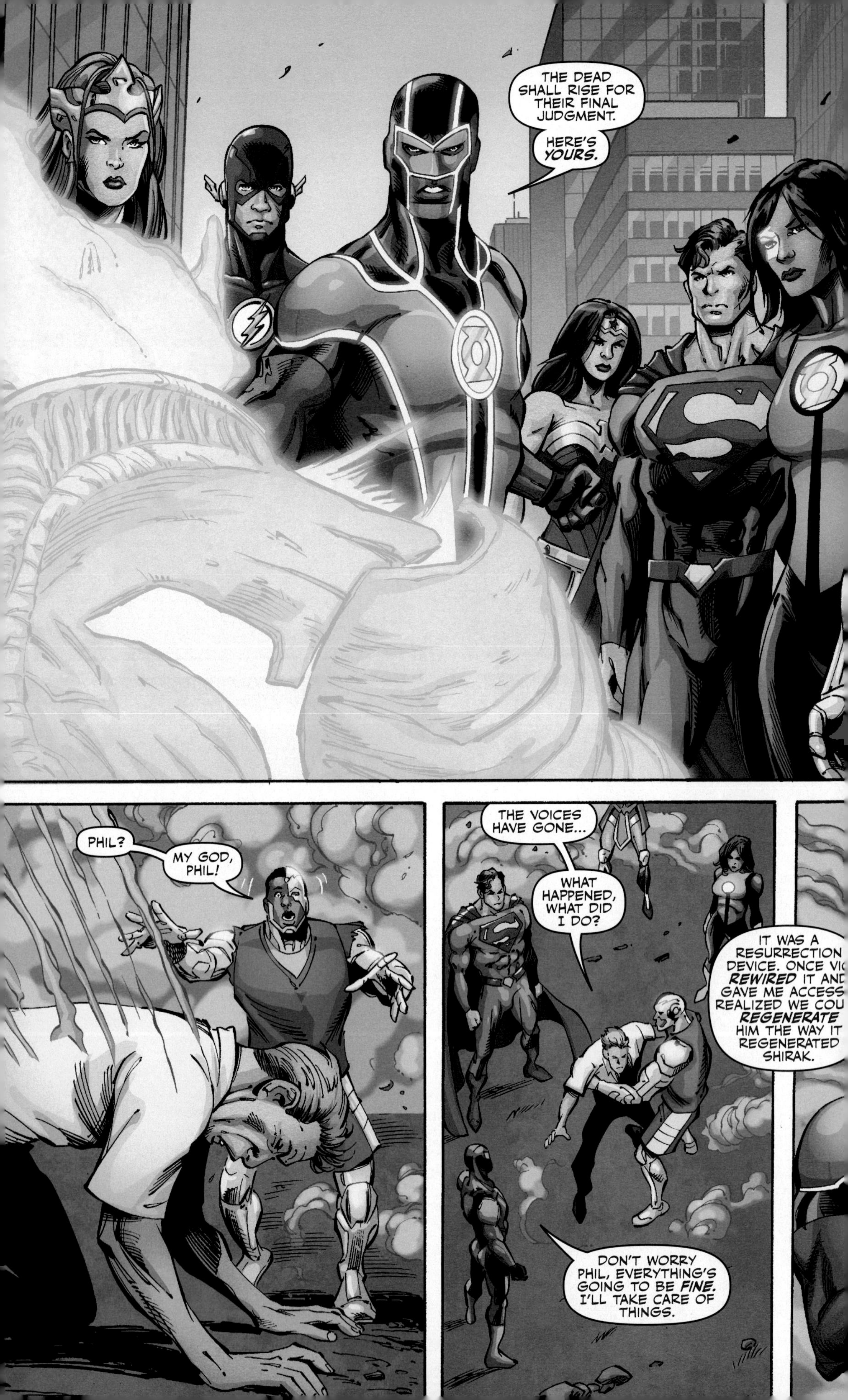
THE DEAD SHALL RISE FOR THEIR FINAL JUDGMENT.
HERE'S YOURS.
PHIL?
MY GOD, PHIL!
THE VOICES HAVE GONE...
WHAT HAPPENED, WHAT DID I DO?
IT WAS A RESURRECTION DEVICE. ONCE VI REWIRED IT AND GAVE ME ACCESS REALIZED WE COU REGENERATE HIM THE WAY IT REGENERATED SHIRAK.
DON'T WORRY PHIL, EVERYTHING'S GOING TO BE FINE. I'LL TAKE CARE OF THINGS.

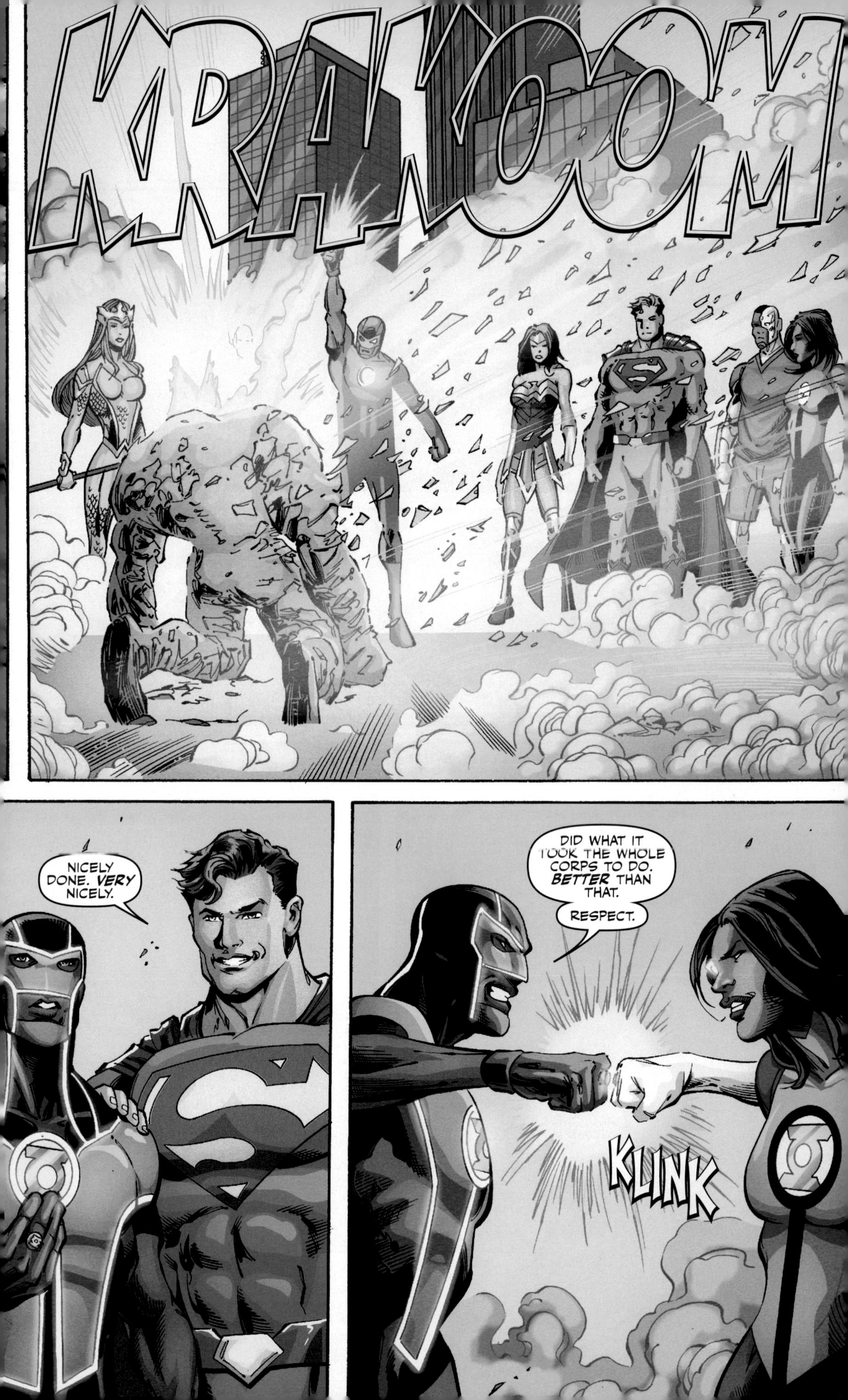

KRAKOOM
NICELY DONE. VERY NICELY.
DID WHAT IT TOOK THE WHOLE CORPS TO DO. BETTER THAN THAT.
RESPECT.
KLINK

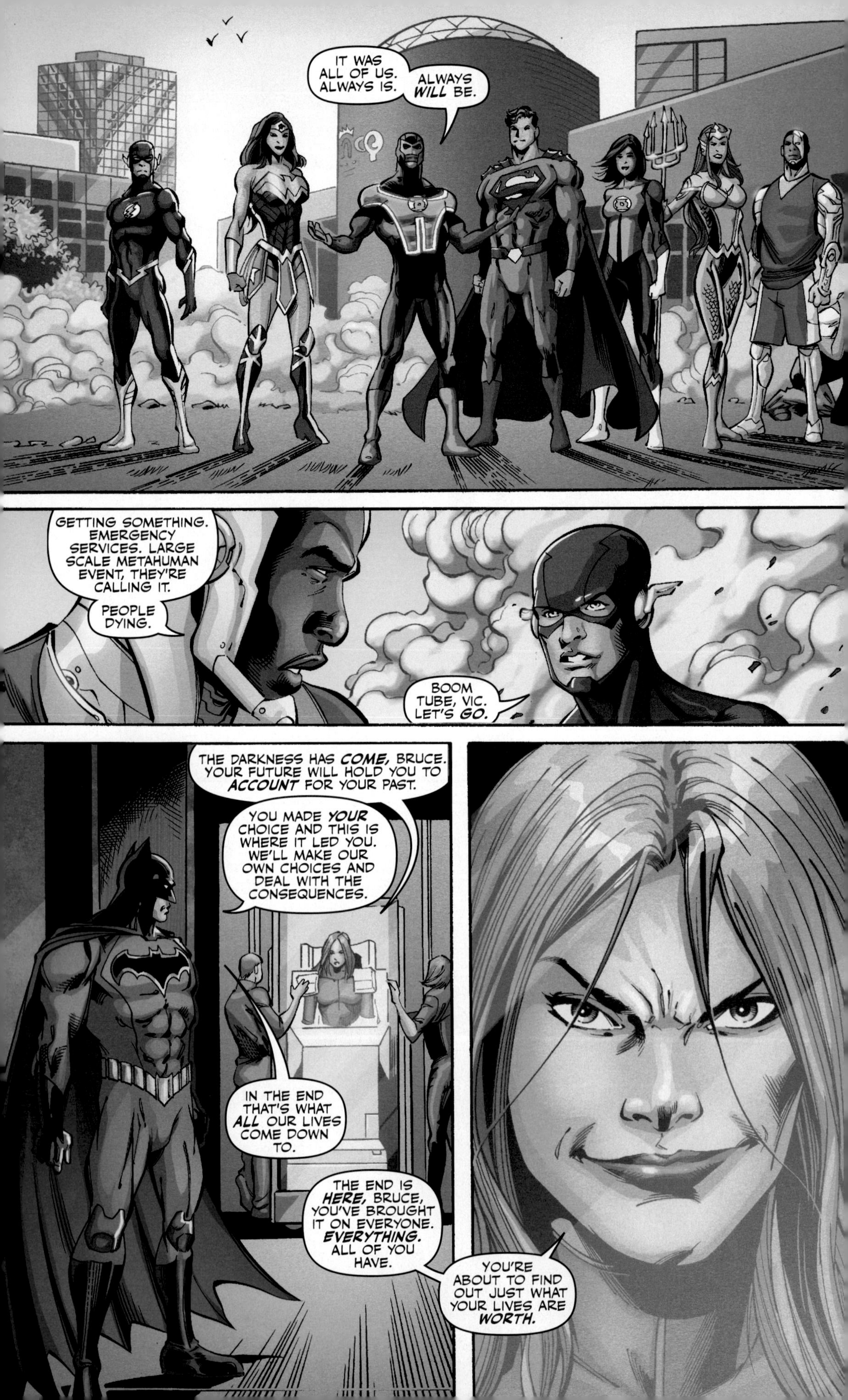
IT WAS ALL OF US. ALWAYS IS.
ALWAYS WILL BE.
GETTING SOMETHING. EMERGENCY SERVICES. LARGE SCALE METAHUMAN EVENT, THEY'RE CALLING IT.
PEOPLE DYING.
BOOM TUBE, VIC. LET'S GO.
THE DARKNESS HAS COME, BRUCE. YOUR FUTURE WILL HOLD YOU TO ACCOUNT FOR YOUR PAST.
YOU MADE YOUR CHOICE AND THIS IS WHERE IT LED YOU. WE'LL MAKE OUR OWN CHOICES AND DEAL WITH THE CONSEQUENCES.
IN THE END THAT'S WHAT ALL OUR LIVES COME DOWN TO.
THE END IS HERE, BRUCE, YOU'VE BROUGHT IT ON EVERYONE. EVERYTHING. ALL OF YOU HAVE.
YOU'RE ABOUT TO FIND OUT JUST WHAT YOUR LIVES ARE WORTH.

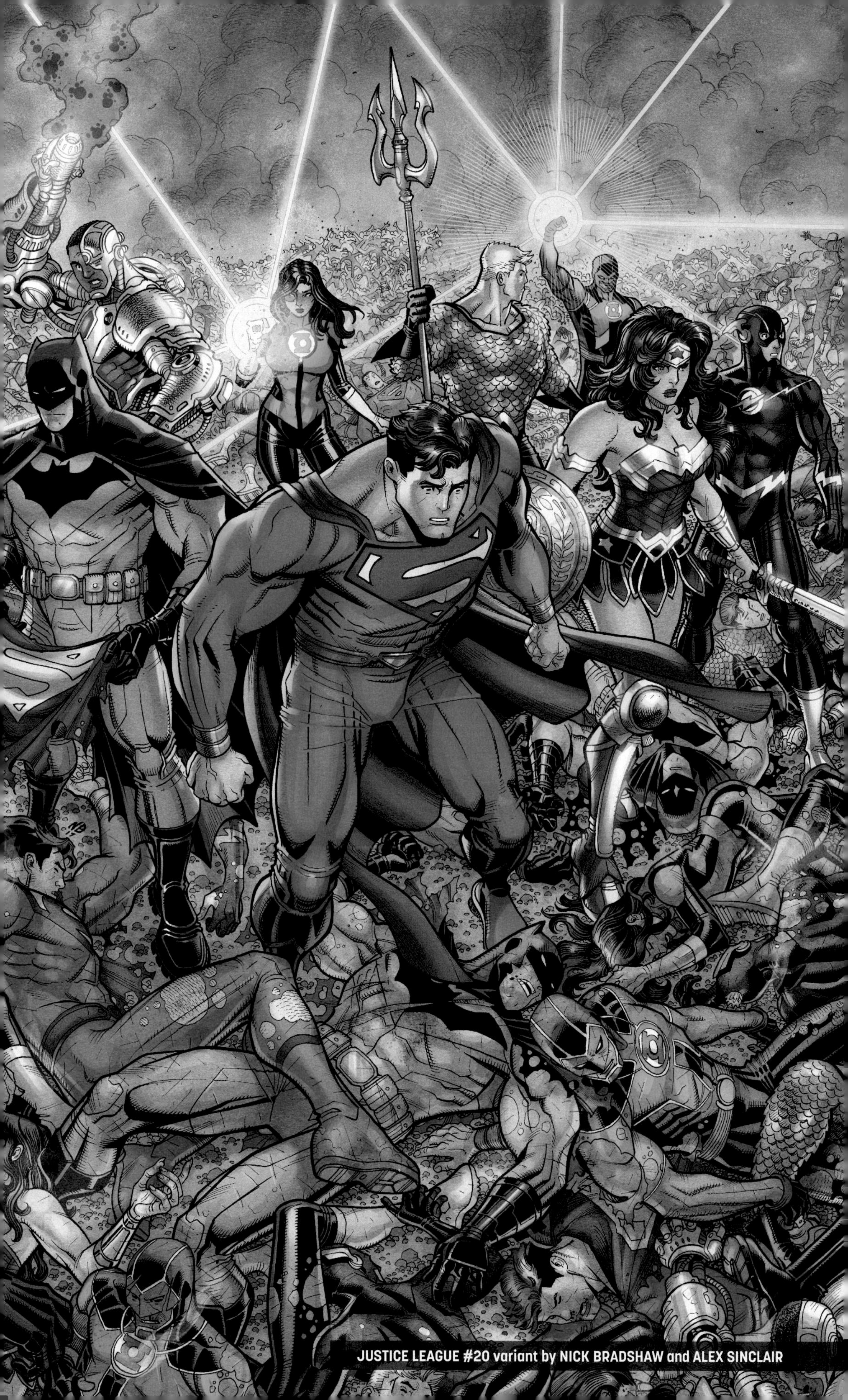

JUSTICE LEAGUE #20 variant by NICK BRADSHAW and ALEX SINCLAIR

JUSTICE LEAGUE #21 variant by NICK BRADSHAW and ALEX SINCLAIR

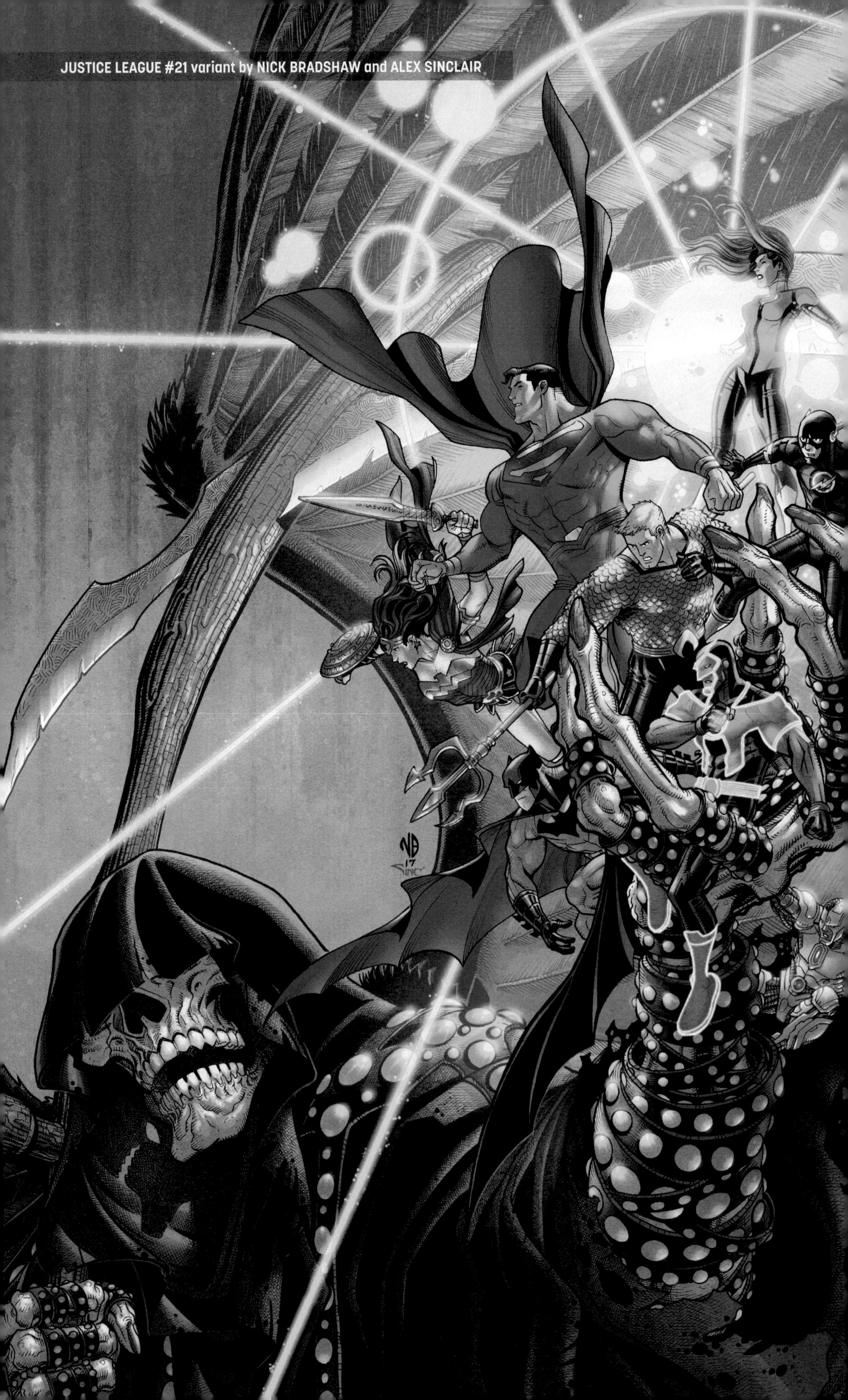

JUSTICE LEAGUE #22 variant by NICK BRADSHAW and ALEX SINCLAIR

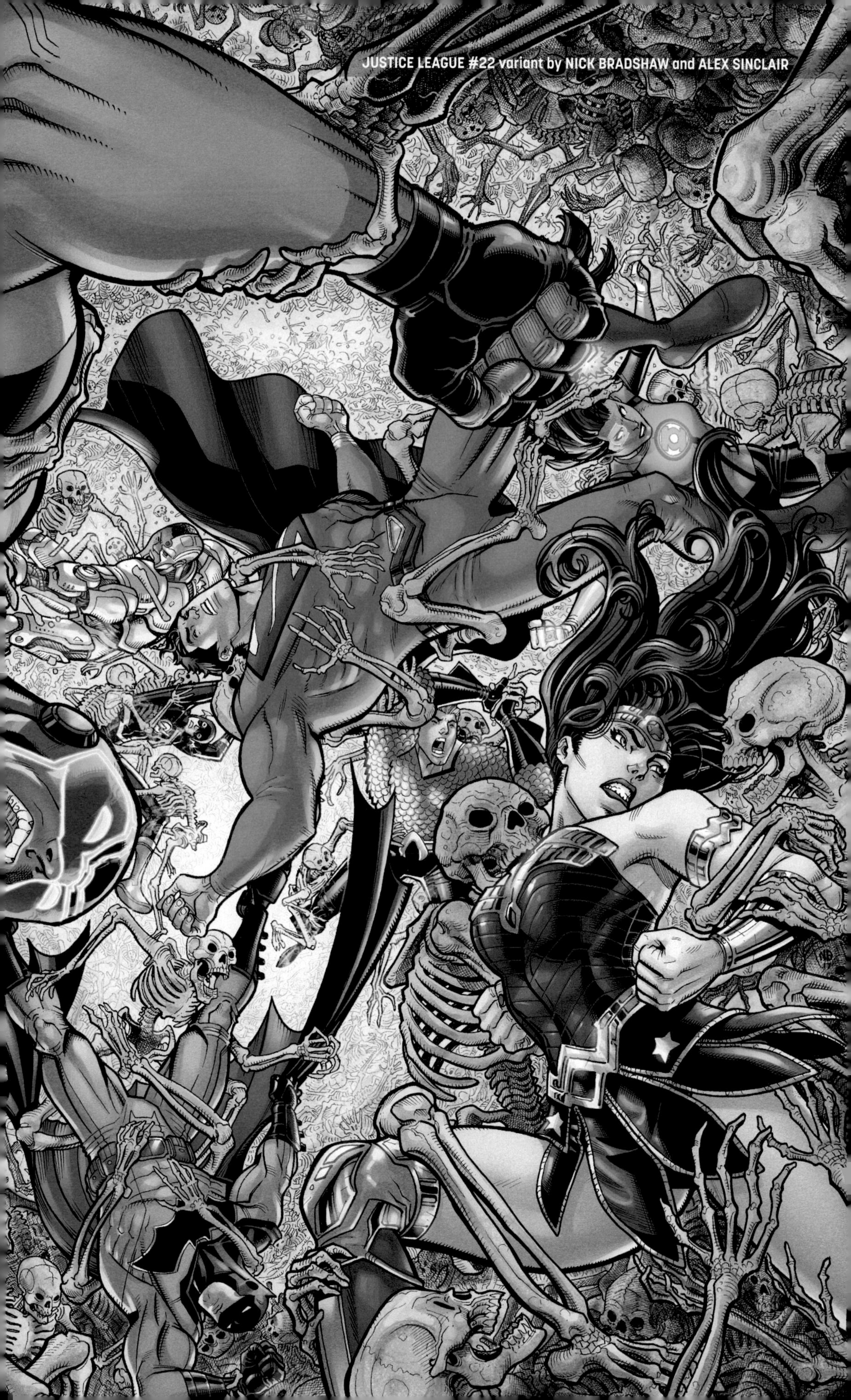

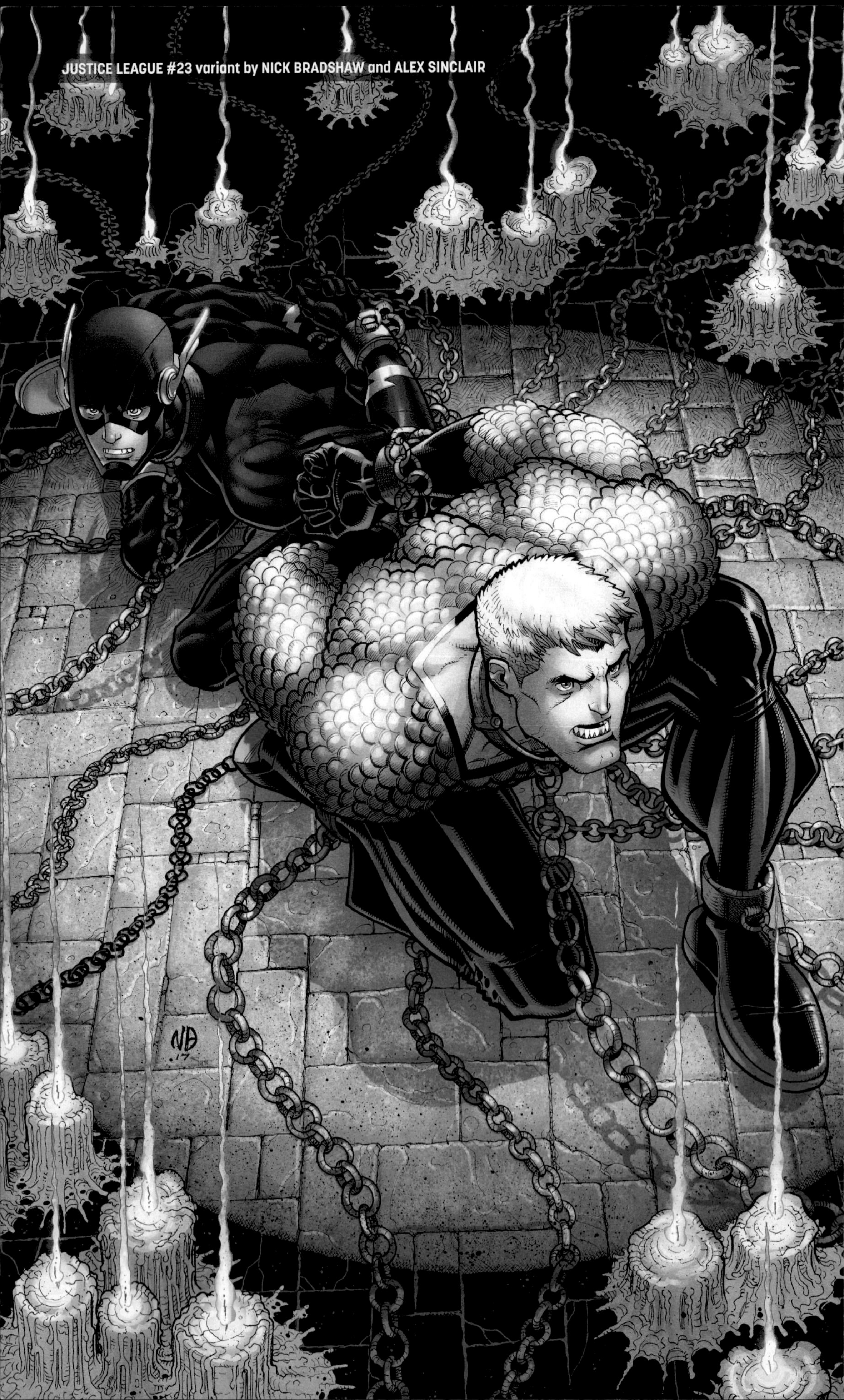

JUSTICE LEAGUE #23 variant by NICK BRADSHAW and ALEX SINCLAIR

JUSTICE LEAGUE #24 variant by NICK BRADSHAW and ALEX SINCLAIR

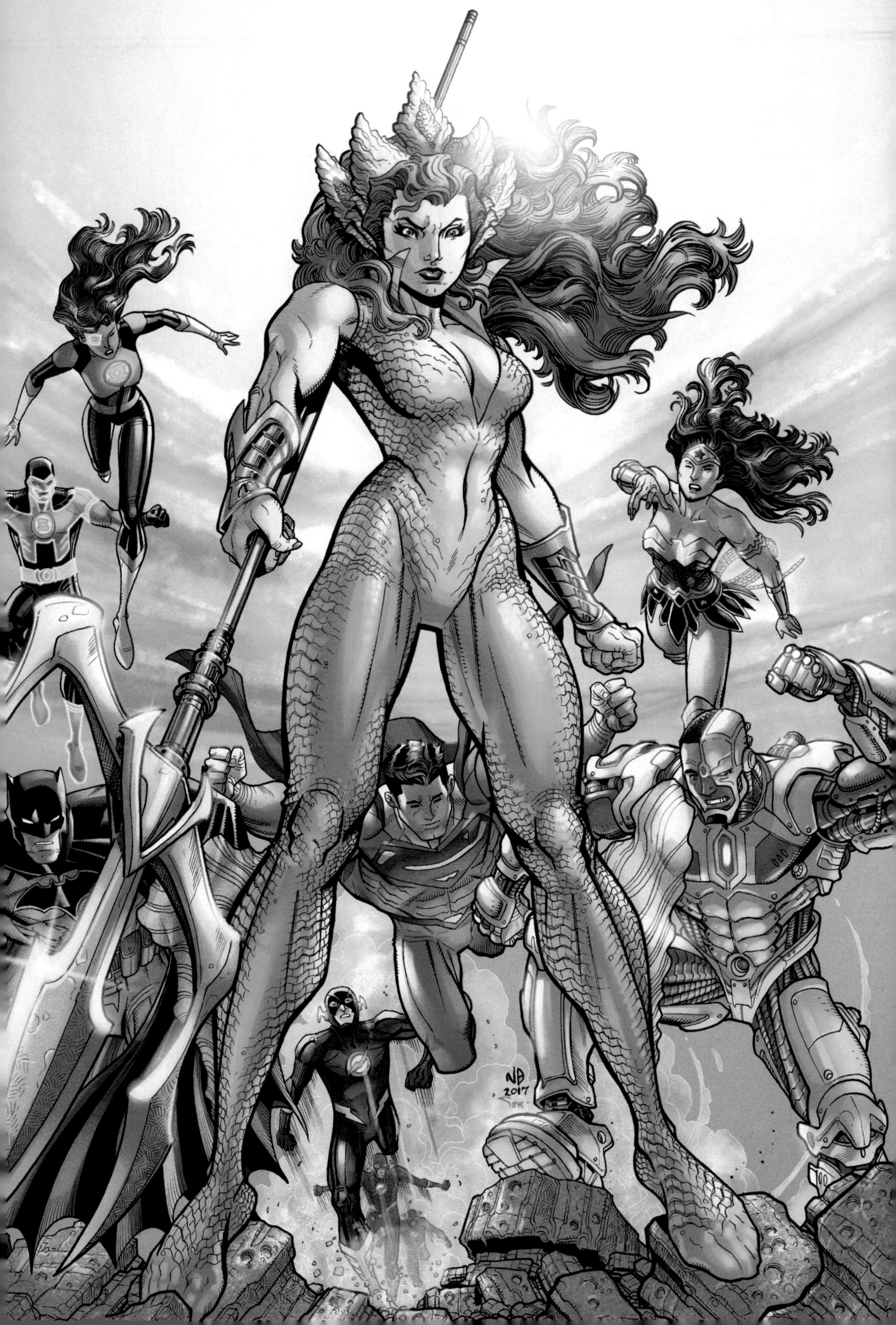

JUSTICE LEAGUE #25 variant by NICK BRADSHAW

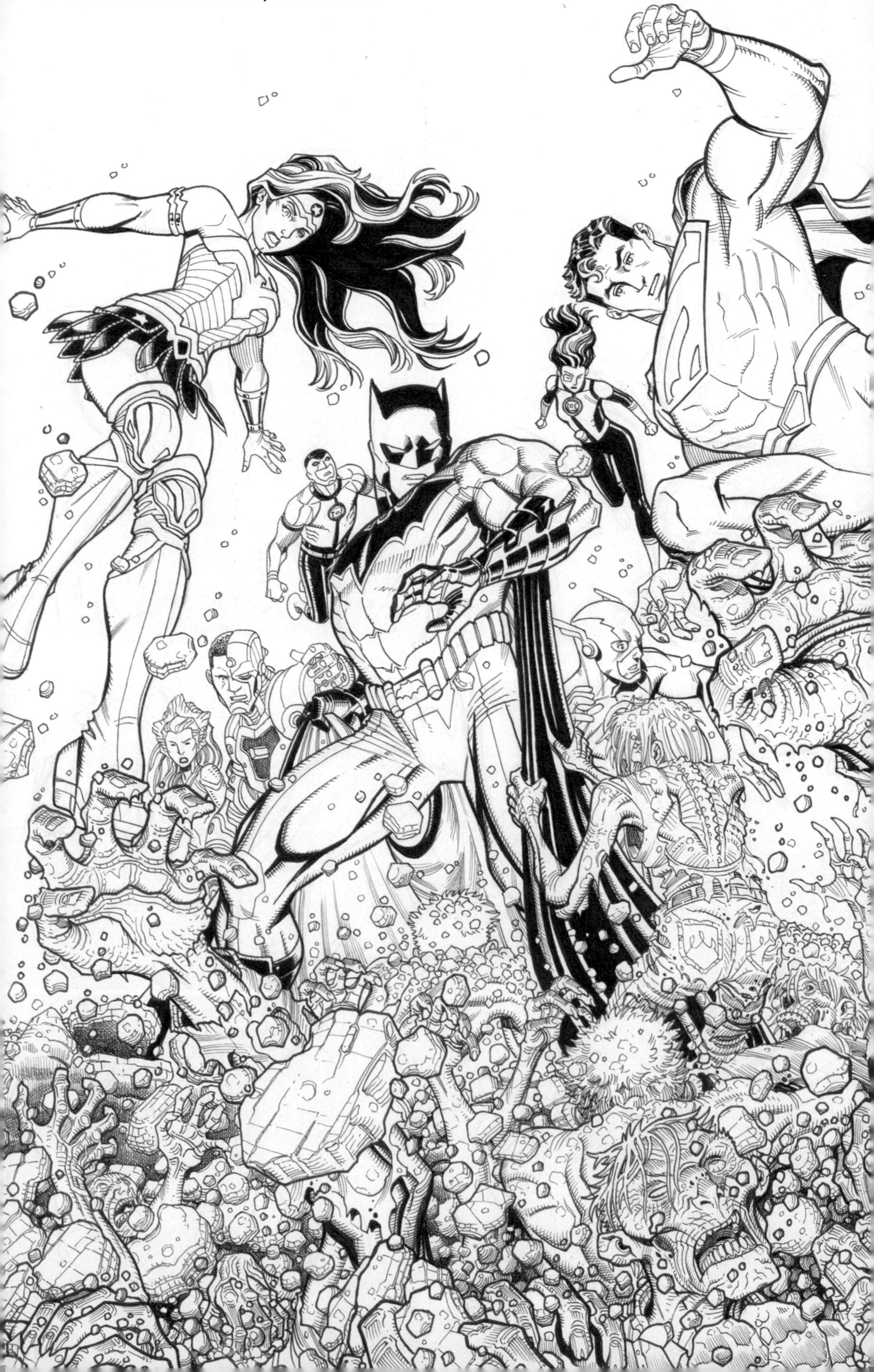

DC UNIVERSE REBIRTH

JUSTICE LEAGUE

VOL. 1: The Extinction Machines

BRYAN HITCH
with TONY S. DANIEL

VOL.1 THE EXTINCTION MACHINES
BRYAN HITCH • TONY S. DANIEL • SANDU FLOREA • TOMEU MOREY

VOL.1 THE IMITATION OF LIFE
JOHN SEMPER JR. • PAUL PELLETIER • WILL CONRAD

**CYBORG VOL. 1:
THE IMITATION OF LIFE**

VOL.1 RAGE PLANET
SAM HUMPHRIES • ROBSON ROCHA • ETHAN VAN SCIVER • ED BENES

**GREEN LANTERNS VOL. 1:
RAGE PLANET**

VOL.1 THE DROWNING
DAN ABNETT • PHILIPPE BRIONES • SCOT EATON • BRAD WALKER

**AQUAMAN VOL. 1:
THE DROWNING**

JUSTICE LEAGUE
VOL. 1: ORIGIN
GEOFF JOHNS
and JIM LEE

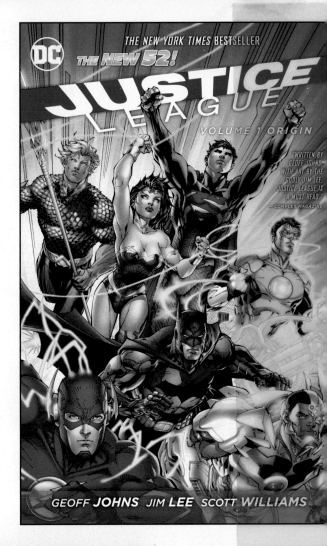

**JUSTICE LEAGUE
VOL. 2: THE VILLAIN'S JOURNEY**

**JUSTICE LEAGUE
VOL. 3: THRONE OF ATLANTIS**

READ THE ENTIRE EP

JUSTICE LEAGUE VO
THE G

JUSTICE LEAGUE VO
FOREVER HER

JUSTICE LEAGUE VO
INJUSTICE LEA

JUSTICE LEAGUE VO
DARKSEID WAR PA

JUSTICE LEAGUE VO
DARKSEID WAR PA